RACISM AND EMPIRE

By the Same Author

Gandhi in South Africa: British Imperialism and the Indian Question, 1860–1914

The British Imperial Experience

British Relations with Sind, 1799–1843: An Anatomy of Imperialism

With Leo Rose and Margaret Fisher: *Himalayan Battleground: Sino-Soviet Rivalry in Ladakh*

RACISM AND EMPIRE
White Settlers and Colored Immigrants in the British Self-Governing Colonies 1830–1910

Robert A. Huttenback

Cornell University Press | ITHACA AND LONDON

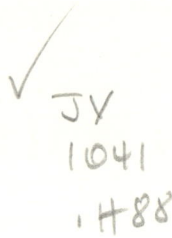

Copyright © 1976 by Cornell University

All rights reserved. Except for brief quotations in a review, this book, or parts thereof, must not be reproduced in any form without permission in writing from the publisher. For information address Cornell University Press, 124 Roberts Place, Ithaca, New York 14850.

First published 1976 by Cornell University Press.
Published in the United Kingdom by Cornell University Press Ltd., 2-4 Brook Street, London W1Y 1AA.

International Standard Book Number 0-8014-0974-8
Library of Congress Catalog Card Number 75-30257
Printed in the United States of America by Vail-Ballou Press, Inc.
Librarians: Library of Congress cataloging information appears on the last page of the book.

FOR MADELEINE

Acknowledgments

As is always the case, this book would not have been possible without the generous help and cooperation of many individuals and institutions. The author especially wishes to thank Charles A. Price of the Australian National University; his colleagues and friends John Benton, Robert Conhaim, Lance Davis, Daniel Kevles, and Robert Rosenstone, who nobly performed the laborious task of reading the first draft of the manuscript and greatly improved it through their advice; the librarians, directors and staffs of the following libraries and archives: Royal Commonwealth Society (London), India Office Library (London), Commonwealth Relations Office Library (London), Public Record Office (London), the libraries of the University of California at Berkeley, at Los Angeles, and at Santa Barbara, the library of the California Institute of Technology, the library of Birmingham University, the Mitchell Library and Archives Office of New South Wales (Sydney), the Latrobe Library and Victoria Archives (Melbourne), the Battye Library and Western Australia Archives (Perth), the National Archives of New Zealand (Wellington), the Alexander Turnbull Library (Wellington), the Queensland Archives (Brisbane), the Archives of Tasmania (Hobart), the Archives of South Australia (Adelaide), the Australian National Library (Canberra), the Commonwealth Archives Office (Canberra) and its Melbourne depository, the libraries of the Universities of Adelaide and Melbourne, the Public Archives of Canada (Ottawa), the Provincial Archives of British Columbia (Victoria), and the Archives of the Republic of South Africa. Finally, the author would like to thank Malvine Baer and Edith Taylor, who typed the manuscript; Kay Scheuer of Cornell University Press, who so ably edited it; Carol Pearson, who prepared the index; his wife, who from time to time allowed him to abandon home and family to do research in the far corners of the globe; and the California Institute of Technology, which helped to provide funds.

Brief sections of this book appeared in two articles, "No Strangers within the Gates: Attitudes and Policies towards the Non-White Residents of the British Empire of Settlement," *Journal of Imperial and Commonwealth History*, I, May 1973, and "The British Empire as a 'White Man's Country'—A Comparative View of Racial Attitudes and Immigration Legislation in the British Colonies of White Settlement," *Journal of British Studies*, Autumn 1973. The sections on South Africa draw upon the author's previous book, *Gandhi in South Africa: British Imperialism and the Indian Question, 1860–1914* (Cornell University Press, 1971).

ROBERT A. HUTTENBACK

Pasadena, California

Contents

	Introduction	13
1	Colored Labor in the Pre-Restriction Era—The Contract System	26
2	The Immigration Question—The Battle Joined	59
3	The Immigation Question—A Solution Found	139
4	White Colonist versus Colored Immigrant	195
5	The Classic Example—"White Australia"	279
	Conclusion	317
	Bibliography	327
	General Sources	327
	Australia and New Zealand	329
	Canada	338
	South Africa	341
	Index	349

RACISM AND EMPIRE

Introduction

In the decades of "prestige imperialism," when the thought of the Union Jack flying over so many foreign lands swelled the hearts of millions of Englishmen, the tread of army boots and the rattle of musketry imparted to rich and poor alike the vicarious thrill of being subject and citizen of an empire on whose possessions the sun literally never set. But if the Empire was God-ordained, as many thought, it was certainly not the product of clearly conceived policy or some governmental master plan emanating from the corridors of Whitehall. Rather, the aphorism that the Empire was founded in a fit of absence of mind was nearer the truth, for religious deviationists, commercial adventurers, and jailers in quest of sites for prisons were more often than not the founders of British colonial settlements.

Given such a history, it is not surprising that enthusiasm for Empire grew but slowly in Britain and that no lofty rationale for imperial advance was forthcoming for many years. Eventually, humanitarianism, evangelical Christianity, and the "civilizing mission" associated with "bearing the white man's burden" combined to produce an imperial philosophy of sorts—a rather ill-defined dedication to "fair play," and an official determination that all subjects of the crown, and to a lesser extent aliens, regardless of race, color, religion or ethnic background, should be equal before the law.

The common conception of Empire was reflected in an article published in the *North American Review* of April, 1846,

"Wherever her [Britain's] sovereignty has gone," the writer, David Wells, contended,

two blades of grass have grown where one grew before. Her flag wherever it has advanced has benefited the country over which it floats; and has carried with it civilization, the Christian religion, order, justice and prosperity. England has always treated a conquered race with justice, and what under her law is the law for the white man is the law for his black, red and yellow brother. . . . If injustice is done him, the English courts are open to him for redress and protection as speedily and impartially as to any white man.[1]

Even Gandhi after almost two decades of conflict with the white settlers of South Africa maintained his faith in the imperial philosophy. "Though Empires have gone and fallen," he averred, "this Empire perhaps may be an exception and . . . is an Empire not founded on material but on spiritual foundations. That has been my source of solace all through. I have always believed there is something subtle, something fine in the ideals of the British Constitution. Tear away those ideals and you tear away my loyalty to that Constitution; keep those ideals and I am ever a bondman." [2]

But how viable were those ideals Gandhi so much admired? The disparity in strength between Great Britain and the extra-European world made it easy for liberal motives, sincerely conceived, to degenerate into feelings of racial and national superiority. The attitude of Sir Francis Younghusband, the leader of the British invasion of Tibet in 1904, was not atypical. He wrote in *The Heart of a Continent:*

No European can mix with non-Christian races without feeling his moral superiority over them. He feels, from the first contact with them, that whatever may be their relative positions from an intellectual point of view, he is stronger morally than they are. And

1. David Wells, "Great Britain and the United States: Their True Relations," *North American Review,* CLXII, Apr. 1896.
2. M. K. Gandhi, *The Collected Works of Mahatma Gandhi,* (Delhi, 1958–), XII, 505, quoting the *Cape Times,* Aug. 20, 1914. Hereafter referred to as *Works.*

facts show that this feeling is a true one. It is not because we are any cleverer than the natives of India, because we have more brains or bigger heads than they have, that we rule India; but because we are stronger morally than they are. Our superiority over them is not due to mere sharpness of intellect, but to the higher moral nature to which we have attained in the development of the human race.³

Britons in the mid-nineteenth century were developing a sense of racial uniqueness. Historians of the period, no doubt influenced by the precepts of social Darwinism and the continental racial theorists, "discovered" the roots of an Anglo-Saxon genius as far back as the fifth century in the liberties of Saxon freemen. These liberties, it was contended, were brought by Saxon invaders to the British Isles, where they survived the Norman conquest and other vicissitudes to flourish once again in Victorian Britain. What we may call "Anglo-Saxonism" assumed the existence in England of a homogeneous people blessed, since the earliest times, with superior physical and mental attributes.

At the heart of Anglo-Saxonism lay the conviction that the Anglo-Saxon (British) race possessed a special capacity for governing itself (and others) through a constitutional system which combined liberty, justice and efficiency. It was a gift that could not be transferred to lesser peoples such as Indians, who could never understand parliamentary democracy, and Frenchmen, who were always in a political mess. In fact, the British constitution was so remarkable that history was deemed to have to come to an end in Britain, in contrast to troubled places like the Balkans, which were still "in history." British superiority was not the result of anything as easily definable as education, climate or the imperatives of economics or geography; it was due rather to the unique attributes of the British race.

As the nineteenth century progressed the term "British race" was heard ever more frequently. "I believe that the British race

3. F. E. Younghusband, *The Heart of a Continent* (London, 1896), 396–97.

is the greatest of governing races the world has ever seen," proclaimed Joseph Chamberlain, the secretary of state for the colonies at the turn of the century. "I say that it is indeed a craven and poor-spirited creature who despairs of the future of the British race." [4] Or, as Cecil Rhodes put it more lyrically while wandering across the South African veldt: "As I walked, I looked up at the sky and down at the earth, and I said to myself this should be British. And it came to me in that fine, exhilarating air that the British were the best race to rule the world." [5]

Sir Charles Dilke, the prominent Liberal politician, epitomized much of this feeling in his book *Great Britain,* the story of his mid-century tour of "Saxondom." Dilke saw America as the agent of Anglo-Saxon domination and predicted a great racial conflict from which "Saxondom will rise triumphant." "China, Japan, Africa and South America must soon fall to the all-conquering Anglo-Saxon. . . . Italy, Spain, France, Russia, become pigmies by the side of such a people." And it was all for a higher purpose: "The power of English laws and English principles of government is not merely an English question—its continuance is essential to the freedom of mankind." [6]

Dilke's vision of the future was not much different from that of Cecil Rhodes, who in the first draft of his will spoke of "the extension of British rule throughout the world . . . the colonisation by British subjects . . . of the entire continent of Africa, the Holy Land, the Valley of the Euphrates, the islands of Cyprus and Candia, the whole of South America, the islands of the Pacific not heretofore possessed by Great Britain, the whole of the Malay archipelago, the sea-board of China and Japan." [7]

Even that most complicated of nineteenth century Englishmen, Benjamin Disraeli, who considered himself, among other

---

4. J. L. Garvin, *The Life of Joseph Chamberlain* (London, 1933–1951), II, 27, quoting The *Times,* Nov. 12, 1895.
5. Basil Williams, *Cecil Rhodes* (London, 1938), 55.
6. Sir Charles Dilke, *Greater Britain* (London, 1869), 230, 572–73.
7. Quoted in R. A. Huttenback, *The British Imperial Experience* (New York, 1966), 102.

things, a member of the Jewish "race," wrote in his *Tancred* that England's greatness was purely "an affair of race. A Saxon race protected by an insular position, has stamped its diligent and methodic character on the century. . . . All is race; there is no other truth." [8] It was a view echoed by Anglo-Saxonists across the water in America. For example, Theodore Parker, the liberal Unitarian minister and militant abolitionist, said he looked "with great pride on this Anglo-Saxon people. It has many faults, but I think it is the best specimen of mankind which has ever attained great power in the world." [9]

Feelings of uniqueness led inevitably to a sense of racial and national superiority. In the minds of many, "Nigger" really did begin at Calais—or Dublin. Irishmen were cursed by a double indictment, judged to be both low-class and members of an inferior—the Celtic—race. They were condemned as dirty, emotional, shiftless, untrustworthy, undisciplined, and unstable. Edith Balfour, who married Alfred Lyttelton, a future secretary of state for the colonies, wrote of the Irish, "They are like children still listening to old fairy stories while their bread has to be earned; they are like children who are afraid to walk alone, who play with fire, who are helpless; like children who will not grow up." Disraeli had previously written with surprising venom that the Irish "hate our free and fertile isles. They hate our order, our civilisation, our enterprising industry, our sustained courage, our decorous liberty, our pure religion. This wild, reckless, indolent, uncertain and superstitious race have no sympathy with the English character. Their fair ideal of human felicity is an alternation of clannish broils and coarse idolatry. Their history describes an unbroken circle of bigotry and blood." [10]

8. Quoted in L. P. Curtis, Jr., *Anglo-Saxons and Celts* (Bridgeport, 1968), 30.
9. Quoted in George M. Fredrickson, *The Black Image in the White Mind* (New York, 1971), 100.
10. Quoted in Curtis, 53, 50–51.

To a lesser extent Jews, Frenchmen, Italians, Portuguese, and others were disdained. A writer as sophisticated as John Buchan did not like Germans and was mystified by the French, and his characters disapproved of the "Portugooses." Italians were always "Dagos." Buchan was too subtle a writer to reflect the kind of anti-semitism characteristic of the late nineteenth and early twentieth centuries. Yet in *The Three Hostages,* Richard Hannay visits a nightclub where "fat Jews and blue-black dagos" danced cheek by jowl.[11]

Within the spectrum of Anglo-Saxon prejudice, it was clearly better to be English than Irish, but even more important to be white rather than black. Irishmen and other non-British Europeans might be the objects of opprobrium, but they were at least not as strange and different as the peoples of Africa and Asia. Many early British anthropologists were convinced of the Negro's inferiority. And in most cases the judgment was heavily biased by physical appearance. The *Church Missionary Intelligencer* in 1869 admitted that "it is the hue of the negro's skin which, in the eyes of modern anthropologists, forms an inseparable obstacle to his admission within the pale of our species." [12] Blackness connoted evil, and the negative effect of the Negro's color was exacerbated by other factors such as thick lips, kinky hair, and the generally primitive state in which the African lived. But Indians, scions of a culture as rich as or richer than the Anglo-Saxons', were no less victims of prejudice based largely on color.

Of all the indigenous peoples within the British Empire, only the Maoris were accorded anything approaching equal treatment before the law. One suspects this was because they were never defeated in the field and were, as a consequence, credited with virtues not usually ascribed to conquered native peoples—nobility of character, intelligence, fine physical bearing, and, of

11. John Buchan, *The Three Hostages* (London, 1934), 156.
12. Quoted in Christine Bolt, *Victorian Attitudes to Race* (London, 1971), 132.

course, courage. J. W. Fortescue, the historian of the British Army, reported that British soldiers considered the Maori "on the whole, the grandest native enemy that [they] had ever encountered." [13]

The literature of the day, and especially books dealing with the imperial adventure, provide an accurate barometer of public sentiment. For H. Rider Haggard whiteness was a prerequisite for both beauty and any kind of exalted status. Kipling's reservations about "lesser breeds without the law" are well known. Buchan in a familiar passage in *Prester John* has the white hero speak of knowing the

> meaning of the white man's duty. He has to take all risks, reckoning nothing of his life or his fortune and well content to find his reward in the fulfillment of his task. That is the difference between white and black, the gift of responsibility, the power of being in a little way a king; and so long as we know this and practice it, we will rule not in Africa alone but wherever there are dark men who live only for the day and for their own bellies.[14]

G. A. Henty wrote chiefly for young boys, and his description of the native African is reminiscent of Edith Balfour's view of the Irish. Negroes, asserted Mr. Godenough in *By Sheer Pluck,* were

> just like children. . . . They are always laughing or quarreling. They are good-natured and passionate, indolent, but will work hard for a time; clever up to a certain point, densely stupid beyond. The intelligence of an average negro is about equal to that of a European child of ten years old. A few, a very few, go beyond this, but these are exceptions, just as Shakespeare was an exception to the ordinary intellect of an Englishman. They are fluent talkers but their ideas are borrowed. They are absolutely without originality, absolutely without inventive power. Living among white men their imitative faculties enable them to attain a considerable amount of civilisation. Left alone to their own devices they retrograde into a state little above their native savagery.[15]

13. Quoted in Huttenback, 57.
14. John Buchan, *Prester John* (New York, 1938), 245.
15. G. A. Henty, *By Sheer Pluck* (New York, no date), 117.

As for Indians, they could be brave and loyal but little more. No "native" could possess the basic morality and "character," "pluck," "dash," and "good-fellowship" that were so distinctly British.

It is not surprising that Englishmen in the metropole tended to be aware of Irishmen more than they were of Asians and Africans. There were after all few colored persons in Great Britain, and the Irish question was a continuing sore. In America, however, it was the Negro who was perceived as a threat to Anglo-Saxon dominance. In 1862, a largely Republican House committee concluded in an official report "that the highest interests of the white race, whether Anglo-Saxon, Celt, or Scandinavian, require that the whole country should be held and occupied by these races alone. The Anglo-American looks upon every acre of our present domain as intended for him and not for the negro." William H. Seward, when a senator, contended: "The white man needs this continent to labor upon. His head is strong and his necessities fixed. He must and will have it." [16]

In time negrophobia became justified by the discovery in the Negro of savage lust and inehxaustible sexual potency. He was by the turn of the century judged a "brute" and "a fiend, a wild beast, seeking whom it may devour." The description of the events preceding a lynching, written in 1901 by George T. Winston, show how over the years the image of the Negro had changed from an inferior, servile creature into a dangerous menace.

When a knock is heard on the door, [the Southern woman] shudders with nameless horror. The black brute is lurking in the dark, a monstrous beast, crazed with lust. His ferocity is demoniacal. A mad bull or a tiger could scarcely be more brutal. A whole community is frenzied with horror, with the blind and furious rage for vengeance.[17]

As in America, the Anglo-Saxon settlers in the British colonies found they did not have leisure for the niceties and fine dis-

16. Quoted in Fredrickson, 146, 141.   17. *Ibid.*, 276, 278.

tinctions of prejudice. A sort of Gresham's Law of racial and ethnic animosity saw to it, in areas where there were men of color, that the white man directed his hatred almost exclusively against them. Only when all the inhabitants of a region were white were white minorities subjected to a high degree of disdain and the disadvantages associated with it. Thus Irishmen in England were considered part of a despised lower order whereas in the colonies they were members of the ruling elite.

Observers and critics of the British Empire have often been willing to turn a blind eye toward the generally illiberal policies of South Africa because in their view the racial equation there was unique. The fact that the rest of the Empire of Settlement acted similarly has been largely ignored. These colonies, throughout much of the nineteenth century, became the destination of non-Europeans from "friendly" states such as China and Japan and from another part of the British Empire—India. As in South Africa, a strong resentment developed against these new arrivals, based principally on the racial precepts of Anglo-Saxonism but in part also on the workingman's fear of losing his job to "cheap" labor from Africa and Asia.

Two sets of principles were clearly on a collision course. On the one hand marched the concept of what Burke had called "the natural equality of mankind at large," which, under the influence of nineteenth-century liberal humanitarianism and the evangelical movement, had turned into the concept of trusteeship and the imperial philosophy of a nonracial empire, all of whose subjects were equal before the law. Emerging on the other hand was the determination of the British settlers in South Africa, Australia, New Zealand, and Canada that theirs must be a "White Man's Country."

Joseph Chamberlain manifested the ambivalence in many British minds when he spoke to the premiers of the self-governing colonies upon the occasion of Queen Victoria's Diamond Jubilee in June 1897. His words held something for everybody. As a good Anglo-Saxon he identified with the colonies' fear of being inundated by nonwhite immigrants. "We quite sympathise," he said,

> with the determination of the white inhabitants of these colonies which are in comparatively close proximity to millions and hundreds of millions of Asiatics that there shall not be an influx of people alien in civilisation, alien in religion, alien in customs, whose influx, moreover, would most seriously interfere with the legitimate rights of the existing labour population. An Immigration of that kind, must, I quite understand, in the interests of the Colonies, be prevented at all hazards, and we shall not offer any opposition to the proposals intended for that object.

As a minister of the crown, however, charged with the protection of the imperial philosophy of equality, Chamberlain asked his listeners "also to bear in mind the traditions of the Empire, which makes no distinction in favour of, or against race or colour; and to exclude, by reason of their colour or by reason of their race, all Her Majesty's Indian subjects, or even all Asiatics, would be an act so offensive to those people, that it would be most painful, I am certain, to Her Majesty to have to sanction it." [18]

Owing to its somewhat haphazard growth, the British Empire lacked the administrative and structural continuity apparent in more planned enterprises such as the French and German Empires. In the differing circumstances associated with colonial acquisitions, London acted with its usual pragmatism. Thus the Empire by mid-nineteenth century consisted of possessions at varying levels of constitutional development and blessed with a great variety of governments. Protectorates, totally dependent colonies, colonies with representative government (some with elected and others with official—ex-officio and appointed—legislative majorities) all fell under the aegis of the Colonial Office. At the top of the ladder of imperial constitutional development stood those colonies that had been granted responsible

---

18. C. 8596, 1897 *Proceedings of a Conference between the Secretary of State for the Colonies and the Premiers of the Self-Governing Colonies.*

government. This meant that the governor received his instructions from the leader of the majority party in the legislature and maintained only a limited power to reserve legislation for Whitehall's scrutiny. Responsible government was granted to Canada in 1848 and in ensuing years to all the constituent parts of the Empire of White Settlement—the Australian colonies, New Zealand, and South Africa.

One question with which this study will deal is how far Whitehall was prepared to go to preserve "the traditions of the Empire, which makes no distinction in favour of, or against race or colour." This concern constitutes a minor chord, however, rather than the dominant one. Even before the advent of responsible government, there was considerable doubt that Britain had either the will or the ability to interfere in the internal affairs of its colonies on a consistent basis. What responsible government did was to add constitutional impediments to natural reticence and to make British intervention essentially illegal except in matters of imperial or international concern. To be sure, the right to disallow colonial legislation remained, but a sort of imperial common law precluded its use except on rare occasions. As for the Government of India, it maintained a certain independence from Whitehall and claimed the right to speak for British Indians wherever they might be. This meant that Calcutta could prescribe the conditions under which indentured Indians were allowed to emigrate and staunch the flow to any place that failed to maintain an acceptable corpus of protective legislation. Over the emigration of free Indians and the status of those no longer under contract, the Government of India had little or no control and its interest in their well-being was at best limited.

Our chief concerns, therefore, lie more with the colonies of settlement themselves than with Great Britain, and with colored immigrants rather than indigenous peoples. Although to a lesser extent than in Britain itself, the white population of these colonies was remarkably homogeneous. The Afrikaner and

French populations of South Africa and Canada, respectively, marked notable breaks in the pattern, but even they, although differing with their Anglo-Saxon neighbors on many issues, did not do so on matters of race. Indeed, the Afrikaners were much more extreme than the British, while the French Canadians were too preoccupied by the convolutions of their own identity crisis to care greatly about anything else.

The book is divided into five major sections. The first four treat comparatively major issues as they manifested themselves in Australia, Canada, New Zealand, and South Africa. Chapter 1 discusses indentured or contract labor which, because it implied only the temporary residence of imported nonwhite workers, was deemed by many of the colonists an ideal solution to perennial labor shortages. That the remedy was not all that it seemed was manifested chiefly in the case of South Africa. Chapter 2 introduces the question of free colored immigration to colonies that did not want these "undesirables" and the various stratagems used to keep them out. Chapter 3 deals with the birth of the "Natal formula" (more commonly known as the literacy or language test), its reception in Whitehall, the various guises in which it appeared, and the uses to which it was put by the colonies of white settlement.

But if the "Natal formula" finally provided the weapon to keep free colored immigrants out, it must be remembered that many thousands had already settled in the Empire before their entry was blocked. And indentured Indians in Natal could and did continue to remain in South Africa as free men even after the advent of the "Natal formula." Chapter 4 accordingly analyzes the position of nonwhite immigrants who were legitimate residents of the colonies of settlement.

In no other constituent part of the Empire did the "Natal formula" and its ancillary legal abutments reach the state of refinement and sophistication that they did in Australia after the creation of the Commonwealth in 1901. The fifth part of the book, consequently, devotes itself to "White Australia" and, to a lesser extent, "White New Zealand."

Many years after Mahatma Gandhi had left the shores of Africa forever, General Smuts, his chief adversary in the struggle over Indian rights, wrote, "It was my fate to be the antagonist of a man for whom even then I had the highest respect." But Smuts went on to "frankly admit that his activities at that time were trying to me. . . . Gandhi raised a troublesome issue. We had a skeleton in our cupboard." [19] That "skeleton," as it came to light in the various cupboards of the self-governing British Empire, is the subject of this book.

19. Quoted in R. A. Huttenback, *Gandhi in South Africa* (Ithaca, N.Y., 1971), 330.

1 Colored Labor in the Pre-Restriction Era— The Contract System

All the British colonies of settlement—Canada, Australia, New Zealand and South Africa—were from the first deeply committed to the dream of becoming outposts of the "British race." The only settler to be encouraged to sail to the new lands were British-born denizens of the home islands who shared the ethnic roots and world view of the colonies' white populations. Cruel reality and the laws of economic necessity have, however, a way of eroding and diluting even the most firmly held beliefs, and as labor became an ever more compelling need in the vast and sparsely settled imperial lands, entrepreneurs came to the realization that the reservoir of manpower in Britain willing to settle overseas was not great enough to fulfill the demands. Besides, the ease of acquiring land, as Edward Gibbon Wakefield so clearly saw, invited the dispersal of what white population there was and prevented the establishment of a labor pool upon which employers could draw. And in the only colony with a large native population, Natal, the tribes resident in the territory were unwilling to provide continuous and reliable labor.

Given such a dilemma, the colonial establishments, much to the chagrin of the nascent working population, either actively encouraged or at least failed to prevent the arrival of laborers and others such as miners from the densely populated zones of Asia. Thus, in the second half of the nineteenth century and the first part of the twentieth, Chinese and Japanese immigrated to Australia and Canada. A handful of Chinese landed in New Zealand, and tens of thousands of Indians migrated to South Africa. A few Indians sailed to Australia and New Zealand, while natives of the Punjab in northern India began arriving in British Columbia at the turn of the century.

The desire for Asian immigrants originally manifested itself in Australia. As early as 1829, Robert Gouger of South Australia, soon to be the territory's first colonial secretary,[1] wrote that if laborers were imported from Canton, new lands could be exploited. Even willing to countenance Chinese land ownership, Gouger wanted to lend the necessary capital and encourage the growth of Chinatowns. Thinking "procreative power" a most important commodity, he hoped to make it possible for the wives and children of Chinese immigrants to follow them. Land grants should be made dependent on the Chinese settler providing a certain number of Chinese laborers. Nothing, however, came of the proposal.[2]

What the colonial entrepreneurs really had in mind was indentured or contract labor, not free immigrants. Thus New South Wales, the senior Australian colony, initially turned to India for help. In 1836 efforts were mounted to import Indian coolies into New South Wales, and between October 1836 and May 1837 a stream of memoranda was submitted to the legislative council. A certain John MacKay estimated that it would cost £11 to import a male Indian and £8 to ship a female. He thought that most, if not all, the "wealthy colonists of respectability" would be willing to pay half the costs of importing "coolies" if the government would underwrite the remainder. Furthermore, the scheme would involve a lot less expense than

---

1. The colonial secretary was the chief administrative officer of a colony and is not to be confused with the secretary of state for the colonies.
2. Margaret P. Rendell, "The Chinese in South Australia and the Northern Territory in the Nineteenth Century" (M.A. thesis, University of Adelaide, 1952), 45.

the aided passage offered Europeans.[3] As one writer averred, "There is one great advantage to be derived from the Indian character, they are temperate and are particularly trustworthy where sobriety is absolutely necessary." [4] On May 24, 1837 a group of flock owners wrote the colonial secretary that because of the shortage of British immigrants, they wanted the governor to send to Bengal for shepherds, cowherds and household servants who should be of "sober, honest and industrious habits." They again offered to share the costs with the government.[5]

Downing Street was less than enthusiastic about the sheep men's proposal. Lord Glenelg, the secretary of state for war and the colonies, wrote Governor Sir George Gipps that the introduction of Indian laborers in any numbers could not but have an adverse effect on the colony. The Indians would be considered inferior by the rest of the colonists, and this creation of a degraded element in the population would place agricultural labor in such disrepute as to discourage emigration from England.[6] But despite the Colonial Office's opposition and the awesome administrative efficiency of Gipps, some laborers from both India and China were imported into New South Wales by private entrepreneurs. When a handful of Indians also found their way to South Australia, Lord Stanley, who had taken over at the Colonial Office, could contain himself no longer. He pointed out that Her Majesty's Government had always opposed the introduction of Indian laborers into the Australian colonies and that consequently he could not countenance the system in the case of South Australia.[7]

The Colonial Office had an ally in the small but growing

3. CO 201/61, N.S.W. 2370, no. 98, Bourke to Glenelg, June 17, 1837, encl. 3.
4. *Ibid.*, Remarks upon the Employment of Indian Labourers out of Their Country by J. R. May, esq.
5. *Ibid.*, flock-owners to colonial secretary, Sydney, May 24, 1837.
6. CO 202/37, Entry Book, no. 46, Glenelg to Gipps, Dec. 14, 1837.
7. CO 13/24, no. 21, Grey to Stanley, Feb. 22, 1842; no. 50, Stanley to Grey, Aug. 23, 1842.

working population. On August 4, 1843, for instance, Stanley wrote Gipps that he was in receipt of a petition from persons in Sydney "principally of the working class," inveighing against the possible importation of laborers from India under an officially sanctioned scheme. The secretary of state reported that the petition had been "very graciously" received by the Queen. The petitioners were to be informed that "No measure [was] in contemplation for permitting the Emigration of Coolies into New South Wales." [8]

But though Whitehall and its representatives in the colonies could rail against the importation of colored labor, there was really very little they could do about it as long as the immigration was handled privately. Although all requests for government support were peremptorily refused, 270 Chinese nonetheless arrived in New South Wales between 1846 and 1849.[9] And Governor Sir Charles Fitzroy could not help but report that Chinese in Sydney had easily found profitable employment as servants, gardeners and shepherds, "and have generally proved to be an industrious and harmless class of men—giving satisfaction to their employers." [10]

Chinese law specifically forbade Chinese emigration, and the governments of Great Britain and New South Wales disapproved. Nevertheless, the *Cadet,* a British vessel, in November 1849 sailed from Amoy for Sydney with 150 Chinese laborers aboard, while the *London* set sail from Hong Kong with 230 more.[11] The Colonial Office, in minuting, wearily concluded that it did not know what to do, especially as the governor of New South Wales had failed to reply to a dispatch on the subject.[12] As a matter of fact, colored laborers from many parts of the world were quietly landed in New South Wales. For exam-

8. CO 13/48, no. 122, Stanley to Gipps, Aug. 4, 1843.
9. CO 201/416, N.S.W. 1101, no. 203, Fitzroy to Grey, Oct. 3, 1849.
10. *Ibid.*
11. CO 201/420, F[oreign] O[ffice] to C[olonial] O[ffice], Dec. 20, 1849, encl. J. W. P. Farrow (Manilla) to Palmerston, Sept. 25, 1849.
12. *Ibid.,* minuting.

ple, natives of Singapore were imported into the Geelong district as shepherds. In the course of time, a number ended up in Melbourne jail as vagrants, and the superintendent consequently felt constrained to urge the implementation of legislation to inhibit colored immigration or, failing that, the passage of laws to protect the public from expenses resulting from it.[13]

The Colonial Office was willing to countenance almost any immigration scheme that did not involve the importation of colored labor. In early 1852 the Madras East India Society proposed to send, at its expense, twenty Eurasian males between the ages of eighteen and thirty to New South Wales. If the experiment were successful, the society hoped to send more and to receive financial assistance from the government. Lord Grey, then the secretary of state for war and the colonies, approved the proposal and saw no reason why New South Wales should not devote a limited portion of its land fund to subsidize the immigration of "persons of semi-European origin" [14] from India, providing they were "of the right type." The first consignment in due course arrived and was successfully absorbed by the colony. Employers were enthusiastic about the scheme, and they wrote the governor "that there is ground for believing the majority of the persons to be descendants of soldiers, sailors, and other public servants, who thus have an additional claim for consideration." [15] There is, however, no evidence of any further shipments of Eurasians from India. Throughout the British Empire, any contamination of white blood was bound to exact its toll. As the *Madras Commercial Chronicle* wrote: "Australia offers ample opportunity for further colonisation, and the Eurasians are as free as others to take advantage of it, but they must bear with them a large measure of those very

13. CO 201/416, N.S.W. 1101, no. 203, Fitzroy to Grey, Oct. 3, 1849, encl. superintendent to colonial secretary, July 11, 1849.
14. CO 201/458, Madras East India Society to Grey, Feb. 25, 1852; CO to Lt. Governor C. Latrobe, no. 40, July 17, 1852.
15. CO 204/36, Memorial of Landholders, Flockmasters, Merchants and others residing in N.S.W. to Sir Charles Augustus Fitzroy, July 16, 1852.

qualifications, in which they are most deficient, namely, energy, perseverance, and a disregard for hardships. Wanting these . . . the East Indian Emigrant will inevitably fail. He must hold his own with the vigorous and resolute, the enduring and hardy Anglo-Saxon." [16]

Still, employers persisted in their efforts. In 1853, Thomas Duncan of Sydney came to an agreement with a Chinese known as Tam Hoch for the importation of Chinese into the northern districts of New South Wales.[17] After their arrival they were described as an undesirable lot. The dearth of females brought about problems with the Aborigines, and the Chinese were accused of "unnatural crimes."[18] Furthermore, it was alleged, they broke their agreements as soon as they discovered how much labor was receiving on the open market. H. H. Browne, the New South Wales agent for immigration, thought the Chinese too delicate for the Australian climate, but on the other hand referred to "their well known beastly habits and revengeful temperaments when either thwarted or annoyed."[19] Governor Fitzroy saw no need to act, as he was convinced that the adverse experience of importers would prevent the arrival of any more contract laborers in northern New South Wales.[20]

By and large Fitzroy's assessment was accurate not only for New South Wales but for the whole continent, although virtually all the Australian colonies made sporadic attempts to import Asian labor. South Australia, for instance, was an immense province which between 1863 and 1911 included within its jurisdiction the vast Northern Territory reaching up to Darwin (also known as Port Darwin and until 1911 as Palmerston).

16. CO 204/36, imm. agent to colonial secretary, June 15, 1852.
17. CO 201/467, no. 167, Fitzroy to Grey, Dec. 30, 1853. The area referred to became part of Queensland when that colony was established in 1859.
18. *Ibid.*, encl. W. A. Duncan, act. govt. resident, Brisbane, to H. H. Browne, agent for imm., Oct. 27, 1853.
19. *Ibid.*, Browne to colonial secretary, Dec. 15, 1853.
20. CO 201/480, col. land and em. office to H. Merrivale, May 20, 1854.

This huge tropical wilderness was sufficiently inhospitable to repel virtually all white settlers. Consequently, acts were passed in 1878 (Act 163) and 1882 (Act 140) to allow for the immigration of Indian laborers. These laws, however, aroused little controversy, as the complex protective machinery demanded by the government of India doomed them to sterility from the first. Besides, Indians were never deemed a threat, at least in South Australia. They were natives of a British dependency and were thought disinclined to immigrate.

The same could not be said of the Chinese. Although the laborers of the south lived in dread of their arrival, the entrepreneurs of the north saw them as the only salvation for the region, especially after 1871 when gold was discovered at Pine Creek (N.T.). In April 1874 J. C. Coates, secretary of a large number of mining companies in the Northern Territory, wrote the commissioner of crown lands requesting government support for the acquisition of cheap labor capable of withstanding the rigors of the climate. Coates suggested that Captain Bloomfield Douglas, R.N., who was familiar with the Northern Territory, be sent to Singapore by the outgoing mail to secure the services of some two hundred coolies whose number should include some skilled gardeners to grow vegetables to keep the whole contingent healthy. A list of the various companies and the number of Chinese immigrants they would be willing to employ was enclosed with the letter. The government accepted Coates's proposal, and Captain Douglas in due course returned with the two hundred coolies, each of whom had been signed to a two-year contract.[21] This single shipload appears to have been the beginning of Asian immigration to the Northern Territory. A recession in the nascent mining industry brought matters temporarily to a halt, however, and the numbers of Asian laborers imported into the territory throughout its history as a part of South Australia were small, although large enough to arouse

21. Rendell, 45–46.

working men and political leaders in the south and some of the European settlers in the north.

Of all the Australasian colonies, Western Australia was, in its early years, perhaps the most anemic in terms of population—not to mention labor. As had its sister colonies, it turned its eyes towards Asia for relief. Despite the disapproval of the Colonial Office,[22] Governor Irwin, noting a credit balance of £82. 8s. 2d in the colonial treasury, determined in 1867 to send the *Champion* to Singapore for Chinese coolies. The vessel duly fulfilled its assignment but returned with domestic servants rather than the needed farm labor. It was consequently sent back the following year to collect a more suitable cargo. The census figures for 1868 revealed a population of 4,642 Europeans and 90 Asians.[23]

Between 1870 and 1880 Western Australia mounted several efforts to introduce Chinese coolies into the colony. In 1874, for example, the legislative council authorized the governor to spend such amounts as he considered necessary for immigration purposes, including up to £1000 on the importation of Chinese or Javanese coolies.[24] In anticipation of their arrival and to prevent any major misadventure, the legislature passed an imported labor registry act in 1874. The measure was designed to control the transportation of coolies under indenture. Ships' masters were asked to furnish passenger lists and other details before landing any Chinese, and it was hoped in this manner to avoid the problems experienced by the eastern colonies during the gold rush and poll tax periods (see Chapter 2). The precautions were, however, unnecessary at this time, as the importation scheme met with little success. In 1878 the legislative council decided to invest £4,500 in the acquisition of coolies and

22. CO 397/7, W.A. Entry Book, no. 13, Grey to officer admin. the Govt. of W.A., Feb. 29, 1848.
23. Bonnie Hicks, "A Study of a Minority Group: The Chinese in Albany," W.A. Archives, Battye Library, 1967, Chap. 3, 1.
24. J. S. Battye, *Western Australia: A History, From its Discovery to the Inauguration of the Commonwealth* (Oxford, 1924), 318–19.

only £2,500 in European immigrants. But owing to the opposition manifested in many quarters to the idea of coolie immigration, only fifty Chinese ever actually arrived that year, and experience with them gave rise to considerable further controversy. The evidence, however, was positive enough for the council, in 1879, to vote a further £2,000 for the importation of Chinese coolies. The noted historian of Western Australia, J. S. Battye, states that Governor Orde was sufficiently impressed by the negative arguments to prevent implementation of the scheme.[25] But the government gazettes for the period indicate that the governor called for applications from employers interested in Chinese labor and that this notice was repeated in 1880.[26] It was the paucity of the demand rather than the governor's attitude which prevented action. In late 1880 the demand increased, with results that will be discussed later.

As in the other Australasian colonies, large commercial interests such as the pearlers of Shark's Bay wanted Chinese coolies, while the laboring element did not.[27] Be that as it may, the few Chinese in Western Australia were treated with little respect. A certain Ah Coo was horsewhipped by his employer and left without food for several days. Ah Fuk was turned out and left essentially destitute for two weeks.[28] Minuting, probably by the governor and the colonial secretary, concluded that legal action against the employer would be useless. They were more concerned that penniless Chinese introduced by settlers not fall to the care of the government.[29]

The only major exception to Fitzroy's perception occurred in Queensland which, as the most equatorial of the Australian

25. *Ibid.*
26. Brian DeGaris, "The History of Asian Immigration into Western Australia," W.A. Archives, PR 3186, 4.
27. W.A. Archives, chief secretary's office, 1265–1880.
28. *Ibid.*, 1394–1881, Thomas Plow, detective sergeant, to detective office, Perth, 19/5/81.
29. *Ibid.*, J. H. Clarkson, govt. resident, Roeborne to Lord Gifford, Oct. 20, 1881, minuting.

colonies, was well suited for the development of tropical and subtropical agriculture, particularly the raising of sugar cane. The colony was sparsely populated in comparison with New South Wales and Victoria, and as a plantation economy demanded a large and constant supply of labor, it came to feel a need for agricultural workers unmatched by any of the other colonies.

Like its sister dependencies, Queensland at the outset looked towards India and China for relief. From the first, petitions pointed out that the rigors of a tropical climate necessitated special treatment for the colony if it were to prosper.[30] The Colonial Office, in contrast to its attitude towards other Australian colonies on the same question, was not unsympathetic. Minuting of December 10, 1860, explained:

> In the early days of Australia, and at greater distances from the Tropic, I am inclined to believe that it was a wise policy which resisted occasional projects to import coolies from India. It is no light gain to have acquired in those vast regions a purely British population, approaching already to a million souls, unmixed with inferior races or feeble half castes. But this great advantage being secured, it would probably be neither practicable nor expedient to attempt to refuse permission to import Coolies into a new Australian colony, situated in a hotter zone than the others, and affording some prospect of yielding, if sufficient labour can be commanded, the all important benefit of a supply of cotton.[31]

And, indeed, it was cotton on which Queensland based its hopes for salvation, rather than sugar.

Queensland's governor in the early 1860s was Sir George Bowen, a fervent advocate of both cotton cultivation and imported Asian labor. With missionary zeal he preached the true word and attempted to convert nonbelievers to the Faith. Whereas most Australian governors were importuned by their constituents on the imported labor issue, Bowen reversed the process. In early 1860 he addressed an open letter to the colo-

30. CO 234/2, Q. 1616, Bowen to Newcastle, Dec. 18, 1860.
31. *Ibid.* Newcastle, in minuting of Dec. 24, agreed.

nists of Queensland in which he contended, "The introduction of Asiatic labour would be to Queensland what machinery has been to England, elevating the European labourer to the rank of merchant, and the mechanic to that of an employer, and contributing to a marvelous degree to the well-being of every class of society." [32]

With the interruption of the cotton supply from the southern United States, Queensland became the major supplier of cotton to British mills. Bowen urgently requested the Duke of Newcastle at the Colonial Office to support a scheme for the immigration of Indian laborers to Queensland,[33] and the secretary of state, in turn, convinced his counterpart in the India Office to sanction immigration to Queensland on the same basis as to Mauritius and the West Indies. In other words, working conditions, diet, and length of contract had to be precisely defined and a return passage to India guaranteed.[34] With this news in hand, Bowen did not follow the usual path of awaiting the passage of necessary legislation but instead gained legislative sanction for the issuing of administrative regulations to govern an immigration program. As he wrote the Colonial Office, it would have taken at least twelve months to pass the necessary act of parliament, and such a delay at the commencement of a major effort to cultivate cotton would have been disastrous, "especially to those English Capitalists who propose to grow cotton in Queensland with the aid of Asiatic labour. It would, in fact, amount to a virtual prohibition of the employment of their enterprises in the promising field of this Colony." [35] When the Government of India pleaded that there was not enough labor for the needs of India herself, Bowen found himself unconvinced, as Queensland had recently been asked to contribute

32. I. H. Moles, "The Indian Coolie Labour Issue in Queensland," *Journal of the Historical Society of Queensland*, V, no. 1, 1953.
33. CO 234/3 Q. 5593, no. 20, Bowen to Newcastle, Apr. 16, 1860.
34. CO 423/1–Q. Entry book, no. 15, Newcastle to Bowen, Apr. 26, 1861.
35. CO 234/4, col. sec.'s office to Bowen, Sept. 26, 1861; no. 55, Bowen to Newcastle, Sept. 27, 1861.

funds "to save millions of their Hindoo fellow-subjects from positive starvation."[36]

With progress on the Indian front slow, Bowen turned his attention towards China. He contended that the immigration of Chinese families would remove many of the objections that the white colonists harbored toward the exclusively male Chinese community. Besides, the presence of Chinese labor on plantations would increase both the demand for European artisans and the flow of capital into Queensland.[37]

But while Bowen continued to wax eloquent on the promise of Queensland cotton cultivation and to circumvent established procedure to gain his end—the importation of Asian labor—the Colonial Office was becoming increasingly disenchanted with the enthusiastic governor, because he seemed totally unwilling to go beyond vague schemes and to pass the kind of protective legislation for Asian immigrant labor demanded by both Her Majesty's Government and the Government of India. "I cannot help observing," Newcastle wrote to Bowen,

> that your Government in their natural and laudable desire to develop the resources of Queensland appear to me to have overlooked in some degree, the responsibilities which attach to those who induce multitudes of ignorant persons to leave their homes, sometimes with their women and children, in order to seek a new country which may or may not be fitted for them. It is not unnatural that having no experience of the misery and disaster which in such large operations is found to result even from a trifling oversight, they should consent to run risks the extent of which they do not entirely realise rather than appear to thwart the desires of those whose immediate interests they represent.

The secretary of state then gently chided Bowen for having ignored previous warnings "which were suggested by a very large and minute experience of the dangers attendant on the announcement and progress of immigration.[38] Away from the dip-

36. CO 234/6, Q. 2822, no. 4, Bowen to Newcastle, Jan. 10, 1862.
37. *Ibid.*
38. CO 234/1, no. 12, Newcastle to Bowen, Apr. 20, 1862.

lomatic constraints of official correspondence, Newcastle confided to minuting, "Sir G. Bowen has in this matter endeavoured to 'stand a march' on the Sec. of State and the Indian Govt. or has allowed his zeal and anxiety for immigrant labour to outrun his discretion and that attention to details of the subject which the interests of the Colony itself as well of the Coolies absolutely require." [39]

Partially restoring his credit with Whitehall, Bowen was able to gain passage through the Queensland legislature of Act 25 of 1862—"An Act to Give the Force of Law to Regulations for the Introduction and Protection of Labourers from British India"—which was superior in many ways to its counterpart in colonies already importing Indian laborers. Under these conditions and as the immigration scheme envisaged no expenditure of funds by the Government of Queensland, the measure received the royal assent.[40] For a number of reasons, however, not the least of which was the inability of the Government of India to pass enabling legislation until 1864, Act 25 remained essentially a dead letter.

Nevertheless, Bowen fought on. In forwarding anti-labor importation petitions from Brisbane and Ipswich to Newcastle, the governor contended that they were "really got up by a few individuals, generally without any stake in the country who seek to make political capital by trading on the prejudices of the mass of the working men in our towns," who now regarded Asian labor as the British working man had once viewed the introduction of machinery.[41] As time went on, favorable peti-

39. CO 234/7, L. and E., Q. 859, Murdoch to Sir Frederick Elliot, minuting by N., 2/2.
40. CO 234/7, L. and E., Q. 9911, Murdoch to Elliot, Oct. 10; CO to I[ndia] O[ffice], Oct. 13; IO to CO, Oct. 27, 1862. The law had the usual guarantees required by the Government of India, such as paid return passage at the end of five years' (three years' indentured) service, a minimum of 25 percent of the immigrants to be women, adequate health facilities, etc.
41. CO 234/6, Q. 9289, Bowen to Newcastle, July 18, 1862.

tions were passed on without comment, while negative ones were ascribed to the prejudices of the unthinking artisans of the southern towns. Gleefully, Bowen pointed out that one of the petitions, which he considered typical of those opposed to Asian immigration, had been "covered . . . with stains of rum and tobacco juice . . . [as] the 'Anglo-Saxon' who had been paid to collect signatures to the petition denouncing the 'immoral and heathen Asiatic,' had unfortunately himself got drunk in some public-house, while engaged in procuring names. I greatly fear that the condition of the documents is an evidence of the sort of means by which these demonstrations are too often managed." [42]

With the prospects of Indian immigration becoming ever dimmer, Bowen once more turned his gaze on China. In October 1863 he wrote Newcastle that the British consul at Canton had informed him that he could easily obtain Chinese labor for Queensland. Would this be permissible? The secretary of state, although opposed, did not veto the proposal, but pointed out that as the consul in question was about to be recalled to England, Queensland would have to set up its own recruiting establishment in Canton. "You will probably prefer to forego," Newcastle conjectured, "the services of Chinese immigrants rather than incur the cost of carrying on Immigration on so expensive a scale." [43]

China did, indeed, turn out to be another dry well. But the resolute governor never faltered in his resolve to make Queensland the cotton producing center of the world. He contended Asian labor would never supersede white and invoked expert testimony which declared that "With a sufficient supply of Asiatic labour, Queensland alone could . . . grow cotton sufficient in quantity for the supply of the whole world, and superior to that produced in any other country." [44]

42. CO 234/7, Q. 10338, no. 48, Bowen to Newcastle, Aug. 17, 1862.
43. CO 234/8, Q. 12171, no. 54, Bowen to Newcastle, Oct. 4, 1863; 234/9, Q. 9734, Newcastle to Bowen, July 25, 1863.
44. CO 234/10, Q. 9734, Bowen to Cardwell, Aug. 10, 1864.

Ultimately, Bowen's enthusiasm for cotton and Indian and Chinese labor immigration came to nought. No Indian coolies or pigtailed "celestials" were ever to make their appearance in either the numbers or the form desired. And the end of the American Civil War shattered the dream of Queensland's preeminence in cotton forever. In a sense, however, Bowen's vision of the future had been remarkably accurate. Much of the economic future of Queensland did lie in plantation agriculture, but the crop was to be sugar instead of cotton.

As the sugar industry expanded and mineral resources were unearthed in the late 1860s and early 1870s, the pressure on the government to import labor increased. In view of this development, Queensland again made periodic attempts to induce the immigration of Indian coolies. From the floor of the Assembly, Thomas Henry Fitzgerald of Wickham contended that Indians made ideal laborers and that the language problem was not acute with them. He urged the implementation of a scheme to admit Indians in numbers sufficient to offset the labor shortage.[45] The colonial secretary contended that the labor supply in the colony was more than adequate to meet its needs,[46] but it soon became clear to the government that this assessment of the situation was incorrect. In August 1874 Lord Normanby, then the governor, consequently wrote Lord Carnarvon, the new secretary of state, that his government had determined to sanction Chinese immigration and had asked him to communicate with Her Majesty's consul at Amoy on the subject. Colored labor, the governor contended, was vital to the successful cultivation of sugar; without it settlement of the north must cease, the sugar industry die, and the white man lose a remunerative area of employment. Clinton Murdoch, at the emigration board, in minuting, pointed out that as Her Majesty's Government had forced the Portuguese to cease shipping Chinese from Macao, the Queensland proposal was not without potential em-

45. Queensland *Hansard*, July 7, 1874.   46. *Ibid.*

barrassment. Indian immigration involved no such problem.[47]

It was all of little moment. When Sir William Cairns (described by a contemporary as looking like a mute at a funeral) replaced Lord Normanby as governor, he informed London that his ministers did not wish to continue conversations on the Chinese immigration scheme, for even as things stood, the influx of Chinese prospectors was causing animosity in the ranks of white labor. Within a month, the governor expressed himself still more strongly. Not only had his government never favored Chinese immigration, but the cabinet was in fact against it. Cairns claimed that his ministers were ignorant of what Normanby had written. "The Government are opposed to any action that would savour of encouragement to Chinese Emigration." [48]

It appears that the first sixty South Sea Islanders were introduced into Queensland in 1862 (although a similar number had been imported into New South Wales as early as 1847) by Captain Robert Towns, a Sydney skipper, member of the legislative council in New South Wales and the owner of a cotton estate in northern Queensland that came to be known as Townsville. A few other employers followed Towns's example, and within three years about 1,200 islanders were working on Queensland plantations. When news of the enterprise reached London, it gave rise to a controversy that was to last for several decades.

From the first days of evangelical humanitarianism, its prophets had zealously striven to bring the word of Christ to the natives of the islands of the South Seas and to protect them from those who would take advantage of their innocence. It was inevitable that a major conflict would erupt between the planting interests in Queensland and the prophets of Clapham Sect, who

47. CO 234/34, Q. 12706, no. 36, Normanby to Carnarvon, Aug. 3, 1874; minuting of Apr. 11, 1874.
48. CO 234/35, Q. 7305, no. 30, W. W. Cairns to Carnarvon, Apr. 10, 1875; Q. 8386, no. 40, Cairns to Carnarvon, May 7, 1877.

were not about to see their victory over slavery dissipated by a new form of servitude in the Pacific. It was an issue that affected Parliament, with its strong Christian constituency, more than most imperial questions, and legislation designed to control the excesses of the labor trade periodically reached the statute books.[49] When the working population, ever fearful of cheap labor, joined the opposition to Polynesian importation, the Queensland Government was forced to increase its efforts to keep the labor trade itself and the treatment islanders received in the colony above reproach.[50] It was an enterprise in which the authorities at Brisbane were never very successful. Kidnapping, murder, and other excesses continued to be the order of the day.

In 1883 there were according to various estimates between 11,400 and 14,000 islanders in Queensland.[51] Some of them had completed their terms of indenture but had not returned home. They hardly constituted a threat to the white working man. But such was the sensitivity on the labor question that 733 residents of Mackay, on the north coast of Queensland, petitioned the legislature for relief from the threat of competition from time-expired islanders. It was contended that the islanders took jobs away from white men; that they reduced the supply of colored labor on the sugar plantations by going into other lines of work; that they drank too much, became disorderly and endan-

49. Pacific Islanders' Protection Act of 1824, Act 4, Geo. IV, c. 96. Pacific Islanders' Protection Act of 1872, 35 and 36, Vict., c. 19. Pacific Islanders' Amendment Act of 1875, 38 and 39, Vict., c. 51.
50. Queensland Acts 47 of 1868 and 17 of 1880.
51. 13,967 according to CO 263/83, 1884, p. 1420. O. W. Parnaby, *Britain and the Labor Trade in the Southwest Pacific* (Durham, 1964), 204, listed the following statistics as to the numbers of islanders present in Queensland in any given year:

Date	Numbers	Date	Numbers
1868 2 March	1543	1891 5 April	9428
1868 31 Dec.	2127	1892 1 Jan.	8627
1869 31 Dec.	2135	1893 1 Jan.	7979
1870 18 June	2033	1894 1 Jan.	7489
1871 1 Sept.	4336	1895 1 Jan.	7853
1875	4441	1895 31 Dec.	8163

gered the public; and that, furthermore, they corrupted their indentured fellows by teaching them to drink. The petitioners begged the legislature to limit the employment of even free Polynesians to tropical agriculture and asked that anyone who hired a time-expired islander become liable for the cost of the return passage in substitution for the original employer.[52]

Sir Samuel Griffith and his Liberal Party won an overwhelming victory in the colonial election of 1883, based on his strong opposition to the island labor traffic. The legislature as a consequence passed Act 12 of 1884, which amended the Pacific Island Labourers Act of 1880 (no. 17). Several sections of the original act had been designed to mollify the European working population. Article 2 had defined a "Pacific Islander" or "Islander" as "A native, not of European extraction, of any island in the Pacific Ocean which is not in Her Majesty's dominions, nor within the jurisdiction of any civilised power." Islanders were to be confined to employment in tropical or semi-tropical agriculture which was defined as "The business of cultivating sugar-cane, cotton, tea, coffee, rice, spices, or other tropical or semi-tropical productions or fruits and of rendering the products thereof marketable." Although article 4 exempted islanders employed in the pearl or bêche-de-mer fisheries of Queensland from the workings of the act, article 7 provided, among other

1876	1 May	5108	1896 31 Dec.	8444
1877		5874	1897 31 Dec.	8224
1878		5869	1898 31 Dec.	8485
1881	3 April	6348	1899 31 Dec.	8795
1883		11443	1900 31 Dec.	9324
1886	1 May	10037	1901 31 March	9327
1887	1 Jan.	8723	1902 31 Dec.	8878
1888	1 Jan.	8200	1903 31 Dec.	8614
1889	1 Jan.	7580	1904 31 Dec.	7879
1890	1 Jan.	8115	1906 10 April	6389

In 1906, 691 held exemption tickets under 47 Vict., no. 12, and under the Commonwealth Act, no. 22, 1906. Commonwealth Act, no. 16, 1901, required that the remainder be returned to the islands.

52. CO 236/83, 1886, p. 1453.

things, that no license to import islanders would be issued to any employer, "unless the applicant proves to the satisfaction of the Minister that he is engaged or has made provision for engaging in tropical or semi-tropical agriculture, and that the islanders whom he desires to introduce are intended to be employed in such agriculture only."

The new act went even further. Again, for the benefit of the working class white voter, the measure was at pains to clarify what was meant by "tropical or semi-tropical agriculture." It "shall mean field work in connection with the cultivation of sugar-cane, cotton, tea, coffee, rice, spices, or other tropical or semi-tropical productions or fruits." Islanders were specifically excluded from eligibility for employment as engineers, engine drivers, enginefitters, blacksmiths, wheelrights, farriers, sugar-boilers, carpenters, sawyers, splitters, fencers, bullock drivers, mechanics, grooms, coachmen, horsedrivers or carters except in connection with field work, and domestic or household servants.

But the limitation of employment to tropical and semi-tropical agriculture applied only to indentured islanders. What of those who were free? Article 10 took care of this contingency: "From and after the first day of September, one thousand eight hundred and eighty-four, it shall not be lawful to employ any Islander, except under agreement for service . . . nor except in tropical or semi-tropical agriculture." Exemption from many of the workings of the act was, however, provided for Polynesians who had been in Queensland for more than five years. To protect the islanders, government approval was required for all masters and mates engaged in the Pacific Island labor trade, and remuneration based on the number of islanders placed under contract was expressly forbidden. Violation of this condition could result in forfeiture of the vessel concerned. Article 9 forbade the sale of firearms, ammunition and explosives to islanders who had often, it was said, unleashed reigns of terror when they returned home with small arsenals of modern weapons.

Sir Anthony Musgrave, who became governor of Queensland

in 1883, held views different from those of many of his predecessors. He expressed deep concern about the new Polynesian act. Some sections were very clearly desirable, but others, he thought, might well be judged breaches of good faith inasmuch as they arbitrarily withdrew privileges from a class of persons particularly under the protection of Her Majesty's Government. In addition to an official despatch, Musgrave wrote confidentially:

There is very little humane consideration for the unfortunate Polynesian labourer among either of the political parties. The object on the one side (now in power) is to prevent his competing with white labourers; and the unjust restriction of his freedom which is effected by the act is received by the other side of the house with more or less favour because it will drive more into cultivation in which so many of that party are interested. I cannot disguise from myself the fact that the Polynesians are simply looked upon as slaves would be, though not treated with the care which would be bestowed upon them if they were real property. The mortality is very great.

And indeed recent returns indicated that 695 out of 13,697 had died in 1883. This figure constituted a total mortality of about five percent and was, the governor contended, probably an underestimation. On the Homebush plantation near Mackay, 69 out of a total Polynesian work force of 600 had died in a single month. In Mackay itself, islanders were dying in the streets. The whole labor question was clearly an imperial responsibility, Musgrave contended. Whitehall should make use of the knowledge that Queensland very much needed Polynesian labor, it being clearly nonsense to assume all labor needs could be satisfied by white men.[53]

The Colonial Office agreed with Musgrave's contentions but felt it could not interfere with the internal affairs of a colony blessed with the privileges of responsible government. The gov-

53. CO 234/44, Q. 6961, conf., Musgrave to Derby, Mar. 13, 1884. It was estimated in 1901 that of the 50,500 islanders imported up to 1895, at least 10,000 had died in Queensland. A. T. Yarwood, "Attitudes Toward Non-European Migrants," in F. S. Stevens (ed.), *Racism: The Australian Experience* (New York, 1972), I, 151.

ernor, however, was not to be deterred. A few weeks later he again wrote, contending that the new law could not possibly be effective given the attitude of his ministers. Murder, rape, and kidnapping were still the order of the day in the islands, and conditions were little better in Queensland itself. The governor enclosed a copy of the *Wide Bay and Burnett News,* referring to the inhuman treatment of islanders in the new hospital built there for them.

Colonial Office minuting indicated a greater degree of caution:

> I am a little doubtful of Sir A. Musgrave's discretion in forming a judgement on these matters—When party politics and press writing run as high as they do in Queensland the Governor must always be on guard against being misled, and I fear he is too ready to believe that the traders and planters are worse than they really are—and of course his opinions are known in the colony. There are enough outrages and evils connected with the traffic and we may be glad to see it abolished, it is difficult enough to get at the truth, but I cannot swallow the Wide Bay and Burnett News as all truth.[54]

Musgrave was right in assuming that the Polynesian act would do little to control the occurrence of excesses. Public sentiment made it very difficult to punish even those few offenders who were apprehended and convicted. When two members of the crew of the *Ethel* were convicted in 1885, eight of the jurymen asked for the commuting of their sentences.[55] In the case of the *Hopeful,* five crewmen received sentences ranging from seven years to life, and a sixth was sentenced to death. The judge refused the jury's recommendation for mercy and was submitted to the most intense pressure to change his stand.[56] And, of course it required the most overwhelming evidence to

---

54. CO 234/44, Q. 6951, no. 25, Musgrave to Derby, Mar. 10, 1884, minuting by Herbert, Fiddes and Derby; draft tel., Mar. 24, 1884; Q. 9691, conf., Musgrave to Derby, Apr. 24, 1884; minuting by Bramston.
55. Queensland Archives, Col. 410.
56. *Ibid.,* chief secretary to governor, Nov. 26, 1889, encl. minister of justice to chief secretary, Oct. 10 and 21, 1889.

gain a conviction from a white jury for acts committed by their fellows against men of color.

Parliamentary opinion in Queensland was made clear in debates on the law of 1884. Charles Chubb contended that Kanakas had no rights save to earn wages and be protected from injury and that hence the bill was perfectly fair to them. John Ferguson of Rockhampton asserted that "They never passed an act of Parliament without someone suffering, and surely to goodness they were there to legislate for the people of Queensland and not a few hundred blacks!" [57] But regardless of the low esteem in which islanders were held by virtually all members of the legislative assembly, the house still divided into those who favored the continued importation of Polynesians—the planters and their supporters—and the representatives of the urban working class, who strongly opposed any immigration of colored labor.

The political pendulum tended to swing first toward one group and then back to the other. In 1885 the foes of Kanaka labor under Griffith were still in the seats of power, and the Queensland legislature consequently passed Act 17 of 1885, which stipulated that the importation of Polynesian labor into Queensland "should not be continued after the year one thousand eight hundred and ninety." As Henry Jordan of South Brisbane exclaimed at the second reading of the measure: "I rejoice in the fact that the people of the colony have said at last that they will not have black labour. This Parliament was sent here generally on the understanding that black labour was to come to an end." [58] The tide was to turn, however, and in 1892 not only the governor, Sir Henry Norman, but the majority in the legislature and even Premier Griffith, who had reversed his

57. Queensland *Hansard*, Feb. 22, 1884. "Kanaka" was a Polynesian word meaning "man." The islanders referred to themselves by this term, and it soon became an appelation used by the white Australians to describe all island laborers.
58. *Ibid.*, Oct. 15, 1885.

stand because it had proved impossible to replace colored labor with white, favored the planter interest. Consequently Act 38 of that year, "A Bill to Further Amend the Pacific Island Labourers Acts, 1880–1885," extended the definition of "tropical or semi-tropical agriculture" to include "the work of handling sugar cane." Employers were required to support workers whose contracts had expired until they reindentured or were returned to their native lands. New regulations for the protection of the islanders were to be promulgated, covering medical care, food, pay, conditions on labor vessels, the return passage, increased government supervision, and even rites for the deceased. The most important stipulation of Act 38 was, however, contained in article 3, which removed the prohibition on the importation of island labor.[59]

Norman, who claimed never to have heard of a case of ill-treatment of an islander in Queensland and who asserted that excesses in recruiting were few and far between, eagerly awaited London's response. It was not long in coming. "We must admit," Colonial Office minuting read, "that these Regulations look very well on paper. It remains to be seen whether Queensland officials will report irregularities or Queensland juries convict." [60] But Act 38 was nonetheless sanctioned, although the letter bearing the news to Norman urged constant vigilance on the part of the governor and expressed the by now empty faith

---

59. Colonial Office minuting read: "The missionary interest is already up in arms against the movement, but the demands of the north . . . will no doubt prevail. If properly regulated the labour is legitimate enough." CO 234/53, Q. 621, no. 13, Norman to Knutsford, Feb. 13, 1892. Minuting c. 30/3/92.

60. CO 234/53, Q. 15015, no. 85, Norman to Knutsford, June 15, 1892; Q. 12890, no. 65, Norman to Knutsford, May 20, 1892, minuting by F. F. (Frederic Fuller, a first-class clerk in Colonial Office Department Two, which dealt with Queensland). First-class clerks were high ranking officials in the nineteenth-century Colonial Office. The upper hierarchy consisted of the secretary of state, two undersecretaries (of whom the permanent undersecretary was by far the more important), three assistant undersecretaries and several first- and second-class clerks.

of Whitehall that the laws and regulations would be rigorously applied to avoid the abuses so common in former years.[61]

The passage of Act 38 and the imminent renewal of island labor importation into Queensland brought the old foes back to the battle lines. The missionaries once more stormed the barricades defended by the planters and their allies. The Colonial Office was again caught squarely in the middle. When Norman forwarded a favorable report on the labor trade by Dr. Montgomery, the Bishop of Tasmania, W. H. Mercer of Colonial Office Department Two, which dealt with Queensland, minuted in relief: "This is very satisfactory. In fact it completed the evidence in favour of the contention that the traffic is now carried on in a legitimate manner." [62] The *Melbourne Argus,* in December 1893, carried a long series of articles by a reporter who had accompanied a recruiting vessel on its voyage. He was favorably impressed.

But if the Colonial Office thought that battle was over, it was guilty of wishful thinking. The missionary societies were not yet willing to give up the fight, and crimes and inhuman acts of one sort and another were sufficiently frequent to prevent the Pacific Island labor question fading from view. In April 1895, for instance, Norman wrote to Lord Ripon concerning the *William Manson.* The crew of the vessel had clearly been guilty of kidnapping. The master was acquitted by a Queensland jury, however, while the agent, who had attacked a village while drunk and had kept several island women on board the ship for two months against their will, merely lost his position.[63] There seems little doubt that the jury acted irresponsibly, but their conduct was pale in comparison with that of the judge who in his instructions to them stated: "There were peculiarities in the case which did not rise in all cases. For example, a great number

61. *Ibid.,* CO draft of June 30, 1892.
62. CO 234/54, Q. 25026, no. 212, Norman to Knutsford, Nov. 25, 1892; minuting by Mercer, 3/1/93.
63. CO 234/61, Q. 9737, no. 28, Norman to Ripon, Apr. 24, 1895.

of witnesses were South Sea Islanders, coloured men—uneducated men, men unacquainted with religion and the other sanctions which bind white men to the truth." [64] The Colonial Office was appropriately aghast. "I fear," minuting contended, "we shall not be able to justify to Parlt. our present position in allowing Queensland boats to kidnap men and women from islands under the protection of the British Crown, and this consideration is not weakened by the admission of Govt., in public Despatch that the trial, in this case appears to have been a miscarriage of justice." [65] And as was predictable, it was moved in Parliament on November 8, 1895: "That the Queensland Kanaka traffic is against the best interests of the people of Queensland and ought to be discontinued." [66]

The conflict over island labor was destined to continue for many more years. At heart it was a matter of attitude—of emotional reaction which could be regulated by no ordinance or law. Archibald Forbes, writing in the *New Review,* gave what at that time must have passed for a highly sympathetic view of the Pacific islander in Queensland:

The Polynesian seems to me by nature a cheerful, bright sort of fellow. If he is not so in his island home he soon takes on this complexion when he comes to Queensland. When you look at him he grins responsively; when you speak to him he smiles all over his head. He is a likeable fellow, and has an instinctive politeness and cordiality. He will run of his own accord to open a gate for you; or to hold your horse. He seems and is spoken of as a willing workman; he does his work with a light heart, and takes a manifest interest in it. . . . He gives little trouble. . . . There is a good deal in him of feudal instinct. He becomes exceedingly attached to his master, if the latter is a considerate master. . . . After he has gone home for a "time expired" engagement he very often returns to another on the same plantation.

64. C. 7912, Sept. 1895.
65. CO 234/61, Q. 9737, no. 28, Norman to Ripon, Apr. 24, 1895, minuting by Fuller.
66. CO 234/62, Q. 22865, no. 106, Norman to Ripon, Nov. 9, 1895.

Clearly not a fellow to be taken very seriously, with the virtues more of a dog than a man. But despite his seemingly unthreatening nature, the Kanaka must be rigidly limited:

Resolute officials must be held to the duty of seeing to it that there shall be no more bed-making, table-waiting, boot-cleaning, grooming, carriage-driving etc. done on the plantations by Polynesians who should be restricted to tropical or semi-tropical agriculture. The time expired Polynesian must be summarily bundled off to his island on the expiry of his engagement. But his alternative to this deportation must be that, as soon as his term shall have expired, he must enter on another.[67]

Useful, even necessary, was the general view of the Kanaka when properly employed. Utilized in the wrong manner, he was a danger to the well-being of the white working population. Either way he was not the equal of the white man, and it was the Queenslander's abiding faith in this basic truth that made it so difficult to control the labor traffic. As Colonial Office minuting noted, "It is hopeless to expect a jury of intelligent Queenslanders to convict when there is chiefly 'black' evidence and where blacks alone are concerned as sufferers." [68]

Whereas nearly all the Australian colonies were possessed of enterprises demanding considerable amounts of labor, New Zealand was peopled largely by small farmers and developed no entrepreneurial class clamoring for indentured workers. The situation in Canada was, on the other hand, more reminiscent of Australia, but white labor, particularly in British Columbia, managed to prevent the introduction of a significant number of contract laborers. In 1897 even the threat was removed when the Dominion Parliament passed Chapter II, "An Act to Restrict the Importation and Employment of Aliens," which prohibited the importation of most kinds of foreign contract labor.

67. Archibald Forbes, "The Kanaka in Queensland," *New Review*, vol. VI, no. 37, June, 1892.
68. CO 243/61, Q. 9737, no. 28, Norman to Ripon, Apr. 24, 1895, minuting by Fuller, 13/6.

As has already been noted, it was a plantation economy that required the largest concentration of unskilled labor. In Australasia, only Queensland found itself dependent on subtropical agriculture. Throughout the rest of the British Empire, however, the model repeated itself many times, perhaps most notably in Natal, which came under the British flag in 1843. The colony initially eeked out a precarious existence, as no precious metals or gems were discovered in significant quantities and attempts to raise cotton and coffee were disappointing. It was only when sugar was first rendered from cane in 1851 that the key to a better life was found. Within seven years the sugar industry was firmly rooted in Natal, and only the same lack of labor already encountered in Australia—for the local Africans were in general disinclined to work for any length of time on the coastal plantations—blocked the path to the establishment of a truly prosperous settlement.

The experience of other sugar-growing colonies pointed the way to a solution. Long before Natal or Queensland had planted their first cane, the islands of the West Indies and Mauritius had invested their future in sugar. Wed to a plantation economy, they faced extinction after the emancipation of the slaves in 1834. In desperation, these colonies turned for rescue to that great reservoir of manpower, India. In contrast to the later experience of Queensland, they met with success and a vast program for the importation of indentured labor was begun.

In 1859 Natal faced a particularly severe labor crisis, and petitions inundated the colonial administration demanding "the introduction *by the Government* of Coolie labourers." [69] The legislative council appointed a select committee to consider the petitions, and the committee's recommendations led to the introduction of three bills into the legislature designed to end Natal's labor shortage once and for all. These became Natal

69. L. M. Thompson, *Indian Immigration into Natal (1860–1872)*, (Cape Town, 1952), 12.

Laws 13, 14, and 15 of 1859. The first granted validity to contracts made outside Natal in places other than British India. Its purpose was to allow the development of a variety of sources for contract labor. The second enabled the Government of Natal to bring workers from India "at the public expense" under conditions similar to those obtaining in other colonies already importing Indian labor. The third empowered private persons to introduce Indian laborers into Natal at their own expense.

The second of the three measures was the only one to arouse much debate, because its implementation required considerable government expenditure for the benefit, its opponents claimed, of only part of the colony's population. Opposition to the law was in fact slight, but the arguments surrounding its passage opened a controversy between coast planters and up-country settlers that was to be a running sore until indentured immigration came to an end in 1911.

The terms of Natal Law 14 of 1859 required Indian immigrants intended primarily for the sugar fields of the colony to complete five years of indentured service. At the end of five years the immigrants were to become free, and ten years after their arrival in Natal they became eligible for a free return passage to India, although the governor could, at his discretion, commute the cost of the fare (approximately ten pounds) into a grant of crown land, if an immigrant so desired. Nothing in the legislation forced immigrants to return to India at the end of ten years, and section 9 of the law stated: "On the expiration of the first five years after his introduction into this colony every Coolie immigrant . . . shall be at liberty to hire or dispose of his services, or to change his residence, in the same manner as any other labourer, not being a Coolie immigrant."

The new system saved Natal from economic ruin, but its functioning was far from smooth, and the first groups of immigrants, repatriated in late 1870 and 1871, carried back to India tales of mistreatment and indifference. They told officials that because of illegal fines and withheld wages they had been almost completely without money, and complained of floggings, inadequate medical attention, and an inability to get their grievances fairly heard by magistrates, most of whose interpreters, they said, were biased against them.[70] The first reaction of the Indian authorities was to review their own policies, and India Act VII of 1871 tightened the regulations concerned with the recruitment of Indian labor for the various British colonies. More significantly the viceroy wrote the secretary of state for India, "We cannot permit emigration thither [Natal] to be resumed until we are satisfied that the colonial authorities are aware of their duties towards the Indian emigrants and that effectual measures have been taken to ensure that class of Her Majesty's subjects full protection in Natal." [71] It was a position in which Her Majesty's Government concurred.[72]

With its plantation economy now heavily dependent on Indian labor, Natal reacted by appointing a commission to investigate the situation. The "Coolie Commission Report," as the commissioners' findings were termed, recommended the abolition of flogging as a punishment, improved medical services, and, most important of all, the appointment of a protector of Indian immigrants—the coolie immigration agent created by earlier legislation shorn of his offensive title and armed with vastly increased powers. These recommendations were implemented by Natal Law 12 of 1872, and both the Government of India and Whitehall then acquiesced to a resumption of indentured Indian immigration to Natal.

Over the years, as vessel after vessel deposited its human cargo on the quays of Durban, the number of Indians in Natal steadily grew, because most time-expired "coolies" did not re-

70. Huttenback, *Gandhi in South Africa*, 9.
71. N[ational] A[rchives] of I[ndia], Dept. of Rev. Ag. and Comm. (Em.), no. 11, viceroy in council to sec. of state, May 10, 1872. Quoted in Natal leg. counc. sess. paps., 1872.
72. N[atal] A[rchives], no. 155, sec. of state to gov. of Natal, Mar. 14, 1872.

turn to India. Instead, they took advantage of their rights, commuted their fares home into grants of land during the years when that practice was permitted, and remained firmly planted in Natal. By 1891 the colony's population included 41,142 Indians, 46,788 Europeans and 455,984 Africans.[73]

The increasing number of Indians in Natal excited the interest of the Government of India, which, among other things, concluded that Indian laborers were underpaid and that excessive deductions were made from their wages in time of sickness.[74] The viceroy also voiced concern that streams used by Indians were polluted and that some Indians were employed as domestic servants, which required them to work on Sundays in violation of their contracts.[75] Worse, the protector, of all people, was in 1876 arrested for shooting and killing an indentured Indian.[76] When his successor tried to obtain land grants for over two hundred time-expired Indians entitled to them, his plea went unanswered.[77]

In 1855 the Government of India's concern combined with a depression in the sugar industry to prompt the appointment of another commission—this time under the chairmanship of Mr. Justice Wragg—which was instructed to restudy the whole Indian problem. Its report, which appeared in 1887, was a doc-

73. Natal census of 1891.
74. CO 179/144, June 30, 1882. Encl. Govt. of India, Dept. of Rev., Ag. and Comm. (Em.), no. 16, viceroy to sec. of state, Apr. 18, 1882.
75. NA, sec. of state to gov., Feb. 20, 1883. Governor H. Bulwer replied that Sunday work was indeed a violation of their terms of indenture, but that Indians considered employment as domestic servants a privilege and that it would be difficult to reverse the existing situation. He hoped that the Indian Government would sanction the continuing use of Indians as domestic servants (*ibid.*, gov. to sec. of state, Aug. 5, 1882, Jan. 3, 1883). Bulwer also reported efforts to pass legislation limiting the pollution of rivers and streams (*ibid.*, Jan. 16, 1883). And he agreed that the sixpence-a-day deduction from the pay of Indians who were sick was a heavy burden on them during the first two years of indenture, and indicated that he would attempt to have this condition changed (*ibid.*, May 19, 1883).
76. NA, gov. to sec. of state, Jan. 11, 1877.
77. NA, protector's report for 1880.

ument of little consequence. The complaints of both Indians and whites received only superficial attention, and the commission had few recommendations to offer, although such matters as marriage and divorce, the pollution of streams, the magisterial powers of the protector, prison regulations, the disposition of the estates of deceased Indian immigrants, Sunday labor and other irregularities on certain estates, the use of alcoholic beverages, and the question of adequate rations for female laborers fell under its scrutiny.

On one significant issue—the rights of Indians already in Natal—the commission placed itself firmly on record, however. When it was proposed that Indians whose indentures had expired would have to return to India immediately, Commissioner J. R. Saunders replied: "I wish to express my strong condemnation of any such idea. What is it but taking the best of our servants and then refusing them the enjoyment of their reward, forcing them back (if we could but we cannot) when their best days have been spent for our benefit. Where to? Why? back to the prospect of starvation from which they sought to escape when they were young. Shylock-like taking a pound of flesh and Shylock-like, we may rely on it, meeting Shylock's reward." [78]

Whatever its weaknesses and strengths, the Wragg Commission Report opened a major debate on the Indian question in Natal. One extreme of popular opinion was well summed up in the words of the chairman of the Victoria County Planters' Association: "I am glad to say that the increasing number of free coolies now renting land will keep many of them here as useful and enterprising colonists. . . . They . . . are most industrious, working morning, noon, and night." [79] On the other hand, the up-country farmers strongly opposed indentured immigration. To them it seemed an unreasonably large draw on

78. NA, Wragg Commission Report, Chap. XLIV, 100.
79. Protector's report for 1875, chairman Victoria County Planters' Association to protector, Dec. 12, 1874.

the colonial revenues from which they gained no appreciable advantage. A letter addressed to the editor of the *Natal Witness,* the newspaper that represented their views, was indicative of their continuing hostility. "There are no greater thieves than Coolies," the writer opined, "imported for the sole use of the coast planters and for whose importation the up-country districts have to pay a large sum of money annually." The Indians were not in need of protection, the paper editorialized; "It is rather the European community that requires protection against the heathen coolie." [80]

But despite the grumbling of the up-country farmers and other opponents of imported Indian labor, the people of Natal generally appreciated the usefulness of the indentured Indians. Although most of them did not return home at the end of the required ten years' labor, when they became eligible for a free return passage, they tended to continue their role as unskilled workers and to enter other professions, such as domestic service, which supported rather than competed with white enterprise. In 1875 Sir Garnet Wolseley, then the administrator of Natal, wrote the Colonial Office concerning formerly indentured Indian laborers: "It may be confidently expected that . . . they [will] not only supply the planters with labour but to a large extent furnish the colonists generally with indoor servants for whom there is a pressing want in the province." [81] In other words, indentured Indians were welcome so long as they stayed in their place and did not aspire to rights such as the franchise, which the colonists felt should be reserved for white men.

With the exception of Natal, contract labor had little permanent effect on the demographic profile of the colonies of white settlement. Although the Transvaal, in the years after the Anglo-Boer War, contained a large number of indentured Chinese laborers (over 50,000 at one point), they were virtually all repatriated by 1910. Even in Natal, it was not the presence of

80. *Natal Witness,* July 20, 1877; July 10, 1876.
81. NA, admin. to sec. of state, June 1, 1875.

the indentured or even the formerly indentured Indian which brought matters to the crisis point. Rather, it was the advent of the free Indian immigrant, who, because he threatened white economic dominance, brought about a three-sided confrontation among the Government of Natal, Her Majesty's Government in London and the Government of India.

The animosity towards colored labor that gradually became apparent had complex roots. The upper and middle classes of the white population were prepared to tolerate the imported workers so long as they either returned home at the end of their contracts or limited themselves to areas of labor where they in no way competed with members of the higher social orders. The white working man was more deeply concerned about nonwhite competition, for the colored laborer was prepared to work for less, for longer hours, and often more diligently and effectively. But although the economic factor was a real one at all levels of white society, the animosity felt towards the colored man can be only partially explained by it. More significant, and overriding all other considerations, was the xenophobia and race hatred of the Anglo-Saxon.

2 The Immigration Question—
The Battle Joined

Indentured and other contract labor brought into a colony as a convenience to the employer, if not the working man, was one thing. The influx of free colored immigrants was quite another. As the legal structure of the Empire in mid-century placed no impediments in the way of immigration within the Empire or from abroad, the large number of non-British immigrants brought to Australia by the discovery of gold not only changed the history of that continent but ushered in a series of problems that were to manifest themselves also in New Zealand, Canada and South Africa.

Although the first finds were in New South Wales proper, the real treasure lay further south, near Port Phillip, in that portion of the colony which had been granted a separate existence, as Victoria, the previous year. In autumn 1851, when the Ballarat and Bendigo fields were discovered, the population of Victoria was 97,000 settlers and 6,000,000 sheep. Into the new colony totally unprepared for their advent, there suddenly poured wave after wave of prospectors. By February 1852 there were 40,000 diggers at Bendigo Creek alone.[1] A high percentage of the new arrivals were Chinese, and strong feelings against them soon became apparent. Accused of being filthy and of carrying loathsome diseases, they were also said to contribute nothing to the community because they lived off the smell of

1. C. E. Carrington, *The British Overseas* (Cambridge, 1950), 486.

the proverbial oiled rag and sent all their profits home.² Pressure on the government mounted as the white population of the goldfields became progressively more incensed. It was clearly a case of racial animosity rather than economically motivated fear, for the Chinese either worked claims abandoned by Europeans or engaged in placer operations as opposed to the hard rock mining practiced by the white miners.

In July 1854 the European miners at Sandhurst, Victoria, planned a major anti-Chinese demonstration, but as it was scheduled for July 4, it had to be postponed because of "the indignation . . . the North Americans expressed at the anniversary of their independence having been selected for the disturbance." The delay allowed the governor, Sir Charles Hotham, to summon an additional fifty mounted troops and thus to frustrate the designs of the white diggers.³ A protest planned for Castlemaine, about twenty-five miles from Sandhurst, was also prevented.⁴ When Hotham went on a tour of the Victoria goldfields in September 1854, he wrote Lord Grey at the Colonial Office, "I found an orderly, well-conducted people—particularly in the observance of the Sunday." The governor noted a large proportion of women in the population (always considered a sign of morality and stability), schools of every denomination, people of all kinds, and "an appearance of tranquility." Hotham was travelling incognito, but, he reported, when his true identity was discovered, "thousands flocked" to his presence "and then burst forth the shouts of loyalty to Her Majesty, and cries of attachment to the old country, such as can hardly be imagined, the scene ending by a procession of diggers being formed to accompany Lady Hotham and myself to our quarters—a distance of full a mile and a half."

2. CO 311/14, Dec. 11, 1856. As a matter of fact, the Chinese sent some 117,000 ounces of gold (valued at approximately £465,000) to China in 1856–57. By comparison, Victoria in 1856 produced gold valued at £12,214,976.
3. CO 309/26, no. 87, Hotham to Newcastle, July 17, 1854.   4. *Ibid.*

Given the polyglot, international, and largely disaffected population of the goldfields, one wonders whether Hotham was the victim of self-delusion or some monstrous practical joke. The miner, he felt, was "a lover of order, and good government . . . of loyalty and duty." The governor could not say too much in praise of the "true hearted" diggers so full of loyalty who when properly led would always be "amenable to reason . . . [and] deaf to violence." Leadership was a matter of class and breeding for "discrete officers will always possess the influence which education and manners everywhere obtain." [5]

The Government of Victoria voiced its determination to preserve law and order, but it could not prevent a considerable number of anti-Chinese demonstrations during which Chinese were frequently injured, their property destroyed, and their claims appropriated as they were driven from the mining communities. Nor were the governor and his ministers particularly sympathetic to the Chinese. Hotham wrote the Colonial Office in mid-1854: "the inroad—for I can call it nothing else—of the Chinese, has increased to an alarming extent. No longer do one, or two vessels laden with Asiatics, present themselves in this port [Melbourne], but a number of no less than 340 Chinese per week have arrived bringing with them the intelligence that more are coming or in the words of the Commission appointed to enquire into the State of the Gold Fields that 'all are coming.'" [6]

Happily, the Duke of Newcastle provided the key to the Chinese problem as perceived by the Australian colonies. In letters to the governors of Victoria and New South Wales,[7] Newcastle purported to be concerned about the conditions under which Chinese travelled to Australia. He urged the governors to remain vigilant, "and in case any serious abuses should come to

5. CO 309/26, Hotham to Grey, Sept. 18, 1854.
6. CO 309/33, no. 80, Hotham to Sir William Molesworth, June 15, 1855.
7. CO 411/1, no. 12, Newcastle to Latrobe, Jan. 29, 1853; CO 202/60, no. 22, Newcastle to Fitzroy, Feb. 5, 1853.

light, or appear probable, to propose to the Legislature an act imposing penalties on all ships bringing immigrants to New South Wales in which it may appear that a sufficient proportion of space had not been allotted to the Emigrants or an adequate issue of provision made regularly to them throughout the voyage or that the Ship had left China in an unseaworthy state." Whether he so intended it or not, the secretary of state's letter supplied the Australian colonies with an ingenious device for excluding Chinese without offending either the imperial sensibilities of the Colonial Office or the international sensitivities of the Foreign Office.

Victoria Act 39 of 1855 in consequence stipulated that no vessel might carry immigrants in excess of a ratio of one to every ten tons of burthen. A fee of ten pounds was to be exacted from every immigrant landed, and the governor was empowered to place further levies on immigrants to pay for the administration of the act. To make the purpose of the law absolutely clear, an immigrant was defined as "any male adult native of China or of an island in the Chinese seas or any person born of Chinese parents."

Hotham, as a product of the Liberal age, clearly felt some guilt at his allowance of Act 39. He said the action ran counter to his true nature, but that circumstances left him no choice. To salve his imperial conscience, the governor felt impelled to initiate a plan under which care was provided for Chinese in Australia who became ill or "decayed." Hotham also intended to nominate three "protectors" whose duty it would be to adjudicate disputes in which Chinese became involved and to direct the economy of the villages in which it was intended to house the Chinese. A tax, not to exceed twenty shillings, was to be levied on all Chinese, from the proceeds of which the protectors, interpreters and police were to be paid and a reserve established for the construction of a hospital and a home for the aged and infirm. Failure to pay the tax made a Chinese liable to a £5 fine or two months' imprisonment.⁸ Regulations promulgated in 1856 implemented the governor's scheme. The first seven Chinese villages, each with its own headman, were established at Bendigo, and others were created later in adjacent goldfields such as Ballarat and Castlemaine.⁹

The passage of Act 39 of 1855 failed, however, to ameliorate the situation on the goldfields. The measure did little more than inhibit Chinese immigration by sea. It did not prevent Chinese coming overland from South Australia (10,325 crossed the border in 1857 alone [10]), and it did virtually nothing to reduce the number of Chinese already at the diggings. In June 1857 trouble erupted on the Buckland goldfield. A European who was either drunk or pretending to be so entered a Chinese store and begun insulting and physically accosting the occupants. After a time they turned on him and forcibly expelled him from the premises. The European called for assistance, and a general attack was made on the Chinese camp. Nine tents were burned, one Chinese severely beaten, and property estimated by the Chinese to be worth between £1200 and £1500 taken. A crowd of about one hundred miners watched as a group of from twelve to twenty others did the damage.¹¹

About a month later, after a public meeting on the same goldfield passed a series of anti-Chinese resolutions, thirty or forty of the participants went up the creek to the first Chinese encampment. There they laid about them with a will. Property was indiscriminately destroyed and the Chinese driven down

8. CO 309/33, no. 80, Hotham to Sir William Molesworth, June 15, 1855.
9. CO 311/15, Regulations for the Chinese on the goldfields, ordered printed, Dec. 2, 1856.
10. P. C. Campbell, *Chinese Coolie Emigration to Countries Within the British Empire* (London, 1923), 52.
11. Victoria Archives, box 652. F. C. Standish, protector, to resident warden, Nov. 11, 1857. The European population of the goldfield was estimated at 700–800.

the creek pursued by the constantly increasing mob. Although the marauders never numbered more than a hundred, a large and appreciative audience stood in support. Proceeding from encampment to encampment, the mob eventually drove some two thousand Chinese over the Buckland River crossing place, a good seven miles from where the whole affair had started. Other than firing three shots before crossing the river, the Chinese, most of whom were armed, made no resistance. Without any of their belongings, they were in a deplorable condition, terrified and hungry. Many had been brutally beaten and three apparently murdered, though the coroner ruled they had died from the cold and previous disease. Estimates showed 751 tents, 30 stores and the Joss-House (perhaps the largest and best building in the district) were destroyed. The total loss of property was placed somewhere in the vicinity of £8000 to £9000. Many Chinese storekeepers were also robbed, sometimes of as much as £200.

To its credit, the government, in the person of the resident warden, did its best to induce the Chinese to return and to guarantee them protection. At the same time it actively pursued and prosecuted the perpetrators of the act. By the beginning of August about three hundred and fifty Chinese had trickled back to the Buckland, but they left again in haste on August 3, as the result of a European miners' meeting and the departure of the police to give evidence at the trial of those accused of having participated in the July riot. The resolutions passed at the meeting, attended by about a hundred of the most influential miners, came to light on August 2 and could not have inspired much confidence in the breasts of the Chinese. The meeting condemned all those who had robbed Chinese. On the other hand, it expressed sympathy for miners who had been forced to leave their homes and to "endure hardships and fatigue to escape the law, on the late expulsion of the Chinese." A committee was also elected to make contact and consort with other branches of the Anti-Chinese League already established in the colony.¹²

The Government of Victoria met the continued anti-Chinese agitation on the goldfields by passing Act 41 of 1857, "An Act to Regulate the Residence of the Chinese population in Victoria." The new law stipulated that within fourteen days of its passage, each alien Chinese would have to obtain a license for which he must pay £1 every other month. If the license were not obtained, a Chinese could be fined £10 and in addition lose the protection of the law for any mining claim or business establishment he might hold.

Act 41 was too much for many of the more moderate settlers, especially the commercial and professional men who frequently stood to prosper from the Chinese presence. On January 18, 1858, over fifty European inhabitants of Ballarat, including the superintendent of police, many members of the miners' council, wardens, bankers, ministers, doctors, and even the keeper of the jail, petitioned the governor for redress on behalf of the Chinese. They pointed out that the Chinese were not only forced to live in special locations but that they were expected to pay £10 for permission to set foot in the colony, £1 for a miner's right, and now the new mulct for the so-called license or "protection ticket." A second petition signed by a further sixty Europeans testified to the "orderly and sober and peaceable conduct and industrious habits of the Chinese resident on the Ballarat Gold Fields."

The governor minuted on the petition that he thought the protectors might be allowed to exempt Chinese who really did not have enough money to pay for a protection ticket. But he was chastized by his ministers. The premier noted: "As the object of the act passed last session is to discourage the residence

12. Victoria Archives, file on the Buckland riots of 1857, resident warden, Beechworth, to chief secretary, Melbourne, July 10 and Aug. 5, 1857.

of Chinese in Victoria I consider that any interference with its operation would frustrate the intention of the Legislature in passing it. No doubt certain cases of hardship may occasionally occur, but did such cases not arise the whole act would be inoperative."[13] At least, in March, when some Chinese stores were burned down in Canton Lead and Mount Ararat, a board of investigation recommended compensation because the Chinese involved held protection tickets.[14] But the Chinese in general saw little advantage to complying with the law and were commonly successful in evading the exactions it prescribed. They refused to pay the license fee and as they tended not to file claims and only to work land unwanted by Europeans, the loss of legal protection for their holdings was of little moment.[15]

Act 41 was a failure in many ways. Violence against the Chinese persisted,[16] and further discriminatory legislation was demanded by some elements of the population.[17] On the other hand, the European moderates continued to inveigh against the law,[18] an effort in which they were joined by the Chinese themselves, who complained that Act 41 was passed when the goldfields were prosperous, but that by 1859 the average Chinese was earning only one-half a penny weight of gold per day.[19]

13. Victoria Archives, chief secretary's records, box 685, file E. 58/898. Petition by European residents, Ballarat; minuting of Jan. 25, 1858.
14. *Ibid.*, box 685, file E. 587/2458, Mar. 22, 1858.
15. *Ibid.*, G. Western, Chinese protector, to resident warden, Avoca. Jan. 23, 1858; Feb. 24, 1859, warden in charge, Avoca, to chief secretary, Melbourne, informing him that 212 Chinese had taken out licenses since Jan. 1, 1859.
16. In April 1859 the European miners again attacked the Chinese in Buckland, killing one of them.
17. Victoria Archives, chief secretary's records, box 704, 1859–1863, file J. 59/1266, John McIntyre to chief secretary, July 14, 1859.
18. *Ibid.*, box 704a, Chinese protectorate, 1861–1863, file 60/N990, petition c. Jan. 18, 1862; petition from Melbourne Chamber of Commerce to chief secretary May 13, 1862.
19. *Ibid.*, box 704, 1859–1863, file J. 59/1266, petition of Chinese residents at Ballarat to Sir Henry Barkly, July 21, 1859. Also box 704a, Chinese Protectorate, file 60/N990, reg, Feb. 1, 1860, Chinese petition of Feb. 1860.

When the Chinese asked for educational facilities by virtue of the fact that they paid a special tax,[20] the government tersely responded, "No funds." [21]

In early 1859 the Victoria legislature passed Act 80, "To consolidate and amend the laws affecting the Chinese emigrating to or resident in Victoria." There was little that was new in the measure,[22] but in conjunction with the act of 1855 and the South Australia law (Act 3) of 1857 it essentially halted the flow of Chinese into Victoria and placed rigid controls on those already there. The census of 1861 indicated that of the 540,322 persons in the colony (228,181 or 42 percent on the goldfields), 24,732 were Chinese, whereas four years earlier their numbers had been estimated at 35,000.[23] Succeeding census reports were to indicate a constant decrease in the numbers of Chinese in Victoria.

By September 1861, Chinese immigration seemed to many a

20. *Ibid.*, box 704, 1859–1863, Chinese petition of Feb. 1860. The Chinese also complained about the export tax on gold.

21. *Ibid.*, box 704, 1859–1863, file J. 59/1266, Rev. C. Searle to chief secretary, Feb. 10. Minuting by J. D. (?)S., 26/2/59.

22. It provided for the registration of Chinese and their movement, when desirable, from district to district under regulations promulgated under the act. Failure to register or to obey government instructions could result in a fine of up to £5. Chinese were to continue to pay £10 if they arrived in Victoria by sea, and the fee was set at £4 for those arriving overland. The annual license fee was lowered to £4. Immigration restrictions remained largely the same as those established under Act 39 of 1855. The Victorian gold miners' resentment at the failure of the colonial government to provide any form of local self-government had resulted in much agitation and some violence. As a consequence the government had established boards made up of miner representatives who had jurisdiction over most of the affairs of the goldfields. Act 80 allowed Chinese to obtain miners' rights but not to vote for representatives on the mining board. They could not, of course, be members. Although Act 170 of 1861 repealed most sections of Act 80 of 1859, the prohibition against Chinese with miners' rights or other pertinent legal documentation voting for or being members of mining boards was retained and reiterated in Act 32 of 1862.

23. Of the 24,732 Chinese reported in the 1861 census only eight were female.

dead issue. The anti-Chinese legislation had left a bad taste in the mouths of the more liberal and well-educated members of the Victorian ruling class, and it ran counter to the spirit of the recently concluded Anglo-Chinese treaty (1860). The government consequently determined to repeal much of it. There was not universal consent in the legislature. A Mr. Grundy contended that he, for one, "would never consent to see this colony overrun by hordes of ugly moon-faced Chinese." Another member (Mildred) said he would oppose the third reading of the bill because he believed the Chinese an immoral and "crime-committing people" who tolerated if not encouraged infanticide.[24] Nevertheless, Act 170 repealed those sections of Act 80 of 1859 which dealt with the entry and residence of Chinese, the tonnage ratios and the penalties attached thereto.

The rising and ebbing of the tide of anti-Chinese sentiment in Victoria caused the passing and subsequent repeal of several pieces of discriminatory legislation. Finally, Act 259 of 1865 revoked legislation of the previous year but, as had earlier laws, empowered the governor to make regulations concerning the registration of Chinese immigrants and their removal from any district. It also maintained the restrictions attached to miners' rights in Chinese hands.

Once introduced into Australia, the Chinese quickly spread to all the other colonies, and the cycle of riots, petitions and discriminatory legislation already encountered in Victoria repeated itself. New South Wales Act 3 of 1861 was designed on the Victorian model to regulate and restrict the immigration of Chinese. The effect of the measure was almost immediate. Whereas the census of 1861 had shown 12,988 persons of Chinese birth, that of 1871 dropped the figure to 7,220. The Chinese proportion of the colony's population during this period was reduced from 3.71 percent to 1.34 percent. By 1867 the trend was sufficiently clear to allow the legislature, following Melbourne's example, to assuage its conscience and to heed the

24. Victoria *Hansard,* Sept. 24, 1861.

pleas of the liberal section of the community, which complained that the existing situation "only tends to lower our prestige as an intelligent and civilised people." [25] Act 8 of 1867 consequently repealed the restrictive legislation of 1861.

Although the Chinese threat to South Australia was hard for the unpracticed eye to detect—only twenty-one persons of Chinese birth entered the colony between 1836 and 1855 while but eleven more did so in the next five years [26]—the legislature in Adelaide passed restrictive legislation based on the Newcastle formula in 1857 (Act 3), only to repeal it (Act 14) four years later.[27] As for Queensland, it did not pass a Chinese immigration act until 1877 (Act 8).

As already noted, not all the white settlers of Australia thought the Chinese presence an abomination. J. A. Patterson in his *Goldfields of Victoria in 1862* devoted a chapter to them. "I think I may say," he wrote, "that the conclusion at which I have arrived—that these people are a valuable addition to our labourers on the gold-fields—is shared by all who look at the Chinese question, as it develops itself in Victoria, apart from the prejudices of race, and the undefined and ignorant ill-will that is occasionally found to exist between peoples and tribes not so remote to each other as Saxons and Chinese." Patterson went on to describe Guilford which, with five to six thousand inhabitants, had long been the main Chinese camp in Victoria. Although he found the streets narrow and primitive, he was generally filled with admiration for what he considered the camp's cosmopolitan life. Much of what Patterson had to say was clearly exaggerated and secondhand, but his notes about Guilford at its height make an interesting contrast to the de-

---

25. CO 204/99, petition, c. March 1866. 26. S.A. census of 1861.
27. In 1878 nearly all the Chinese in South Australia were in the Northern Territory. Their number was placed at 980 as compared with 830 Europeans (CO 13/136, S.A. 12096, Administrator Way to CO, S.A. no. 33, Aug. 7, 1878). The census of 1891 counted 3,997 Chinese in South Australia out of a total population of 310,426; 2,597 of these were adult males in the Northern Territory.

scriptions of the Chinese and their quarters more usually encountered:

> In the days of its greatest glory, "the Camp" had its permanent theatre and circus performers, and in every street in it—its temples devoted to Joss were numerous. All the arts flourished in it—down to the making of alloyed gold—as they did at home. The restaurants, the tea-houses, the gambling salons, the cobblers' stalls, the tailors' shops were as they are in Canton; and the student of the Chinese language and literature, manners and customs, politics and laws, might have studied and graduated here as well as in Pekin itself. There were shops for literature and shops for art; there were scholars to write your letters and interpreters to read them; there were doctors, and perhaps quacks, with peculiar rules of practice and medicine to wit—surgeons of whom it could not be said they had "too much sawee." [28]

The Reverend W. Young prepared a report on the Chinese population of Victoria in 1868. He found the Chinese industrious, patient, persevering, and thrifty, but he bemoaned their lack of wives and general immorality. Fortunately the good reverend saw a solution: "The grand instrument to be employed for the effectual reformation of these people is, unquestionably, the teaching of the truths of God's Holy Word, and preaching the gospel of Christ to them." [29]

But kind words about the Chinese, however condescending, were certainly the exception rather than the rule. A more representative view was that of W. D. Ponder, a newspaper man and a member of the South Australia House of Assembly, who wrote in his diary:

> Chinamen, as a rule are ingenious and industrious: but generally speaking they are also ignorant, superstitious and loathesome. Their ingenuity and industry is shown by the beautifully carved ornaments they manufacture and the fearfully heavy loads they carry: whilst their ignorance and superstition is proved by their conduct

---

28. J. A. Patterson, *The Goldfields of Victoria in 1862* (Melbourne, 1862), 130–35, copy in the Mitchell Library, Sydney.

29. CO 311/69, report on the Chinese population by Rev. W. Young, 1868.

at the time an eclipse of the sun or moon is occurring, at earthquakes and on many similar phenomena of nature. Any one who has seen these opium-smoking heathen (and who has not) does not require to be told that they are dirty and loathesome, for the fact is self-evident.

The "celestials" or "rice eating people" or "John," as Ponder preferred to call the Chinese, came from the "flowery land," home of "small-footed beauties." He deemed "lack of women [as the] primary cause of John's vicious life and immorality . . . (although even the most ardent friend of the Mongolian race cannot defend some of their filthy doings). . . . Must we sit quietly and see our country usurped by the flat-nose barbarians?" Ponder asked, and promptly answered, "Never . . . Away with maudlin sentimentality, and let us put such restrictions upon the yellow skins as will keep them in their own celestial land for they are not wanted in South Australia." [30]

The Chinese for their part did what little they could. Ming A. Ching, an interpreter, wrote an official attached to the chief magistracy in Hong Kong: "Now dear Sir, will you not, as soon as you receive this, with your bright pencil, send a petition to Sir John Bowring, Knight, Commander of Hong Kong, to let Her Majesty of England know that the Chinese have been here afflicted? Now that the treaty is made and our empire is as hers, will she not stretch out her strong arm and pull back the oppressions? If your bright pencil brings us relief and liberty, will you not have done great and wisely?" [31] Tu Lin Pow petitioned the New South Wales assembly for compensation and redress because his store had been burned to the ground and property worth £600 destroyed. Ah Sue acted similarly, not only because he had lost property, large amounts of gold dust and money in bank notes, but because he claimed to have had his hair cut off and "a portion of flesh removed from his skull." Simon Sangling

---

30. 1878 entry in Ms. diary of W. D. Ponder, S.A. Archives.
31. Quoted in the *Aborigines Friend and the Colonial Intelligencer,* V. 1859–1866, 166–68, Mitchell Library.

had been driven from his tent at Lambing Flat along with his European wife and their young children. He had lost everything and had been beaten. The mob had cried "cut off his tail," but since he had no queue, they had emptied his purse and stolen two nuggets and his pocketknife besides. The police had done nothing, Sangling charged; although they and the commissioner for crown lands later expressed their regret at the incident. He now asked for relief from the assembly. Tom Me, What Young and Yue You also petitioned the assembly,[32] but to little effect.

The white settlers in New Zealand, some hundreds of miles to the southeast of New South Wales, had emerged from the same ethnic and cultural milieux as their cousins in Australia, and they saw the world and the Chinese threat through similar eyes. A few casual Chinese immigrants drifted into New Zealand in the early 1850s. But there was no serious influx until the discovery of gold in Otago brought the first "rush" from Victoria in 1866. The census returns of the following year showed a Chinese population of 1,219, a total which increased to 2,641 in 1871 and to 4,816 three years later.[33]

But long before the Chinese appeared in New Zealand in any numbers, the handful that were there became the victims of the usual animosity. As early as 1857 an anti-Chinese committee had been formed in Nelson to fight the "Mongolian Filth," even though there were no Chinese in the district.[34] As the Otago diggings became exhausted, the Chinese in small numbers drifted into the nascent towns of Wellington and Dunedin, where they set themselves up as market gardeners and fruiterers. The ire of the white laboring class was thus added to that of the

32. CO 204/77, Tu Lin Pow to assembly, ordered printed, Sept. 20, 1861; Ah Sue to assembly, no date; Simon Sangling to assembly, July 30, 1861; Tom Me, What Young and Yue You to assembly, ordered printed, Sept. 12, 1861.
33. Ng Bickleen Fong, *The Chinese in New Zealand: A Study in Assimilation* (Hong Kong, 1959), 15.
34. *Ibid.*, 16.

miners, even though the Chinese tended to enter callings which complemented rather than competed with European enterprise. The cries of indignation sounded familiar: "We are free men, they are slaves! We are Christians, they are heathens! We are Britons, they are Mongolians!" [35] Although many merchants, as in Australia, saw advantages to the Chinese presence,[36] the *Lake Wakatipu Mail* accurately summed up the prevailing attitude when it wrote, "All classes agree that the Chinese are eating up the inheritance that we should leave for our race in the future." [37]

The Daily Telegraph described the arrival of the first Chinese in Dunedin: "His reception was noisy and appeared rather to disconcert Johnny, who took to his heels and scudded up the street at a rapid pace." [38] *The Otago Witness* of February 8, 1868, rendered a pitiful description of what befell the only Chinese working in Naseby. "A crowd of drunken hooligans cut off the pigtail of Ah Pack, stripped off most of his clothes, and closed him in a large cask and rolled the terrified fellow about the town. The police took him into custody, but the poor fellow had gone partly out of his mind and wandered about the country looking for his Chinese friends." [39]

In August 1871 the New Zealand House of Representatives established a select committee of thirteen members to investigate the whole question of Chinese immigration to New Zealand. The committee heard countless witnesses and collected vast quantities of evidence. The usual negative arguments were paraded forth. Chinese were pagans. They were immoral and trapped young girls into catering to their vile appetites. They were gamblers and thieves, uncivilized barbarians who were filthy in habit and style of living. Chinese spoke no English, they did not understand British law or customs, and they did

35. *Ibid.*, quoting the *Otago Daily Times*, Aug. 17, 1871.
36. *Ibid.* The Dunedin Chamber of Commerce wanted to encourage the Chinese to work the mines abandoned by Europeans c. 1864–65.
37. *Ibid.*, 161, quoting the *Lake Wakatipu Mail*, May 17, 1871.
38. *Ibid.*, 27, quoting the *Daily Telegraph*, June 2, 1863.   39. *Ibid.*

not intend to settle in New Zealand. They took wealth out of the colony, and if allowed to enter freely they would soon overwhelm the European population, drive them out of work because of the low wages they demanded, and then became more bold and arrogant in their demeanor.[40] Nevertheless, the committee after due deliberation concluded that the Chinese were industrious, frugal and orderly; that they were neither immoral nor dangerous; that they did not introduce any special form of infectious disease; and that in general they constituted a useful form of labor. Furthermore, the Chinese came without their families intending to return to China after they had saved £100 or more, and "In view of the foregoing the Committee are of the opinion that there have been no sufficient grounds shown for the exclusion of the Chinese; and that no sufficient case has up to the present time been made out to require the Committee to propose that legislative action should be taken having for effect the exclusion of the Chinese or the imposition of special burdens upon them."[41]

The minutes of the proceedings indicated that the committee was often far from unanimous in its conclusions. For instance when one member (Fitzherbert) moved a resolution which in the end comprised the last few lines of the committee's report as quoted above, it passed by a vote of only five to four.[42]

New Zealand may not yet have been ready to move against its small Chinese population. On the other hand, the Australian colonies, as we have already seen, did not feel similarly constrained. Essentially unimpeded by Whitehall, they, as well as London, seemed to have conveniently forgotten that Article 1 of the Treaty of Nanking (1842) had stipulated that the subjects of Great Britain and China would enjoy full security and pro-

---

40. CO 211/53, ad interim report (no. 11) of the Chinese Immigration Committee.
41. *Ibid.*, H-5B, final report of the Chinese Immigration Committee.
42. *Ibid.*

tection of their persons and property within the dominions of the two powers. The convention of friendship between Great Britain and China signed in Peking on October 24, 1860, was even more specific. It proclaimed in its fifth article that as soon as ratification of the treaty were exchanged:

His Imperial Majesty the Emperor of China will by Decree command the high authorities of every province to proclaim throughout their jurisdiction that Chinese choosing to take service in the British colonies, or other parts beyond the sea, are at perfect liberty to enter into engagements with British subjects for that purpose, and to ship themselves and their families on board any British vessel at any of the open ports of China; also that the high authorities aforesaid shall, in concert with Her Britannic Majesty's Representative in China, frame such regulations for the protection of Chinese emigrating, as above, as the circumstances of the different ports may demand.

But despite the successful flouting of the two treaty documents and the resulting erection of an apparently effective legal barrier to Chinese immigration, Australian fear of invasion by the "yellow peril" did not die. In fact, slowly and almost unconsciously, the individual colonies came to realize that security lay in mutual support and joint action.

It was labor that provided perhaps the first examples of cooperative effort against the Chinese. The years after 1870 saw a great rise in union power, ushering in the classical labor-capital conflict in which capital became ever more enamored of a colored immigrant work force and labor developed a paranoid fear of it. One of the first groups to become organized were the goldminers, and they were, of course, particularly sensitive to the Chinese presence. In February 1872, the miners at Bendigo, Victoria, formed the Bendigo Miners' Union. Diggers in other areas followed suit, and in September 1873, miners at Clunes formed themselves into a union. One week after the establishment of their organization, the Clunes miners went out on strike against the Lothair Mining Company. After three months, the company attempted to break the deadlock through the use of nonunion Chinese labor.

On the evening of December 8, news reached Clunes that a large number of Chinese were about to leave Ballarat and Creswick for the Lothair Mine. The Ballarat *Courier* of December 10 described what followed:

> Nearly the whole population turned out to join the demonstration of resistance. After about five hundred men, members of the Miners' Association, had marched round the town, headed by the Clunes Brass Band, and armed with pick-handles, battens and waddies of various descriptions, nearly the whole male population, and a good many women—to say nothing of the boys . . . took up their residence in the street, or at the doorways, waiting the arrival of the Mongolians.[43]

After what must have seemed an interminable delay, the coaches filled with Chinese arrived with an escort of troops. They were met with barricades and a shower of stones. A general melee ensued, at the end of which the authorities capitulated. The coaches, still with their Chinese passengers on board, were sent rumbling back whence they had come, and the senior police officer present promised that no further attempts would be made to introduce Chinese labor into the mines of Clunes.[44]

The government condemned the miners but took no action and the company was forced to accede to the union's demands. More important, the newly formed Amalgamated Miners' Association was able, a few years later, to force the Victoria mines department to insert a clause in every mining lease issued which stipulated that Chinese labor would not be recognized as fulfilling the labor covenant.[45]

The European miners had led the way, the goldfields having seen the earliest concentration of Chinese on the continent. But with the decline of goldmining as a viable occupation, the diffu-

---

43. Geoffrey A. Oddie, "The Chinese in Victoria, 1870–1890" (M.A. thesis, University of Melbourne, 1959), 37.
44. *Ibid.*   45. *Ibid.*, 38.

sion of Chinese into other professions increased, and the unions became alarmed. That no real problem existed was manifested by the population figures. In Victoria, for instance, the number of Chinese residents dropped steadily. In 1871 the Chinese had numbered 15,669. By 1875 the total had dipped to 11,251 and five years later to 8,486.[46] The facts were that virtually no new Chinese immigrants arrived, and that without women no children could be born, while at the same time many Chinese returned home and others died.

The New South Wales Trades and Labour Council was formed in 1871, bringing the nascent labor movement to full life. In 1878 the new organization flexed its muscles by calling a seamen's strike in Sydney to protest the hiring of Chinese by the Australian Steam Navigation Company which intended to use them in tropical waters at rates of pay considerably below those it had agreed to pay members of the seamen's union. The threat to white labor was clear, and the sympathy and cooperative action the strike aroused in the major cities of Australia and New Zealand [47] was a harbinger of things to come—joint action to fight the "yellow peril."

The seamen's strike became inextricably intertwined with the whole Chinese question, and on October 2, 1878, a public meeting in Sydney resulted in the forwarding of a petition with 14,701 signatures to the legislative assembly. The petitioners were largely working men, and they wished to "call the attention of your Honourable House to the degrading and immoral actions practiced in our midst by semi-barbarians." The Chinese, it was claimed, were disgustingly dirty and frequented

---

46. CO 313/60, Victoria Blue Book, 1880.

47. In November 1878 the Australian Steam Navigation Company began employing Chinese at the rate of £2-15-0 per month as opposed to the £6-8-0 it had agreed to pay unionized white men. In time the company essentially capitulated to the strikers. A major motivating factor was the Queensland Government's decision to withdraw its mail subsidy and to make future awards conditional on the exclusive employment of white labor.

houses of prostitution (in contrast to the virtuous European working man), all of which resulted in the "dissemination of infextious and loathsome Eastern diseases."[48] Another meeting attended by 4,000 persons from all over the colony was held at the Haymarket in Sydney on November 30.

Again, not all the sentiment was anti-Chinese. The so-called "celestials" were active in their own behalf. L. Kong Meng, Cheok Kong Cheong, and Louis As Mouy were the authors of a short piece entitled *The Chinese in Australia, 1878–79*. It was a singularly literate appeal for the kind of fair play that the British Empire was ostensibly all about. It compared British and Chinese society to good effect and pointed to the heavy use of opiates in Britain, the homeland of most of those Australians who so strongly disparaged the Chinese use of the pipe. Furthermore, the essay contended, British men knocked down their wives, an indignity to which a Chinese husband would never submit his spouse.[49] A petition to the assembly signed by 229 Chinese asked why they and their countrymen should be singled out for bad treatment. They were good and sober citizens and besides, Great Britain and China were on friendly terms.[50] A certain James Fullerton, LL.D., and three others requested better treatment for the Chinese because "some of the Chinese in this colony make a credible profession of Christianity" and efforts were being mounted to instruct others.[51]

On the other hand, it was clear where the majority stood, and petitions directed against the Chinese poured into the legislature—196 signatures from Bombala, 481 from Balmain, 1,655 from Hunter River, 244 from Tenterfield, and 422 from Plattsburg. Anti-Chinese organizations such as the Working Man's Defence Association and the National Chinese League bur-

48. CO 204/187, 1878–79.
49. L. Kong Meng, Cheok Hong Cheong and Louis Ah Mouy, *The Chinese in Australia, 1878–79*, (Melbourne, 1879). In the collection of the Mitchell Library.
50. CO 204/187, Chinese petition, ordered printed, Feb. 19, 1879.
51. *Ibid.*, ordered printed, Feb. 7, 1879.

geoned.⁵² In 1879, at the first Intercolonial Trade Union Congress held at Sydney, a motion against "Asiatic Immigration" was unanimously passed.

All of this played into the hands of one of the most astute politicians ever to grace the Australian scene, Sir Henry Parkes, the premier of New South Wales. When a politician can unite personal conviction with political expediency, he is twice blessed indeed. Henry Parkes was a devout white supremacist and passionately anti-Chinese. But he also saw in the Chinese question the key to the political loyalty of the urban working class of New South Wales. With public agitation continuing unabated, Parkes took advantage of a slight increase in Chinese immigration to New South Wales in 1880–1881 to sound the tocsin and to call for an intercolonial conference on the Chinese threat to all of Australasia.

He had chosen the proper moment. South Australia, even though 1881 census returns showed only 347 Chinese in the colony proper, was seething with indignation. And the same could be said of Victoria. There the Chinese population had steadily declined from 15,079 in 1870 to 8,486 a decade later.⁵³ Nevertheless, despite the proven effectiveness of existing legislation, the legislative assembly increasingly turned its attention to the Chinese question. On May 19, 1880, it passed a motion asking the governor to provide the House with copies of all correspondence with the imperial government concerned with the Chinese in Victoria. Eight days later a similar motion was carried and figures were demanded concerning such matters as the amount of gold exported from the colony by the Chinese and the drain on the treasury attributable to Chinese lepers and lunatics.⁵⁴ Agitation continued throughout the session.

On June 11, 1880, Parkes wrote to A. H. Palmer, colonial secretary of Queensland, predicting that the Chinese menace

52. Co/187, 1878–79 and/195, 1879–80.
53. CO 313/60, Victoria Blue Book, 1880.
54. Victoria *Hansard,* May 19 and 27, 1880.

would increase. The immigrants were all bound by some unknown authority, he contended, and not really free. They were the cause of social mischief and resented by all Australians. Common action was imperative to save the situation.[55] Palmer reacted negatively to the invitation to attend the proposed intercolonial conference. He asserted that the poll tax had completely halted the influx of Chinese and that hence, from Queensland's point of view, no further action was necessary or desirable. But the other colonies, most notably Victoria in the person of its chief secretary (premier), Graham Berry, placed increasing pressure on Queensland. Berry, the self-proclaimed champion of the working man, was as stoutly anti-Chinese as Parkes, and his words, when added to those of his colleague in Sydney, took their toll. Although Palmer reiterated that the Queensland Chinese Immigration Act of 1877 was highly effective,[56] and indeed the Chinese population in the colony did continue to fall,[57] Queensland, in the long run, could not hold out against the pressure and agreed to attend the intercolonial conference.

Tasmania, not having any known deposits of gold, counted only 844 Chinese in its population of 115,705 in 1881. According to the Tasmanian census of that year, 238 of these worked in the tin mines, and 146 were market gardeners. Many of the rest were farm laborers. Nevertheless, Tasmania accepted the invitation to attend the conference.

Despite the mere handful of Chinese present within its borders, New Zealand reacted positively to the proposed Chinese conference. The chief prophet of Anglo-Saxonism in the legislature was Richard Seddon, who had developed a hatred

55. CO 236/71, 1880.
56. *Ibid.*, Palmer to Parkes, June 22, 1880; colonial secretary, Queensland to chief secretary, South Australia, Sept. 20, 1880; Berry to Palmer, Sept. 13, 1880; Palmer to Berry, Sept. 23, 1880.
57. Between July 1880 and April 1881, for instance, the number of Chinese in Queensland dropped from 13,234 to 11,200, CO 236/75 1881, p. 1133.

for the Chinese on the goldfields of Victoria. In some ways he was not unlike his Australian counterparts, Henry Parkes and Graham Berry. The contemporary historian and critic, Vernon Scurrah, thought that Seddon was almost a fanatic on the question of Asian immigration. He was so intent on the salvation of the working man that he completely dismissed over half of mankind because they had colored skins. Seddon would have bundled all Asians already in New Zealand back to their countries of origin with little ceremony. "There was in his attitude little of the charity we expect from great souls." Seddon "saw nothing good in the Asiatics; to him they were degenerate, immoral, filthy and a festering sore in the economic life of the country," and he would "rid the country of them." [58]

Seddon was warmly supported by Sir George Grey, who as a governor of New Zealand during the Maori troubles and as an observer of the confrontation of Bantu, Boer and Briton while governor of Cape Colony, had become sensitive to the kind of population heterogeneity which connoted massive cultural and economic differences. Grey, who had returned to New Zealand after a career of service to the crown and had even become the island colony's prime minister for a short time, was convinced that "if a mixed race of inferior order be allowed to spring up and become the ruling power . . . there can be little hope of a high degree of civilisation ever prevailing." [59]

As a consequence of such sentiment, a Chinese immigration restriction bill was introduced into the New Zealand Parliament in July 1880. It was the second attempt to pass a law of this type, an earlier effort having failed in the previous session. The debate was heated. William Hutchinson, representing the city of Wellington, for instance, agreed that in theory people should have the right to settle where they pleased. But one also

58. Fong, 19–20, quoting Scurrah.
59. N.Z. Archives, Appendices to the Journals of the House of Representatives, D–3, 1879, "Memorandum on the Immigration of Chinese into the Colony." Presented to both Houses of the General Assembly by command of His Excellency; written by Sir George Grey, price 3d.

had the right to protect oneself against loathsome disease, and that was what the Chinese constituted vis-à-vis New Zealand. When a more liberal member compared the plight of the Chinese in New Zealand with that of the Irish, Seddon rose in astonishment and anger. "To compare the Irish with the Chinese," he roared, "was an insult to every Irishman in the colony. Go to an Irishman on the gold fields and ask him whether a Chinaman was his equal or not. He would tell you that the Chinaman was a 'baste and nothing more than a long-tailed baste.' . . . There was about as much distinction between a European and a Chinaman as that between a Chinaman and a monkey." As has already been noted, the Irishman, although despised in Britain, was white and hence privileged in the Antipodes. Sir George Grey once again entered the fray. He strongly backed the proposed bill. "Why not," he asked, "let the people of New Zealand—a European race—keep themselves as pure a European race as they possibly could?"

But the time was not yet. And Seddon was obliged to pick his way carefully in order to avoid offending the Maoris, who were after all not without political power. He had to make sure that he specified particular groups rather than general categories of peoples for his attention, for he did not want the Maoris to identify with his intended victims. As it was, Major Te Whereo, representing Western Maori, "could not agree to this Bill, because honourable members would perhaps turn round and deal with the Natives in the same way." Robert Reid, like Seddon from Hokitika, probably represented the majority opinion of the day when he averred that he was no friend of the Chinese, but that he saw no need for a bill so extreme as the one proposed. After all, the committee report of 1871 had pointed out that the Chinese were certainly no menace to the colony, nor were they the carriers of infectious diseases. They were, rather, industrious, frugal and orderly.[60] Owing to the lack of a sufficiently broad base of support, the bill was withdrawn on

---

60. N.Z. *Hansard,* July 8, 1880.

July 29, 1880. That there really was a Chinese problem in New Zealand was open to genuine doubt. Official records indicate Chinese immigration to New Zealand took a major drop after 1871 and that by the mid-1880s more Chinese were departing the colony than were arriving.[61]

The least developed of the Australasian colonies was Western Australia, and its lack of enthusiasm at the prospect of the intercolonial conference on the Chinese question was consequently not surprising. The colony had not only imported small numbers of Chinese in the past, but the governor was convinced that a limited program of Chinese immigration was worth pursuing. The divergence of views between Western Australia and the eastern colonies was part of a pattern that was to continue. Western Australia was isolated from the more populous centers of the continent by thousands of miles of arid desert and often saw its own interests in conflict with those of its distant neighbors.

As the intercolonial conference approached, the eastern Australian colonies attacked Western Australia's attitude towards Chinese immigration. Governor William Robinson staunchly defended Western Australia's policy in a letter to the secretary of state, Lord Kimberley. He pointed out that the Chinese laborers had been imported into the colony with the permission of the Colonial Office, and he did not see why the eastern colonies should force their Chinese policy on "this distant and exceptionally situated colony." Western Australia had imported 50 coolies from Singapore in 1879, and it now proposed to accept a similar number. The effort was on a very small scale and the governor did not see how it concerned the other colonies.[62] He disparaged the charge that Chinese had made their way eastward from Western Australia and voiced confidence that Her Majesty's Government would not, as the eastern colo-

61. Fong, 21. In 1876, for example, 112 Chinese arrived and 453 left.
62. There were, anyway, only 914 Chinese in Western Australia as late as 1891, according to the census of that year.

nies demanded, close the ports of a crown colony to a people free to come and go through British ports, just as Englishmen were at liberty to pass through the Treaty Ports.[63] Nevertheless, the governor did depute the chief justice of the colony, who was in Melbourne at the time, to represent Western Australia at the conference as an observer.

The conference convened in Sydney in January 1881. It was chaired by Sir Henry Parkes, and representatives from all the Australasian colonies were in attendance. On January 19 the assembled delegates passed the key resolution: "That this Conference resolves that the introduction of Chinese in large numbers into any part of the Colonies of Australia is highly undesirable, and recommends uniform legislation on the part of all the colonies to restrict the influence of Chinese into these colonies." Subsequently, the conference attacked the policy of Western Australia which, under the terms of a government notice of December 28, 1880, had announced its intention of importing another small consignment of Chinese laborers. The conference demanded action by Her Majesty's Government, pointing out that the petitioners represented over 2,500,000 souls and Western Australia only 30,000. To further its aim of gaining a reversal of the Western Australia action, the conference deputed Parkes, Graham Berry of Victoria and William Morgan of South Australia to sail to England in order to petition the secretary of state in person.[64]

Western Australia was furious. The *Western Australian* of January 25 defended the government's position and asserted, "it is well-known that the anti-Chinese crusade in Victoria and South Wales has been nothing more than a claptrap bid for the votes of the working population of the larger towns." Western Australia would have preferred British to Chinese workmen, but other shores tended to be more attractive to Englishmen.

63. CO 18/194, W.A. 4665, no. 26, Robinson to Kimberley, Jan. 25, 1881.
64. CO 211/99, New Zealand-Intercolonial Conference held at Sydney.

The paper could not decide whether the demand for imperial action was a joke or not. The governor, however, had no such doubts. "The incident," he wrote Kimberley, "is a piece of impertinence almost unparalleled in political affairs. . . . The Eastern Colonies . . . can all unite in a petty piece of meddling busy-bodyism towards the internal affairs of Western Australia." It was a view with which the secretary of state tended to agree,[65] and the conference delegation consequently returned from London refreshed, no doubt, by the bracing sea voyage but otherwise empty-handed.

Rebuffed by Whitehall, the Australasian colonies were nevertheless able to set about ordering their own houses. Parkes mounted the attack in New South Wales on several fronts. He first invoked the ever-present fear of the introduction of smallpox by Chinese immigrants. On rather dubious evidence, Parkes wrote Graham Berry in Melbourne: "A case of undoubted smallpox reported this morning. House and all concerned placed in quarantine."[66] Soon rumors of more cases were abroad, and the other colonies were informed of New South Wales's dilemma. "I have the honour to inform you," Parkes wrote his colleagues, "that within the last forty-eight hours some undoubted cases of smallpox have been discovered among the population of Sydney."[67]

Keeping up the façade, Parkes next telegraphed the colonial secretary of Hong Kong: "Smallpox having been introduced here by Chinese recently arrived, this Government has by Proclamation notified that Hong Kong and all ports of China will be treated as places from which all vessels arriving in Sydney will be quarantined."[68] Three days later the Government of Hong Kong replied in some mystification: "Health Officer re-

    65. CO 18/195, W.A. 9083, no. 57, Robinson to Kimberley, Apr. 11, 1881; minuting by Kimberley on 17/4268.
    66. N.S.W. Archives, box-Chinese Immigration, 1880–1881—4/829.1–4, Parkes to Berry, June 15, 1881.
    67. *Ibid.*, Circular to other colonies from Parkes, c. June 16, 1881.
    68. *Ibid.*, Parkes to colonial secretary, Hong Kong, June 17, 1881.

ports Hong Kong free from all evidences of infectious or contagious disease, and that out of 3,585 Chinese he examined this month as emigrants, none was suffering from smallpox. The Governor therefore hopes that quarantine will not be enforced against Hong Kong." [69]

But Parkes kept up the pressure. He wrote Berry that New South Wales intended in its proposed legislation to provide for the placing of all vessels with Chinese on board into quarantine "whether any contagious or infectious disease shall have prevailed or existed on board at any time during the voyage or not," [70] to raise the penalty for evasion of the act to £100 per occurrence, and to change the ratio of Chinese to ship burthen from one Chinese for every ten tons to one Chinese for every one hundred tons. Parkes hoped that Victoria would follow suit.[71] A New South Wales proclamation required all ships from China and Hong Kong to be detained at the quarantine station at Port Jackson, "until they receive practique from the Health Officer." [72] When the vessel *Ocean* arrived, she was consequently detained although there was no sign of sickness aboard.[73]

There was an air of fraud to the whole business as was evidenced by a telegram Parkes sent to officials of the other colonies only a few days after his original sounding of the alarm. In it he reported no new cases of smallpox had developed since June 19 and that the boy mentioned in his original message to Berry was now convalescent.[74] Still, the game had been worth

69. *Ibid.*, act. colonial secretary, Hong Kong to colonial secretary, N.S.W., June 20, 1881.
70. Article 2 of the draft Chinese act of 1881. This section was not included in the final version of the law.
71. N.S.W. Archives, box-Chinese Immigration, 1880–81—4/829.1–4, Parkes to chief secretary, Victoria, June 27, 1881.
72. *Ibid.*, procl. dated June 17 in N.S.W. Government Gazette Extraordinary.
73. *Ibid.*, Memo. from the colonial secretary, July 1, 1881.
74. *Ibid.*, M. 18251, June 23, 1881.

the candle. The Australian public and especially that of New South Wales was now nervous and apprehensive, a state of mind which was to facilitate the passage of the restrictive legislation Parkes so ardently sought.

Parkes was always willing to exploit the Chinese immigration issue. But why had he become so frenetically active in early 1881? The answer lay in a note he had written the inspector-general of police, asking for some statistical information on Chinese recently arrived in New South Wales. The reply shocked him. Since January 1, 1881, 2,404 Chinese had arrived and only 529 had left or were about to leave the colony. The police report outlined the reasons for the increased influx:

There are mainly three causes to account for the large number of Chinese who have arrived recently. The first is that the Chinese generally emigrate shortly after their New Year which happens about the end of January or the beginning of February. The second is the flattering reports that returned miners have given of their success at the tin and gold mines of this Colony and Queensland; and the third is the difficulty of obtaining employment of any kind in California at present, in consequence of the anti-Chinese agitation that has been going on there for some time.

"The Australian Colonies," the statement concluded, "are evidently increasing in popular favour among the Chinese as several of the immigrants had mortgaged their farms and gardens to enable them to pay for their passage here." [75]

It is little wonder that Parkes sprang into action. Australia was not to take second place to California in its determination to exclude the Chinese. The thought of New South Wales and Australia as havens for "celestials" unable to survive in California must have exercised the premier no end. That the census of 1881 placed the total number of Chinese in New South Wales at 10,205—only 1.36 percent of the population—was clearly con-

75. *Ibid.*, M. 85212, Parkes to inspector general of police, Apr. 20, 1881; Robert Anderson, inspector, and A. Johnston, sub-inspector, to George Read, superintendent in charge, and forwarded to inspector general, Apr. 21, 1881.

sidered beside the point; the dark hue of the future was all too evident.

The fears of Parkes and his constituents, as well as the resolutions of the intercolonial conference, had now to be translated into action. When once again a bill to curtail Chinese immigration to New South Wales was introduced into the legislature late in 1881, the public greeted the news with acclaim. One pamphleteer who signed himself Timothy Wobblechops strongly urged Parkes on his course. "Is it for this [the Chinese presence in Australia] British pluck and energy procured us these noble regions?" Wobblechops asked. "Is it for this Britons and other Europeans have torn themselves from those nearest and dearest to them and crossed the wide sea? Is it for this natives were born and reared in the country? 'Oh!' I say again, 'may none of us live to see the like!' " [76]

Sydney's two major newspapers remained true to their previous stances. The *Morning Herald* attacked Parkes's racism. "To fine a free man for arriving in a free country is a detestable piece of legislation." As for Parkes, he "would be popular just now if in Southern Russia he was hounding the people against the Jews, or if in Ireland he was stirring up hatred against the Saxon. But a humane statesman would rather assuage than embitter the barbaric enmities, and it is the duty of a Government to labour as far as possible to prevent a popular burst of feeling, when it tends towards injustice or cruelty, from getting permanently recorded on the Statute-book." The paper continued at length, pointing out that the number of Chinese in New South Wales had dropped from 20,000 to 9,000 without the benefit of legislation such as that proposed.[77] Contending it was unfair to blame the Chinese for the presence of smallpox as the disease was more prevalent in London than it was in Sydney, the *Herald* said the Chinese were exemplary citizens. The proposed

76. J. Hurst (ed.), *The Chinese Question in Australia, 1880–81* (Sydney, 1880), 7.
77. *Sydney Morning Herald*, Aug. 9, 1881.

restrictive legislation was "utterly indefensible, and in any British community is so strikingly at variance with the general principle of our race in its dealings with mankind, that it acquired from our history a peculiar degree of repulsiveness." [78]

In contrast, the *Sydney Daily Telegraph* supported the Government:

> It is all very well indulging in sentimental talk about the equal rights of men, and these should be respected. But there are occasions and circumstances which render it necessary that we should remember that charity begins at home. The Chinese question involves a real danger. The small number at present in the colony may not be much injury to it, but a large influx would be a curse to the country. There are very few Chinese of the better class among those who leave their country, and it is well-known that the Chinese in the colonies demoralise those Europeans brought into contact with them.

The *Telegraph* concluded that "the Chinaman is no doubt a man and a brother; but it would be better for himself and his Australian brethren if he stayed at home in his own country." [79]

In Parliament, Parkes presented his case with care, taking advantage of both the liberal self-image and the prejudices of his colleagues: "I am willing to admit," the premier intoned, "that legislation of this kind is undesirable. I am as anxious as any can be that we should maintain the boast that whoever steps upon our shore shall find an asylum here. I am as anxious as any man can be that this land shall be a refuge for the oppressed, the poor, and the struggling from every part of the world. . . . Notwithstanding this, I feel that times arise when the law of self-preservation is superior to every other law."

Parkes contended he had no sympathy for those who painted the Chinese as immoral and depraved. "On the contrary, I have at all times maintained that so far as I could judge, they were an industrious, a thrifty, and a law-abiding people." But he op-

78. *Ibid.*, Aug. 11, 1881.
79. *Sydney Daily Telegraph,* July 30, 1881.

posed their presence in Australia nonetheless: "I object to them, in the first place, because they do not assist in the permanent settlement of the country. I object to them, in the second place, because they are a class of persons who cannot possibly have any real sympathy with British progress, and with the development of those principles at which we all aim in promoting the progress of a British population. I object to them also on account of the vast numbers of the nation to which they belong."

Parkes was now under full steam. He discussed the evil of Chinese competition for the white laborer, the lack of women among the immigrants, and the degree to which the Chinese constituted a social threat. He even invoked the American experience, pointing out that the Chinese constituted only one in 476 of the American population as compared with a figure of one in 50 for New South Wales and one in 19 of the European male adults in the colony. New South Wales wanted no inferior or subservient class within its population. All citizens should be permitted to share the same privileges and to intermarry freely. The intimation was that Chinese could never aspire to this state. The premier concluded his oration with a rhetorical question: "Is it part of our duty to encourage or to throw open the gates of the country to the inundation of persons who in no sense come to assist us in founding an empire, but who come here to better as far as they can their own condition, intending to return to their country?" [80] Clearly, the answer, in Parkes's view, had to be no, and most of the speakers that followed supported the premier, emphasizing the inferiority of the Chinese race. A few stalwarts continued to object on the basis that the proposed measure was "un-British," but they were soon swept aside.

The governor, Lord Loftus, informed the Colonial Office of the course of events. He reported that proposed legislation

80. N.S.W. *Hansard,* July 13, 1881.

would, through quarantine regulations and heavy penalties for violations, so discourage shippers that they would no longer venture near New South Wales with Chinese passengers and that hence, although it was nowhere explicitly stated or established in the contemplated law, the Chinese would, in fact, be totally excluded from the colony. Loyal to his constitutional role, however, the governor pointed out that the draft bill did not run counter to any treaties and that public opinion was overwhelmingly behind the government. Opposition from the imperial government, he contended, "might give rise to urgent remonstrances and be attended with very serious consequences." [81]

Once more the imperial philosophy of equality and the determination of a colonial white population to violate it were in confrontation. Whitehall clearly wished to extricate itself from a familiar and embarrassing dilemma. Colonial Office minuting noted the frequent reference in the assembly debates to the words of Newcastle, who had said, "if the right to obstruct Chinese immigration is conceded, it is perhaps better that the obstruction be directed to prevent the arrival of the immigrants than to discourage or harass them after they are arrived." [82] It was advice New South Wales was clearly following, and hence disallowance of the measure would be most difficult.

The actual provisions of Act II of 1881, "An Act to restrict the Influx of Chinese into New South Wales," were as follows: article 3 established a ratio of Chinese to tonnage at 1/100. Masters violating this stipulation were liable to a fine of £100 per offense unless they could prove the suspect was a British subject, a difficult assignment indeed. For although the measure did, in fact, exempt British subjects from its workings, this con-

---

81. CO 201/595, N.S.W. 15311, no. 103, Loftus to Kimberley, July 12, 1881.

82. CO 201/595, N.S.W. 16853, no. 123, Loftus to Kimberley, Aug. 10, 1881. Minuting by W. H. M. (W. H. Mercer).

cession to Whitehall's imperial spirit was essentially meaningless. At the end of article 10, which dealt with Chinese British subjects, stood the disarming statement that "a certificate of the Governor of any British Colony or of a British Consul shall be sufficient evidence of the claim of such Chinese to exemption under this section." As natural-born British subjects held no certificates and as governors and consuls were not in the habit of signing such documents for Chinese in any case, the protection afforded by this clause was at best illusory.

Other sections of the bill required the payment of £10 for every Chinese permitted to land or arriving in the colony overland. Any Chinese attempting to enter New South Wales without paying the entrance tax was liable to a £10 penalty and the master of the vessel on which he arrived to a £50 charge even if the immigrant absconded. To further secure the colony against the illegal entry of Chinese, each master had to submit a list to the senior customs officer at his port of entry, specifying, to the best of his knowledge, the name, place of birth, the apparent age, the ordinary place of residence, the date and port of embarkation, and the calling or occupation of every Chinese on board his vessel. A maximum penalty of £200 was provided for nondelivery of the document.

Had it not been for the intercession of the legislative council, the bill would have been still more stringent. The council argued against the inclusion of a highly restrictive quarantine clause, the stipulation that Chinese obtain either poll-tax payment certificates or exemption certificates, and a prohibition on Chinese ownership of land. As Parkes was anxious to get the bill read into the law, he conceded the council these points. Faced with the reality of the act passed by both houses of the New South Wales legislature, Edward Wingfield, one of the assistant undersecretaries, represented the official Colonial Office view when he admitted the act was more stringent than legislation passed in other colonies but that inasmuch as the council had obtained the removal of the quarantine, real estate, and certification clauses, Her Majesty's Government would have no alternative but to allow the measure.[83]

Henry Parkes may have been the prime mover in the anti-Chinese legislative campaign, but faithful to the resolutions of the Sydney conference, most of the other Australasian colonies closed ranks with New South Wales. Victoria Act 723 of 1881 was promulgated on December 24 and South Australia followed suit with Act 213 of the same year.

In New Zealand, Seddon, the "King Dick" of the small wage earner, was becoming an increasingly powerful figure in politics. After the Sydney conference, his views on the Chinese question were to carry the day. Even though the Chinese population of the colony, according to the census of 1881, had reached only 5,004, Acts 47 of 1881 and 34 of 1888, identical in virtually all respects to similar Australian legislation, were overwhelmingly passed by the legislature.[84] In June 1882, however, a private member introduced a bill to bar all Chinese from the goldfields,[85] but withdrew it before it could reach a second reading.

New Zealand public opinion was probably quite fairly represented in the *New Zealand Times* (published in Wellington) which wrote:

It [the Chinese question] is not a mere question of today's emergency . . . but the ever present contingency of hordes of Chinese swooping down upon the colony the moment sufficient inducement offers. Let there be another revival of gold-mining industry, an

---

83. CO 201/595, N.S.W. 870, no. 178, Loftus to Kimberley, Nov. 29, 1881; minuting by E. W. (Edward Wingfield) on N.S.W. 2011.

84. Under the terms of Act 47 of 1881, the ratio of Chinese passengers to vessel tonnage was established at $\frac{1}{10}$. A penalty of £10 was prescribed for every violation. Entering Chinese had to pay £10, and the owner of the immigrant ship was liable to a fine of up to £20 for each evasion plus forfeiture of the vessel. Exemptions from the workings of the act were provided for resident Chinese, as was a system under which resident Chinese could absent themselves from New Zealand temporarily and be permitted to return without penalty. Act 34 of 1888 in article 4 established a ratio of Chinese passengers to ship tonnage at $\frac{1}{100}$.

85. N.Z. *Hansard,* June 16, 1882.

event well within the bounds of probability, and the news would be instantly wired to Chinese ports and every vessel available would quickly swarm with living cargoes of Chinamen, bond slaves to speculators, who would bring them here as means of personal profit, and not as aids to colonisation. And in their train would come a host of evils and demoralisation, the very chance of which it were well to avoid.[86]

Seven years later the governor of New Zealand, Sir William Jervois, who had recently been transferred from South Australia, tried to explain the colonial attitude to his superiors in London—not an easy task as the number of Chinese in New Zealand had actually decreased by 462 since 1881.[87] The dispatch to Lord Knutsford, the secretary of state, was a long one but the governor summed up his view towards the end of the message: "It is their [the Chinese's] qualities of thrift, frugality and industry that render them peculiarly obnoxious to the working man, who has no patience for people that are content to rise earlier in the morning, work harder all day, and be content with smaller profits than himself." [88]

Tasmania and Western Australia, of all the Australasian colonies, traditionally maintained the most liberal attitudes towards their Chinese residents, but this is not hard to understand in view of the fact that the 1891 census showed less than 1,000 Chinese in either. Yet in 1887 Tasmania, largely in deference to its sister colonies, passed an act to restrict Chinese immigration which bore all the familiar trappings.[89] Western Australia

86. *New Zealand Times,* July 9, 1880.
87. N.Z. *Hansard,* Dec. 16, 1887.
88. CO 209/248, confidential, Jervois to Knutsford, May 16, 1888.
89. Under the provisions of Tasmania Act 9 of 1887, the master of a vessel was to keep a complete list of Chinese aboard his ship, specifying their names, places of birth, apparent ages, ordinary places of residence, ports and dates of embarkation and callings or occupations. A ratio of one Chinese for every 100 tons of ship burthen was established, and it was made applicable to all vessels arriving in Tasmanian ports even if they did not land any of their passengers. Chinese who were allowed to land would have to pay the familiar £10 entry tax, and the law provided for the usual penalties on the master and owner up to and including

acted similarly when the discovery of gold in payable quantities in 1886 caused a dramatic change in the colony's attitude. And once infested by the anti-Chinese virus, Western Australia fell a total victim to the disease.

The government introduced a Chinese immigration restriction bill based on the by now well-worn pattern established by the eastern colonies. S. Burt, speaking for the government in the council, contended the law was necessary in view of the flood of Chinese to the Kimberley goldfields. To strengthen his argument, he pointed out that the Western Australia goldfields were closer to China than any heretofore discovered on the continent. The bill as it finally emerged was slightly less stringent than the legislation of most of the other colonies, however, and indeed several members of the council complained about this.[90] The ratio of Chinese to ship tonnage was established at 1/50 rather than the more conventional 1/100. The usual £10 landing tax was to be assessed, but the punitive clauses of the act were somewhat less severe than usual. To insure against the wrath of the guardians of the imperial gospel in London, the law, in letter rather than in administration, applied only to alien Chinese.[91]

In summary, then, it can be said that within a few years of the Sydney conference all the Australasian colonies had stringent Chinese immigration restriction acts on their statute books. They were, however, not yet sated. That the strangers in their midst were at worst inoffensive and at best highly desirable settlers did little to diminish the zeal of the white colonists. In late 1883 the New South Wales legislative assembly received a report on the Chinese population of the colony by Martin Brennan, a sub-inspector of police. Brennan was im-

---

forfeiture of the vessel. British subjects were to be exempted from the workings of the law, but again it was incumbent on a Chinese to prove that he was, indeed, a British subject.

90. *W.A. Hansard*, July 6, 1886.

91. Act 13, 1886. The measure was refined and strengthened by Act 32 of 1893.

pressed by the Chinese thirst for education, and urged that Chinese children be allowed to attend government schools. Sanitary conditions in the Chinese quarters were indeed poor and living accommodations cramped, but Brennan concluded, "that the Chinese are the most industrious race in the world is a proposition which no one who knows them thoroughly could question, and the Chinese of this Colony, with few exceptions, stand in the estimate of discriminating men as deserving that character; as gardeners they have no equals, and Europeans are indebted to them for a thorough knowledge in the raising of vegetables etc." All in all, Brennan visited 942 different sites where Chinese were housed and his report was in general laudatory.[92]

Clearly, the sub-inspector's sentiments ran counter to those commonly held, and that he had not changed the opinion of the Chinese population entertained by most members of the assembly was manifested by the words of Richard W. Thompson of West Maitland, who delivered himself of a judgment somewhat different from Brennan's. All the Chinese had to be removed from the colony. He did not want them even as vegetable growers though "they had been held up as a pattern in that capacity." Not only were the Chinese filthy, they were "abominable liars." Worst of all, they were a moral danger in at least two ways. "They . . . interfere[d] with grown-up people by underselling them . . . [and] they interfered with our children, male and female, in such a way as would be disgusting to talk about even in this Assembly." Finally, Thompson hoped that the government would approve "an absolutely restrictive tax" on Chinese immigrants and that every evasion or attempted evasion would be met "with the severest penalties."[93]

Of course, the crusade for a White Australia was only the cutting edge of a more general form of xenophobia prevalent not only in the Antipodes but throughout the British Empire.

92. CO 204/237, report on Chinese camps by Martin Brennan, Nov. 15, 1883.
93. N.S.W. *Hansard,* Feb. 16, 1886.

When A. C. Gregory rose in the Queensland legislature to denounce the admission of Germans into the colony, he spoke for many of his fellow colonists. "Our own people are here already," said the honorable member,

> and great attempts have been made to prevent any other nationalities coming into the colony. The cry against coolies has been made a watchword, and everything has been done in order to prevent their introduction into the colony; and obstructions have also been placed in the way of the introduction of Polynesian Labourers. We have also tabooed the introduction of Chinamen; and now we are asked to consent to the introduction of a people who are certainly as different from our own, both in language and customs as any of those to which we have so strongly objected.[94]

Still, it was the Chinese question which was viewed with the greatest alarm, and despite the legislative triumphs of the early 1880s, increased apprehension was again everywhere evident in the second half of the decade. Into this generally explosive atmosphere once more strode the chief political beneficiary of the campaign for total Chinese exclusion—Sir Henry Parkes, still the premier of New South Wales. Although the Chinese population of the senior colony was at no higher a level than it had been in 1861 and only a few hundred more than in 1881,[95] Parkes was determined to see further common intercolonial action against the Chinese threat. In late 1887 he fired his opening shots in a letter to Duncan Gillies, the premier of Victoria. Joint action by all the Australasian colonies was a matter of urgency, Parkes contended, for the Chinese inundation was a continuing threat.

Warming to his task, Parkes wrote a circular to Queensland, South Australia, Tasmania, and New Zealand calling for common action. The premier was sweet reason personified. He disparaged those who contended that the Chinese were an inferior race. He opposed their entry into Australia not because of their

---

94. Queensland *Hansard* (Council), Oct. 8, 1884.
95. N.S.W. census of 1861, 1881, 1891.

degraded character but for social and political reasons. Common customs, common language, and common faith in jurisprudence cemented society together, and "it is inadvisable and fraught with serious evils to allow sharply defined class distinction to grow up in these colonies."

The reactions to his proposal must have cheered Parkes. Even Tasmania was positively inclined and replied, "However selfish it may appear to cry 'Our country for our own people,' the cry is in accordance with the instincts of nations and indeed, is in accord with the sacred instincts of the families where 'kith and kin' are sheltered to the exclusion of strangers." [96] Parkes must also have been encouraged by the continuing support of his position by newspapers and periodicals. A contemporary issue of *Chambers' Journal of Popular Literature, Science and Art* reiterated the usual arguments against the presence of "John" in Australia. He failed to bring his women, would not assimilate or settle, and was addicted to opium and gambling: "The Chinaman makes not the slightest effort to rise to the superior level of his new surroundings, but merely transfers his Asiatic mode of living to the Antipodes." But the heart of the matter lay elsewhere, in the journal's eyes: "The last, and from the utilitarian standpoint the weightiest count in the indictment against the ubiquitous Mongolian, is that he slowly throws the white man out of employment and secures to himself a monopoly of certain favoured departments of mechanical industry." He lives off a handful of rice in ugly and crowded quarters, and,

on the gold fields, "John" is detested with a widespread bitterness that has frequently found expression in open violence. He exasperates the European diggers by rarely, if ever, searching out gold for himself, and by coming in vast crowds wherever the white man makes a discovery of the precious metal. He thus reaps a harvest that he has not assisted to sow. He profits by the pioneering enterprise of the European without exposing himself to any of its attendant risks and dangers. . . .

96. CO 204/273, Parkes to Gillies, Nov. 4, 1887; Parkes circular to other Australasian colonies, Nov. 8, 1887; Fysh to Parkes, Nov. 25, 1887.

They have already between forty and fifty thousand of these objectionable aliens in their midst, and they see clearly that the thousands will gradually grow into millions.[97]

The last accusation was, of course, well wide of the mark. It has already been pointed out that the Chinese, in contradistinction to European miners, engaged in placer rather than hard rock mining, or worked abandoned sites.

With the summoning of another intercolonial conference on the Chinese question still not assured, Parkes determined not to await the resolutions of the impending assemblage, but to draft legislation for New South Wales immediately. In this he was urged on by Gillies, who asserted that the existing New South Wales legislation was not sufficiently stringent. Victorian law, he pointed out, stipulated that proof of British citizenship must satisfy the collector of customs, a provision not reflected in any New South Wales measure. In case Parkes should not have understood what Gillies had in mind, the Victorian premier went on to say: "The Collector of Customs or other authorised officer would of course *not be* satisfied that the Chinese carried in the vessel *are* British subjects so that the provision with reference to carrying only one for every 100 tons will apply to them as well as the ten pounds poll tax." Gillies was willing to share one further thought with Parkes. He emphasized that there was nothing to prevent the Government of New South Wales from naming certain ports in orders-in-council which would for the next six months be closed to any vessel carrying Chinese passengers. Alternatively, the government might declare that ships bearing Chinese passengers would be quarantined for any period up to six months which the governor in council might decide.[98]

So inspired, Parkes's government determined on the final solution of the Chinese immigration question, an ambition which

97. *Chambers' Journal of Popular Literature, Science and Art,* fifth series, July 21, 1888.
98. N.S.W. Archives, box 4/884.1–4, Gillies to Parkes, Nov. 30, 1887.

was to be at least partially achieved by the provisions of a bill that was to become Act 4 of 1888.[99] The Colonial Office proved surprisingly tractable. John Anderson, one of the second-class clerks, minuted:

The nature of the anti-Chinese legislation is a social measure of self defence—not against the unruliness of the Chinese but against his practice of working for wages on which an Englishman could not exist. The matter is one entirely within the competence of the Colonial Legislatures and H.M.'s Government can do nothing even if they wished. This is perfectly well known to the Chinese.

At the same time to humour them we may send a circular to all Colonies in which Chinese are established calling for info. as to any exceptional legislation concerning them, its objects and results, and inform the F.O. that we have done so.[100]

Not unaware of the embarrassment connected with increasingly stringent immigration legislation which exposed Australian prejudice to world scrutiny, New South Wales and the other Australasian colonies would have preferred the Chinese question to have been resolved by British diplomatic initiative.[101] But Her Majesty's Government was reluctant so to act. Sir Robert Herbert, the permanent undersecretary at the Colonial Office, was more sensitive to the complexities of the whole issue than his subordinate, John Anderson. "This is an extremely delicate and difficult question," he minuted. The solutions "suggested by the Australians are very stringent and seem to me to be the embodiment of the views expressed in Bret Harte's 'Heathen Chinee', i.e., the fear of being ruined by Chinese cheap labour." The Colonial Office should be careful not to encourage the existing Australian policy. Lord Knutsford agreed with Herbert's views but with typical Colonial Office pragma-

99. CO 204/273, Papers associated with the Chinese Immigration Restriction Bill of 1888.
100. CO 201/607, Parl., C. 5448, FO to CO, Dec. 21, 1887, minuting by J. A.
101. CO 201/608, conf., Aust., no. 129, Parl., C. 5448, Aug. 1888, minuting.

tism noted that if all the Australian colonies acted in unison, Her Majesty's Government would really be left with very little choice.[102]

No doubt cognizant of the prevailing attitude, the Australasian colonies intensified the negotiations designed to lead to another intercolonial conference. Queensland's Premier Griffith, for instance, wrote his counterpart in Victoria that much as he favored British diplomatic conversations with China, he wondered what would prevent Chinese, despite an anti-immigration policy by their government, from first sailing to some port of the "Eastern Archipelago" and then to Australia. "I think therefore that it is highly important that the several legislatures should take immediate action in the way of Legislation." [103]

Duncan Gillies, not surprisingly, answered a New South Wales telegram in terms that clearly expressed support for Parkes's scheme:

I beg to inform you that this Government are of opinion that the influx of Chinese to Australia should be discouraged as far as possible. They think . . . that it is undesirable that there should be any considerable portion of the population to whom the ordinary rights of citizenship cannot be conveniently granted and the difference between Asiatic and European civilisation is so great that both forms cannot practically exist together in the same country. For this and other obvious reasons, which it is unnecessary to state in detail, they think it is very desirable that stringent laws should be enacted in *all* of the Colonies with the object of restricting as far as practicable immigration from China.[104]

Gillies's message coincided with his Government's assertion that many Chinese were using fraudulent naturalization papers to avoid paying the poll tax, or so it was claimed. The Government of Victoria therefore determined to issue no more natu-

102. CO 201/608, N.S.W. 6390, tel., CO to Lord Carrington, Apr. 3, 1888, minuting by Herbert and Knutsford, 6/4.
103. Queensland Archives, Col. 13, Griffith to Gillies, Apr. 7, 1888.
104. *Ibid.*, Gillies to Parkes, Nov. 2, 1887.

ralization certificates to Chinese unless it was absolutely satisfied as to the bona fides of the applicants.[105] What this meant, in effect, was an end to the naturalization of Chinese.

South Australia felt similarly afflicted, and its premier, Thomas ("Honest Tom") Playford, wrote Gillies an iluminating letter. "Under these circumstances," he explained,

we have discontinued the issue of naturalisation certificates to Chinese, and do not propose to recognise any certificates not granted by this Colony. Of course, the naturalisation certificates of one Colony have no effect beyond the territorial limits of that Colony, and although we should be glad to recognise your certificates, as no doubt you would ours, you will probably consider that, for mutual protection against a people whose lower orders are skilled in fraud, it will be wise to repress our natural inclinations in this respect.

There is an additional difficulty, so far as the Colonies are concerned, as regards Chinese who, being natives of Hong-Kong, are natural-born British subjects, but we hope by an alteration of our Act, so as to make the Customs officer the sole judge in the matter, and by rigid exercise of discretion, to practically shut the door to evasion of the Act.[106]

The visit of an official Chinese investigating commission under the leadership of General Wong Yung Ho in April and May of 1887 did little to decrease the intensity of anti-Chinese feeling. Still, it must have been a shock for Australian officials to encounter, for the first time, the sophistication of upper-class Chinese. As the visitors entered Darwin harbor, they were met by the senior local official, the resident, Mr. Parsons. The *Northern Territory Times* of April 4 described the scene: "His Mightiness (Yee Toon) after digesting the view of the Government Residence, slowly relieved himself of the following remark: 'In proportion as it becomes hidden by the surrounding foliage, so do the architectural beauties of the edifice become

105. Victoria Sessional Papers, 1888, Chinese immigration, Gillies to Playford, July 20, 1887.
106. *Ibid.,* Playford to Gillies, Aug. 15, 1887.

manifest to the beholders.' Mr. Parsons has not yet recovered from the shock."[107]

When the commissioners reached Melbourne, they were presented with a memorial by the Chinese community. It was a persuasive document. On a per capita basis, it contended, the Chinese contributed more to the colonial coffers than any other segment of the population. Not only were they subjected to a poll tax upon entry, but imported items for Chinese use were taxed at a rate several times higher than imports intended for the European population. The government contended that the Chinese should pay more because their presence necessitated additional police. But, the memorialists pointed out, the Chinese rate of arrest per thousand was 15.73 compared with 42.516 for the European population. "The Chinese," the writers concluded,

were singled out for such a yoke of national ignominy and dishonour which, even in the darker days of the Roman Empire, was only reserved for the vanquished, never for the subjects of a Friendly Power—to say nothing of one in actual alliance. . . . Your Excellencies can well imagine what outcry would be raised against Chinese perfidy if a Briton were thus treated in China, yet such is precisely the treatment meted out by these dependencies of the British Crown, in direct violation of all international law and usage, and in contravention of the Treaty engagements entered into by the Governments of the two Empires.[108]

When the Chinese delegation's report to its government resulted in an official protest by Lew Ta-Jên, the Chinese minister in London, the Australian colonies, and particularly New South Wales, determined to exert the greatest possible pressure on Whitehall to find a diplomatic solution to the problem of Chi-

107. Oddie, 114–15.
108. Victoria Sessional Papers, 1888, Chinese immigration, General Wong Yung Ho and Ü Tsing, Imperial Commissioners to Sir Henry Loch, June 13, 1887, encl. Lowe Kong Meng and 46 other Chinese to the Commissioners, June 3, 1887.

nese immigration into Australia. Lord Carrington, the governor of New South Wales, in a long letter urged the conclusion of a treaty with China along the lines of the Sino-American treaty (1880), which essentially excluded Chinese labor from the United States. Carrington then attempted to summarize the sources of Australian anxiety. The proximity of China to Australia combined with the opportunities perceived by the Chinese to exist on the continent roused the fear of Chinese inundation in every Australian breast. All Australia was determined to preserve the British character of its civilization. "There can be no interchange of ideas or religion or citizenship, nor can there be intermarriage or social communion between the British and the Chinese." The fundamental issue was that "the working classes of British people in all the affinities of race are directly opposed to their Chinese competitors. . . . There can be no sympathy, and in the future it is to be apprehended that there will be no peace, between the two races." Carrington closed his message with his Government's "renewed expressions of our loyal attachment to Her Majesty," but with the threat that if the Chinese question was not settled by diplomatic means, "the Australian Parliaments must act from the force of public opinion in devising measures to defend the Colonies from consequences which they cannot relax in their efforts to avert."

The inspiration for Carrington's letter was not hard to find. Parkes, on the previous day, had written Gillies:

There can be no doubt whatever that we have just ground for appealing to the Imperial Government to take up the great contention of these Australian Colonies against the continued influx of Chinese labourers. If we are part of the Empire, as self-governed colonies excluded from all participation in the making of Treaties, we have an indisputable right to expect the Imperial Government to consult and protect our separate and peculiar interests in this matter (which does not reach Her Majesty's subjects in Great Britain) by the exercise of the powers of Treaty on our behalf. . . . All the inconvenient and possibly exasperating consequences of legislation by different Australian Parliaments would be avoided by the Empire in this highest capacity dealing with the subject.[109]

It was a contest in the avoidance of responsibility. The Colonial Office hoped it could hide behind the façade of responsible government as the rationale for countenancing colonial legislation repugnant to the imperial philosophy of fair play and equality before the law. The colonial governments were determined, if possible, to shift the burden to Whitehall as an imperial obligation.

Carrington had certainly been right about the increasing tensions in Australia. It was more a matter of emotion than reality, for immigration figures gave no cause for concern. In South Australia, for instance, fear of the Chinese overrunning the ruby fields of the Northern Territory was prompted by a largely unsubstantiated telegram from the resident to the premier, which was made public.

> Guides being advertised for the conduct of 500 Chinese to the McDonald Range ruby fields. This movement is supported by the Chinese storekeepers, . . . and if legal means exist should be stopped. Once landed in the centre of Australia they will spread over all the colonies. . . . A powerful syndicate of Hong Kong and Canton merchants exists to pour Chinese into this port so long as it is open. There seems to be a general impression in China that access to the East is about closed, and they are making for Port Darwin in shoals. . . . The Chinese question has reached an acute stage and must be firmly handled.[110]

The explosion came on April 27, 1888, when the steamer *Afghan,* with 268 Chinese from Hong Kong on board arrived at Port Phillip Heads in Victoria. The health officer gave the vessel a clean bill of health, and it then proceeded up the bay to Williamstown, where it dropped anchor. That same afternoon the *Melbourne Age* wrote that "a large number of them [the

109. CO 881/8, CO confidential print 129, Aus., Lew Ta-Jên to Salisbury, Dec. 12, 1887; Carrington to Knutsford, Mar. 31, 1888; tel., Parkes to Gillies, Mar. 30, 1888.
110. Oddie, 53–54.

Chinese passengers] claim the right to enter Victoria on the ground that they are naturalised British subjects [60 of the 67 who wished to land asserted they were residents of the colony], and others professed their willingness to pay poll tax to obtain the privilege." [111] Public indignation, long tenuously held in check, burst forth in full fury. The Trades Hall Council organized a deputation to the premier which it asserted represented from thirty to forty thousand workers. Mr. Trenwith, the leader of the delegation, "hinted at a popular rising if the Chinese were permitted to land," and the crowd of over 1,000 that gathered at the wharf amply illustrated his point.[112] When an anti-Chinese meeting was hastily assembled at the Melbourne town hall, the *Age* reported that "there was an enormous attendance . . . the whole of the available accommodation in hall being occupied." Speakers from many trades and callings harangued the throng and the *Age* of the following morning captured the spirit of the meeting in an editorial. "Our allegiance is to our own population first," the paper intoned, "and we cannot be bound by any consideration to abstain from legislation which the moral welfare of the population demands." [113]

With a general election approaching, the Government of Victoria immediately agreed to satisfy the demands of its vocally anti-Chinese constituents. When 48 of the Chinese presented British naturalization papers, government officials concluded that they were fraudulent.[114] "In fact some of the papers appeared already to have done service two or three times over." [115] (The government indeed had some basis for suspicion. Geoffrey Serle notes that there was a remarkable correlation between

111. *Ibid.*, 72, quoting the *Age*, Apr. 27, 1888.   112. *Ibid.*, 73.
113. *Ibid.*, quoting the *Age*, May 2 and 5, 1888.
114. Victoria Sessional Papers, 1888, Chinese immigration, Gillies to Loch, May 2, 1888.
115. CO 881/8, CO conf. print 129, Aus., no. 80, Loch to Knutsford, May 10, 1888.

naturalization certificates issued in one year and new arrivals the next. For instance, 519 Chinese were naturalized in 1883 and 557 Chinese immigrants arrived in 1884. Comparable figures for 1884 and 1885 were 601 and 670, and for 1885 and 1886, 1,178 and 1,108.[116]) As the *Afghan* weighed 1,439 tons, 254 of the Chinese on board, according to the government, were not entitled to land, and the master and owner of the vessel were liable to an immense fine. The government was not at all anxious to exact payment and let it be known that if the *Afghan* left Melbourne without discharging *any* of its passengers, no more would be said of the matter. The captain of the *Afghan*, of course, had no choice but to submit to the government's "persuasion" and to comply with what was essentially an illegal order. And the government compounded its culpability when it proclaimed:

The Governor with the advice of the Executive Council pursuant to the provision of the Acts relating to the Public Health and of the several orders in Council thereunder, declaring Hong Kong, Singapore, together with Chinese and other Eastern ports infected, has, by order made on the 1st day of May 1888, directed that all intercolonial and other vessels bringing Chinese passengers to any port in Victoria be detained by the Health Officer of such port until such vessel and passengers by severally released by the said office.[117]

On the very day the proclamation went into effect, another vessel, the *Burrumbeet*, arrived in Melbourne with 14 Chinese on board who intended to land in Victoria. They immediately fell afoul of the proclamation and were placed in quarantine near Point Napean, "under a strong charge of constables." [118]

The governor, Sir Henry Loch, experienced imperial administrator that he was, did his best to restrain his ministers, but to no effect. He reported to the Colonial Office that he would

116. Geoffrey Serle, *The Rush to be Rich* (Melbourne, 1971), 297.
117. N.S.W. Archives, box 4/884. 1–4 second supplement to Victoria Government Gazette of Apr. 27, 1888.
118. Oddie, 72–75, quoting The *Age*, May 4 and 5, 1888.

have interfered more actively, but the law had only been "strained" and not broken.[119]

After Victoria had successfully repulsed the Chinese onslaught, the scene of action shifted elsewhere. In South Australia, the collector of customs at Adelaide prevented 55 Chinese on board the steamer *Menmuir* from landing on May 6 because it was a Sunday. The next day, at a special cabinet meeting, the government, encouraged by the usual public meeting, again prevented the landing of the Chinese. Through the attorney general, the tortuous and specious reasoning of the cabinet was announced: "No attempt has been made to land any Chinese from the 'Menmuir' and it is not anticipated that any will be, as the time prescribed by the Chinese Immigration Act for the payment of the poll-tax expired with the passing of the first customs entry, and all entries have been passed. No payment or landing would now be permitted nor will either be permitted." [120]

The *New Zealand Mail* in its weekly edition of May 11, 1888, was highly critical of some of the anti-Chinese excesses in Australia. It was confident that, "we in New Zealand can keep clear of so unworthy a mode of action." Yet the paper would "leave no stone unturned to check the Mongolian immigration, which although hitherto not very formidable in New Zealand, threatens speedily to assume alarming dimensions now that America is understood to be legally closed as a Chinese immigration ground, and Australia—although illegally—also." And the same issue carried the story of how the citizens of Aukland had induced the government to prevent the landing of Chinese passengers on board the *Te Anau,* a procedure which was repeated in Dunedin.

Meanwhile, the *Afghan,* on May 4, sailed northward to Sydney, where the reception its passengers received was even more

119. CO 881/8, CO conf. print 129, Aus., sec. and conf., Loch to Knutsford, May 10, 1888.
120. Rendell, 152.

tumultuous than their welcome in Melbourne. A large public meeting was immediately held at the town hall where the usual resolutions were passed. The next day a procession of 5,000, headed by the mayor, marched to Parliament and demanded to see the premier. When he was unavailable, the mob invaded the building itself. Parkes was probably far from displeased. The uproar would enable him to place additional pressure on the British Government for diplomatic settlement of the Chinese question and would increase the chances of Colonial Office allowance of stringent new anti-Chinese legislation. While Parkes was preparing his next move, the passengers on board the *Afghan,* soon joined by another contingent recently arrived on the *Tsinan,* languished in Sydney harbor. A Chinese delegation led by the prominent local businessman, Quong Tart, called on the premier, but to little avail. It was an impasse which was destined to be solved by action of the courts.

In both New South Wales (*Ex Parte Lo Pak*) and Victoria (*Chun Teeong Toy* v. *Musgrave*), legal proceedings were begun. Fearing an adverse decision, the Government of New South Wales relaxed its attitude slightly. On May 21, the collector of customs endorsed the exemption certificates of twenty-two Chinese on board the *Afghan,* five from the *Tsinan,* six from the *Menmuir,* and four from the *Guthrie.*[121] Two days later, the supreme courts justified the government's apprehensions by ruling that fifty-seven Chinese from the various vessels should be released.[122]

The litigation in Victoria involved one of the *Afghan's* passengers, who had been refused permission to enter the colony and was consequently suing the collector of customs, A. W. Musgrave. The plaintiff, Chun Teeong Toy, asserted that the master of the *Afghan* had offered to pay the £10 poll tax on his behalf but that the collector had refused to accept payment be-

121. N.S.W. Archives, box 4/884. 1–4, acting inspector general of police to principal secretary, May 21, 1888.
122. *Ibid.,* box 4/884. 1–4, ruling by supreme court of New South Wales, May 23, 1888.

cause the government had ordered him not to allow any Chinese to land. The court ruled in favor of Chun. The colony of Victoria, it asserted, did not enjoy the right of exclusion which was part of the Royal Prerogative, for that right had not been transferred to the colonial ministers by the constitution act. Hence Victoria could not exclude "alien friends." Furthermore, Victoria's own legislation provided no basis for exclusion. A master could be fined for bringing an excessive number of Chinese to the colony's shores, and Chinese immigrants could be forced to pay a poll tax, but nowhere was total exclusion provided for in law. With regret, Mr. Justice Williams concluded, "It leaves us in this most unpleasant and invidious position, that we are at present without *legal* means of preventing the scum or desperadoes of alien nationalities from landing on our territory, whenever it may suit them to come here." [123] When Victoria appealed the decision to the privy council, in the House of Lords, the Empire's highest court, however, it was reversed on the basis that an alien had no legal right expressible by action, to enter British territory.[124]

Parkes must have been secretly delighted with the march of events. His resolute determination to stem the Chinese tide made him the darling of the white population. And the action of the colonial courts marked him as that favorite British hero, the virtuous man waging the gallant fight and doomed to defeat by powers over which he had no control. The Federated Seamen's Union of Australasia addressed the premier in terms of admiration and respect:

Sir:
As the members of the Federated Seamen's Union throughout the colonies expressed in their unions' meetings an earnest and unanimous desire to congratulate you and your colleagues on the resolute and determined attitude assumed by the government on which you

123. CO 311/159, 1888, 1095, c. Oct. 1888.
124. Huang Tsen-ming, *The Legal Status of Chinese Abroad* (Taipei, 1954), 38.

are the distinguished and honoured head, I am instructed to forward a copy of the resolution as carried at our meeting on Monday evening last by acclamation.

The resolution lauded the premier and his government for their "resolute protection of our race and country from an invasion of innumerable hordes of Chinese. . . . We believe that you have the support and voice of the people of this Colony and all Australians who have a spark of patriotic feeling within them." [125]

Parkes effectively exploited the rumors that the British Government had no intention of using diplomatic channels to rescue Australia from the Chinese menace to increase his support at home and to place additional pressure on Whitehall to countenance the highly restrictive Chinese immigration measure (Act 4 of 1888) that the New South Wales legislature had passed. Carrington telegraphed the Colonial Office: "Telegrams in newspaper three days ago announce that Imperial Government declines to entertain negotiations with Chinese authorities requested on question of Chinese immigration. Though Cabinet Ministers deny authenticity, much feeling already manifest, and fomented by all press correspondents. I feel certain Cabinet Ministers will be compelled to introduce restrictive measures of a grave character if news is confirmed. I think it is my duty to inform you of a steady increase of intensity of feeling." [126] The fact of the matter was that the Colonial Office insisted negotiations with the Chinese be attempted for the very reason that a failure to do so would have such an adverse effect in Australia. The Foreign Office was willing to comply, although Lord Salisbury informed his counterpart at the Colonial Office that "the information . . . received from China leaves very little hope

125. N.S.W. Archives, box 4/884. 1–4, Federated Seamen's Union of Australasia to Parkes, May 23, 1888.
126. CO 881/8, CO conf. print 129, Aus., Carrington to Knutsford, Apr. 26, 1888.

that the Chinese Government will concur in stipulations of the kind suggested." [127]

Tempers in the New South Wales Parliament ran high at the supposed attitude of Her Majesty's Government and the rumored reservation of the Chinese immigration restriction bill by the governor. John McElhone of Upper Hunter spoke with rising passion: "I say we should insist upon our right, and we should again and again, press legislation, and tell the home Government in plain terms that, unless they will legislate for the protection of our own social interests in this matter, and to prevent the Chinese from coming among us, we should sever our connection with England and act independently." McElhone suggested that New South Wales had been too conciliatory in the past and urged the implementation of a 1/1,000 ratio of Chinese passengers to ship tonnage in the future. Henry Copeland of New England, in contrast, took a more imperial view, worrying about the effect of current events in the colony upon Sino-British relations.[128] Parkes himself delivered a singularly pugnacious speech. In times of extreme danger, he exclaimed, a government must not be afraid to break the law. "Why, a government that stood in fear of technical observance of the law in any such case as that would be swept away, and deservedly swept away." Parkes made good use of his talents for invective and hyperbole. Sixty thousand Chinese, he implied, were taking the bread out of the mouths of Australian working men and their families. While appeals for British diplomatic intercession were being ignored, ship after ship was arriving in Sydney filled to the gunwales with Chinese. "We can bear remonstrance," he said, "we can meet argument, we can make good our case against the world; but we cannot patiently stand to be treated with the frozen indifference of persons who consider some petty quarrel in some petty state of more importance than the gigantic inter-

127. CO 201/609, N.S.W. 8485, FO, Apr. 30, 1888, R. W. H. (Herbert); FO to CO, Apr. 30, 1888.
128. N.S.W. *Hansard,* May 16, 1888.

ests of these magnificent colonies." Having led his listeners, step by step, to a peak of emotional frenzy, Parkes appealed "to gentlemen in all quarters of this House—I appeal to every section of my fellow country-men throughout the land—to support us in this effort to terminate a moral and social pestilence, and to preserve to ourselves and our children, unaltered and unspotted, the rights and privileges which we have received from our forefathers." [129]

When Sir George Dibbs, a former premier and Parkes's bitter opponent, accused him of disloyalty to the mother country, Thomas Wilker of Northumberland rose to the premier's defense and in the process, no doubt, represented the views of the vast majority in the chamber.

> The Premier has shown a manliness and independence which I never expected of him; because he is protecting the rights and liberties of the working population of New South Wales, and he is protesting willful insult from the home government. He virtually says, "I am ready with my life to defend the high prerogative of self-government. I am ready with my life, in defiance of all that may be brought to intimidate a man, to warp the statesmanship of a man, and limit his courage and honesty—in spite of all that I am determined to protect the population of the Colony, and that the will of the people shall rise even higher, if need be, than the men-of-war in the harbour or the representative of the Crown in our country." That is a manly course of action.[130]

The doughty Dibbs was, however, not to be deterred, and he moved a vote of censure on the government. He accused Parkes of being "a mean, despicable dastardly man," and in anger exclaimed: "One's blood boils that such disloyalty could be shown by a gentleman who receives so much at the hands of his sovereign." Needless to say, the motion lost by a count of five ayes to fifty-one noes.[131]

After Carrington asked whether he should give the royal assent to the Chinese immigration restriction bill, Frederic W.

---

129. *Ibid.*   130. *Ibid.*, May 17, 1888.   131. *Ibid.*, May 23, 1888.

Fuller, a first-class clerk in the North American and Australian department, hastily minuted, "of course assent cannot be refused"; while Herbert added, "Any delay in authorising the Royal Assent would gravely increase the present strong feeling in the colony and prove almost certainly prejudicial to any prospect of a full consideration of the question and of a settlement on moderate terms." [132] Parkes had played his cards well, and Act 4 of 1888 in due course gained the royal assent despite provisions that ran counter to the liberal axioms of the British imperial philosophy.

The law in its final form was in many ways more severe than its early drafts. Article 1 repealed the act of 1881. Article 2 legitimized the illegalities associated with the detention of the *Afghan* and the other vessels bearing Chinese immigrants: any officials "who may have committed any act in preventing the landing of Chinese, or otherwise in relation to Chinese immigrants, or to vessels carrying such immigrants since the first day of May, one thousand eight hundred and eighty-eight, are hereby indemnified, and shall in all Courts of Law in New South Wales and elsewhere be held harmless in respect thereof." Article 3 stipulated that any Chinese not already naturalized who left the colony was subject to all the restrictions of the act upon his return. Other articles demanded the usual list of Chinese to be prepared by the master of the vessel bearing them, lowered the ratio of Chinese to ship tonnage to 1/300 (1/1,000 in the initial version of the bill), and raised the penalty on the master to £500 for each Chinese passenger in excess of this ratio. The poll tax on Chinese immigrants was raised to £100, and those Chinese who were permitted entry were in article 11 specifically prohibited from becoming associated with mining without the express permission of the minister (which would, of course, never be forthcoming). Finally, article 15 provided the usual meaningless sop for the Colonial Office. Chinese who

132. CO 201/608, N.S.W. 9782, tel., Carrington to Knutsford, May 17, 1888, minuting of May 17.

were British by birth and could so prove by means of a certificate signed by the governor of a British colony or a British counsel were exempt from the workings of the act along with holders of bona fide New South Wales naturalization certificates and those with exemption certificates as provided for in the act of 1881. The naturalization dictum was again a direct slap at London. Nevertheless, Knutsford minuted tiredly, "We cannot practically disallow the act." [133]

Her Majesty's Government now found itself in the unenviable position of being caught between the pugnaciously anti-Chinese Australasian colonies and an incensed Chinese government. On the *Afghan* matter, Lord Salisbury could only weakly write to Lew that the Chinese aboard the *Afghan* had not been allowed to land in Melbourne or Sydney in conformity with colonial regulations, and the foreign secretary was forced to admit, "I am not acquainted with the text of those regulations." Lew was not to be easily mollified. He quite properly pointed to the illegality of the actions of the Victorian and New South Wales Governments. "Having caused a study of the statutes to be made, I am advised that, in none of them, bristling as they are with pains and penalties directed against Chinese subjects, is there a single provision empowering the Executive to prohibit the landing of immigrants who are prepared to pay the stipulated poll-tax." [134] As has already been shown, there was little the British Government was prepared to do. The Australasian colonies drew a good deal more water in Whitehall than the representative of the dying Ch'ing Empire.

The British authorities were, however, willing to intercede where they could do so without cost. The intercolonial conference on the Chinese question was scheduled to open in Sydney on June 12, and the Colonial Office was willing to try to influ-

133. CO 201/608, N.S.W. 17416, Agent-General, Aug. 20, 1888, minuting by Knutsford, 6/10.
134. CO 881/8, CO conf. print 129, Aus., FO to Lew Ta-Jên, May 18, 1888; Lew Ta-Jên to Salisbury, May 16, 1888.

ence the proceedings. Herbert minuted that the negotiations with China which the Australasian colonies desired were dependent on the actions of the conference, as the Chinese bill recently passed in New South Wales essentially made diplomatic progress impossible. He thought that the conference should be reminded of the possibilities of increased trade with China, "which is likely to afford a specially valuable market for Australian produce," and he suggested a course of action which might satisfy both the Chinese and Australians:

> The Chinese Government has specially objected to legislation declaring that Chinese subjects are to be treated differently from the subjects of any other power, and . . . it seems desirable to consider whether laws and regulations equally restricting the immigration of oriental and other coloured foreign labourers into the Colonies may not meet the requirements of the case, observing that if thus placed on the same footing with other nations not of European race China might be willing to agree to conditions more or less similar to those of the treaty with the United States, and to the limitation of the numbers permitted to embark for any Australian Colony in that year.[135]

Knutsford pointed all this out in a telegram to the Australasian colonies which concluded: "It should be clearly understood that while Her Majesty's Government will be prepared to consider any representations from Conference, they are not at present able to give any assurance that negotiations with Chinese Government can be opened, as it depends on nature of proposals to be made to that Government; but I confidently believe that Conference will endeavour to conciliate susceptibilities of Chinese Government as far as practicable." [136]

The Colonial Office's overtures received a prompt and hostile reply. Sir Thomas McIlwraith, the Liberal premier of Queensland, stated that the Queensland cabinet was unanimous in disapproving of Knutsford's suggestion that all foreign laborers be

135. CO 13/145, S.A. 10754, tel., May 29, 1888, minuting by Herbert, May 29, 1888.
136. *Ibid.*, Knutsford to all Australasian colonies, June 6, 1888.

placed on a similar legal footing, while Parkes pointed out that Australian exports to China amounted to only £16,000 out of a total export trade valued at £38,700,000. He trusted that the Australian colonies would gain the cooperation of Her Majesty's Government "in their endeavour to prevent their country from being overrun by an alien race who are incapable of assimilation in the body politic, strangers to our civilisation, out of sympathy with our aspirations, and unfitted for our free institutions, to which their presence in any number would be a source of constant danger." [137]

The conference of 1888, like that of 1881, was the instrument of Sir Henry Parkes, its chairman. The most significant of its resolutions was the determination to draft a common anti-Chinese law immediately. The colonial governments feared diplomatic negotiations between Great Britain and China would take such a long time that a Chinese immigration of massive proportions might take place in the interim. The conference was still anxious to aid in the conclusion of a Sino-British treaty and to that end was willing to eliminate the poll tax on entering Chinese. But as a *quid pro quo* it wanted Her Majesty's Government to induce the crown colonies of Hong Kong, Labuan, and the other Straits Settlements to prohibit the emigration of all Chinese to the Australasian colonies unless they were students, merchants, officials or travellers. "The Chinese who may claim to be British subjects in those colonies," Carrington wrote, "are very numerous, and the certainty that their migration hither was prevented would give great satisfaction." [138]

The conference bill as it emerged failed to exempt British subjects from its provisions, although it did not apply to any person duly accredited to an Australasian colony, or to the crew of a vessel not being discharged, or to persons or classes of per-

137. CO 282/124 Tas., McIlwraith to J. M. Macrossan, June 14, 1888; Parkes to Knutsford, no date.
138. CO 881/8, CO conf. print 129, Aus., tel., Carrington to Knutsford June 14, 1888.

sons from time to time exempted.[139] Article 5 established a permissible ratio of one Chinese passenger for every 500 tons of vessel tonnage and set a maximum fine of £500 for each violation. Article 12, as a concession to the Colonial Office and because it was no longer really necessary under the provisions of the act, eliminated the poll tax.[140]

New South Wales undertook to amend its own bill to bring it into conformity with the conference measure,[141] although it never in fact did so. But not all the colonies favored the proposed law which each of them was to enact. New Zealand was not represented, and P. O. Fysh, the premier of Tasmania, thought that the situation was not so desperate that Her Majesty's Government should not be given the chance to act diplomatically. He felt further restrictive legislation would harm imperial interests, and he took exception to the exclusion of the wives of resident Chinese under the terms of the conference bill and to the failure to respect the rights of Chinese British subjects.[142]

Despite the small chances of success that remained, given the severity of the conference bill, the British Government determined to attempt to reach a diplomatic accord with the Government of China. On June 22, the Colonial Office enclosed its version of a possible draft treaty. It provided for the right of officers of the government, teachers, students, merchants, travellers, "or [those] belonging to other classes than that of labourers as hereinafter defined . . . [to] be freely admitted to visit, pass through, or reside in all possessions, provinces, territories, or places under the sovereignty or protection of the other, without let or hindrance; and . . . [to] receive from the Government of the place in which they may be, all proper assistance and pro-

139. Article 2.
140. CO 236/10, Queensland, Chinese immigration, correspondence and proceedings of conference respecting.
141. CO 881/8, CO conf. print 129, Aus., tel., Carrington to Knutsford June 15, 1888.
142. *Ibid.,* Fysh to Knutsford, June 15, 1888.

tection." Laborers were to be admitted only to those possessions of the contracting powers which declared themselves open for such immigration and then under rules regulating their number, conditions of residence, and employment. Herbert, in forwarding the Colonial Office draft to his counterpart in the Foreign Office, wrote: "Lord Salisbury will observe that, in order not to wound the susceptibilities of China, the stipulations contained in these articles avoid all mention of the exclusion of Chinese from Australia, and put both countries on an equal footing in respect of the privileges and disabilities of their subjects." [143]

The Colonial Office was too cowed by the conference and the events immediately associated with it even to hold out for the rights of Chinese British subjects. And this, at least, had been *sine qua non* in the past. In writing to the Foreign Office, the Colonial Office explained that, "if, at the instance of Her Majesty's Government, one or more of the Colonies should now depart from the agreement of the Conference, and make an exception in favour of British subjects, it is to be apprehended that the forgery and falsification of certificates of origin would be actively resumed and fresh complications introduced." [144]

It soon became clear that the Foreign Office's pessimism concerning the possible outcome of negotiations with China was well founded. On July 5 Lew again strongly protested the treatment of the Chinese in Australia. He drew upon a long catalog of horrors, referring to the corpus of anti-Chinese legislation, the *Afghan* affair, and the proceedings of the Chinese immigration conference. "I protest," he wrote, "against Chinese subjects resorting to Her Britannic Majesty's dominions being stigmatized by being made the object of special legislation which the Australasian Colonies have not thought fit to apply to, I do not say to the subjects of other nations generally, but even to the fugitives who escape from confinement in the adjacent posses-

143. CO 881/9, CO conf. print 130, Aus., CO to FO, June 22, 1888.
144. *Ibid.*, CO to FO, June 26, 1888.

sions of a foreign state." Nor were immigration questions his only concern:

> In New South Wales and Victoria, a Chinese sailor forming part of the crew of a ship in harbour, cannot accompany his shipmates ashore, on pleasure, without incurring a penalty of £10, or on default of payment, 12 months' imprisonment. This is an act of illiberality and invidiousness, which I believe is without parallel in any country, and is certainly out of place between two countries like China and Great Britain, the magnitude and variety of whose interests require their relations should be of the most cordial and intimate nature.[145]

The British ambassador in Peking, Sir John Walsham, was, surprisingly, optimistic. He telegraphed Salisbury that if the Australasian colonies would refrain from passing any further restrictive legislation, the Chinese would agree to a formal arrangement under the terms of which there would be free admission of Chinese other than laborers to the colonies, while the latter group would be limited to one for every 500 tons of ship burthen. The poll tax would be eliminated. The persons and property of Chinese residents of Australia to visit China and return would be preserved.[146] So far it would seem that the grounds for an amicable arrangement were, after all, visible. But when the Chinese Government changed its view of the acceptable ratio of Chinese immigrants to ship tonnage from 1/500 to 1/300,[147] all hope dimmed.[148]

145. *Ibid.*, Lew Ta-Jên to Salisbury, July 5, 1888.
146. *Ibid.*, tel., Walsham to Salisbury, Aug. 13, 1888.
147. *Ibid.*, tel., Walsham to Salisbury, Aug. 30, 1888.
148. The British Government did actually negotiate a draft treaty with the Chinese, but it contained the 1/300 ratio rather than the 1/500 figure the Australian colonies preferred. Although the agreement turned out to be stillborn, its various provisos are of interest as they show just how far the Australian colonies would have been willing to go if the ratio of Chinese to ship tonnage could have been successfully negotiated. Government officials, teachers, students, merchants, and travellers, when provided with proper certification, were to have been allowed either to visit or to reside within the territories of the two contracting parties. Laborers were to have been admitted under conditions framed by the

If it had not been evident before, the events of 1888 made it embarrassingly clear that the Colonial Office was largely impotent to influence the Australasian colonies on the Chinese question. Frustration was the order of the day in Parliament, to the degree that Australia and its Chinese dilemma received any attention at all. In the House of Commons on August 9, 1888, Sir George Campbell asked Sir John Gorst, who was representing the government: "Whether he had noticed that Sir H. Parkes used the following words in the New South Wales legislature, not once but twice:

'Neither for Her Majesty's ships of war, nor for Her Majesty's representative on the spot, nor for the Secretary of State for the Colonies, do we intend to turn aside from our purpose, which is to terminate the landing of Chinese on these shores for ever, except under the restrictions imposed by the Bill, which will amount and are intended to amount to practical prohibition'?"

Gorst's answer was evasive. He retreated under cover of the assertion that the act in question had not arrived from Australia.

With the exception of the delegates from Western Australia and Tasmania, both of which had recently passed new immigration restriction legislation, and for that matter New South Wales itself, the representatives of the Australasian colonies returned to their homes to pass the conference Chinese exclusion bill into law without delay. Queensland determined to improve on the severe measures already on the statute books. Under the terms of Act 22 of 1888, the penalties which could be imposed on masters were increased. Chinese crewmen were no longer exempted, and a master could be imprisoned at hard labor for a year if a Chinese crewman escaped from his ship. Worst of all, article 10 provided for the possibility of life imprisonment for

---

host nation. It was also understood that there would be no more poll tax on Chinese of any class and that Chinese laborers already in Australia would have the right to leave and re-enter the continent. Victoria Archives, Premier's Secret Papers, 88/3786, conf., Sept. 14, 1888. CO 201/608, Tsungli Yamen to Walsham, Aug. 27, 1888.

a Chinese who entered the colony illegally. Sir A. H. Palmer, the former colonial secretary who was now administering the colony, admitted to being severely disturbed by the bill. He wrote Knutsford: "I beg leave to direct your Lordship's attention to clauses 9 and 10 of this Bill. I have pointed out to my Chief Secretary [premier] that these clauses impose imprisonment for life. He contends that no ministry would carry them out—that they are in fact more in the nature of a standing threat than anything else; but I have strong objections to any such power being given to any ministry or any man."

Knutsford in his reply noted that the Queensland draft bill varied in significant ways from the measure agreed upon at the conference. Before tendering advice to Her Majesty, he would be interested in knowing the colony's reason for pursuing such a course of action. Boyd Morehead, the premier, pointed out that by resolution of the conference the conference bill could be modified by each colony according to its needs. Queensland had seen fit to increase the severity of the conference measure because of the colony's long seaboard and the easy access its many ports gave to the goldfields.[149]

Colonial Office minuting by Herbert followed a familiar pattern. "I am inclined to think that it may be better not to argue the matter further with Queensland Ministers," the permanent undersecretary wrote, "but to rely, as Lord Salisbury supposes we may rely, upon the intention of the Colonial Government not to administer the law with extreme severity." [150] It was an assumption that had been proved bankrupt time and time again.

What amounted almost to a ritual dance now ensued. Knutsford suggested a few minor amendments such as the reduction

149. CO 881/9, CO conf. print 130, Aus., Palmer to Knutsford, November 6, 1888; conf., Knutsford to Palmer, February 13, 1889; Norman to Knutsford, May 4, 1889, encl. Morehead to Norman, April 25, 1889.
150. CO 234/50, Q. 1475, FO to CO, July 23, 1889, minuting of July 25.

of the penalty on the master should a Chinese passenger abscond. The secretary of state bound himself to gain the royal assent should the Queensland ministry make the necessary amendments. The governor, Sir Henry Norman, responded that his ministers were prepared to cooperate, but as the parliamentary session was closing, there was not time to act. Knutsford in turn telegraphed the canonical reply: "It would have been preferable to precede sanction given to Bill by further legislation but, nevertheless, if your Ministers undertake to pass Bill amended early next session I will advise Her Majesty to assent now." It was a bargain Queensland was happy to accept, and Norman telegraphed the secretary of state: "Ministers promise to introduce Bill amended next session. Leader of the Opposition promises cordially to assist." [151]

When the Queensland legislature passed the amending measure (Act 29 of 1890) the following year, it fell far short of the commitment made to the Colonial Office. The master of a vessel, one or more of whose Chinese crew absconded, was still liable to a fine of £500 per violation which could not be reduced by judicial action.[152] As John Bramston, one of the assistant undersecretaries, minuted: "If a Chinese sailor dies in [port] the Master of the ship will be fined £500, by a magistrate who has no option." [153] Norman admitted that the actual wording of the amended passage was not what the secretary of state had prescribed but argued, "I think the Bill as worded will sufficiently express what is desired." Knutsford weakly asked for further amendment in keeping with the original agreement between

---

151. CO 881/9, CO conf. print 130, Aus., Knutsford to Norman, July 31, 1889; tel., Norman to Knutsford, rec., October 5, 1889; tel., Knutsford to Norman, October 10, 1889; tel., Norman to Knutsford, rec., October 19, 1889.

152. *Ibid.*, tel., Norman to Knutsford, August 22, 1890.

153. CO 234/52, Q. 7123, Feb. 23, 1891, minuting of 14/4. The reason for this was that, under the terms of article 2 of the revised measure, the same number of Chinese crewmen who entered a Queensland port had to leave it.

the Colonial Office and Queensland, but to this the colonial government would not agree.[154] And there, as was almost always the case, the matter ended.

Victoria, with Act 1005 of 1888, "For the Further Restriction of Chinese Immigration," essentially passed the conference bill as it was into law. Western Australia, even though its colonial secretary, Sir M. Fraser, thought it unnecessary,[155] finally followed a similar course; as did South Australia [156] in a law (Act 438 of 1888) which was continued indefinitely under the terms of Act 534 of 1891. The debate on the measure was notable chiefly for a poem read into the record by the Honorable L. Glyde, part of which ran as follows:

> The high price clumsy, lazy whites
> Were no match for this saffron chap,
> And they now deplored that when he snored
> They had raised him from his nap.
> They raved and tore and wept and swore
> To drive him home again,
> But never one inch would the Pagan flinch
> For it paid him to remain.[157]

New Zealand had not attended the conference (its delegate had arrived too late) and had, furthermore, passed a Chinese restriction measure just a few weeks before the conference convened. Governor Jervois was, however, one of the few British officials to view the relations between the Australasian colonies and the Colonial Office honestly. No doubt this was in large measure the consequence of an unusually broad administrative experience. He had toured the Empire extensively and had already been governor of the Straits Settlements and, of course, South Australia. "The truth is," Jervois wrote, "that the draft

154. CO 881/9, CO conf. print 130, Aus., conf., Norman to Knutsford, August 22, 1889; no. 61, Knutsford to Norman, November 27, 1890; no. 18, Palmer to Knutsford, Feb. 23, 1891.
155. W.A. *Hansard* (Council), Nov. 6, 1888.
156. Act 3 of 1889.   157. S.A. *Hansard*, Aug. 4, 1888.

bill is simply an attempt to paralyze Imperial initiative on the question, and to reduce Imperial intervention to a simple registry of the decrees of the Conference." The Colonial Office was outraged. Frederic Fuller termed Jervois's contention that imperial initiative was paralyzed by the conference "far fetched," and clearly lined himself up on the side of the conference. "The abstentions of N. Zealand and Tasmania will not wreck the scheme," he wrote. "It is an attempt of the tail to wag the dog." [158]

But Jervois had been quite right, and when the governor of South Australia had the ill grace to ask whether he should allow the colony to deprive Chinese British subjects of the right to land, the Colonial Office's position was stripped bare of all pretense. Herbert minuted:

I think we had better reply somewhat to the effect that H.M. Govt. do not think it necessary at this stage of the question to urge that there should be a distinction in the uniform law between Chinese who are British subjects and those who are not. . . . There are not many who would be likely to come in that capacity and British nationality might be strictly defined. We have sanctioned Australian anti-Chinese Acts which make no exception in favour of Chinese British subjects—and in some other acts Chinese British subjects have been exempted from their operation. I think we may safely, pending treaty negotiations, prevent Chinese British subjects from leaving Hong Kong for Australia and consider at leisure what should be the rule under the treaty.[159]

But no treaty was ever concluded and no colonial laws amended as a consequence.

The influx of Chinese into Canada was also due to the yellow metal—California gold. Within a decade of the first strikes, there were over 10,000 Chinese in California, and by 1880 the

158. CO 209/248, N.Z. 16818, conf., Jervois to Knutsford, July 10, 1888, minuting of Aug. 20, 1888.
159. CO 13/145, S.A. 12608, tel., Robinson to Knutsford, June 25, 1888, minuting by Herbert, June 25, 1888.

census placed 105,465 Chinese in the United States, the vast majority being in California. It did not take long for Chinese immigrants to find their way northward into Canada. Some ten years after the discovery of gold in California, more modest strikes at Carsiar and Cariboo in British Columbia began to attract them to that province, both from California and from China itself. By 1881 there were 4,350 "celestials" in British Columbia (out of a total population of 50,000) and their numbers more than doubled to 9,400 (out of a total population of 98,000) in ten years.[160]

The white citizens of British Columbia took just as dim a view of the new arrivals as their Australian cousins. Despite the usual labor shortage, they bent all their efforts to closing British Columbia to the unwanted orientals. Again, the anti-Chinese sentiment was not universal. Employers in general welcomed them, and the contractors pushing the Canadian transcontinental railway westward did so particularly. As a consequence, it was to take some years before the Canadian Parliament would pass legislation in the direction desired by most of the settlers in British Columbia, and it would never act energetically enough to satisfy the province. The Pacific coast was a long way from Ottawa, and although political considerations forced some attention to the province's concerns in the capital, the fact remained that the Chinese were concentrated in the western province and few legislators or officials in Ottawa found it easy to identify with British Columbia's plight. Besides, there was always the railway, the necessary chain to tie together the sprawling federation. Sir John A. Macdonald, the prime minister, put it this way:

I share very much the feeling of the people of the United States and the Australian Colonies against a Mongolian or Chinese population in our country as permanent settlers. I believe that it is an alien

160. Stanislaw Andracki, "The Immigration of Orientals into Canada with Special Reference to the Chinese" (Ph.D. dissertation, McGill University, 1958), 48.

race in every sense, that would not and could not be expected to assimilate with our Aryan population, and therefore, if the temporary necessity had been overcome and the railway constructed across the continent with the means of sending the European settlers and labourers into British Columbia, then it would be quite right to join to a reasonable extent in preventing the permanent settlement in this country of Mongolian, Chinese or Japanese immigrants.

"At present," concluded Macdonald, "it is simply a question of alternatives: either you must have this labour or you cannot have the railway." [161]

Nevertheless, the House appointed a select committee on Chinese labor and immigration. The evidence of many witnesses had a familiar ring. Chinese were dirty, disease-ridden, and had curious habits and customs. They degraded the jobs they undertook to such an extent that no white person would assume them. For example, it was impossible to get white servant girls to immigrate to Canada. Furthermore, Chinamen contributed nothing to the revenue, sent all their earnings back to China, and lived off the smell of the familiar oiled rag. The member of Parliament from Cariboo (Thompson) reported, "I think we have not over half-a-dozen Chinese women in New Westminster all told. They are all prostitutes, and it is a notorious fact that nearly all the Chinese women who come to British Columbia are prostitutes—and I believe to the Pacific Coast generally. . . . There is scarcely a Chinaman who comes to British Columbia but brings with him the most virulent form of syphilis." When Senator William Macdonald appeared before the committee, he also preached a familiar line: the Chinese, he said, "are not so desirable a class to have in the country as Europeans. They are of irregular habits, and their mode of living is altogether different from ours. . . . They do not mix up and affiliate with our people, and it is not desirable that they should do so." A certain F. J. Barnard thought that the Chinese, "while they earn your money and are appointed by your enterprise and

161. *Ibid.*, 26–27; Canada *Hansard*, 1882, 1477.

industry, . . . take no part whatever in your political advancement, or in your social and moral condition. They are aside altogether from us—just as much as a steam engine is aside from a human being." A petition from British Columbia signed by 1,497 persons was read into evidence. It asked on behalf of the laboring class of the province that the Canadian Parliament pass a law preventing the further immigration of Chinese and prohibiting their employment on the transcontinental railway. The committee, when its report was issued, concluded that Chinese immigration ought not to be encouraged and that Chinese should not be employed on public works financed by the Dominion.[162] But as yet the Dominion was not prepared to take action.

In the meantime, agitation in British Columbia continued to increase, even though the 1880–81 census showed that there were only 4,383 Chinese (4,350 in British Columbia) in the entire Dominion, out of a total population of 4,324,810. Noah Shakespeare, a notorious Sinophobe, became the president of a recently formed anti-Chinese association, and an increasing number of petitions and resolutions poured into the provincial legislature. If the furor was intense in 1880, when the increase in the Chinese population over the previous five years had been small, one needs but little imagination to conceive of what it became during the following half decade. In 1881 the Canadian Pacific Railway commenced construction in earnest, and in the four years after 1881, 15,701 Chinese arrived in British Columbia.[163] On March 16,1882, Lieutenant Governor C. T. Cornwall sent to Ottawa a resolution of the British Columbia House of Assembly which urged that the Canadian Pacific Railway should be allowed to employ only white labor in the province. J. H. Pope, on behalf of the government, could only reply that there were no means of forcing the contractors to use white in-

162. CO 45/490, Report of the Select Committee on Chinese Labor and Immigration, 1879.
163. Canada Sessional Papers, 1886, Returns concerning Chinese.

stead of Chinese labor and no funds to underwrite the increased cost that would result from the policy recommended by British Columbia.[164]

In July a public meeting in Victoria drafted a resolution which was sent to the governor general, the Marquis of Lorne, by the indefatigable Noah Shakespeare, now the mayor of the city. "Your petitioners," it read, "view with dismay the rapid and ever-increasing influx of Chinese into this Province. . . . Their presence in our midst is an unmitigated evil and prevents the influx of white population.

"Unless some immediate and urgent steps are taken to restrict this heathen invasion, the rapid deterioration and ultimate extinction of this Province as a home for the Anglo-Saxon race must ensue." [165]

The following month, the provincial executive council, with the approval of the lieutenant governor, wrote to Ottawa in a similar vein. The document asserted:

that the employment of Chinese as carried on is practically establishing a system of slave labor.

That at the present time there are about twelve thousand Chinese here, and that more than one-half of that number are employed on the Canadian Pacific Railway. That Chinese labor being largely employed, drives white labor from seeking work thereon. That Chinese as a class are injurious to a young community, as they trade almost exclusively among their own people, send all their earnings to Asia, introduce loathsome diseases and demoralizing habits, put the authorities to constant expense endeavoring to suppress crime and granting charitable aid to their sick and infirm. . . . They are a non-assimilating alien race.[166]

In 1883 Noah Shakespeare was elected to Parliament by Victoria and, having reached the font of all power, he immediately set to work. On April 30 he rose to move that the House favor, in principle, the passage of a law similar to the Australian Chinese immigration restriction acts of 1881. Macdonald again

164. *Ibid.*, 1883, Paper 93.   165. *Ibid.*   166. *Ibid.*

wondered what alternate supply of labor was envisaged to replace the Chinaman. When the answer to that question was forthcoming, he rumbled, the House could pass any law it wished, but until then it should reserve action. The motion was consequently negatived on a division.[167]

But Shakespeare was not to be easily discouraged, and in less than a year he returned to the attack, this time tabling a motion calling for the prohibition of all Chinese immigration into British Columbia. The prime minister was still reluctant to act. He cautioned the honorable members about the danger of possible interference with the China trade now that the railroad was nearing completion. He wanted to delay action and to appoint a Royal Commission. In the long run, however, he relented, and Shakespeare's motion was passed with the words "restrict and regulate" being substituted for "prohibit" and "Canada" replacing "British Columbia."[168]

Meanwhile, British Columbia in 1884 passed "An Act to Prevent Chinese Immigration," which made it unlawful for Chinese to enter the province and provided penalties for contravention. British Columbia based this extraordinary arrogation of power on article 95 of the British North America Act, which empowered provincial legislatures to make laws governing agriculture and immigration into their provinces. The legislature, however, chose to ignore the rest of the section, which declared that the Government of Canada might from time to time make laws governing the same subjects vis-à-vis the provinces and that

167. Canada *Hansard,* Apr. 30, 1883.
168. *Ibid.,* Mar. 19, Apr. 2, 1884. Shakespeare did not, of course, represent the unanimous view of the British Columbian members in the Dominion Parliament. J. Homer of New Westminster, for instance, averred that: "Almost every industry in British Columbia at the present time, is more or less dependent on Chinese labour, more particularly the coal mining, the salmon canning and the contractors of the Canadian Pacific Railway. To place restrictions upon Chinese labour before making any provisions to replace it with white labour, would be, in my opinion, a very serious mistake, for it might be the means of crippling those industries for years to come." Andracki, 30, quoting Canada *Hansard,* 1883, 904.

any provincial law regarding immigration or agriculture would have effect only so long as it were not repugnant to any act of the Dominion Parliament. The British Columbian law was as a result disallowed by an order in council of April 8, 1884.[169]

Despite British Columbia's chagrin, the Dominion limited itself to appointing the Royal Commission on Chinese Immigration that had been approved by Macdonald. J.-A. Chapleau, Canada's secretary of state, was placed at its head, and John Hamilton Gray, a justice of the supreme court of British Columbia, was the other member. As the report, issued in the following year, put it, "The object of the Commission . . . [was] to obtain proof that the principle of restricting Chinese immigration is proper and in the interests of the Province [British Columbia] and of the Dominion." The evidence on the negative side had been heard before. The chief justice of British Columbia, Sir Matthew Begbie, and many employers were highly favorable to the Chinese.

The commission took evidence from all over the world and particularly from the United States, and its conclusions and recommendations were markedly moderate. Chapleau asserted that, "Chinese labor is a most efficient aid in development of a country, and a great means of wealth. As a railway navvy the Chinaman has no superior, and his presence in California has given the State a start many years ahead and added incalculably

---

169. P[ublic] A[rchives] of C[anada], Governor General's Secretary's Office, General Correspondence regarding Asiatics, file 226, Canada no. 69, Apr. 15, 1884, draft Lansdowne to Derby, encl. minister of justice (A. A. Campbell), Report to the Governor General on British Columbia Bill 15, Apr. 7, 1884. The minister commented on British Columbia's basis for action: "Having reference to the condition of Canada at the time of the union of the Provinces the undersigned is of opinion that the authority given by the 95 section of the British North America Act is an authority to regulate and promote immigration into the Province and not an authority to prohibit immigration.

"A law which prevents the people of any country from coming to a Province cannot be said to be of a local and private nature. On the contrary it is one involving Dominion and possibly Imperial interests."

to its material prosperity; while in British Columbia Chinese labor has been attended by great advantages to the Province and the same excellent effects would, most likely, for many years from now follow its utilization."

On the other hand, Chapleau admitted that the Chinese were "a non-assimilable race, clearly marked off by color and national and race characteristics." Chinese brought down wages. They competed with female white servants and were capable of taking over whole industries. Yet they were as moral as the rest of the population, did not become public charges, and in general took care of themselves. Chinese merchants were honorable and capable men whom British Columbia should welcome, as they would be of great benefit to the province. In conclusion, Chapleau urged Parliament to act with a light hand to regulate the immigration of Chinese into Canada (a $10 entrance fee was recommended) but not totally to exclude them.

Commissioner Gray was equally mild. He also thought that the Chinese were fine workers and that they were able to cultivate land on which the white man could grow nothing; besides, he pointed out, the country was hardly over-populated. His final words summed up the spirit of the whole report. He recommended "moderate restriction based upon police, financial and sanitary principles, sustained and enforced by stringent local regulations of cleanliness and preservation of health." [170]

The Chapleau Commission Report, when it was made public, infuriated British Columbia. One of the provincial members in Parliament (Baker) asked whether "any hon. gentlemen in the House . . . would like to live in the same room as a Chinaman?" When a voice from the chamber responded in the affirmative, Baker continued with some heat: "You would? Then there is no accounting for taste. I think, from what we know of the Chinese race, what we know personally, and what has been told us in this House by those who represent constituencies

170. CO 45/580, S49, Report of the Royal Commission on Chinese Immigration, 1885.

where those individuals so largely predominate, there is sufficient to convince us that they are a most undesirable class to be brought into our midst, and that they will never become permanent settlers." [171] Breathing defiance and offended virtue, the British Columbian legislature, in 1885, again passed the Chinese immigration restriction act [172] disallowed by Ottawa the previous year. Predictably, it met the same fate.

Lord Lansdowne, now the governor general, wrote to the Colonial Office that British Columbia's animosity was rooted in the white settlers' annoyance at the failure of the Chinese laborers to spend their earnings in the province rather than in indignation at their "beastly habits" or the unsanitary conditions in which they supposedly lived. He went on to contend that, "but for the presence of Chinamen in B. C. the greater part of her public works could not have been carried out." He pointed out that it cost $125 to transport a worker from old Canada to the western province, and that it was this fact rather than a disinclination to work next to Chinese that kept white labor from entering British Columbia in greater numbers.[173]

But Lansdowne and his government realized that British Columbia would have to be accorded some satisfaction if open violence in the province were to be avoided. On April 13, 1885, Chapleau introduced a bill "to restrict and regulate Chinese immigration." The measure established the principle of an entrance tax on Chinese but mentioned no amount, as the sponsor wished this to be determined by the house. The minister did, however, specify that the ratio of Chinese to ship burthen was to be established at 1/10.[174] In this the government had clearly misjudged the temper of the British Columbian members, who found the proposed tonnage proportion totally unacceptable.

171. Canada *Hansard,* July 2, 1885.
172. Statutes of B.C., Chapter 22, 1885.
173. PAC, Governor General's Secretary's Office, General Correspondence regarding Asiatics, file 226, draft, Lansdowne to Derby, Apr. 5, 1884.
174. Andracki, 52, quoting Canada *Hansard,* 1885, 1038.

The bill was consequently withdrawn and replaced by another which was assented to on July 20, 1885.[175] The measure was directed against all persons of Chinese origin regardless of the possibility that they might be British subjects. It did not, however, cover Chinese who were already residents of Canada, members of the diplomatic corps or other governmental representatives and their suites, tourists, merchants, men of science, and students with certificates of identity and visas. The law was very reminiscent of early Australian legislation. A ratio of one Chinese for every fifty tons of burthen was specified, as was a $50 entrance tax. A $50 fine was prescribed for every Chinese over the statutory limit, and contravention of the law could cost a ship owner up to $1,000 and forfeiture of the vessel. The usual certificates for Chinese who had paid the tax and permits for Chinese residents wishing to absent themselves temporarily from the country were provided for in the law.

The Chinese Immigration Restriction Act was revised and amended by Chapter 35 of 1887, which exempted "any woman of Chinese origin who is the wife of a person not of Chinese origin" from the workings of the act [176] and made provision for

175. CO 44/144, chapter 71, 1885. A minor conflict erupted over the date upon which the act would come into effect. The original version of the law had specified Jan. 1, 1886, but the British Columbian representatives contended that the time lag would allow employers to make significant last-minute importations of Chinese labor. Part of the act consequently came into effect in the month after its passage and the rest on Jan. 1, 1886. Andracki, 53–54.

176. This clause was inserted because a certain Mr. Moore, an "Englishman of standing," according to Prime Minister Macdonald, had been forced to pay the entrance tax on his wife, who was Chinese. The case became a minor *cause célèbre*. But when an attempt was made to extend the exemption to the wives of Chinese immigrants in order to encourage the immigration of Chinese families, the prime minister responded: "The whole policy of this measure is to restrict the immigration of Chinese into British Columbia and into Canada. On the whole it is considered not advantageous to the country that the Chinese should settle in Canada producing a mongrel race and interfering very much with white labour in Canada."

The original House version of the bill removed the exemption on

Chinese in transit across Canada to be excused from the payment of the entry fee if they travelled under special regulations made by the minister of customs. British Columbia thought the Dominion legislation was much too mild, but the fact remained that while nearly 4,000 Chinese entered between January 1 and August 20, 1885, only 235 arrived between August 20, 1885 and January 31, 1886, and 688 departed.[177]

British Columbia's own efforts to bar nonwhites from the provincial labor force continued unabated even though there were in 1891 only 8,910 persons of Chinese birth in the province (despite the heavy influx between 1881 and 1885) out of a total population of 98,173, and not yet enough Japanese or East Indians to be enumerated.[178] In view of the continued frustration of provincial efforts to achieve nonwhite and particularly Chinese exclusion, the pressure on Ottawa constantly increased. Letters, petitions and memorials flooded into the Dominion Parliament and government offices. Complaints were directed particularly at the steamships of the Canadian Pacific Railway plying between Vancouver and Hong Kong, which, it was asserted, consistently brought more Chinese than the law allowed to the western shores of the Dominion.

British Columbia also claimed that many Chinese arrived in the province with forged certificates attesting to Canadian residence. The committee of the Canadian privy council agreed that this presented a problem, as the actual holders of the documents were probably the blameless victims of unscrupulous entrepreneurs and to send them back to Hong Kong when they had used all their savings for the passage seemed harsh and unfair. The privy council admitted that Chinese immigrants with

---

Chinese merchants, but the Senate would not countenance the change. Andracki, 59.

177. Canada Sessional Papers, 1886, Returns concerning Chinese. Average arrivals between Jan. 1886 and Dec. 1889 fell to 700 per annum (without departures being taken into account).

178. Canada census, 1891.

forged certificates had indeed been allowed to land, an action, the committee conceded, "equivalent to allowing the steamers to land so many immigrants more than they are entitled to carry." But, as has been said before, Ottawa was separated from Vancouver by most of a continent, and it seemed at that time less important to please British Columbia than to preserve the growing trade with China and to prevent the diversion to other steamship lines of traffic then in the hands of the subsidized Canadian Pacific.[179]

Nevertheless, Parliament was prepared to take some action on British Columbia's behalf, and Chapter 25 of 1892 established a new certification procedure for Chinese residents of Canada leaving the country on a temporary basis. Any Chinese before departure would have to register at the point of exit, leaving sufficient details to ensure future identification. Upon his return, providing it took place within six months, the Chinese would have his $50 entrance tax refunded if he could convince the controller that he was in fact the same person who had registered upon leaving. The abolition of the certificates as established under the act of 1885 and their replacement by a register was designed to put an end to the transfer of certificates or the use of forged ones to evade the established ratio of immigrants to ship tonnage. The new system had the unfortunate effect of increasing the discretionary power of immigration officials. The 1885 law had declared the possession of a certificate *prima facie* proof of the right to enter Canada without the pay-

179. PAC, Orders in Council, R.G. 2, series 1, V. 490, Department of State, J. A. Felton, secretary Vancouver Trades and Labour Council, to J. A. Chapleau, secretary of state, Aug. 14, 1891. The assistant general manager of the Canadian Pacific Railway in a letter of July 8, 1899 to Sir Wilfrid Laurier, the prime minister (PAC, Laurier Papers 35130) gave it as his opinion that an increase in the amount of the entrance tax from $50 to $200 would eventually prevent Chinese from coming to Canada and consequently also end the traffic in the opposite direction. A later letter of Jan. 26, 1900, foresaw the possible collapse of the line (Laurier Papers, 41460, J. J. Shaunessy, Canadian Pacific Railway to Laurier).

ment of the entrance tax. Under the new system, the ability of a returning Chinese to land in Canada was dependent upon his success in proving his identity "to the satisfaction of the Controller" with the register, maintained by the controller, as the only source of evidence.[180]

Once again leading the anti-Asian agitation was organized labor. A resolution of the Dominion Trades and Labour Congress declared the Chinese "a menace and an undeniable danger to the moral, social, political and material interests of Canada." Not only should their admission to the Dominion be totally halted, but a special $100 annual tax should be imposed on Chinese already resident in Canada whose names and addresses were to be maintained in a special register. In addition, "like laws respecting the importation, immigration and registration of Japanese [should] be enacted."

The resolution was based on a communication from the Vancouver branch of the Congress. "Chinese immigration is still the burning question of the day," it stated, "and the more we see of them the more we are convinced of the great curse they are on this country. Incapable of improvement, they are nothing better than filthy harbingers of disease. Morality, they have none. Christianity they cannot conceive of except as a huge joke." Furthermore, the letter continued, the diseases the Chinese bore were so mysterious that "physicians have been hopelessly baffled in their attempts to accurately diagnose [them]." Worst of all, the Chinese took advantage of white women:

They are also adept druggists in their own way, and as servants they have ceaseless opportunities of adulterating food with drugs unknown to white men, thus placing the female members of the household at their disposal and unscrupulous will. We hear of many divorces having been occasioned in the various cities of the coast by employing Chinamen to do the housework. . . .

Another point to show their cuteness. Whenever they go to school (Chinese school) it is always a white female teacher: no case of them

180. Andracki, 66–69.

studying English under the tutorship of a white man has yet been noticed.[181]

The privy council was as usual not particularly sympathetic to British Columbia's plight. It felt that the will of the petitioners, "must . . . insofar at least as exclusion is concerned be held to be subordinate to the obligations solemnly entered into between two great and friendly nations, and that no action should be taken which could be construed by the Imperial Government as inimical or as infringing upon treaty rights." The council went on to hold "that in view of the commercial relations of Canada with China it is not expedient to change the provisions of the Chinese Immigration Act as it at present exists; nor to take any action that might be considered by the Chinese Government as an evasion of the spirit of Treaty obligations or as an unfriendly act." [182]

The history of anti-Asian attitudes and legislation in the Empire of Settlement before the last decade of the nineteenth century, as manifested in the foregoing pages, indicates a common resolve to exclude large classes of nonwhite immigrants from the imperial domain. Yet, despite such stratagems as the passenger to tonnage ratio and the poll tax, no sure method had been devised to achieve the desired end without interfering with the policies of the Foreign Office or shattering the fragile hypocrisy surrounding the imperial philosophy of equality. That a formula calculated to satisfy all needs was after all available will become clear in the next chapter.

181. PAC, Orders in Council, R.G. 2, series 1, V. 566, Sept. 4, 1893 (P.C. 38), encl. George Gagan, secretary Vancouver Trades and Labour Council to George Dower, secretary-treasurer, Dominion Trades and Labour Congress, Sept. 1, 1892.
182. *Ibid.*, V. 566, Sept. 6, 1893 (P.C. 38).

3 The Immigration Question—
A Solution Found

Natal, of course, shared the Australasian colonies' and Canada's determination to bar the entry of free colored immigrants. But its problem was complicated because the colony desired at the same time to insure itself a continuing supply of indentured laborers. As has already been noted, the only natives of the subcontinent to enter Natal in the early years of Indian immigration were indentured laborers. Although Indians whose contracts had expired and who had chosen to remain in the colony in time caused some uneasiness, they worked almost entirely at occupations where they did not compete with whites, and it was their number and the rights they acquired when they were free, not any economic threat, which affronted the white colonists.

The free Indian, or "Arab" as he came to be known, who began arriving in Natal in the 1880s, changed everything. He was financially independent and rather than hiring himself out as a laborer, he entered commerce usually as the proprietor of a general store. Here he did business not only with Indians but with the white colonists and Africans as well. Now, for the first time, Indians were competing directly with white men. As the "Arab" tended to operate very efficiently and, with the help of relatives, on a small margin of profit, he inevitably began driving white shopkeepers into liquidation. For the colonial housewife, regardless of her racial attitudes, shopped where prices were best, and more often than not this was at her local "Arab's."

In 1880 there were 7 "Arab" shopkeepers in Durban; by 1885 there were already 40.[1] The census of 1891 listed 598 Indian storekeepers, centered in Durban (132), Pietermaritzburg (74), Umlazi (67), Inanda (63), and Ladysmith (60). Another group whose occupation must have been very similar to "storekeepers" was designated "traders" by the census. They numbered 172, with 53 in Newcastle, 51 in Pietermaritzburg, and 29 in Durban. Still, the "Arabs" constituted only a small percentage of the total Indian population of some 41,000 (about equal to the European population), the vast majority of whom continued to perform unskilled labor though their numbers also included many fishermen, hawkers and market gardeners, as well as sixty-six cigar makers, six engine drivers, three constables and one hangman!

The combined threat of an increasing number of ex-indentured Indians permanently settled in Natal and the intrusion of the "Arab" for the first time aroused real alarm among the white colonists. The ex-indentured Indians had to be tolerated, for they were the particular responsibility of the Indian Government, and the Natal authorities were most careful to avoid a confrontation that would endanger the vital supply of Indian labor. The "Arabs," on the other hand, came to Natal of their own volition and were not covered by most of the protective legislation promulgated for the benefit of their indentured brethren. The colonial government had therefore only to bear in mind the general imperial responsibility of the Colonial Office and practice a certain degree of circumspection vis-à-vis the India Office and the Government of India in moving against them.

This Natal at first failed to do. Instead it met the issue head on, attempting to exclude free Indians from the colony explicitly, and this course of action naturally offended the sensibili-

---

1. *Natal Blue Book,* 1880, 1885.

ties of the imperial authorities in London.² The second attempt at legislation designed to exclude free Indians was much more tactful. Act 14 of 1897, "To place certain Restriction on Immigration," was technically nonracial. Qualifications for entry into Natal were to be based on property (£25) and knowledge of a European language, with judgment of language ability to be a matter of discretion on the part of the immigration officer. This simple device, the education test, was in its various manifestations to be known as the "Natal formula." In the case of Natal, Act 14 was to be administered in such a way that Europeans were to be judged eligible to enter Natal while all Indians were not.³ The prime minister made its purpose quite clear when he told the legislature: "It never occured to me for a single minute that [the act] should ever be applied to English immigrants. . . . Can you imagine anything more mad for a Government than that it should apply to English immigrants? The object of the bill is to deal with Asiatic immigrants." [4]

Although the governor of Natal, Sir Walter Hely-Hutchinson, clearly stated to Joseph Chamberlain that "the main object of the proposed law is to prevent Natal from being flooded by undesirable immigrants from India," the secretary of state was able blandly to inform the Indians of Natal that "the Immigration Restriction Act . . . does not affect British Indians as such." [5] The Colonial Office's real view of the matter was reflected in a message sent to the India Office: "Some form of legislation in restriction of Indian immigration was inevitable in Natal; and the Secretary of State was of opinion that it was desirable that a law should be passed in that colony in a form which was not open to objection that it persecuted persons of a

2. Natal Leg. Ass. Sess. Paps., speech by the prime minister on the immigration act, L.A. no. 5, 1st. Sess., 1st Parl., 1897.
3. NA, Ind. Coll., Govt. House Paps., IO to CO, July 21, 1897.
4. See note 2.
5. NA, gov. to sec. of state, Jan. 11, 1897; no. 99, sec. of state to gov., Nov. 12, 1897.

particular race." [6] To bring further calm to Colonial Office nerves, the framers of the act had provided that exemptions from its workings could be granted by the governor. But during the first year the act was in operation, only twelve Asians were exempted—five Indian servants of the 5th Lancers, three Indian teachers, three Mauritius Creole servants, and one Indian servant for the Addington Hospital.[7]

As has already been noted, the British Government had the right to disallow all legislation passed by the British colonies in South Africa, but in practice, after a colony attained responsible government, the Colonial Office interfered only in matters of imperial concern. Despite an imperial philosophy dedicated to the equality of all British subjects regardless of race, Whitehall found it difficult to interfere with the will of a white colonial government, even if that government represented only a small minority of the colony's total population. The situation was, moreover, fraught with emotional ambivalence, for it must have been difficult for Englishmen in the nineteenth century, not the most tolerant of ages, to have felt in their hearts that Africans and Indians were really the equals of white men.

Natal's position was less uncertain. The prime minister had no doubt as to what the British Government's attitude should be on the question of free Indian immigration:

> If it became a question as between the colonial Empire and the Indian Empire, then I say, without the least reserve, that the interest of those of British extraction must be preferred to the interests of those of Indian extraction. . . . If you allow them [the Indians] to make it [Natal] a paradise for Indians, you will find that, as far as Europeans are concerned, it is an exact antipode of paradise. . . . We mean to preserve this fair land, as far as we can, for those who are now in the Colony, to maintain it, as far as it is possible, as a British Colony, and not to have the whole of

---

6. NA, Ind. Coll., undersec., CO to undersec. IO, Oct. 2, 1897.
7. Natal Leg. Ass. Paps., L.A. no. 19, 2nd Sess., 2nd Parl., 1898, July 7, 1898.

the conditions of the country submerged under an Asiatic wave of immigrations.[8]

The Government of India was in many ways a distinct constitutional entity. Yet, despite its considerable power, it was frequently disinterested and usually ineffective. The best it could normally manage was to call the attention of the Colonial Office to colonial laws it viewed as being detrimental to the welfare of overseas Indians. Besides, the Indian authorities identified indentured immigrants as their chief concern, and they were unwilling to take a strong stand in defense of the rights of free immigrants.

One of the factors preventing Calcutta from acting with greater effect was the sympathy felt by many high officials in India for the white settlers of Natal. For instance, J. Westland, the finance member of the viceroy's council, strongly supported Natal's immigration philosophy. "I cannot see any reasonable foundation," he wrote, "for the doctrine that when we conquer a race or nation by the force of arms, the people of that nation acquire rights as against members of the conquering race who happen to have cast their lot in tropical or sub-tropical colonies." J. Woodburn, another member of the council, took a similar position. He thought that if Indians "were admitted [to Natal] on terms of absolute equality, the British would be elbowed out."[9]

But the Government of India was at best an interested party. It was in Whitehall that the responsibility clearly rested. And the British Government found itself increasingly caught between anti-Asian white minority regimes in South Africa, liberal opinion in Britain and national indignation in India. The

---

8. *Ibid.*, L.A. no. 5, 5th Sess., 1st Parl., 1897; speech by the prime minister, Mar. 25, 1897.

9. NAI, Govt. of India, Department of Rev. and Ag. (Em.), Aug. 1897, proc. 12, note by J. Westland, Oct. 26, 1897; note by J. Woodburn, Mar. 15, 1897.

Times felt that Natal Indians had been persecuted by the legislature of Natal. "They have been wantonly assaulted in the streets and been unable to obtain redress from the courts. They have been robbed and outraged and reviled for presuming to exist at all . . . and they have been persistently denied the status of citizens." [10]

To exacerbate the situation, frequent questions and debates on the subject of the Indian condition in South Africa occurred in Parliament, the attack often led by Indian members.[11] On October 11, 1897, Dadabhai Naoroji, the "grand old man of Indian politics," remarked in a letter to Chamberlain, "we are repeatedly told that we are British subjects, quite as much as the Queen's subjects in this country, and not slaves and I always look forward with hope to a fulfillment of these pledges and Proclamations . . . and I pray that it may be a reality and not remain a romance."[12] A Colonial Office minute dealing with the Natal Indian question summed up the British dilemma: "The whole subject is perhaps the most difficult we have had to deal with. The Colonies wish to exclude the Indians from spreading themselves all over the Empire. If we agree, we are liable to forfeit the loyalty of the Indians. If we do not agree we forfeit the loyalty of the Colonists." [13]

Embarrassed and frustrated, the British Government compromised, insisting that the letter of any particular law be nondiscriminatory but paying little attention to the spirit. Such was the case with the Immigration Restriction Act and with Act 2 of 1897, "An Act to Amend the Laws Relating to Quarantine." On the surface the Quarantine Act looked like a perfectly reasonable piece of legislation, but section 2 of the law, which allowed the colonial health authorities to prevent the landing of healthy Indians who had not been exposed to infection, con-

10. The *Times*, Aug. 27, 1894.   11. *Hansard*, Aug. 16, 1900.
12. NA, Ind. Coll., no. 102, sec. of state to gov., Nov. 13, 1897, encl. Naoroji to Chamberlain, Oct. 11, 1897.
13. CO 179/202, CO, Domestic, no. 4900, received Mar. 6, 1897, minuting by F. S., June 17, 1897.

vinced the Indians that it was another legislative stratagem designed to stop them from entering Natal. A quarantine order, the law read, "shall extend to a ship having on board passengers who have come from a proclaimed place, notwithstanding that they may have embarked at some other place, or that the ship has not touched at the proclaimed place."

Indians were, of course, even less welcome in the two Dutch republics of the Transvaal and the Orange Free State than they were in Natal. Even with British victory in the Anglo-Boer War, Indians did not gain the right to enter the Orange River Colony (as the Orange Free State was called after the Peace of Vereeniging) or find the possibility of entering the Transvaal much improved. Part of the reason lay in the changed status of the Dutch population. Whereas the Afrikaners had been citizens of a foreign state before the war, they were now British subjects. And the British Government, which had intervened on the part of Indians against the Republican governments, now changed its stance. As Lionel Curtis, the prominent imperial statesman, explained, the British Government before the war exerted itself on behalf of the Indians, "just as it would have . . . on behalf of any other British subjects in any other foreign country." At that time, it had held no responsibility to the white inhabitants of the Republic. When the Transvaal was annexed to the British crown, however, "the imperial Government undertook, and rightly undertook, to administer the country themselves." To continue to maintain a pro-Indian attitude, "would violate obligations . . . imposed upon it through unforeseen circumstances towards the European inhabitants of the Colony." [14] Nevertheless, the British authorities prevented the promulgation of some of the more extreme measures favored by the crown's new subjects. As Chamberlain put it, "for measures passed at this juncture His Majesty's Government cannot dis-

14. T[ransvaal] A[rchives], Curtis to Duncan, Aug. 3, 1906, encl. Curtis to Patrick Russell, Aug. 3, 1906.

claim direct responsibility." [15] And he implied that for laws passed after the advent of responsible government, the situation would be reversed.

The Transvaal was granted responsible government in December 1906. At the initial session of the newly constituted legislature, the government introduced an Asiatic Law Amendment Bill requiring the registration of all Indians in the Transvaal as a means of checking "illegal" entry. The bill (Act 2 of 1907) was passed with unseemly haste (within twenty-four hours, to be exact), and the news of this event was joyously proclaimed throughout the Transvaal. The member from Barberton (Loveday) almost certainly represented all white colonists when he called the act "the first step to stop what may mean the extinction of the white races in this country by immigration from the East. It has been rightly stated," he continued, "that this measure should appeal to every individual in this country, and it does appeal to every individual." [16] His Majesty's Government duly sanctioned the measure. "They [the British Government]," the secretary of state wrote to Lord Selborne, the governor of the Transvaal, feel "that they would not be justified in offering resistance to the general will of the Colony clearly expressed by its first elected representatives; and I am accordingly to inform you that His Majesty will not be advised to exercise his powers of disallowance with respect to the Act." [17]

To reinforce Act 2 of 1907, Act 15 of the same year established the "Natal formula" as a means of controlling unwanted immigration into the province. Section 2, subsection 1, stipulated that "Any person who when asked whether within or outside this Colony by a duly authorised officer shall be unable through deficient education to write out (from dictation or

15. TA, sec. of state to high comm., Dec. 10, 1906.
16. Transvaal *Hansard*, Mar. 21, 1907.
17. NAI, Papers with Acts, India Act XIV of 1914, sec. of state to gov., May 9, 1907.

otherwise) and sign in the characters of an European language an application for permission to enter this Colony or such other document as such officer may require," would be deemed a prohibited immigrant. The Asiatic Law Amendment Act and the Immigrants Restriction Act were designed to supplement each other. Subsection 4 of section 2 of the latter law implied that all Indians who had not registered under the provisions of the former would be considered prohibited immigrants, and section 8 forbade such persons from acquiring licenses to trade and to own or lease property. For the Indian community it was all too much, and the attacks of the now responsible Transvaal Government on their position resulted in the first *satyagraha* campaign.

The *Times* of January 6, 1908, in a rare moment of insight, remarked:

As a nation we have little reason to be proud of the treatment now being meted out to our fellow subjects in the Transvaal. . . . If the Republican Government chastised the Indians with whips, since the annexation of the Transvaal they have been chastised by scorpions. . . .

The wrongs of the Transvaal Indian community will soon be known and brooded over by the dumb millions who look to us as all-powerful in India, and, when evil is done, will be used for all they are worth by the agitators against our rule. And the worst of it is that their grievance will be just. Nor can we wash our hands of the business merely by casting the responsibility on the Colonial Government, for Mr. Harold Cox points out with undeniable force that His Majesty's Ministers specially reserved the right of the Imperial Government to deal with questions of this nature.

The conflict over Indian registration and immigration restriction was a struggle more of principle than of substance—for instance, the Indians fought only for the admission of six "highly educated" Indians per year as of right rather than a more extensive concession. Nevertheless, it was destined to rage intermittently for some seven years.

Although the chief area of conflict had, after the Anglo-Boer War, shifted to the Transvaal, Indian immigration continued to be an issue in both Cape Colony and Natal. By 1904 there were 8,489 Indians in the Cape—a figure not greatly different from the Transvaal's—but because of the Cape's traditionally more liberal attitudes they posed a less acute problem there. Nevertheless, in 1902 an immigration restriction act (Assembly Bill 57), admitted by the governor, Sir Walter Hely-Hutchinson (formerly the governor of Natal), to be based on the Natal act, was introduced into the legislature. The law did not specifically mention Indians; it was, however, obviously aimed at them. The usual European language test was prescribed, but European illiterates could be excused from it, an explicit inequity that led the Colonial Office to threaten to disallow the measure.[18] The governor replied: "Ministers have given the required assurance that they will introduce a Bill next session to amend the existing Bill by omitting the word 'European' from the clause." [19]

The Cape immigration restriction act was much less harsh than those of the other South African colonies. Only Indians desiring permanent residence were affected, and an Asian deemed a prohibited immigrant was not punished but merely sent back to his port of origin at the colony's expense, with £3 in his pocket.[20] It would be a mistake, however, to conclude that this more liberal law was enacted in the Cape without difficulty. Strong pressure from the colonial secretary, Sir P. Faure, reflecting the will of the Colonial Office, was required to remove a clause stipulating that "any Asiatic who is not granted a

18. *Ibid.*, Mar. 1903, procs. 19–20, tel., sec. of state to gov., Dec. 8, 1902. The effectiveness of the act can be attested to by the following figures: in 1903, 1,646 Asians entered Cape Colony; by 1908 the number had fallen to 387. In 1909 the figure was 445, and in 1910–1911 between 400 and 500. Even the reduced numbers, when compared with comparable figures for the other South African colonies, indicate the greater liberality of the Cape measure.

19. CO 48/567, tel., gov. to sec. of state, Dec. 12, 1902.

20. CO 48/568, Laws and Regulations Applicable to Immigrants of Asiatic Race, prepared by Mr. Advocate Morgan Evans, Jan. 30, 1903.

special permit of immigration into the Colony by the Governor on the recommendation of the Minister" was a prohibited immigrant. During the debate, a liberal Dutch member of the opposition, J. W. Sauer, had claimed, "There were 240 millions in India and there were Chinamen who were British subjects who would come into this country to an extent which would swamp it. After all, to them it was a matter of no importance whether a Chinaman was a British subject or not. The point was that they did not want to see Asiatics come here, introducing social, economic, and political trouble in this country, and they would do that whether they were British subjects or not." [21]

When the Customs Union Conference at Bloemfontein (March, April 1903) voted to favor the importation of indentured Asian labor into South Africa primarily to speed the development of the Transvaal, discussions in the Cape legislature became more heated and emotional than otherwise would have been the case. A successful resolution in the House of Assembly condemned the conference's action and called attention to the fate of Natal which, it was claimed, had been turned into an Asian colony.[22]

When the Colonial Office grew impatient at the failure of the Cape Government to alter the immigration restriction act, the governor replied that amendment was for the present politically unfeasible, the threat of Chinese coolies being imported into the Transvaal to work on the railroads and in the mines having excessively aroused feelings of fear and resentment. The prime minister, J. Gordon Sprigg, now wanted to wait a year, during which passions were expected to cool.[23] For the moment, as the *South African News* wrote on December 8, 1903: "He must be a dullard or a pro-Asiatic magnate who could note the solid stately buildings of the Paarl, the spacious gardens, above all the sturdy race which inhabits the district, and not feel the enormity of the treason to South Africa of which the importation party is

[21]. Cape *Hansard*, Nov. 12, 1902.   [22]. *Ibid.*, July 2, 1903.
[23]. CO 48/572, tel., gov. to sec. of state, Aug. 3, 1903.

guilty." It was the fear of ex-indentured laborers filtering into the Cape from the Transvaal that sparked the colony's antagonism. Should the Chinese immigration scheme for the Transvaal be sanctioned, Sprigg proclaimed, "it will be the duty of the government here to submit to the Legislature the measures which they consider necessary to prevent the entry of Asiatics from the neighbouring Colonies into the Cape Colony." [24]

In 1904 the Cape legislature passed a "Bill to Prevent Introduction of [non-British] Chinese into Cape Colony," but it was hardly the promised amendment of the immigration act of 1902. Upon being addressed in regard to this oversight, the governor could only reply,

> In view . . . of the tone of recent discussion that has taken place in the House of Assembly as well as in the Legislative Council on the question of Asiatic immigration Ministers cannot admit that the condition of things is in any way improved. Under the circumstances therefore Ministers regret that they do not feel justified in recommending that steps be taken in the direction desired during the present session of Parliament and would accordingly ask that the matter be allowed to stand over for the present.[25]

When, in 1906, a "Bill to Amend the Law placing Restrictions on Immigration and providing for the Removal from the Colony of Prohibited Immigrants" was finally passed, the exemption for European illiterates still remained, and despite their undertaking to amend the Immigration Act of 1902 so as to provide parity for Asians, the Cape ministers were quite arrogant in their defense of the status quo. "To omit the word 'European'," they claimed, "would be to extend that privilege [the exemption from the language test] to all Nationalities and Races, . . . a course which does not commend itself to Ministers as being in the interests of the Colony; and, as has been explained above, they have found it necessary to adhere in the amending bill to the terms of existing laws so far as it involves

24. CO 48/573, minuting by Sprigg, Dec. 9, 1903.
25. CO 48/576, gov. to sec. of state, Apr. 12, 1904.

the principle now in question." ²⁶ Hely-Hutchinson wrote to the Colonial Office: "I feel quite sure that if Ministers could possibly have met your wishes about the Immigration Bill, without gravely risking the existence of the government, they would have done so." ²⁷

The new act (no. 30 of 1906) actually eroded the situation further. The old law had stipulated that all persons domiciled in South Africa were not to come under its jurisdiction. The law of 1906 exempted only those "persons born in South Africa" and "persons of European birth domiciled in South Africa." Nevertheless, the governor explained that while "it must be admitted that in principle these distinctions are to be regretted . . . in practice they involve little, if any, real hardship." ²⁸ The Colonial Office registered a feeble protest.²⁹ It wearily concluded, however, that "H.M.G. is in a weak position. If the Bill is reserved and assent refused, the Cape will fall back on the Act of 1902 which is no less objectionable." H. C. M. Lambert, one of the first-class clerks, minuted: "The matter is not of enough importance I think to justify us in trying to force the Cape Government to risk its existence," ³⁰ and the whole question of amending the immigration act of 1902 in the manner promised died with a whimper. The prime minister, Dr. L. S. Jameson, informed Hely-Hutchinson that "Ministers have the honour to give assurance that section 4(g) [the domicile clause] of the said Act will be administered in a liberal and equitable manner, so as to fully safeguard the interests, lawfully acquired by Asiatics residing in the Colony." ³¹ The Colonial Office accepted this

26. CO 48/585, prime minister to gov., May 31, 1906.
27. NAI, Govt. of India, Dept. of Comm. and Ind. (Em.), Feb. 1907, proc. 13–15, gov. to sec. of state, June 5, 1906.
28. CO 48/586, gov. to sec. of state, Aug. 21, 1906.
29. NAI, Govt. of India, Dept. of Comm. and Ind. (Em.), Feb. 1907, procs. 6–9, minuting on gov. to sec. of state, Aug. 21, 1907.
30. CO 48/585, minute paper 22660, June 25, 1906, minuting of July 3, 1906.
31. NAI, Govt. of India, Dept. of Comm. and Ind. (Em.), June 1907, proc. 1, prime minister to gov., Feb. 20, 1907.

new undertaking, and the India Office reluctantly agreed, remarking that "the Secretary of State for India in Council can only . . . trust that section 4(g) will be interpreted in a liberal and equitable manner." [32]

How "liberal and equitable" the law's administration was to be was indicated by a proclamation of August 30, 1906, which declared that

from and after the date hereof, it shall not be lawful for any Arab, Indian or other Asiatic of whatsoever nationality, to enter any of the territories aforesaid (namely, the Transkei, including Gealakaland; Tembuland, including Emigrant Tembuland and Bomnanaland; Pondoland, including East and West Pondoland; Port St. John's; Griqualand East;) without a special permit signed by the Resident Magistrate, or by his order, and approved by the Chief Magistrate of the Transkeian Territories.[33]

In Natal, Act 30 of 1903 refined the colony's design for keeping free Indians out. Again, Indians were not mentioned in the legislation. Exclusion was to be effected by the manner of the law's administration. An immigrant seeking admission to Natal would have to fill out in some European language an application to enter the colony, "to the satisfaction of the Minister," [34] and the minister was to prove a very hard man for an Indian to satisfy. The India Office recommended that the language requirement be changed to "English or some European language selected by himself [the immigrant]," [35] but it was not seriously

---

32. CO 48/588, IO to CO, Nov. 14, 1906. For many of the colonists the immigration act of 1906 was not sufficiently strong. During debate on the measure in the house of assembly, S. C. Cronwright-Schreiner moved that a clause forbidding the entry of Asians into Cape Colony be inserted into the bill, but the house negatived the motion by a vote of 67 to 23. Cape *Hansard,* Aug. 14, 1906.

33. *Cape of Good Hope Government Gazette,* Aug. 30, 1906, proclamation issued by Maj. Gen. Edmunds Smith Brook, officer administering the colony.

34. Section 5a.   35. CO 179/230, IO to CO, no date.

offended when its suggestion was ignored. The other South African colonies, which had resolved at the Bloemfontein Customs Conference that "the permanent settlement in South Africa of Asiatic Races would be injurious and should not be permitted," [36] had nothing but praise for Natal's action.

The Natal Indians, however, were alarmed. To them the immigration act of 1897 had seemed harsh enough.[37] Yet the new measure was still more restrictive. The earlier law had required an immigrant to fill out a simple form in the characters of some European language. Now he had to write out any application that the immigration officer might choose to dictate. The age at which children attained their majority was lowered from twenty-one to sixteen years, thus making it more difficult for them to join their parents in Natal. Five years' indentured service, which in the past could have constituted the establishment of domicile, would no longer do so, and three years' free residence would in the future be required to establish domicile instead of two. The chairman of the Natal Indian Congress stated at a public meeting: "We thought all our troubles would vanish by a magic wand—that we would breathe free, that we would succeed in waking the colonies up to a sense of their Imperial Duty. But all these hopes seem but a dream. The awful reality is that our struggle for existence has only just com-

---

36. Procs. of the So. Af. Customs Conf., Mar. 19, 1903, resolution 11.

37. *Natal Mercury*, June 25, 1903. Actual figures on the working of the immigration act of 1897 were as follows: in 1897, 254 Indians (as opposed to 8 Britons) were excluded from Natal, and 1,103 Indians allowed to land. Of this last number, all but 10 were able to prove former domicile. In 1898, 925 Indians were not permitted to disembark (as opposed to 25 Britons); 400 Indians were allowed to land, of which number 240 proved former domicile. In 1899, 494 Indians were excluded from Natal under the workings of the act; 470 were allowed to land, of which number 306 proved former domicile. In 1900, 364 Indians were excluded and 712 allowed to land; 508 proved former domicile. In 1901, 3,311 Indians were excluded and 1,583 admitted; 1,138 proved former domicile. NA, encl. in report of Natal delegates to Sir Denzil Ibbetson, Feb. 9, 1903.

menced. . . . In 1902 alone Mr. Smith excluded 3,907 of our countrymen." [38] His statement ended with an eloquent plea:

> They proudly call Natal the most loyal British colony in South Africa. They are members of the British Empire and have sworn allegiance to the old flag. The same flag waves over us. We belong to the same family. We provide seasoned, well-trained soldiers to fight the Empire's battles. Our loyalty is proverbial. Our sobriety, our industry, our law abiding character are acknowledged even in this Colony. We have accepted the principle most dear to them: viz., that they shall have the right to regulate immigration so long as they do not thereby slight a whole race. . . . In the name of humanity, justice, fair play, in the name of the British Constitution, I ask them to stay their hand, and give us rest, to which we are fairly entitled.

When the Union of South Africa was established in 1910, the "Natal formula" was again invoked. The Union Immigrants Regulation Act (no. 22) of 1913 in section 4(1)(b) stipulated that a prohibited immigrant was "any person unable, by reason of deficient education, to read and write in any European language to the satisfaction of an immigration officer, or, in the case of appeal, to the satisfaction of the [immigration appeal] board; . . ." The Indians consequently discovered that the creation of the new federation only extended and increased the impediments to immigration under which they suffered.

While the South African colonies immediately recognized the advantages of the "Natal formula," it was to take their Australasian counterparts somewhat longer. Not until the conclusion of the intercolonial conference of 1888 and the passage of essentially uniform Chinese immigration restriction legislation did the Australasian colonies turn to questions of race and color over and beyond the Chinese problem. Then the presence of small groups of non-Chinese Asians began to cause increasing

---

38. *Natal Mercury*, June 25, 1903.

concern. For instance, there were some 1,500 Asians in the north coast districts of New South Wales, many of whom were "Hindoos." And throughout Australia, the itinerant merchant (nearly always an Asian) made an attractive target. In the New South Wales Assembly, Mr. Suhey of Darlington asked: "Is it not a fact that Afghan, Indian and Cingalese hawkers from time to time threaten helpless women and metaphorically speaking, force them to buy their goods at the point of a knife?" Auguring things to come, Suhey went on to ask:

> What is there to prevent the Government from refusing these Asiatics licenses to trade? We have at present time not only Chinese doctors, Chinese lawyers, and Asiatics in almost every profession and every species of handicraft, but the coloured races are now absorbing a great many lines of ordinary trade. A large share of the grocery business has almost passed into the hands of coloured aliens. . . . We say we believe in a "white Australia," and yet the records we have of mixed marriages between coloured aliens and persons of white blood and of various kinds of illicit connections are so horrible that I can do no more than just refer to them on this occasion.[39]

The fact was that those who dreamed of a "White Australia" were beginning to realize that they were beset by dangers on all sides. The Chinese menace appeared under control at last, and there seemed only a finite number of "Hindoos," Afghans, Syrians, and Cingalese. To be sure, the Kanaka question in Queensland remained unresolved, but it was felt that Australian union, which must inevitably come, would lead to its solution. Suddenly, however, it was perceived that a new and more dangerous group of colored aliens was insinuating itself into this frontier bastion of white Anglo-Saxon civilization. The Japanese, according to the Queensland census of 1891, had numbered only 49. By the time of the next census (1901) there were 2,269. And they were different from their fellow Asian immi-

39. N.S.W. *Hansard,* July 7, 1897.

grants. They came not from a weak nation victimized by European exploitation, but from a state just beginning to flex its industrial and military muscles and destined to become a major factor on the world scene. The Reverend A. C. Smith, the convener of heathen missions in Queensland, in 1894 wrote a description of the Japanese immigrants he had encountered which would have chilled the blood of any defender of a white Australia: "The Japanese are very quick, smart and industrious. . . . I attended a weekly night class of these Japanese. . . . They rapidly acquire our language, and after a few lessons become beautiful writers. Their introduction, however, is a matter of regret, for they will form formidable competitors with white industry in any industry they please." [40]

The greatest area of Japanese penetration was in the pearl-shell fisheries of Thursday Island and Torres Straits, and in March 1894 the colonial secretary asked the governor to request Whitehall to communicate with the Japanese Government with a view to placing a check on Japanese immigration to Queensland. The Government of Queensland felt that the Japanese had already established so tight a grip on the pearl-shell industry that further immigration would probably cause such a wave of animosity that the government might not be able to protect the Japanese against "vexatious treatment." The Colonial Office duly solicited the Foreign Office's cooperation,[41] and the latter agency held a preliminary conversation with the Japanese minister, Viscount Aoki. The matter was put quite subtly. Aoki was warned that excessive Japanese immigration to Queensland might arouse public resentment, and the minister, in turn, promised to communicate the information to his government.[42]

The whole issue was a delicate one, as the British and Japa-

40. CO 234/60, Q. 20190, no. 123, Norman to Ripon, Oct. 8, 1894, encl., Rev. A. C. Smith to Women's Presbyterian Mission Union.
41. CO 234/59, no. 19, Norman to Ripon, Mar. 22, 1894, encl. col. sec. to Norman, Mar. 21, 1894; CO to FO, May 3, 1894.
42. CO 234/60, FO, Q. 9575, FO to CO, May 31, 1894.

nese Governments were in the final stages of negotiation for a treaty of commerce and navigation (signed in London on July 16, 1894), the articles of which ran counter to what Queensland desired both in spirit and in fact. The first article assured the subjects of both Great Britain and Japan respectively "full liberty to enter, travel, or reside in any part of [the] dominions and possessions of the other contracting party." The treaty then went on in its third article to guarantee reciprocal commercial and navigational rights. Although article 19 specified that the treaty did not apply to British self-governing dominions unless they chose to adhere to it within two years, it nonetheless severely circumscribed the role Her Majesty's Government could play as a broker between the Australasian colonies and the Imperial Japanese Government.

The Anglo-Japanese treaty was the subject of discussion at an Australasian premiers' conference in 1896, and nonaccession to the instrument was decided upon. Nevertheless, Queensland, of all the colonies, determined that it would be to its commercial advantage to sign a protocol with the Japanese Government whereby it joined the mother country, in 1897, as a party to the treaty of 1894. The protocol did, however, guarantee "that the stipulations contained in Articles I and III of the above-named Treaty shall not in any way affect the laws, ordinances, and regulations with regard to trade, the immigration of labourers and artisans, police, and public security, which are in force or may hereafter be enacted in Japan or in the said Colony of Queensland." It was perhaps an act of cynical expediency. Sir Samuel Griffith wrote with considerable honesty about the racial attitudes of Australians and other Anglo-Saxons: "The strong feeling of antipathy to Asiatic races that is now so marked a feature of the British speaking people in America and Australia seems to be a modern phenomenon. History records no instance of similar race hatred." Griffith went on to ascribe this racial antipathy to economic factors, but his example was not particularly convincing: "That this is the real ground of opposition is illustrated by the fierce objection that was made to the proposal made in 1890 to introduce Italian labourers into Queensland; their standard of comfort was thought to be lower than the normal standard of Australia." [43]

The fact was that most Australians were strongly opposed to Japanese immigration, and nowhere was this more true than in Queensland where the labor movement had been galvanized by the socialist, William Lane, who, in his papers, the *Boomerang* and the *Australian Worker,* invoked the terrible danger of Asian competition to the Australian working man. Queensland's planters and the pearlers of Thursday Island, on the other hand, were in desperate need of just the kind of labor the Japanese could supply. The Government of Queensland, in this instance, however, sided with labor, and although it had come down in favor of Kanaka importation and signed the protocol with Japan, it was determined not to countenance the further immigration of Japanese workers. In refusing applications for Japanese labor, the government admitted to being "guided by the fact that the sentiment of the people of Queensland is wholly opposed to the introduction into the colony of Japanese or other Asiatic alien labour, [a position] in which the Government itself shares." [44]

No doubt the government's anti-Japanese stance was at least partially reinforced by reports such as the one filed by John Douglas, the government resident on Thursday Island and former premier of the colony. Douglas informed his superiors there were fifty-three Japanese prostitutes within his jurisdiction and that they were now applying for a special lease to allow "the formation of a settlement for the purpose of promiscuous sexual intercourse," which he hoped the government would not

43. Sir Samuel Griffith, "Australia and the Coloured Races," *Review of Reviews,* IX, May 1894, 577–78.
44. Queensland Archives, PRE 102, Henry S. Dutton, undersec., to govt. resident, Thursday Island, Apr. 28, 1894.

countenance.⁴⁵ Although Douglas pointed out that the Japanese Government did not sanction the immigration of prostitutes and that the women were smuggled in from Hong Kong, it was a fine point which probably had little impact in Brisbane.

Disagreement over immigration rules and procedures was destined to continue for some months. In the meantime, anti-Japanese pronouncements became increasingly frequent in the Queensland Parliament. Henry Daniels of Cambooya declared:

> This Japanese difficulty has arisen in the first instance from bringing black labour for the sugar industry. It seems to me that we are going to pay too big a price for the sugar industry—in fact, more than the industry is worth. To say we cannot prevent Japs coming here in large numbers because Japan happens to be a first-class power is absurd. What has Japan done to be called a first-class power? She has simply whipped China, who was in a thoroughly disorganised state at the time of the war.

Charles McDonald of Flinders continued in the same vein. "Hon. members tell us," he said, "that the Japanese are not what they were a few years ago. They were then an insignificant people; nobody took any notice of them, but since they have defeated a few Chinamen in some sort of scramble they had, all the pluck is knocked out of the lot of hon. members on the other side, and they think we should not attempt to pass any law to prevent this undesirable class of people coming along. Where is their boasted British pluck now?" ⁴⁶

The Japanese Government was not slow to react. Using the lever of increasing commercial profit accruing to the colony from the treaty relationship, it kept constant pressure on the authorities in Brisbane. On November 18, 1899, K. Iijima, the Japanese consul at Townsville, suggested that much of the sting could be taken out of Queensland-Japanese relations if it were

---

45. *Ibid.*, tel., John Douglas, govt. resident, Thursday Island, to undersec., Home Office, July 19, 1898.
46. Queensland *Hansard*, July 20, 1897.

just agreed that the Japanese population (which he estimated as being between 4,000 and 5,000) be stabilized and maintained at its present level.[47] Having received no answer for several months, Iijima wrote again in more explicit terms on June 12, 1900. The consul suggested: (1) that vacancies left on Queensland sugar plantations by departing Japanese be filled by new Japanese immigrants (up to the level specified in his previous letter); (2) that the vested interests of Japanese on Thursday Island be respected and that the renewal of rights or their transference to other Japanese not be impeded (again, the limits previously mentioned were to obtain); (3) that a subconsulate be established on Thursday Island; and (4) that the Japanese Government undertake that it would in future allow no laborers or artisans into Queensland without the permission of the colony's government.[48] When the premier, James Dickson, finally replied, he was willing to accept Iijima's proposal in principle, although he disagreed with the consul's figures. His government was, however, willing to stipulate a Japanese population in Queensland of 3,247 (Dickson's assessment of the Japanese population in 1900), providing no more than 25 Japanese came on any one vessel. Iijima promptly accepted the compromise on behalf of his government, and a *modus vivendi* acceptable both to Imperial Japan and the self-governing colony of Queensland appeared to have been achieved.[49]

A postal conference which assembled in Hobart in 1895 and the intercolonial conference which met in Sydney the following year took the first major steps towards following the implications of Chinese immigration legislation to their logical conclusion. Frightened by rumors of increased Indian settlement

47. CO 234/71, Q. 38036, no. 100, Griffith to Chamberlain, Oct. 11, 1900, corres. on Japanese immigration to Queensland, encl. Iijima to chief sec., Brisbane, Nov. 18, 1899.
48. *Ibid.*
49. *Ibid.*, Dickson to Iijima, Oct. 3, 1900; Iijima to Dickson, Oct. 13, 1900.

along the northern rivers of New South Wales and plans for Japanese colonization along the Victoria River in the Northern Territory, the Sydney conference moved the development of Australasian racial policy a significant step further down the road leading to a white Australasia. The premiers agreed to extend the Chinese immigration restriction legislation of their respective colonies so that it would in future cover not just Chinese but all colored persons.

New South Wales attempted to put this policy into practice through the passage of an act (41 of 1896) which was designed to place under the provisions of the Chinese restriction and regulation act of 1888, "all persons belonging to any coloured race inhabiting the Continent of Asia or the Continent of Africa, or any island adjacent thereto, or any island in the Pacific Ocean or the Indian Ocean, not being persons duly accredited on any special mission to Her Majesty by the Government or ruler of any country, state, or territory, or to this Colony under the authority of the Imperial Government." [50] Although ministers of religion, missionaries, native teachers, tourists, merchants, men of science, and students were exempted from the workings of the act, providing they were supplied with proper accreditation and identification, colored persons in general were stripped of the rights and protection afforded by British citizenships and the act of 1888. Under the new law, they were, regardless of status, to be treated alike.

The *Sydney Morning Herald* of October 14 wondered if the act were really necessary. The *Sydney Daily Telegraph* of the same day was more sure. "It is in no spirit of hostility to coloured aliens that we would exclude them from this community," it wrote;

the question is simply one of protecting ourselves against the growth of an evil which experience teaches that it is easier to prevent than

50. Article 1.

cure. . . . If we want a homogeneous Australia, we must have a white Australia, and ungracious as it may seem, it is a much fairer thing to shut coloured aliens out altogether than invite them to come in, and then refuse them the recognition afforded our citizens. . . . It is not much use . . . to shut out Chinamen, and leave the door open to millions of Hindoos, Arabs, Burmese, Angolese, and other coloured races which swarm in British Asia.

Regardless of the state of public opinion on the measure, it was clearly too controversial to be approved at the colonial level, and the governor duly reserved it for the signification of Her Majesty's pleasure.

South Australia passed legislation (Act 672 of 1896) similar to that of New South Wales, and it was, of necessity, also reserved by the governor of the colony. New Zealand first passed an act (19 of 1896) which increased the poll tax on entering Chinese from £10 to £100 and changed the ratio of Chinese to vessel tonnage from 1/100 to 1/200. This measure received the governor's sanction. A second law (Act 64 of 1896), based on the New South Wales and South Australian models was, however, reserved. Tasmania was the only other colony at this time to follow the Sydney conference's resolution in the form of Act 55 of 1896, and it too was reserved.

Joseph Chamberlain had meanwhile been coming under increasing pressure, both foreign and domestic, to control the embarrassingly xenophobic tendencies of Britain's Australasian dependencies. In his moment of need, the secretary of state was introduced to the wonders of the "Natal formula," and decided to make it the focus of his meeting with the premiers of the self-governing colonies which was scheduled for London in conjunction with the celebration of Queen Victoria's Diamond Jubilee. When the Australasian premiers assembled at the Colonial Office in June 1897, Chamberlain determined to convince them of the virtues of the Natal act and of the desirability of replacing the reserved laws of 1896 with similar legislation.

The secretary of state spoke persuasively, and at the end of his oration, he revealed to the premiers a solution to their racial problem that could both satisfy them and preserve intact the letter of the imperial philosophy.

> The Colony of Natal has arrived at an arrangement which is absolutely satisfactory to them. . . . They have adopted legislation which they believe will give them all they want and to which the objection I have taken does not apply, and which does not come into conflict with these sentiments which I am sure you share with us; and I hope, therefore, that during your visit it may be possible for us to arrange a form of words which will avoid hurting the feelings of Her Majesty's subjects, while at the same time it would amply protect the Australian Colonies against the invasion of the class to which they would justly object.[51]

Chamberlain, in his role as secretary of state for the colonies, tended to emphasize, domestically, the position of nonwhite British subjects within the Empire. More troublesome, however, was the status of non-Europeans who were the citizens of "friendly" powers such as Japan. After the conference Chamberlain, as the loyal champion of his colonial constituents, wrote the Foreign Office, the chief object of Japanese pressure, "that if the admission of Asiatics is not at once limited, it would be impossible in communities as democratic as those of Australia to avoid such popular outbreaks against a coloured element as has been experienced in the U.S."[52] John Anderson, now a first-class clerk in Colonial Office Department Two, was worried lest Australian legislative practices result in affronts to nations with whom, under treaty, Great Britain had concluded reciprocal most-favored-nation arrangements. He pointed to such countries as Liberia, Morocco and Persia. Edward Wingfield, Herbert's successor as permanent undersecretary, however, concluded that the Australasian colonies would have their way regarding aliens whether treaties were violated or not, and

---

51. C. 8596, 1897, Proceedings of a Conference between the Secretary of State for the Colonies and the Premiers of the Self-Governing Colonies.
52. CO 418/4, Aus. 9910, CO to FO, Aug. 17, 1897.

Chamberlain minuted: "I agree. We cannot prevent this legislation and we had better let sleeping dogs lie in the case of such powers as Persia, Liberia, etc." [53]

But the Japanese were hardly "sleeping dogs," and they kept up a drumfire of reproach. A letter from the Foreign Office to the Colonial Office of September 6, 1897, must have gone a long way towards reinforcing Chamberlain's contention that the "Natal formula" did indeed provide the way out of a thorny dilemma: "Mr. Secretary Chamberlain will observe," the note read, "that Monsieur Kato is anxious that the restrictions on immigration be made to apply to all foreigners, including Europeans." The secretary of state now increased his efforts to win over the Australasian colonies to his way of thinking.

Although far from optimistic after the conference, Chamberlain managed success in the long run. In Australia and New Zealand, the whole period 1896–1898 was one of continuous debate on colored exclusion. The arguments were familiar. King O'Malley of Encounter Bay in South Australia "only wished those who had said that coloured races were as good as the Whites would go to South Carolina for a night and sleep with a negro with his black woolly hair and his bad breath. The stench would be so great that he would not like to repeat the performance. Asiatics and all inferior races had certain misfortunes which pursued them to their dying day. But the Great Creator had preserved Australia from these people and their leprosy." [54] New Zealand's Richard Seddon, now the island state's prime minister, rose in Parliament and attacked the old enemy. "Every steamer from Australia is bringing a large number of Chinese," he thundered, "and the number of Chinese in the City of Wellington has doubled during the last five years.

53. *Ibid.*, draft no. 47, CO to New Zealand, Aug. 17, 1897, minuting by Anderson, July 14, 1897; by Wingfield, July 17, 1897; by Chamberlain, July 19, 1897.
54. S.A. *Hansard*, Nov. 11, 1896.

... From my experience on the goldfields, from what I know personally, and from what has been brought prominently under my notice, I say they are not a desirable class of colonists." The former prime minister, Sir Robert Stout, who was Seddon's great rival, nevertheless supported him, and would have gone even further: "There is another thing which I think we ought also to have—namely a law against negroes and Kaffirs, just as much as Chinese." William Earnshaw of Dunedin had the final word. "At the same time, while excluding Asiatics," he exclaimed, "we should also exclude Assyrians, Japanese, and negroes. These four races are absolutely out of touch with our civilisation, and they will not mix or blend with our civilisation —the hybrid being worse than the pure race." [55] On the other hand, many members of the New Zealand Legislative Council protested the government's attitude and the passage of discriminatory legislation.[56] But the act to further amend the law regulating the immigration of Chinese was nonetheless passed, even though the Chinese population had dropped to 3,711.[57]

In a slightly different vein, one member of the New South Wales lower house (Ewing) asked what Japan, whom Britain might need "to clip the claws of Russia in the Pacific," would say when its subjects were excluded by a British colony? What of "the men who are at present upholding the British banner on the Afghan hills . . . men who will not be permitted to come here. We use these men in one part of the world to uphold British influence and British power, to maintain the imperial prestige of Britain, in which we participate, and still we will not permit them to come here." [58]

The *Daily Telegraph* of Sydney saw itself as the voice of sweet reason, and perhaps in the context of the times it was. "The

55. N.Z. *Hansard,* June 23, 1896.
56. N.Z. Archives, Govt. House, reg., no. 264/97, N.Z. no. 52, H. J. Miller, speaker of the leg. council, to the Earl of Glasgow, Sept. 3, 1896.
57. Huang, 44.   58. N.S.W. *Hansard,* Nov. 24, 1897.

question is to keep the whole of this island free from the taint of alien blood and unless the five Parliaments of the five colonies legislate to the same purpose, individual effort, no matter how well directed must fail." The paper denied imputing intellectual or moral superiority to the white man. But experience had proved that diverse racial groups could develop to their full potential only when they remained apart. "The races will not blend either socially or politically and where they exist together it is, therefore, impossible to have a homogeneous community. . . . It is the general effect produced by the existence of a multi-colored citizenship that has to be considered, and results prove that this is inimical to the well-being of both races." [59]

In the months between the London conference with Chamberlain and the creation of the Commonwealth of Australia, four of the Australasian colonies—New South Wales, New Zealand, Western Australia, and Tasmania—passed acts based on the "Natal formula," while the others awaited the creation of a common Parliament.[60] The four measures were very similar. All required some sort of language test, ranging from filling out an application to taking fifty words of dictation. Western Australia prescribed English, while New Zealand, New South Wales, and Tasmania allowed other European languages. Only New Zealand provided any protection for British subjects, and even then it was limited to persons of British (including Irish) birth and parentage. Exemptions were generally provided for accredited diplomats, members of Her Majesty's armed forces, officers and men of visiting foreign naval vessels, and wives and children under eighteen of nonprohibited immigrants. To steel themselves and each other, the premiers, in a conference assembled in Melbourne in 1898, resolved "that the Colonies which have not already done so pass an Act on the lines of the Natal Act (on the understanding that the same shall be vigilantly en-

59. Sydney *Daily Telegraph,* Nov. 25, 1897.
60. N.S.W. Act 3 of 1898; N.Z. Act 33 of 1899; W.A. Act 13 of 1897; and Tasmania Act 69 of 1898.

forced), and agreed that if, after trial of that Act, any difficulties shall arise in any colony, then the colonies will join in such further legislation as may be necessary." Sir Hugh Nelson (Queensland) did not join the resolution.[61]

The "Natal formula" had evidently been accepted by the Australasian colonies, and the Colonial Office as *quid pro quo* abandoned its one previously consistent stand—that the rights of British subjects receive at least *pro forma* recognition. The protection of British citizenship had, of course, been violated many times before—most recently, Western Australia Act 40 of 1895 had forbidden the issuing of miners' or business licenses on goldfields to Africans or Asians even if they were British subjects.[62] But that a white British subject had rights not enjoyed by a colored British subject in Australia had never been made so blatantly clear before.[63] Forty-six Sikhs in Perth wrote the secretary of state in dismay. They pointed out that they had risked their lives to protect the British flag, believing that all British subjects were equal before the law. Now that they had immigrated to Western Australia they were, to their surprise, treated as aliens along with "enemies of Her Imperial Majesty" and "Afghans." "We humbly submit that . . . our entry into the Colony is menaced . . . and that our life is made a burden

---

61. S.A. Parl. paps., 1898, no. 24, conference of the premiers, Melbourne, Mar. 1898.

62. This law was made still more severe by Western Australia Act 30 of 1904.

63. Colonial Office minuting by E. H. March, a second-class clerk in the North American and Australasian Department, is revealing. "This is rather unsatisfactory," he wrote, "but so is the whole situation, and now that we have gained our main point about the Immigration Act we shd. perhaps let the Colony have its way about details. It wd. be no kindness to insist on the issue of licenses to Asiatics; if this leads to riots in WA, they would come off second best. We might save appearances by asking the Gov. to tell the petitioners that if a person able to prove himself a Br. subject is refused a license he shd. seek the legal remedy." CO 18/225, W.A. 3501, CO to IO, Feb. 22, 1898, minuting by Marsh, July 6, 1898.

to us by actions of the Colonists." [64] It was a plea that was destined to go unnoticed.

The "Natal formula" as implemented in South Africa and Australasia meant a language or literacy test so administered as to exclude unwanted immigrants. In Canada the principle of exclusion through innocuous legislation allowing vast interpretive latitude was soon accepted, but Canada used devices all its own to achieve the desired ends.

By the end of the nineteenth century, Indians, other than the British themselves the most persistent immigrants in the Empire, and Japanese were joining the Chinese in British Columbia. In the case of the former, the resentment was immediate, and it intensified with the sharp rise in immigration that occurred after 1905. Threats of expulsion caused some unrest in India, where it seemed to many that Indian British subjects were accorded less protection in Canada than Chinese and Japanese foreigners. The Bengali newspaper, *Sanjivani,* wrote:

There is no law under which Indians can be expelled from Canada, and the only fault for which the Government of Canada wants to get rid of them is, that they live very frugally and have compelled the English settler to do the same. . . .

There are many Chinese and Japanese in Canada, but the Canadian Government does not dare do anything to them, because they know how to avenge the wrong. Indians are, however, a subject people, weak and unarmed; so they can be persecuted with impunity. But Indians will not allow such things to go on any longer. They will now take up all their own trade, both export and import, and will not let European merchants monopolise Indian trade. If the Indian settlers of Canada are driven away, there will be a violent agitation in India and no Indian will touch English goods any more;

---

64. CO 18/225, W.A. 4570, Smith to Chamberlain, Jan. 27, 1898, encl. Bishin Singh and 46 Sikhs of Perth to Chamberlain, Jan. 20, 1898. The India Office was not prepared to take a very strong stand on behalf of Indians in Australia. It wrote the Colonial Office urging that Indians be exempted from immigration restriction legislation, but the tone was not one of great concern. CO 418/4, Aus. 15889, IO to CO, July 21, 1897.

and Indians will in this way revenge the wrong that may be done to their countrymen.⁶⁵

The editorial writer exaggerated the favorable position of the Chinese in Canada, but he was certainly correct in assuming that the government of Imperial Japan would, as in Australia, come to the defense of its subjects. Her Majesty's Government as a consequence became increasingly nervous. Although Canada had refused to adhere to it, the Anglo-Japanese treaty of 1894 did guarantee Japanese subjects "full liberty to enter, travel and reside in any part of the British possessions." Japan was also becoming a significant factor in British policy in the Pacific, and Joseph Chamberlain accordingly wrote the Canadian governor general a surprisingly strong letter. He asked Lord Minto to "impress on your ministers that restrictive legislation . . . is extremely repugnant to the sentiments of the people and Govt. of Japan, and you should not fail to impress upon them the importance, if there is any real prospect of a large influx of Japanese labourers into Canada, of dealing with it by legislation of the Dominion Parliament on the lines of the Natal Act which is likely to be generally adopted in Australia."

Chamberlain recognized "the importance of guarding against the possibility of the white labour in the Province [British Columbia] being swamped by the wholesale immigration of persons of Asiatic origin." He also acknowledged the friendly spirit of the British Columbia Government and conceded that, "There is no difference between Her Majesty's Government and the Government of British Columbia as regards the object aimed at by these laws"—a British population in the province. But, as the secretary of state went on to explain, "it is not the practical expulsion of Japanese to which the Government of the Mikado objects but their exclusion *nominatum* which specifically stamps the whole nation as undesirable persons." ⁶⁶

65. I[ndia] O[ffice] L[ibrary], Reports of the Native Press, Bengal, *Sanjivani,* Mar. 19, 1898.
66. CO 42/857, draft Chamberlain to Minto, July 20, 1898.

The Japanese Government did its best to assuage the fears of Oriental inundation which so dominated the thinking of most white British Columbians. When the Japanese consul in Vancouver reported to his superiors that in the first eleven days of April 1900, 4,500 Japanese had arrived in British Columbia, the Japanese authorities limited the issuance of emigration permits to five per emigration agent throughout the country.[67] British Columbia nevertheless passed Chapter 11 of 1900, "An Act to Regulate Immigration into British Columbia," which was the "Natal formula" in its classic form and was in due course (1902) disallowed by Ottawa. Unrepentant, the legislature of British Columbia persisted. Chapters 34 of 1902, 28 of 1905, and 21 of 1907 were repromulgations, with virtually no change, of Chapter 11 of 1900. This policy, although futile, at least convinced the province's white population of their elected representatives' zeal and devotion to their constituents' interests. Concomitantly, a stream of resolutions was directed at Ottawa.[68] Feelings were intensified because Chinese immigration, thought moribund since 1895, resumed as a result of the labor shortage which made it attractive for Chinese laborers to move to British Columbia despite the Dominion entrance tax. In 1900 alone, 4,231 Chinese paid the fee.[69] Victoria urged the raising of the poll tax on Chinese to $500 and the passage of an immigration restriction act based on the "Natal formula." The premier, Richard McBride, threatened to resign if no action were taken.[70]

Although the Dominion Government continued largely to ignore British Columbia's wails of anguish, by the turn of the century the province possessed just enough political muscle to

67. CO 42/857, Canada no. 186, CO to Canada, July 9, 1900, encl. J. B. Whitehead to Salisbury, May 19, 1900.
68. CO 62/57, B.C. Sessional Papers, B.C. Legislative Assembly Resolution of Aug. 14, 1900.
69. R. E. Wynne, "Reactions to Chinese in the Pacific Northwest and British Columbia, 1850–1910" (Ph.D. dissertation, University of Washington, 1970), 498.
70. PAC, Laurier Papers, 36467, McInnes to Laurier, Aug. 13, 1899.

have increasing cognizance taken of its plight. The prime minister found it necessary to promise the people of British Columbia that "the Government would be guided by the opinion of the Liberal members [from British Columbia] as to the immigration of Chinese." And the leader of the opposition also guaranteed his support to the province on the Chinese question. With a Dominion election just around the corner, the governor general, on July 18, 1900, sanctioned Chapter 32 of the Dominion code, an act restricting Chinese immigration. Of greatest significance was section 6, which raised the poll tax on Chinese entering Canada from $50 to $100. The phrase "irrespective of allegiance" was also added to the definition of Chinese persons subject to the act—in other words, British subjects were to be affected by the restrictions contained in the measure. For the rest, however, the act was much the same as the law of 1885, and it is worthy of note that 2,518 Chinese immigrants paid the new mulct in 1901.[71] Meanwhile, census figures for 1901 indicated a nonwhite element in British Columbia of 14,628 Chinese and 4,544 Japanese out of a total population of some 178,000.[72]

The Dominion Government in addition appointed a three-man Royal Commission on Chinese and Japanese immigration under the chairmanship of R. C. Clute of Toronto. The evidence presented was reminiscent of other commissions in other places. In British Columbia, it was contended, the Chinese dominated market gardening, the laundry business, canning, boot, cigar and brickmaking. The Japanese, it was asserted, were gaining control of the fishing industry, small boat building, and the supply of shingle bolts, mining timber and cordwood. When the commissioners filed their report in 1902, they contended, vis-à-vis the Chinese, "that it is impossible for the Province of British Columbia to take its place and part in the Dominion as it ought to do, unless its population is free from

71. Wynne, 498.
72. Provincial Archives of B.C., B.C. Sessional Papers, 1902, 84.

the taint of servile labor." The commissioners agreed with British Columbia that the Chinese were indeed nonassimilable, that they brought down white wages and the standard of living, and that they endangered health. British Columbia should have a "thoroughly British population." Chinese laborers, the commission urged, should be excluded from Canada by treaty supported by legislation, and until this happy state could be achieved, the poll tax on Chinese should be raised to $500. The commissioners were more restrained in their treatment of the Japanese question. They deplored the Japanese hand in the fishing and boat building industries, but limited their recommendations to the passage of legislation based on the "Natal formula" should Japanese policy concerning emigration be reversed.[73]

The difference in attitude towards Chinese and Japanese was a reflection of the amount of weight China and Japan carried on the international scene. China, the Ch'ing Empire withering, its national integrity emasculated by the powers of the West, could only plead for indulgence. When the Chinese Empire Reform Association of Canada petitioned for relief, it expected and received little support from home and was fobbed off by the Colonial Office with the usual platitudes about its memorial being laid before the king.[74]

Of the two pressures on the Dominion Government—that from the Imperial Government in London and that from British Columbia—the latter was obviously the more telling. Ottawa was not prepared to go too far in satisfying the western province's demands, and it continued to be aware of imperial and international considerations. But the realities of domestic politics demanded some concessions. Chapter 8 of the Dominion code which was assented to on July 10, 1903, increased the poll tax on entering Chinese from $100 to $500 while the penalty for a master who allowed a Chinese to land without a permit

73. CO 45/885, Canada Sessional Papers, 1902, paper 54, 400.
74. CO 42/880, 5318, Feb. 6, 1902.

was raised from $200 per violation to $500.⁷⁵ It is worthy of note that in the first half of 1903, 4,719 Chinese entered Canada and that in the second half of the year, the number fell to zero.⁷⁶

As was so often the case in British and colonial legislation, the true flavor of the act of 1903 was to be found in the regulations drawn up under it. The rules governing article 17 of the law stipulated that transportation companies must deposit a bond for any Chinese being transported through Canada to some other place. During the journey Chinese were to be confined at all times to their railway carriages.⁷⁷ In addition, the courts ruled that a Chinese travelling through Canada in bond could not change his destination outside Canada, nor was he eligible for *habeas corpus* while in the Dominion.⁷⁸

With the tide of Chinese immigration apparently stemmed, the white settlers of British Columbia could for the moment direct their full animosity against the Japanese. In January 1902 an Anglo-Japanese alliance was signed, which had the effect of making His Majesty's Government even more anxious to pre-

75. The Canadian Pacific Railway claimed the $500 fee would ruin its trans-Pacific business (Laurier Papers, 71362, general manager, C.P.R., to Laurier, Mar. 21, 1903). British Columbia farmers and canners protested the decision (*ibid.*, 73387, Charles E. Hope to Laurier, May 16, 1903, and 112667, resolution of the Kootenay Fruit Growers Association, Aug. 1, 1906). These negative opinions were opposed by a memorial from the Victoria Trades and Labour Council (*ibid.*, 84318, Apr. 6, 1904).

76. Cheng Tien-fang, *Oriental Immigration in Canada* (Shanghai, 1931), 70. Revisions of the law in 1906 and 1908 made it still more stringent, i.e., increased fines for evasion.

77. PAC, Orders in Council, R.G. 2, series 1, V. 692 (P.C. 1609), Aug. 17, 1904.

78. Huang, 110. The act of 1903 was slightly revised by Chapter 95 of 1906, in which a Chinese immigrant was defined as any person of Chinese origin including any person whose father was of Chinese origin. Article 7 accorded to any Chinese woman married to a non-Chinese the same status as her husband. The general level of fines was raised. Article 10 decreed that any ship coming coastwise via the United States was to be treated as if it had come directly from China. Article 22 required Chinese residents of Canada who had absented themselves from the Dominion for more than twelve months to pay the $500 entrance tax upon returning.

vent egregious insults to an important ally. The Japanese Government was not unaware of the dilemma in which the British found themselves. It had contained Japanese emigration to Canada in 1900 and in the same year that the alliance went into effect undertook unilaterally to prohibit the migration of Japanese laborers for an indefinite period. But the Liberal prime minister, Sir Wilfrid Laurier, still found himself in an unenviable position. He seemed to be placating both the Japanese and Imperial authorities in a period of rising Canadian nationalism. British Columbia was, of course, particularly incensed. The Victoria *Daily Colonist* of June 24, 1903, commented, "Though all Chinese are Mongolians all Mongolians are not Chinese. Sir Wilfrid Laurier makes a distinction between Chinese and Japanese which, so far as their immigration affects this province, is not recognized in British Columbia. The provincial policy is one of the exclusion of Mongolians, the Laurier policy is one of the substitution of Japanese for Chinese." [79]

While the imperial bond appeared at best trivial in British Columbia, Laurier understood that, given existing constitutional arrangements, it placed some real constraints on his freedom of action. Canada might have the power to determine her willingness to adhere to commercial treaties of the Empire, but arrangements involving international politics and strategy remained, until after World War I, the exclusive preserve of London. Furthermore, by 1905 the commercial advantages of the Anglo-Japanese treaty of 1894 seemed sufficiently great to Canada (as they had earlier to Queensland) that the treaty was extended to cover the Dominion under the terms of the Anglo-Japanese Convention of 1905.

With the Japanese a continuing irritant, British Columbia's paranoia was about to be exacerbated by a sudden increase in immigration from India. Before 1905 there was but a mere handful of Indians in Canada. But between January 1905 and September 1907, 3,967 Indians entered the Dominion (of which

79. Andracki, 85.

number 1,274 continued on to the United States),[80] while a further 2,623 arrived in 1908.[81] Of the new arrivals, 90 percent were Sikhs, and they settled in British Columbia. These Punjabis were not the usual sort of docile Indian immigrants from the south and the Ganges plain, who were already a familiar part of the scene in South Africa and many other places, and they worked for the railway and in the lumber and fishing industries. To make matters worse from the white British Columbian's viewpoint, they were virtually all British subjects.

The local inhabitants became increasingly hostile to the new arrivals. They refused to sell them food or fuel, and in the dead of winter the plight of many became desperate. The Dominion minister of the interior suggested that each immigrant be required to have $500 in his possession before being granted admission.[82] The tirades from labor sounded familiar. The Victoria Trades and Labour Council contended:

that the Hindoos by reason of their caste prejudices, peculiar religious convictions, loathsome habits and obnoxious manner of living, can never assimilate with white people or perform the duties of desirable citizens of this Country.

That the country from which they come (India) has long been recognized as a hotbed of the most virulent and loathsome diseases such as Bubonic plague, Smallpox, Asiatic Cholera and the worst forms of Venereal diseases, and however strict the medical examination of our ports may be—there is a constant danger of these people being the means of transmission of diseases to our people.

That the introduction of this class of Cheap Labour will be the means of excluding the very class of labour that is most essential for the progress and prosperity of the country—i.e., white workers.

Industry, the council argued, could afford to pay the wages demanded by white labor. Admitting by implication that there

80. PAC, Records of the Immigration Branch, Dept. of the Interior, R.G. 76, 69/17, P.C. 2059/2060.
81. Andracki, 88.
82. PAC, Records of the Immigration Branch, Dept. of the Interior, R.G. 76, 69/17, P.C. 2059/2060, minister of the interior to the governor general in council, Nov. 27, 1906.

was an overall labor shortage, it urged employers to look to the crowded centers of Britain, "in preference to allowing the admission of a race of people who can never be of any use to Canada as citizens and whose very existence amongst our people would be a menace to the wellbeing of the community." [83]

A. S. Monro, the immigration agent in Vancouver, judged the Indians the most threatening of the nonwhite immigrants to Canada. "As competitors to white labor," he wrote his superiors in Ottawa, "they are the most dangerous we have, and they practically engage in the same class of work as the white laborers do, viz., mill work and street work. They will not engage in domestic labor, gardening or agricultural work that white men leave untouched, but seek the same lines of employment usually followed by the white laborer." When W. D. Scott, the superintendent of immigration, visited Vancouver, he reported that 25 Indians had died from exposure the previous year, an unfortunate episode which was sure to be repeated. Indians, Scott averred, were totally unsuited for immigration to Canada; not only were they wanting in proper social habits and incapable of assimilation into the body politic, but they were unable to survive the climate—an assertion that must have seemed strange to anyone familiar with the Punjab in winter.[84]

Under pressure from the Canadian Government, the Colonial Office requested the cooperation of the India Office, which in turn wrote the Government of India asking the viceroy to publicize the difficulties of life in British Columbia, the harshness of the climate, the lack of employment, and the consequent danger of becoming a public charge and of being deported. As a result, appropriate notification was posted by the department of commerce and industry, the division of the Government of

83. *Ibid.*, George F. Gray, president Victoria Trades and Labour Council to W. D. Scott, superintendent of immigration, Oct. 15, 1906.
84. *Ibid.*, A. S. Monro to W. D. Scott, Aug. 16, 1906; memorandum by W. D. Scott, Oct. 27, 1907.

India with jurisdiction over emigration affairs.[85] Colonel Falk Warren, a former officer in the Indian Army, thought the Indians very desirable immigrants but admitted that public antipathy put them in a most difficult position in regard to shelter, food and work, even though there continued to be a chronic labor shortage in the province. "They are subjects of our Empire," he wrote the India Office, and are yet denied the rights of citizenship by a large proportion of their fellow-subjects." [86] The Bengal newspaper, the *Daily Hitvadi*, wrote that the travails under which Indians suffered in the Transvaal were well known but,

> The condition of those Indians who go to British Columbia or Canada in search of bread is equally lamentable. The Sikhs and Pathans who are now in these two countries are without food or shelter. India's food is eaten by the foreigner, but the Indian who goes in search of food even in distant America, finds starvation staring him in the face. The principle of excluding the foreigner from Canada etc. would have force, if these Canadians and others refrained from earning immense wealth by trading with countries of these foreigners.[87]

The attitude of the British Columbia press was in marked contrast. The Vancouver *World* of November 19 proclaimed its pride in the British Empire: "Rome was made clean by each citizen sweeping dirt from his own door. British Columbians are proud of India, proud of her people, proud to regard them as copartners in the great business of empire, proud of East Indians as boys of the flag. But an East Indian in Canada is out of place." The same issue of the *World* ran an editorial under the headline "THE STRANGER THAT IS WITHIN OUR GATES," which read:

85. IOL, Govt. of India, Procs. of Dept. of Com. and Ind. (Em.), May 7-29, 1907, P. 5174/7682.
86. *Ibid.*, Colonel Falk Warren to the secretary of state for India, Jan. 2, 1907.
87. IOL, Reports of the Native Press, Bengal, *Daily Hitvadi*, Dec. 15, 1906.

The city of Vancouver is entering upon a grave crisis and the exercise of all the skill and diplomacy of its rulers is necessary to carry it safely through the difficulties that press upon it. A horde of peculiar people have been thrown upon our shores in a state of deep destitution. These people are strangers in apparel, in customs and religion. They are victims of the most absurd ideas as to caste as were ever cherished by human beings. Their "society" are more conventional than any that govern Mayfair, and it is deemed degrading for one sort to handle anything that has been in possession of a set lower down in the social scale. In the extremity of poverty and misery the caste humbug is maintained.

Although many of the Sikhs had seen service in the Indian Army and were considered among the best fighting men in the world, the possibility of their joining the provincial militia caused great resentment. The Vancouver *Daily Province* wrote: "Many of the militiamen would consider it an indignity to drill with the Sikhs and some have stated their intention of withdrawing from the ranks if the East Indians are admitted."[88]

The real source of British Columbian concern was clear. Between January 1, 1906, and the end of November, 2,193 Indians had arrived in Canada,[89] and the provincial administration must have feared that the entire population of the subcontinent was about to debouch into Vancouver. To make matters worse, H. L. Streatford, the officiating secretary to the Government of Bengal in the general department, contended that the government's attempts to discourage Indian emigration to Canada were destined to fail as long as wages in British Columbia remained high. He reported that 400 Sikhs had recently sailed on the *Laising* and that Messrs. Gillanders and Arbuthnot, acting as agents for the Canadian Pacific Railway, were said to have sold 1,200 tickets to Punjabis. The railroad was reported to be hiring Sikhs at $2–$3 a day.[90]

Ottawa was beginning to hear Victoria more clearly, and

88. Nov. 19, 1906.   89. Canada *Hansard,* Nov. 28, 1906.
90. IOL, Govt. of India, Procs. of Dept. of Com. and Ind. (Em.), Oct. 13–14, 1907, Streatford to the secretary to the Government of India in the Department of Commerce and Industry, Sept. 9, 1907.

post-1905 immigration laws, regulations drawn thereon, and orders in council reflected a growing sensitivity to the aspirations of the white electors of the province even though British Columbia until 1948 sent only six representatives to Parliament, compared to sixty-five for Quebec and sixty for Ontario. It has already been pointed out that the Dominion developed its own paths to restriction. As in the classic "Natal formula," the object was to leave the government the utmost leeway in the interpretation and administration of a highly flexible and apparently benign piece of legislation. Article 20 of the Immigration Act of 1906 (Chapter 19) stated that the governor in council "may provide as a condition to enter Canada that immigrants shall possess money to a prescribed minimum amount, which amount may vary according to the class and destination of such immigrant, and otherwise according to circumstances." Article 27 forbade the entry of paupers and beggars and those likely to become public charges. Persons becoming destitute could be deported within two years of their arrival in Canada. Article 30 empowered the governor general in council "by proclamation, or order, whenever he considers it necessary or expedient [to] prohibit the landing in Canada of any specified class of immigrants." Articles 69 and 70 provided for a fine of between $100 and $1,000 for masters and railroad companies who landed prohibited immigrants or refused to return them whence they came.

As usual British Columbia did not feel that the Dominion Government was acting with sufficient vigor, and Chapter 21 of 1907 was another attempt to pass a provincial immigration restriction act based on the "Natal formula." Upon hearing the news of its passage, Lord Lansdowne, the former governor general, exclaimed: "Confound those British Columbians! They used to play tricks of that kind even in my time, and we disallowed a number of their bills. Amongst them I remember one which in the guise of a sanitary regulation, forbade the exportation of bones and other animal remains, the real object being to prevent the poor Chinaman from regaining his own country and thence going where good Chinamen go after death."[91] When Lieutenant Governor James Dunsmuir, himself an employer of Asian labor, reserved the measure, the province reverberated with demands for his dismissal by Ottawa.

In the case of the Indians, a further irritant was added to the usual racial antipathy. The Punjabis in British Columbia were among the most vociferous dissenters from British rule in India to be found anywhere in the British Empire. It was among the Indians of the west coast that the *Ghadar* conspiracy of 1914 was spawned, and from the first years of the Indian presence in British Columbia, rumors of seditious activities by Indians filled the press and government reports. A headline in the Vancouver *World* of January 12, 1908, read: "SECRET SERVICE MEN GATHER DETAILS OF THREATENED UPRISING." The article went on to speak of Sikh plans to train revolutionaries, the making and storing of arms, and a huge plot to destroy the British Empire which was centered in the province. The Vancouver *Daily Province* ran a lurid exposé on a bomb factory allegedly run by Indians in Millside, B.C. Sub-headlines scattered throughout the article spoke of "INFERNAL MACHINES BEING TURNED OUT BY EXPERTS FOR USE OF MALCONTENTS IN INDIA . . . CONSPIRACY HATCHED IN SEATTLE . . . SCORES OF TURBANED WORKERS IN SAWMILL AT FRASER RIVER VILLAGE ARE SUBSCRIBING FUNDS TO BUY ARMS."[92] Not surprisingly, the governor general was able subsequently to report to the Colonial Office that there was no truth in the allegations.[93]

Nevertheless, the Indians were a sufficiently difficult group of immigrants for the Dominion Government to leap at an oppor-

91. Quoted in Margaret Ormsby, *British Columbia: A History* (Toronto, 1971), 350.
92. Vancouver *Daily Province,* Nov. 6, 1908.
93. CO 42/921, no. 476, Grey to Crewe, Nov. 24, 1908.

tunity to rid British Columbia of at least some of them. British Honduras, after some preliminary correspondence, declared itself both willing and anxious to welcome some of the British Columbian Sikhs to its shores.[94] The colony was even prepared to defray the passage costs of some 700.[95] But, despite a favorable report filed by an Indian delegation sent by the Dominion Government, the whole affair came to nought when the delegation, upon returning to British Columbia, was forced to recant by Indian "agitators." [96]

With the Indian question in crisis and the future of Japanese immigration to Canada not permanently resolved, Chinese immigration which had dropped to zero in the second half of 1903 after the implementation of the $50 entrance tax, suddenly jumped to 1,482 between July 1907 and March 1908.[97] Once again, the sudden halting of the Chinese labor supply had served to improve the bargaining position of the Chinese already in British Columbia. Within two years of the passage of the Chinese Immigration Restriction Act of 1903, wages for Chinese laborers essentially doubled, making it attractive for Chinese once more to come to Western Canada even at an initial cost of the passage plus $500.[98] As for the Japanese, it was

---

94. IOL, Govt. of India, Procs. of Dept. of Com. and Ind. (Em.), Feb. 16, 1910.

95. British Honduras Ordinance no. 20, 1918, "To Authorise Advances to pay the Passage of Certain Indians."

96. IOL, Govt. of India, Procs. of Dept. of Com. and Ind. (Em.), Feb. 1909, no. 18, tel., sec. of state to viceroy, Nov. 27, 1908.

97. Cheng, 70.

98. Andracki, 123. Chinese paying the $500 entrance tax:

January 1904—June 30, 1904	0
July 1, 1904—June 30, 1905	8
July 1, 1905—June 30, 1906	22
July 1, 1906—June 30, 1907	91

CO 42/935, Jordan to Grey, Apr. 1, 1909. Further figures on Chinese immigrants paying the $500 tax:

April 1907—March 1908	1,432
April 1, 1908—August 31, 1908	1,095

not clear whether the unilateral prohibition on the emigration of laborers effected by the Government of Japan in 1902 was still in operation. During the first years of the twentieth century, essentially no Japanese entered Canada, but in the fiscal year ending in June 1905, 354 Japanese immigrants arrived, and in the following year the number rose to 1,922. Between August 1906 and September 1907, 614 Chinese, 2,474 Indians and 6,406 Japanese landed in the Dominion.[99]

The Chinese clearly constituted only a minor problem; not so the Indians and the Japanese, at least in the eyes of white British Columbia. But to exclude these two groups was fraught with difficulty. The Indians were, after all, British subjects, and Japan was a nation in close alliance with Great Britain and hence the British Empire. Canada had furthermore voluntarily joined in the Anglo-Japanese commercial treaty of 1894. To exacerbate matters, the Government of Japan was extremely sensitive about its national dignity and the rights accorded its subjects abroad. It was helpless to do much anyway, as a large proportion of the new immigrants came not from the home islands but from Hawaii (for example, most of the more than 8,000 Japanese who arrived in British Columbia in 1907). The fact that many of these immigrants (3,619 in 1907) continued on to the United States did little to assuage British Columbia's concern.[100]

In Parliament, with another election approaching, Laurier pointed to great increases in trade between Japan and Canada,[101] while his Conservative rival, Robert L. Borden, appealed to the labor vote. "So far as Japanese immigration is concerned," he declared, "I have already said from the public plat-

99. CO 42/916, 36737, North America (General), conf., James Bryce to Sir Edward Grey, Sept. 14, 1907.
100. Wynne, 403–4.
101. Canada *Hansard,* Sept. 21, 1907. CO 42/913, 39458, Grey to Elgin, Oct. 29, 1907. The total trade in 1907 amounted to $2,601,536 (of which amount imports were valued at $2,017,536). In 1900 the trade had come to less than $350,000. CO 45/1003, Canada, Sessional Papers, 1909, paper 746.

form that at present I regard it as a purely economic question. It is a question between labouring men in British Columbia accustomed to a certain condition of living, and immigrants from China and Japan who are accustomed to other conditions of life, and with whom the labouring men of British Columbia and some of the provinces feel they cannot compete on even terms." [102]

The rising wave of anti-Oriental feeling in British Columbia prompted the establishment of an Asiatic Exclusion League in Vancouver in mid-August. The new organization was inspired by a similar one in the state of Washington, and the expulsion of over a thousand Indians from Bellingham, Washington, many of whom filtered across the border into Canada, prompted what was essentially an Anglo-American campaign against Asians in the Pacific Northwest.

On September 8, 1907, the Vancouver league mounted a demonstration at which, after the playing of "Rule Britannia," an effigy of Lieutenant Governor Dunsmuir was burned to the accompaniment of inflammatory speeches. The meeting took place at the city hall, which happened to be near the Chinese and Japanese quarters of Vancouver. Its passions inflamed, the crowd, numbering some 500, disintegrated into a mob and infiltrated the neighboring precincts that harbored the hated Asians. The invading force soon rose to 700, and in several sallies it damaged stores, offices, hotels, schools, and whatever else fell to hand. At first the Japanese did little to defend themselves and their property. But they eventually reached their limit of tolerance and, arming themselves with sticks, bottles, and knives, fell upon their oppressors, shouting "Banzai!" Laurier remarked to the governor general, Lord Grey, that "the Japs showed fight, turned upon their assailants, and routed them. This is at once a cause for rejoicing and for anxiety; rejoicing because the rowdies got a well deserved licking; anxiety because this may make the Japs very saucy, and

102. Canada *Hansard,* Sept. 14, 1907.

render an adjustment of the trouble difficult." Grey himself was furious and mortified. "In B.C. the people appear to have lost their heads," he told the secretary of state, the ninth Earl of Elgin, while to Laurier he wrote, "I hope the result of the investigation by the Govt. into the causes of this abominable outbreak may be to show that it was not spontaneous but the work of Seattle and other American organisations."[103] (Soon, however, Grey became more sympathetic to the anti-Asian attitude of British Columbia and he wrote Elgin that he feared "the inevitable tussle between the White and Yellow races may come before *we* are ready for it!"[104])

The incident led the Canadian Government to take prompt action. To keep a close watch on anti-Asian groups on both sides of the border, Frank Oliver, the minister of the interior, sent T. R. E. McInnes to report on the activities of the Asiatic Exclusion League and its sister organization, as well as on the Chinese, Japanese and Indians themselves. Of greater significance was Laurier's decision to send the postmaster general, Rodolphe Lemieux, to Japan, to negotiate a "gentleman's agreement" under the terms of which Japan would again voluntarily curtail emigration to Canada. Finally, W. L. Mackenzie King, the future Liberal prime minister, was appointed commissioner to conduct an inquiry. The Dominion Government immediately tendered its deepest regrets to the Japanese Emperor, promising to pay reparations.[105] But to the Chinese it at first offered no compensation, on the strange assumption that treaty obligations bound the government to deal fairly with the Japanese but the lack of a treaty with China made similar treatment of the luckless Chinese unnecessary.[106] Soon, however, under Foreign Office prompting,[107] the Canadian authorities agreed

103. Ormsby, 351.   104. *Ibid.*, 353.
105. CO 42/916, 41758, tel., Laurier to MacDonald, Oct. 12, 1907.
106. CO 42/914, 41581, Grey to Elgin, Nov. 28, 1907.
107. CO 42/916, 1907, contains correspondence between the Chinese Govt. and the Foreign Office and between the Foreign Office and the Colonial Office.

to treat both aggrieved parties equally. All in all, King recommended compensation amounting to some $27,000 for the Chinese victims of the riots and $11,000 for the Japanese.[108]

A few months later, in January 1908, a further incident almost incited a renewed outburst of violence. Three firemen somewhat the worse for wear from drink fell through a shop window in the Japanese section of Vancouver. With memories of the autumn riots still green they were set upon by the local residents and sent to the hospital. The Japanese willingness to defend themselves particularly irked many British Columbians. The chief constable of Vancouver wrote immediately subsequent to the incident:

I'm very sorry for this occurrence as matters were just quieting down after the trouble in September. The Japanese are likely to cause us some trouble in the near future and while I do not think there is much immediate danger it is bound to come sooner or later and the Japs have become so cocky and independent that they will have to be put in their place. I do not know that it is generally known that they can muster in very short notice anywhere from ten to twelve thousand trained men, and should they break loose we would be utterly helpless with our present defense. I do not wish to cause alarm in this matter but it has caused me many an anxious thought of late and I really think that we should have at least three or four machine guns attached to our local corps in this city. Nothing would please the Japs better than to have a reoccurrence of the trouble after being so handsomely compensated for their loss during the last riot. To my mind they were paid ten times more than they should have been.[109]

In Tokyo, Lemieux after intensive negotiations came up with a formula which satisfied both Japan's *amor propre* and the aspirations of the Canadian Government. It was agreed that

108. King visited England in March 1908 and held amicable conversations with His Majesty's Government on the subject of Asian immigration to Canada (Cd. 4118, 1908, "Report of Mr. W. L. Mackenzie King on his Mission to England in Connection with the Immigration of Asiatics into Canada").

109. PAC, Laurier Papers, 135713, chief constable of Vancouver to Colonel Sherwood, Jan. 10, 1908.

Japanese emigration to Canada would be prohibited with the exception of (1) resident Japanese returning to Canada; (2) bona fide servants for Japanese residents; (3) immigrants brought in under contracts approved by the Dominion Government; and (4) agricultural laborers for farms owned by Japanese, who were to be brought in under the same restrictions that prevailed between the United States and Japan—i.e., from five to ten laborers per hundred acres. The Japanese Government assumed that the last two named classes of immigrants would not exceed 400 annually.[110]

On the Indian front, the continuing arrival of "Hindoos" in British Columbia was adding heat to an already explosive situation. On November 11, 1907, the governor general telegraphed London that an outbreak of violence was expected in Vancouver upon the docking of the next vessel bearing Indians in any number. The recent arrival of 900 Indians on a single ship (the *Mounteagle*) at a time when the lumber industry, their chief source of employment, was going on a winter schedule had brought events to a climax. On behalf of his government, the governor general outlined the policy that Ottawa wished to adopt in order to cool the atmosphere. The Canadian privy council had drafted an order in council under the terms of which permission to enter Canada would be denied all Indians who did not have in their possession at least $200.[111] The governor general felt that he would have to sign the order unless he could assure his ministers that the Government of India and the British authorities had resolved (1) to prohibit Indians from sailing for Canada without passports; (2) to limit the number of passports issued to a level not exceeding a number agreed upon by the Governments of India and Canada; and (3) to permit Canada to deport all Indians arriving at Canadian ports

---

110. CO 42/919, 17790, no. 211, Grey to Crewe, May 6, 1908, encl. memorandum by Lemieux, May 5, 1908.

111. The inspiration for this idea had been in the report of the 1908 Royal Commission on Oriental Labor chaired by Mackenzie King.

without passports.[112] Lord Morley at the Indian Office, rather than approving the passport system, left matters in the hands of the Canadian privy council.[113]

The Government of Canada subsequently developed a two-pronged policy to keep British Indians from the Dominion's shores. The first stratagem was an ingenious new concept—that of the "continuous journey." An order in council of January 8, 1908 (P.C. 27), stipulated: "The Governor General in Council is pleased to order and it is hereby ordered that whenever in the opinion of the Minister, the condition of the labour market in Canada is such as to . . . render [it] necessary . . . immigrants may be prohibited from landing or coming into Canada unless they come from the country of their birth or citizenship by a continuous journey *and on through* tickets purchased before leaving the country of their birth or citizenship." There being no direct steamship service between India and Canada, the order in council provided an effective weapon to combat further Indian immigration to Canada—at least until the advent of a direct service by means of charter or regular schedule —and to exclude Japanese from Hawaii as well. Within a few weeks, however, the order in council was judged as *ultra vires* of the legislature (in the case of Behari Lal) because in it the governor general delegated power granted only to him by Parliament.[114]

The government as a result decided to put the new tactic on a more secure footing and on March 26, 1908, the minister of the interior moved the "continuous journey" clause as an amendment to the immigration act of 1906. The minister veiled his purpose in subterfuge, asserting that the amendment was necessary to prevent the possibility of a port such as Hong Kong not admitting a Japanese subject deported from Canada

---

112. CO 42/914, 39809, tel., Grey to Elgin, Nov. 11, 1907.
113. PAC, R.G. 7, G. 21, Governor General's numbered files, no. 332, vol. 2(b), 1908, IO to CO, June 3, 1908.
114. Andracki, 98.

because he was an alien.¹¹⁵ As a further precaution, the Dominion did, after all, promulgate an order in council (May 27, 1908) requiring Asian immigrants to have $200 in their possession.

Lord Crewe, the secretary of state for India, and hence the duly appointed protector of Indian rights, clearly understood the true nature of things when he addressed the Imperial Conference of 1911 in words very reminiscent of Joseph Chamberlain on another occasion:

> I fully recognise, as Her Majesty's Government fully recognises, that as the Empire is constituted, the idea that . . . every subject of the king, whoever he may be, or wherever he may live, has a natural right to travel or still more to settle in any part of the Empire, is a view . . . which cannot be maintained. . . . In the absence of any positive law to the contrary, a British national is probably entitled to claim the right of entry into any part of the British Empire but a competent legislative authority of any part of the Empire may, by positive law, restrict or deny that right of entry.¹¹⁶

Canadian legislation combined with the attitude of His Majesty's Government to the Dominion's satisfaction. Whereas 2,124 Indians landed in Canadian ports in 1907 and 2,623 in 1908, only 6 did so in 1909, 10 in 1910, 5 in 1911, 3 in 1912 and 5 in 1913.¹¹⁷

Meanwhile the Dominion Government determined to buttress its position by a diplomatic offensive of sorts to be led by the peripatetic Mackenzie King. He was appointed Canadian member on the Joint Commission on Opium scheduled to meet in Shanghai. On the way, King first stopped in Washington to confer with Theodore Roosevelt. The President was full of good cheer. He averred that American and Canadian interests were identical on the question of Oriental immigration.

---

115. *Ibid.*, 99–100. The amended law became Chapter 33 of 1908. An order in council of May 27, 1908 (P.C. 932) actuated the clause.
116. Andracki, 103.   117. *Ibid.*, 88.

"Gentlemen," he said, "we have got to protect our working men. We have got to build up our western country with our white civilization and (very vehemently) we must retain the power to say who shall and who shall not come to our country. Now, it may be that Japan will adopt a different attitude, will demand that her people be permitted to go where they think fit, so I THOUGHT IT WISE TO SEND THAT FLEET AROUND TO THE PACIFIC TO BE READY TO MAINTAIN OUR RIGHTS."

Continuing, the President said: "Now, Gentlemen, I don't make threats, but I was once a frontiersman and we had a saying there, 'Don't draw unless you mean to shoot,' so I felt that in the consideration of the issues involved I had to send the fleet to the Pacific. I might say that the fleet is there in the interests of the whole Pacific Coast, the interests of British Columbia as well as those of California, and it is in the interests of Australia as well."

Dr. Thompson [a Canadian member of Parliament] enquired if the Monroe Doctrine applied to the Pacific Coast.

"Yes," replied the President, "and to Australia as well—if it doesn't I'll make it apply."

He then said that we could tell Sir Wilfrid just what he had told us and that the United States would stand by Canada in the settlement of this question. He mentioned the difficulty that Canada had to face, but appreciated the circumstances surrounding the Imperial Treaty, understanding that British interests in India were factors which influenced the Imperial authorities to enter into the convention with Japan. "We also wish to have friendly relations with Japan, but you know self preservation is the first law of nature. I have my troubles here, but I am going to have peace, IF I HAVE TO FIGHT FOR IT." [118]

Not familiar with the President's penchant for hyperbole King got more than he bargained for and beat a hasty retreat. He proceeded on his mission to China, stopping in India to confer

---

118. CO 42/918, Conf. Memorandum: Interview with President Roosevelt at Washington, on Monday, February 10. Present: the President, Roger Smith, M.P., Dr. McIntyre, M.P., Dr. Thompson, M.P., B. C. Nicholas. Whether King was present at this particular meeting or just heard about it is not totally clear. His name did not appear on the list of those attending noted above.

with the government, which declared itself gratified at the "continuous journey" and $200 enactments because they resulted in the exclusion of Indians, "without resorting to invidious legislation aimed particularly at British Indians." [119]

King arrived in Peking empowered to barter the abolishment of the $500 entrance tax, so offensive to Chinese self-esteem, for an agreement based on the Lemieux formula.[120] At first the prospect of success was promising. The British ambassador in Peking informed the Foreign Office that the Chinese seemed sympathetic to the concept of emigration control by means of passports. "This struck me as likely to prove the turning point of the negotiations," he reported, "and although a successful issue is by no means assured, the ground has been so carefully examined, that even should the present attempt to arrive at an arrangement fail, an eventual solution has been greatly facilitated." [121] But although there did indeed seem to be some general agreement between King and his Chinese counterpart, Liang Ten-yen, Acting President of the Chinese Foreign Office (they had, after all, both attended Harvard!), that there should be both a passport system and an absolute limit on Chinese laborers permitted to enter Canada annually (the numbers 400 and 500 were mooted) and that in return for this Chinese concession the Canadian Government would repeal the entrance tax provision, Liang insisted that the conversations could be no more than preliminary and would have to be continued at a later date.[122] Despite their nation's travails, the Chinese maintained their innate sense of superiority. The Canadian (and Australian) attitudes towards Chinese immigrants were consequently particularly irritating, and Liang reflected his government's displeasure. He told King that for "the Chinese govern-

119. IOL, Govt. of India, Dept. of Com. and Ind. (Em.), Mar. 1909, no. 18, Minto to Morley, Mar. 11, 1908.
120. *Ibid.,* Mar. 1909, no. 13, secret letter, Grey to Crewe, Dec. 11, 1908.
121. CO 42/933, 13685, Jordan to Grey, Mar. 17, 1909.
122. *Ibid.,* Apr. 1, 1909.

ment to tell its people they were not to leave China to go to Canada was for the Chinese government to slap its own people in the face that Canada might be relieved from slapping them." "Mr. Liang," King noted, "thought the Chinese were kept out because China was a weak power, that Chinese were excluded while Germans and Greeks and Italians were admitted." [123] King did his best to counter Liang's points, but despite the anticipated conclusion of a draft agreement the talks were never resumed.

In Canada, the whole Asian immigration question became more inflamed as the election grew nearer. Liberals in British Columbia urged action on the government with increasing urgency. A letter to William Templeman, the Dominion minister of revenue, read: "Ottawa blundering [in disallowing the 1907 British Columbia Immigration Act] has cost the B. C. Liberal party heavily and gives it an almost impossible task in the coming campaign to reelect the present representatives. If Dunsmuir is retained, the task, so far as the Island and lower mainland constituencies are concerned, would be altogether hopeless." [124]

The Conservatives were never slow to take advantage of the Asian immigration issue, and Borden made full use of all the standard clichés. He asserted that the Chinese presence would injure the Canadian standard of living and that British Columbia should be occupied "by a large and thoroughly British population rather than one in which the number of aliens would form a large proportion." As for the Japanese, "their presence in large numbers delays the settlement of the country and keeps out intending settlers; and all that has been said in regard to the Chinese applies with equal if not greater force to the Japanese." [125] The *Colonist* of October 25, 1908, printed a telegram

123. *Ibid.*, King resumés of Mar. 10 and 17, 1909.
124. PAC, Laurier Papers, 133487, copy of an extract of a letter to the Hon. William Templeman from F. J. Deane, Dec. 1907.
125. PAC, Borden Papers, vol. 233. "The Question of Oriental Im-

from Borden which read, "The Conservative Party stands for a white Canada, the protection of white labour and the absolute exclusion of Asiatics." Premier McBride, himself a Conservative and the first partisan leader of a British Columbia Government, empowered his attorney general, W. J. Bowser, to reintroduce the "Natal formula" legislation into the provincial legislature. It was again disallowed by Ottawa, and Laurier, although he won the 1908 election, lost four seats in British Columbia.

The combination of the Lemieux agreement, the diplomatic offensive led by Mackenzie King, and the "continuous journey" and $200 provisions of Dominion laws and orders in council prevented the government's losses from being greater. Chapter 27 of the Dominion code, the immigration act of 1910, essentially completed the corpus of immigration legislation Canada felt it needed to keep unwanted immigrants of color from its door. It was drafted in the broadest possible terms so as to allow the subsequent promulgation through orders in council of more specific regulations. Most of what the act contained was not new. It was more a document of consolidation. It did, however, identify a new class of prohibited immigrants. Earlier laws had excluded persons who were physically, mentally or morally deficient. Now a category was created whose constituents could be identified only by subsequent government action. Section 3(i) of the act added to the list of prohibited immigrants: "Persons . . . who do not fulfill, meet or comply with the conditions or requirements of any regulations which for the time being are in force and applicable to such persons under Sections 37 and 38 of this Act." Section 37 allowed the governor in council to establish a minimum amount of money to be required of immigrants "which . . . may vary according to their race, occupation, or destination . . . and otherwise according to the circumstances." Section 38 empowered the governor in council to prohibit the landing of any immigrant who had not come to

migration: Speeches (in part) Delivered by R. L. Borden, M.P., in 1907 and 1908," Vancouver, 4–5, Sept. 24, 1907.

Canada by a continuous journey from his native land. Finally, sub-section c of the same article permitted the governor in council to "prohibit for a stated period, or permanently, the landing in Canada or the landing at any specified port of entry in Canada, of immigrants belonging to any race deemed unsuited to the climate or requirements of Canada, or of immigrants of any specific class, occupation, or character." This last clause was new, and it was so all-encompassing as to cover any loophole the legislators might inadvertently have failed to plug.[126]

According to custom, Parliament delegated a great deal of quasi-legislative power to the government in terms of authority to make regulations and issue orders in council under the act, and it was in these regulations and orders that the real teeth of the measure were hidden. Thus, what Burke called "the decent drapery of life" was drawn over the whole proceeding. An order in council (P.C. 926) of May 9, 1910, repromulgated under the new act the $200 requirement for Asians desiring to enter Canada, "unless such a person is a native or subject of an Asiatic country in regard to which special statutory regulations are in force [China] or with which the Government of Canada has made a special treaty, agreement or convention [Japan]." Another order in council of the same day (P.C. 920) re-established the "continuous journey" regulation.[127]

---

126. The Union of South Africa, in its legislation of 1913, used a similar device to guard against any unanticipated loopholes in its defenses against unwanted immigrants. In clause 4(1)(a) of Act 22 the minister of the interior was empowered to declare a prohibited immigrant "any person or class of persons deemed by the Minister on economic grounds or on account of standards or habits of life to be unsuitable to the requirements of the Union."

127. To further secure Canada against Indian immigration, orders in council of Dec. 8, 1913 (P.C. 2642) and Mar. 31, 1914 (P.C. 897) prohibited the entry into Canada of "artisans or labourers, skilled or unskilled" for a period of four months. The orders were not applied to Chinese until later and not to Japanese at all because of the Lemieux agreement.

As the governor general explained the purpose of the $200 requirement as opposed to the $25 demanded of European immigrants, it was in the view of his government at least in part "to safeguard Canada against a possible influx of an inferior class of immigrants whose influx will lead to lower standards which it is the desire of the Government to raise to as high a level as possible." It was believed "that the regulations adopted by H.M.'s Canadian Government will fulfill the object they have in view, that namely of securing for Canada the reputation of being a country inhabited by a high class of people." [128]

The status of Indians, who were after all British subjects, continued to be a source of embarrassment both in London and Calcutta. Lord Morley at the India Office timidly objected to the immigration bill of 1910,[129] and the Indian community itself determined to send a delegation to London.[130] But it was to no avail. It is perhaps ironical that the Canadian Liberals did, after all, lose the election of September 1911, although the issue that defeated them was the recently signed reciprocity agreement with the United States, not Asian immigration. Be that as it may, Sir Wilfrid Laurier and his government, despite a marked lack of enthusiasm, had forged, for political reasons, the legislative basis for a "White Canada." [131]

In its purest form, the "Natal formula" was simply a means for keeping unwanted immigrants out of a colony through the use of a mechanism which seemed innocuous in legislation. The spirit of the "Natal formula," however, was to find its way into legal enactments which had nothing to do with immigration but rather with the lives of nonwhites who were legally resident in the colonies of settlement. And it is with this subject that the next chapter will deal.

128. CO 42/938, 17257, pvt. and conf., Grey to Crewe, May 23, 1910.
129. CO 42/993, IO 7178, IO to CO, Mar. 9, 1910.
130. CO 42/993, 16667, IO to CO, June 2, 1910.
131. The Canadian census of 1911 listed 19,565 Chinese, 8,587 Japanese, and 2,291 East Indians in British Columbia out of a total provincial population of 392,480.

4 White Colonist versus Colored Immigrant

The "Natal formula" became the basis of immigration restriction policy throughout the Empire of Settlement. It allowed the colonies concerned to bar the stranger from the gates and at the same time to draw the "veil of decency" over the proceedings for the sake of the British Government. But immigration was always but a part of the problem from the white settlers' point of view. What about the nonwhites already established as legal residents? Clearly, they had to be prevented from sullying a "white civilization" whose standards they neither appreciated nor respected and which they could defile so long as they possessed rights such as the franchise, the liberty to compete "unfairly" in business, or even what would seem merely the normal concomitants of bare existence.

As had been the case on the immigration issue, Natal was the first colony to deal in a substantive way with the problems engendered by the actual residence of nonwhites. Pietermaritzburg and Durban subjected Indians to local vagrancy laws, "by which all persons of Colour, if found in the streets after 9 o'clock *without a pass* are liable to arrest as vagrants." [1] Law 21 of 1888, the Registration of Servants Law, classified Indians as members of "an uncivilised race," and Law 20 of 1890 limited the right of indentured Indians and their descendants to drink intoxicating liquor. Moreover, anti-Indian feeling in

---

1. NA, gov. to sec. of state, Sept. 7, 1878. Natal Law 15 of 1869 dealt with vagrancy.

Natal was to find expression in threats and actions that went well beyond the curtailment of the right of some Indians to consume alcoholic beverages.

The franchise in Natal was a highly restrictive one (requiring the possession of £50 in property or the payment of £20 annual rent as a prerequisite for inclusion on the voters' rolls). Although very few Indians were as a consequence eligible (181 in 1882 according to the Protector of Indian Immigrants' report for that year), that even a small number had the legal right to vote was a cause of great fear. On February 3, 1880, one representative (Miller) gave vent to his emotion in the legislative council:

> The only feelings I have in this matter is one of disgust that these men [the Indians] should be on the electoral roll.... Who are these people? The scum of Madras and Calcutta. The idea of them coming here to have the electoral franchise conferred on them is monstrous. It was amongst these men at the last election that bribery took place; they got their half-crown and they voted. It is a most disreputable thing in my opinion to have such men put on the roll.... When this charter was published it was never intended to confer this right on them.

Several times during 1880–1881 legislative assaults were mounted to deprive Indians of the right to vote in parliamentary elections. They were repulsed only through the combined efforts of the governor, the Colonial Office, and the planters, who feared that such an action would prompt the Government of India to end indentured immigration to Natal once and for all. The course of future events was, however, presaged by Colonial Office minuting. The writer (probably Sir Robert Herbert, the permanent undersecretary) said that he did not think "the welfare of either Coolie or Native would be directly promoted by giving . . . [them] votes within the ordinary electorates, their votes could be obtained by treating and bribery, by candidates who had their own ends to serve and who might promise to obtain for them injurious concessions (such as the removal of restrictions on purchasing spirits) and would be obliged in order to obtain their votes to oppose measures disliked by Natives or Coolies but necessary for health and good order." [2]

The first efforts to deprive the Indians of the franchise came at a time of deepening uneasiness about the whole subject of the Indian presence. The major source of animosity was of course the "Arab." With his appearance in Natal, a more self-confident and ambitious element was introduced into the Indian population of the colony. Under "Arab" leadership, Indians for the first time voiced their unhappiness in a petition to the secretary of state for the colonies. They resented the 9 P.M. curfew in Durban and Pietermaritzburg, and they requested that shops be allowed to open on Sunday, the only day on which indentured Indians had free time. They complained about police brutality and the lack of interpreters and Indians on juries in the supreme court. London and Calcutta reacted immediately, and dispatches flowed to Pietermaritzburg demanding an immediate response.[3]

The beginning of Indian political activity and commercial competition aroused the petty bourgeois establishment that held sway in Natal's towns and cities and wielded influence in the council chambers of the colonial capital. Indian merchants were falsely accused of contributing nothing to the general weal and of succeeding in business as a consequence of the squalor in which they lived. Reports from outlying districts sounded the tocsin with increasing urgency. In 1885, for instance, the Lion's Head Division announced: "Complaints continue to be made of the increasing number of Indian traders and hawkers in the district. These people render it impossible for small European

2. CO 179/144, Natal minute paper 1405, Jan. 23, 1882, minuting of Feb. 3, 1882.
3. NAI, Govt. of India, Dept. of Rev. and Ag. (Em.), Nov. 1884, procs. 9–10, "Memorial from the Indian Residents in Natal Relative to Certain Grievances Under Which They Represent Themselves to be Suffering in that Colony."

store-keepers to make a living, and all the Native trade of the Colony is getting into the hands of the Free Indians." [4]

Two rival camps now faced each other—on the one side, the white settlers, members of what Joseph Chamberlain called "the greatest of governing races the world has ever seen"; [5] on the other, the Indians, mostly of humble Hindu origin but leavened by a sprinkling of Muslim merchants of higher standing. Largely deprived of civil and political rights, the Indians aspired to equality under the law, and what would normally have been a far from cohesive community was progressively forced towards cooperation, at least in the political sphere. Moreover, the Indians were just as convinced of the superiority of their cutural heritage as the white man was of his, and they were determined to maintain their own identity as British Indian subjects settled in South Africa. At many levels they did not wish to assimilate with the Europeans, who, despite disdain for their new colored neighbors, could not understand the Indians' failure to wait patiently, hat in hand, outside the shrine of Victorian Anglo-Saxonism.

In 1893, thirty-three years after the first indentured Indian had entered Natal, the colony was granted self-government. It was a moment when the white settlers were united on a number of points vis-à-vis their Indian neighbors, and the colony's new constitutional status made the attainment of these objectives a distinct possibility. In addition to their feelings on immigration restriction, which have already been discussed, the whites agreed that Indian laborers should no longer be permitted to remain in Natal at the conclusion of their contracts. They were determined to close the voters' rolls to those already there. And they sought to impede the licensing of Indians to conduct business in Natal.

4. Mabel Palmer, *The History of the Indians in Natal* (Cape Town, 1957), 46.
5. Garvin, II, 27, quoting the *Times,* Nov. 12, 1895.

As an initial step towards the desired goals, a Natal delegation visited India in 1894 and attempted to gain Calcutta's assent to a plan that would have required the repatriation of all indentured immigrants before their contracts actually expired. In this the delegates failed, but they did gain the Government of India's approval for the passage of a particularly pernicious measure—a £3 tax to be levied on formerly indentured Indians who would not return to their native land. This law, Natal Act 17 of 1895, was never successful in inducing ex-indentured Indians to leave the colony. On the other hand, it was the intention of the framers of the legislation that the fee be collected not only from adults but from minors as well, although this last point was not completely clear in the law. For a family with an average annual income of from £12 to £16, the burden must have been almost unendurable.

The £3 tax measure was only one of the overtly offensive laws and practices frequently condoned by the Colonial Office. "Coolies" were required to register when in a town on the basis of their belonging to an "uncivilised race"; [6] and Law 15 of 1869 had not been disallowed even though its second section stated that "every coloured person [a designation that included Indians] found wandering abroad in a Borough after and before such hours as the Corporation may fix, and not giving a good account of himself or herself, is liable on conviction to hard labour not exceeding three months, or to a fine not exceeding £5." [7] In addition, under the terms of Act 38 of 1896, Indians could drink only on licensed premises and then the liquor had to be served to them in glasses. More significantly, Indians were usually excluded from government high schools,[8] and made liable to arrest unless in possession of a pass.[9] The pass law was

6. Natal Law 21 of 1888.
7. NA, Gen. Conf. Desps. from Natal, gov. to high comm., Cape Town, Aug. 24, 1898.
8. *Ibid.*, Natal no. 7, gov. to sec. of state, Jan. 13, 1909.
9. Natal Act 28 of 1897.

ostensibly enacted to protect free Indians from being apprehended in error. It stipulated that such Indians were entitled to a pass, possession of which was proof that they were not absconding indentured laborers. But because the act gave the police protection from suits for false arrest should they take into custody a free Indian without a pass, its chief effect was to make it mandatory for free Indians to carry passes. Considerable pressure from the British and Indian Governments resulted in the passage of Natal Act 18 of 1898, which provided that an arresting officer was protected from legal action for false arrest only if he apprehended an Indian without a pass "under a bona fide belief or suspicion that he was an indentured Indian." But to prove that such a suspicion was not present at the time of arrest was, of course, impossible.

The removal of Indians from the electoral rolls was still considered a matter of great urgency. In 1894 a bill denying Indians the right to vote in Natal parliamentary elections was read a second time in the legislature, but the Colonial Office would not countenance it as "to assent to this measure would be to put an affront upon the people of India as no British Government could be a party to." [10] But this word from on high did nothing to quench the fires of animosity in the legislative assembly. Asiatics, it was asserted, had no experience in voting, and even the most sophisticated Indians in Durban were said to have become confused by the election procedure. The prime minister thought that there were so many Indians in Natal that the white man might be swamped at the polls, and he even attempted to use a vast petition of protest sent by the Indian community to the secretary of state for the colonies to his advantage. "There are only 10,729 electors already on the rolls of the Colony," he wrote. "Consequently had the Petitioners their desire, at this moment they would form nine-tenths of the elec-

---

10. NA, Natal no. 27, sec. of state to gov., Sept. 21, 1895.

torate." [11] The fact that the property qualifications for the franchise denied the vote to virtually all Indians seemed to have been conveniently forgotten.[12]

With an eye to the future, the prime minister exclaimed that the restriction of the franchise was "a duty we owe not only to ourselves, the Colonists of Natal, but to South Africa." [13] Upon being approached by a delegation of Indians, he disingenuously declared that "the very fact that their people were to be disqualified in the Bill from exercising the franchise was in itself an absolute guarantee that the Government would consider itself under a special obligation to promote their interests." [14]

As in the case of the immigration restriction act, it did not take long for the white colonists of Natal to discern a solution that the Colonial Office could tolerate. Only two years after the rejection of its original franchise act, Natal was able to disenfranchise for the future all Indians, regardless of qualifications, who were not at that time on the voters' rolls. The colonial legislators simply stipulated that those "who (not being of European origin) are Natives or descendants in the male line of Natives of countries which have not hitherto possessed elective institutions," unless exempted by the governor in council, could not vote in parliamentary elections.[15]

With the specific racial terminology removed, the Colonial Office's objections to the measure essentially dissolved. Edward Wingfield, Chamberlain's chief aide, although he personally de-

11. Natal Leg. Assem. Sess. Paps., 1896, L.A. no. 6, Apr. 21, 1896, corres. re. the franchise law, ministers to gov., July 27, 1894.

12. There were at the time 251 Indians on the voters' roll as compared to 9,650 Europeans—a ratio of 1:38.

13. Natal *Hansard*, June 20, 1894.   14. *Ibid.*, July 2, 1894.

15. Natal Act 8 of 1896. Natal considered the bill in its final form a concession to the Colonial Office. The colony's government would have preferred a more extreme measure. Hely-Hutchinson, in urging the bill's prompt ratification by the British Government, wrote to Chamberlain (Chamberlain Papers, JC 10/17/34) on Aug. 19, 1896, that "the Natal Ministers practically adopted a private suggestion which emanated from

plored discriminatory legislation aimed at Indians, concluded that "in the present state of colonial opinion . . . it is impossible in the self-governing colonies to require that British Indians shall be placed in exactly the same position as European British subjects." [16] The secretary of state himself wrote to Natal, "It is manifestly the desire and intention of your Government that the destinies of the Colony of Natal shall continue to be shaped by the Anglo-Saxon race and that the possibility of any preponderant influx of Asiatic voters be averted." [17] As this position was one with which Chamberlain had previously indicated agreement,[18] he was "not prepared to advise Her Majesty to exercise her powers of disallowance . . . [although he was] in communication with the Government of Natal on the subject of preserving the rights of those of Her Majesty's Indian subjects who were already resident in Natal." [19] There was, after all, little reason for objection, Chamberlain contended; nothing in the act specifically excluded either British Indians or other non-Europeans from entering Natal. The law merely excluded natives of countries who had no experience with the democratic election process and were as a consequence "presumably not qualified for the exercise of the franchise," from participation in parliamentary elections. Besides, those already on the voters' rolls could remain enrolled and the measure allowed exemptions from its working under certain circumstances.[20]

Initially the Government of India strenuously objected to the franchise law. It duly pointed out that natives of India and Englishmen stood on a similar footing when it came to voting in Indian municipal, provincial, and supreme council elec-

---

the Colonial Office." The governor felt that any further modification of the bill or any undue delay in its passage would cause the government to fall, as "they would be altogether discredited."

16. NA, Ind. Coll., undersec. CO to undersec. IO, Oct. 2, 1897.
17. Quoted in Natal *Hansard*, May 6, 1896.   18. See note 16.
19. NA, Ind. Coll., Govt. House, CO to Naoroji, Nov. 13, 1897.
20. Quoted in Iqbal Narain, *The Politics of Racialism* (Ahmedabad, 1957), 127.

tions.[21] But in the end, Calcutta also conceded, believing that its primary responsibility remained the indentured Indians and aware that it could not do much about popular sentiment in Natal in any case. The Natal Indians, the viceroy felt, should do what they could to obtain the removal of invidious distinctions, but the Government of India itself had to be careful about interfering with the Natal authorities. "It would be a mistake," he concluded, "to press them on points like the franchise." [22]

Objectionable as were the immigration restriction and franchise acts, by far the most insidious piece of legislation passed in this period was Natal Act 18 of 1897, "To Amend the Law Relating to Licenses to Wholesale and Retail Dealers." As things stood, all shopkeepers had to obtain licenses to conduct their businesses, but the process was a relatively simple one which made it difficult to deny Indians either the initial permit or a renewal. The new act was designed to ameliorate this unhappy situation. All applicants for new licenses and license renewals would in the future be subject to municipal licensing officers appointed by the corporations. By means of this law the municipalities of Natal expected to rid themselves of merchants whom they accused, on the one hand, of underselling Europeans as a consequence of living off the smell of the proverbial oiled rag and of the low wages they paid, and whom they belabored, on the other, for offering salaries "so handsome that several lady assistants in the large drapery establishments in town express a determination to put pride in their pockets and suffer the indignity of being in the employ of an Arab." [23] Act 18 stipulated that all books were to be kept in English and that commercial premises must be maintained in a sanitary state. The

21. CO 179/202, Govt. of India, Dept. of Rev. and Ag. (Em.), no. 2, viceroy in council to sec. of state, Mar. 31, 1897.
22. NAI, Govt. of Ind., Dept. of Rev. and Ag. (Em.), Aug. 1897, proc. 12, note by Elgin, Mar. 19, 1897.
23. Pyarelal, *Mahatma Gandhi: The Early Phase* (Ahmedabad, 1965), 475.

licensing officer was to determine whether these conditions were being met. Appeals were to be allowed to a board made up of municipal officials but not to the courts.

At the outset, the Government of India opposed the licensing act, insisting that Indians be permitted an appeal to the supreme court in licensing cases. As had been the case with the franchise act, however, the Indian authorities soon lost the will to resist and after some vacillation assumed their usual supine position.[24] The British Government was in a much better position than India to object to the licensing act, but it allowed the measure with little hesitation, again on the grounds that it contained nothing specifically discriminatory to Indians, and because it naively accepted the Government of Natal's assurance that the law would be fairly administered.[25]

It was clear that more liberal opinion in the colony had wanted the act only to discourage the influx of more Indian traders, not to penalize those already established. As the *Times of Natal* stated on December 21, 1898, "The Act was passed, not so much with a view to enabling the licensing bodies to deal with the Indians already trading in the Colony, as to prevent others coming here to trade." [26] In fact, however, the municipalities, urged on by European protective societies that burgeoned throughout the colony, and checked neither by the courts nor by the colonial administration, saw the law as a mandate to remove all Indians from their midst. Appeals to the licensing boards received scant courtesy and were nearly always dismissed after only the most cursory hearing. The behavior of the municipal licensing boards was too blatant even for the Colonial Office, and in 1899 Chamberlain wrote Hely-Hutchinson with some pique that he had been assured, when the British Gov-

24. NA, Ind. Coll., Govt. House, IO to CO, Nov. 2, 1897.
25. I.e., that Indians' vested interests would be protected. CO 179/204, IO to CO, July 14, 1898.
26. *Works*, III, 37. Gandhi estimated that there were over 300 store or shopkeepers' licenses and 500 hawkers' licenses issued to Indians in Natal.

ernment had allowed the licensing act, that it would not be harshly enforced and that the vested interests of Indians would be respected. The contrary had, however, been the case and unless the law were promptly amended to allow for an appeal to the supreme court, indentured Indian immigration to Natal would probably come to an end.[27] Had Chamberlain paid any attention to the debates on the measure in the legislative assembly, he might have had less cause to be surprised. "This Bill," a leading member of the assembly (Tatham) had proclaimed, "is a bill which is intended by an indirect method, to get at a direct evil. Let there be no mistake about it at all. . . . The term 'Asiatic trader' is not mentioned in the Bill and yet the meaning is to get at the Asiatic trader." [28]

The record of excesses perpetrated under the shelter of the licensing act is impressive. In Newcastle, for example, the licensing officer, as a matter of course, refused to renew the licenses of all eight Indian traders who had held them the previous year. Their lawyer pointed out, to no avail, that the licensing officer was also the town clerk, and consequently the clerk of the court when the town council sat to hear appeals against the decisions of the licensing officer.[29] The situation in Dundee was similar. C. G. Wilson, the chairman of the local board, frankly stated that "it was their endeavour, if possible, to rid the town of the Asiatic curse. They were not only a curse here, but to the whole colony of Natal." [30]

The position of the Indians in Natal was becoming ever more desperate. They were reviled as "Ramysamy," "Mr. Samy" (both corruptions of the common South Indian name suffix, "swami"), or "Mr. Coolie," and they were referred to as "the Asian dirt to be heartily cursed," or "a thing black and lean and a long way from clean." Indians were damned, spat upon, pushed off footpaths, and hurled from trams. They were the victims

27. NA, Ind. Coll., Natal no. 45, sec. of state to gov., May 19, 1899.
28. Natal *Hansard*, Mar. 31, 1897.   29. *Works*, III, 33–34.
30. *Ibid.*, 35, quoting the *Natal Witness*, Nov. 26, 1896.

of arson and other forms of violence.[31] Anti-Indian meetings were frequent. It was not unusual for Indians to be referred to as "black vermin" who bred like rabbits. One speaker averred that "the worst of it is that we can't shoot them down." [32]

Nor was Natal the only colony to legislate against its Indian residents. By the early 1880s, it has already been noted, both "Arabs" and time-expired indentured laborers were making their appearance in Cape Colony and the Afrikaner republics of the Orange Free State and the Transvaal. In the Cape, the reaction toward the Indians who seeped across the colony's border was mild in comparison to that of the rest of South Africa.[33] In 1892, however, the Cape legislature passed a franchise and ballot act which stipulated that an eligible voter would have to be able to write his name, address and occupation in English. Of greater significance, the bill raised the property qualifications for the franchise from £25 to £75. The secretary of state, Lord Ripon, was soon in receipt of petitions of protest from both colored and Indian objectors.[34] Ripon, after studying the measure, came to feel that the "legislation is contrary to the spirit and tendency of public opinion in the present day." [35] Yet he could not properly veto a technically nondiscriminatory bill passed by the legislature of a self-governing colony, especially as it had already received the governor's assent. The bill consequently was not disallowed by the British Government, despite the personal reservations of the secretary of state.

Three years later, in 1895, the Cape legislature passed an "Act to Amend and Add to the Laws Regulating the Municipal Corporation and Government of East London." This law gave

31. *Ibid.*, II, 1–52.
32. *Ibid.*, 187, Indian memorial to Chamberlain, Mar. 15, 1897.
33. There were some 8,489 Indians in Cape Colony in 1904 and 7,963 in 1921.
34. CO 48/521, minute paper 10341, "Coloured objectors" Nov. 8, 1892; CO 48/524, Port Elizabeth Indians to Ripon, Apr. 17, 1894.
35. CO 48/521, sec. of state to gov., Jan. 27, 1893.

the municipal authorities of East London the power to require the residence of natives and Asiatics in specially designated locations outside the town, and also permitted the passage of municipal ordinances "fixing the hours within which it shall not be lawful for natives and Asiatics to be in the streets, public places or thoroughfares . . . without a written pass or certificate . . . and for fixing such parts of streets and open spaces or pavements of the same on which natives and Asiatics may not walk or be. . . . For regulating and setting apart portions of the rivers and sea where natives and Asiatics may not bathe, and where clothes may or may not be washed." As one witness told the select committee on the bill appointed by the Cape House of Assembly, there was great fear in East London about the possible influx of Indians, who were considered by many to be inferior even to the natives in their habits, customs and morals. There were not many Indians yet, but the municipality wished to be forearmed.[36] Again the British Government did not disallow the act. It was not considered a truly discriminatory measure in a racial sense, as in its final form the law exempted all natives and Asiatics "who are at present or may in future become registered owners of land within the municipality valued for municipal purposes at not less than £75."[37] Perhaps of greater moment in the eyes of the British Government was the feeling expressed by the governor, as spokesman for his ministers, that the Cape would rather secede from the British Empire than brook any interference with what it considered its domestic affairs.[38]

The position of the British Government in regard to the rights of Indians in the two Dutch republics was, of course, more complicated than it was vis-à-vis the British colonies in South Africa. The Orange Free State Act 29 of 1890 prohibited

36. NAI, Govt. of Ind., Dept. of Rev. and Ag. (Em.), Jan. 1898, proc. no. 31, Report of the Select Committee of the House of Assembly on East London's Municipal Bill, printed by order of the House of Assembly, July 1894, hearings on the bill.
37. *Ibid.*   38. CO 48/524, note by Loch, no date.

Indians from owning land or carrying on trade within the republic. The British Government attempted to intercede on behalf of the few British Indian subjects (a mere nine on annual license) only to find that it had no legal basis for interference.

In the Transvaal (South African Republic), Her Majesty's Government had in April 1881, through the Pretoria Convention, conceded the Transvaal "complete self-government subject to the suzerainty of Her Majesty." In 1884 a second agreement, the London Convention, was promulgated in order to increase the Transvaal's jurisdiction over its own affairs. No mention was made in the London Convention of suzerainty, and as the British Government was in future years to base much of its claim to the right to protect Indians in the Transvaal on its position as suzerain, this was a matter of some importance. The Transvaal claimed that British suzerainty no longer obtained from the moment that the London Convention replaced the Pretoria Convention. The British Government, on the other hand, took the position that the London Convention merely amended the Pretoria Convention, and that those articles of the London Convention not specifically altered by the second document were still in effect. To confuse the issue still further, article 14 of the London Convention (which was the same as article 26 of the Pretoria Convention) stipulated that

all persons other than natives, conforming themselves to the laws of the South African Republic
   a) will have full liberty, with their families, to enter, travel, or reside in any part of the South African Republic;
   b) will be entitled to hire or possess houses, manufactures, warehouses, shops, and premises;
   c) may carry on their commerce either in person, or by any agents whom they may think fit to employ;
   d) will not be subject in respect to their persons or property, or in respect of their commerce or industry, to any taxes, whether general or local, other than those which are or may be imposed upon citizens of the said Republic.

Indians were by no means the only British subjects in the Transvaal. Indeed, with the gold mines booming, they were only a small minority.[39] Still, they were in the most difficult position. The first paragraph of article 14 stated that all persons, to be eligible for the rights stipulated, must conform themselves to the laws of the South African Republic. The Republic's basic law, the "Grondwet," clearly proclaimed that colored persons, a designation which included Indians, could not receive the same treatment as white persons and would be subject to special laws. Did the "Grondwet" take precedence over the London Convention, and did the first lines of article 14 thus obviate the guarantees of subsequent paragraphs as far as Indians were concerned? A long and acrimonious correspondence ensued between the British and Transvaal governments,[40] complicated by the suzerainty issue and a general confusion as to what the term suzerainty meant in the first place.

Although the Indian question in the Transvaal was not yet sufficiently significant to play any role in the negotiation and signing of the London Convention, its provisions allowed the Transvaal to deal more forcibly with the situation when the rapid growth of the Indian population between 1881 and 1884 aroused growing anti-Asian feeling in the state. As a first step, and with British concurrence, article 14 of the London Convention was amended so that "African native or Indian or Chinese Coolie immigrants" no longer fell under its protection.[41] Next, the Transvaal Volksraad passed Law 3 of 1885 which prescribed that Indians, amongst others, would in future have to reside in

39. The total Indian population of the Transvaal in 1899 was about 17,000. Of this number, approximately 5,500 were merchants or hawkers. TA, records of the British agent in the Transvaal, agent to the high comm., Mar. 24, 1899.
40. *Ibid.*, records of the British agent in the Transvaal, 1892–1899.
41. C. 7911, Papers Relating to the Grievances of H.M. Indian Subjects in the S.A.R., September 1895, 51, state sec. to Derby; 52, sec. of state to high comm., Mar. 19, 1885.

special locations. Her Majesty's Government immediately protested that the law went well beyond what had been intended by the amendment of article 14 which in its wording was clearly aimed at lower-class Indians rather than the established merchants who were the intended victims of Law 3.[42] When, however, the Transvaal Government in 1886 amended the measure so that the rationale for the establishment of locations became "sanitation," the British Government removed its objections.[43]

But the matter, as it turned out, was far from settled; for when the Transvaal Government interpreted Law 3 to mean the establishment of special Indian locations for purposes of both residence and business, the British authorities returned to do battle. The whole situation was by this time so vague and confused that the two protagonists agreed to submit the case to the arbitration of the chief justice of the Orange Free State, Melius de Villiers. After due consideration, de Villiers ruled that as the British had assented to Law 3 in its amended form, the Transvaal was entitled to administer the measure as it saw fit.[44] Nevertheless, despite its legal victory, the Transvaal did not actually implement Law 3. British suasion kept the Republican Government at bay, and while negotiations were still in progress, the Anglo-Boer War broke out and the South African Republic was relegated to the pages of history.

The war between the British and the Dutch republics which erupted in 1899 seemed to presage the salvation of the Indian community. Mohandas Gandhi, the Indians' champion since his arrival in South Africa in 1893, organized an Indian ambulance corps whose 800 free and 300 indentured members performed with great distinction, and throughout the war Indians contributed their efforts unstintingly in many capacities.

In 1906, Gandhi again led a stretcher company during the Bambata Rebellion in Zululand. Even the anti-Indian governor

42. *Ibid.*, 55, sec. of state to high comm., Feb. 24, 1886.
43. *Ibid.*, 59, act. high comm. to state sec., Pretoria, Dec. 2, 1886.
44. *Ibid.*, 26, 14.

of Natal, Sir Henry McCallum, felt constrained to write a letter of thanks to "Sergeant-Major Gandhi." "I cannot allow demobilisation to take place," the governor wrote,

without placing on record on behalf of the Government my appreciation of the patriotic movement made by the Indian community of Natal in providing a bearer company for service in the field during the rebellion.

2. The number of casualties in our forces have been providentially small and the labours of the company have not therefore been so heavy as they would otherwise have been.

3. At the same time mention has been made to me of the good services rendered by those who volunteered for this service and of the steadiness displayed by them. I should feel obliged if you will be good enough to convey to all ranks who served under your command my best thanks for the assistance they have given.[45]

But if the Indians thought that loyal adherence to the Empire's cause would at last soften the hearts of the white colonists and bring about an improvement in their lot, at least in the conquered territories, they were destined to be sadly disappointed. Whereas the Republican Government had never actually moved the Indians of the Transvaal into locations, the British military governor of Pretoria forced the city's Indians into locations as early as 1901 [46]—an action in which he was supported by virtually the entire hierarchy of British officials who, it must be remembered, were not colonists. Sir Godfrey Lagden, the commissioner of native affairs in the Transvaal, thought "it would be intolerable if the comfort and convenience required by higher civilisation were to be seized and invaded by a lower stratum." [47] W. Wybergh, the com-

45. NA Natal no. 259 of 1906, McCallum to Gandhi, Aug. 7, 1906.
46. TA, no. 126, Trans. to CO, June 28, 1901, encl. supervisor of Ind. imm. to pvt. sec. to the Trans. admin.
Another example of increased stringency under the British can be observed in the matter of leases in Indian locations. The South African Republic had offered 99-year terms while the British allowed no comparable privilege.
47. TA, memo., Lagden to high comm., Jan. 4, in disp. no. 14, Trans. to CO, July 26, 1901. This was the same Lagden who at the South

missioner for mines, enunciated a philosophy very similar to modern apartheid. "What is aimed at," he claimed, "is the avoidance of close personal contact between two races with entirely different ideals and customs and frequently with strong personal antipathies. . . . I believe it is both just, advisable, and practicable . . . to recognise frankly the fundamental differences between European and Coloured races."[48] Patrick Duncan (destined to become a governor general of the Union of South Africa) thought "it might be worth our while to consider the advisability of setting apart certain districts for Indian or Asiatic immigrants, either for indentured labour (as is done in Natal) or, if possible as free settlers. But, except in such districts, it seems to me undesirable to allow Asiatics to settle on the land even as labourers, or to acquire land, unless it is quite clear that such settlement will not tend to dispossess or to keep out white settlers."[49]

Lord Milner, the high commissioner for South Africa and the governor of the Transvaal and the Orange River Colony, felt that any "attempt to place coloured people on an equality with whites in South Africa is wholly impracticable, and that moreover, it is in principle wrong. But I hold that when a coloured person possesses a certain high degree of civilisation he ought to obtain what I may call 'white privileges,' irrespective of colour." That time was far off, however. "For the present," Milner concluded, "there is no prospect whatever of [the above situation] . . . prevailing, certainly as far as Asiatics

---

African Customs Union Conference of March 1903, had moved: "This Conference is of the opinion that South Africa is essentially a white man's country, and the permanent settlement upon the land of Asiatic races is injurious and should not be permitted." Cd. 1640 (1903)—Minutes of Proceedings of the South African Customs Unions Conference, Bloemfontein, Mar. 1903.

48. TA, no. 126, Trans. to CO, June 28, 1901, encl. memo. by Wybergh.
49. TA, memo. on position of Indians in the Trans. by P. Duncan, Feb. 14, 1902.

are concerned. . . . The Asiatics are strangers forcing themselves upon a community reluctant to receive them." [50]

Even had the British Government been more committed to the imperial philosophy of equality than was actually the case, the combination of anti-Indian British minority in the Transvaal and a majority of Afrikaners who saw all men of color as sons of Ham—condemned to a lesser existence—[51] would have made any effective opposition to the emerging policy impossible. To his credit, Chamberlain was less sure of what course to follow than his men in the field. He did, at least, from his vantage point in London, see the problem from an imperial point of view, and he was able to discern that what the Transvaal authorities were essentially proposing was the establishment of the same system formerly espoused by the South African Republic. As he put it: "It would be difficult to defend in Parliament what is . . . practically a continuance of the system of the late Republic." [52] As was so often the case, however, the arguments of "the man on the spot," in this case Lord Milner, wore down Colonial Office opposition. Milner was convinced that until such time as a different policy could be determined, the British authorities had no choice but to administer the laws of the South African Republic, imperfect as they might be.

He won his point, and Government Notice no. 356 of 1903—a repromulgation of Law 3 of 1885 (as amended in 1886), the very law against which the British Government had fought so hard in the decade before the war—became almost the first major act of a British government unhampered by an elected legislature. In the notice, the executive council agreed to respect the vested interests of Indians who were trading outside locations before the commencement of hostilities and to pre-

50. TA, Conf., high comm. to sec. of state, Apr. 18, 1904.
51. The comparatively generous attitude of the South African Republic towards the Indians should, however, be borne in mind.
52. TA, sec. of state to high comm., Aug. 6, 1902.

scribe exemptions for certain educated Indians. But, more significantly, the government promised to "take immediate steps to have bazaars in every town set apart in which Asiatics alone may reside and trade." [53] The notice stipulated that "no new licenses to trade shall be granted to any Asiatic except to carry on his business in Bazaars set apart for that purpose." Although Indians, who had been permitted by the Boer authorities to trade outside locations, could continue to renew their licenses, no transfers were to be permitted; nor was the number of licenses held by any trader to be increased beyond the total granted by the Republic. It is also worthy of note that the £3 residence license fee for which all Indians had been liable under the Republic was retained by the British administration.

Milner fully realized that the position assumed by his government was not without its embarrassments, and he attempted to rationalize his stand. "It is true," he confessed,

that Law No. 3 of 1885 . . . was, at the time of its passing and a number of years subsequently, the object of controversy between the Government of the late Republic and His Majesty's Government. But the late Chief Justice of the Orange Free State, Mr. Melius de Villiers, to whose arbitration the question was referred by the two Governments, came to the conclusion, and declared in his award, that the South African Republic was entitled to give effect to this law. Its provisions had, according to the Arbitrator, received the assent of previous Secretaries of State, and his award was based on that assent. And as the award was accepted by the present Secretary of State, the Government of the Transvaal does not feel justified, at the present juncture, in altering the law, although it intends to interpret it as liberally as possible.[54]

The Indians of the Transvaal, under Gandhi's leadership, rallied against the attacks of those on whom they had hoped to depend as friends. But Gandhi was not totally opposed to the principle of locations, so long as Indians were not *forced* to

53. The Transvaal administration planned the establishment of locations at 54 places at a cost of £10,000.
54. TA, tel., high comm. to sec. of state, May 11, 1903.

reside in them. He demanded only that bazaars should be located in the central business section of any town; that those Indians who had traded outside locations before the war should be allowed to continue this practice; and that Indians should be permitted to purchase property in established bazaars, subject to building and sanitary regulations.[55]

Milner battled on, but his reactions were becoming increasingly defensive. Locations were being selected only in healthy areas which afforded adequate business opportunities, he claimed, and "Asiatics of a superior class" were to be exempted from all special legislation. "The policy of the present Government," Milner declared, "is not directed against colour or against any special race. It is dictated by the necessity of preventing people of a higher degree of civilisation, whatever their race or colour may be, from being degraded by enforced contact with people of lower grade." [56]

But no legislation aimed at low class or disreputable whites ever disfigured the code of laws. The fact was that the white colonists of the Transvaal—Briton and Afrikaner alike—were as determined as their fellows in Natal to curtail the business opportunities afforded Indians. As early as February 1903 the British Indian Association complained to the lieutenant governor that new licenses were being refused to Indians who had traded in the Transvaal before the war and that transfers of licenses were being denied even if the proposed new location of a store was in the same district and street. An Indian, it was claimed, was not allowed to transfer a license to another Indian, thus preventing the sale of a business to anyone but a European. Finally, partners in firms which had traded in the Transvaal before the war were denied licenses to trade in their own names, despite the acquiescence of the firm and the other partners.[57] As one Asian wrote to Milner:

55. *Works*, III, 279, Gandhi to col. sec., Pretoria, Feb. 18, 1904.
56. TA, tel., high comm. to sec. of state, May 11, 1903.
57. TA, Brit. Ind. Assoc. to pvt. sec. to lt. gov., Feb. 25, 1903.

Last year in 1902 I was trading on stand 52 Georgetown as a General Dealer, and at the end of 1902 I found I could renew my license. This week I endeavoured to have my license transferred to stand 4893 Hood Street, Johannesburg, also I made two applications to the Receiver of Revenue, Johannesburg, both have been refused without any reason being given.

Consequently, I have on my hands a large amount of stock, and the refusal has prevented me from earning my living. I therefore beg Your Excellency's good office so that I may resume my business.[58]

At issue also was the question of Indian property ownership in locations. As Gandhi pointed out, Law 3 of 1885 had given Asians unrestricted rights to hold land in the locations that might be established for them. Under British administration locations were being designated in unhealthy areas, far away from towns, and with the most vexatious limitations on freehold and leasehold.[59] In Standerton, for instance, no Indian was to be allowed to occupy a site, even in a location, if he had not previously resided or traded in the town. In Barberton, lots in the bazaar were to be rented on a monthly basis only, and again only to those Asians who were already residing or trading in the town. In Boksburg, tenancy was on a month-to-month basis, and buildings were erected at the builder's own risk.[60] On November 11, 1903, Gandhi's newspaper, *Indian Opinion,* referred to the Klerksdorp district surgeon's statement that the proposed Indian location was thoroughly unsuitable as in the rainy season it would be completely flooded. The town council, in reply, contended that the matter was outside of its jurisdiction as the site had been approved by the government, had been surveyed and declared the Klerksdorp Bazaar.[61]

It was Sir Arthur Lawley, the lieutenant governor of the Transvaal, who put the official position most honestly. "It is true," he admitted, "that the British Government had laid

58. TA, Leon Chong to high comm., Feb. 11, 1903.
59. *Works,* IV, 39–40, quoting *Indian Opinion,* Nov. 12, 1903.
60. *Ibid.,* 61, quoting *Indian Opinion,* Nov. 26, 1903.   61. *Ibid.*

down the dictum, 'that there shall not be in the eye of the law any distinction or disqualification whatever founded on mere colour, origin, language or creed.' " But, he contended, the history of South Africa had been such as to place an impassable barrier between the European and colored races. At one time the British Government had supposed that all peoples were equally capable of civilization, and on the basis of this belief it had strongly defended the rights of British Indians in the Transvaal. But, he went on to say, "I do not think that the consequences which must ultimately result from such a policy were realised at the time. To-day, the Government cannot fail to perceive the effects on the social composition of the country which have resulted from concessions made to British Indians in the past, or to see clearly what will be the consequences of making still further concessions." [62]

What Whitehall's attitude was to be was made clear in a letter from Lord George Hamilton, the secretary of state for India, to Lord Curzon, the viceroy. "Chamberlain is not unfriendly," Hamilton wrote, "but he is greatly impressed with the intense and universal hostility which exists among white traders and working classes against free Asiatic immigration, and he is apprehensive that, if he exercises pressure beyond a certain point, his action will be so resented as to set on foot a movement of secession from the British Empire." [63]

To confuse the situation still further, the supreme court of the Transvaal, in the case of *Motan v. the Transvaal Government*, heard in May 1904, expressed consternation that a British Government had adopted the position of the South African Republic in requiring that Indians both trade and reside in locations—the very contention it had always denied in its interpretation of Law 3 before the Anglo-Boer War. In discussing the law, the chief justice, Sir James Rose-Innes, ruled that its provisions relegated Indians to certain streets, wards,

62. TA, lt. gov. to high comm., Apr. 13, 1904.
63. IOL, Curzon Paps., F. 111/162, sec. of state to viceroy, May 28, 1903.

and locations only for purposes of residence. "The mischief purported to be aimed at was the insanitary mode of life in the midst of an European population—not an inconvenient competition with European traders." Rose-Innes concluded with a final rebuke to the colonial authorities. "Under the circumstances," he contended, "it does strike one as remarkable that without fresh legislation the officials of the Crown in the Transvaal should put forward a claim which the Government of the Crown of England has always contended was illegal under the Statute and which, in the past, it has strenuously resisted." [64]

Meanwhile other less far-reaching matters continued to insinuate themselves onto the scene. Many of them were rooted in municipal by-laws which never came under the scrutiny of Whitehall. The introduction of a draft municipal bill into the Transvaal legislature in 1908 prompted questions in the Imperial Parliament to which the colony's prime minister, Louis Botha, promptly replied. He pointed out that power to make by-laws "prohibiting the use of the sidewalks of any public street . . . by *coloured persons* who are not respectably dressed and well conducted" was a municipal rather than colonial prerogative. The purpose of such restrictions, he explained, was to guard "against the danger of . . . [European] women and children being jostled off the pavement by unsavory and ill-mannered coloured people." In fact, Botha insisted, these regulations were rarely enforced.[65]

Under the definitions clause of Act 35 of 1908—"To Consolidate and Amend the law relating to Prospecting and Mining for Precious Metals and Base Metals and to provide for matters incidental thereto"—Indians were defined as colored persons and were prohibited from dealing in precious metals (section 114). They could not hold or sublet property

64. Johannesburg *Star* (weekly edition), May 14, 1904.
65. TA, minute no. 463, July 29, 1908, encl. in gov. gen. to sec. of state, Aug. 3, 1908.

on proclaimed ground (section 130), nor could they reside on proclaimed ground except in bazaars or locations (section 131) —the only exception being for the bona fide servants of white men (section 130). Once the secretary of state was assured that the rights of colored persons already in the mining areas would be protected and that the governor would have the right to exempt individuals from the workings of the law, he gave the measure his blessing.[66] The Government of India limited itself to protesting the failure of the mining bill to differentiate between the various levels of Indian society. Had the law applied only to so-called lower-class Indians the viceroy and his advisers would have been perfectly satisfied.[67] Transvaal Act 32 of 1908, the Shop Hours Act, was a disguised form of attack on Indian merchants. Debate on the measure indicated that it was directed against peddlers, hawkers, and those in the retail business who, by working long hours, competed too successfully with white merchants.

As was the case in Natal and the Transvaal, competition from Indian trades in the Cape aroused the ire of their white counterparts, who constantly demanded action from the legislature. Consequently a bill to regulate the trade of general dealers was introduced into the house of assembly. In its initial version the measure very much resembled its Natal counterpart. Appeal to the courts was allowed only when the cancellation of an existing license was the issue. In the case of new licenses the decision of the licensing court was to be final. The law as it emerged from committee and as finally passed in the form of Cape Act 35 of 1906—"To Regulate the Trade of General Dealers and to Amend the Law Relating to Stamp Duties and Licenses"—was obviously not directed toward Indians already in business but at those who would apply for

66. TA, sec. of state to gov., Dec. 28, 1908.
67. NAI, Govt. of India, Dept. of Comm. and Ind. (Em.), July 1908, proc. 1, minuting of July 6, 1908.

permits to trade in the future. No mention was made of existing licenses. But applicants for new licenses could appeal only to the municipal council, village board, magistrate, or assistant magistrate if their applications were denied by the licensing officer. The question of appeals to higher judicial authority was conveniently ignored.

The Indians of Griqualand West immediately addressed the secretary of state. They were convinced that "the Bill is aimed solely at British Indians and other non-European persons, and that as such it draws a clear distinction between the European and non-European sections of His Majesty's subjects in this Colony and whilst conferring certain rights and privileges on the former, withholds these self-same rights and privileges from the latter. That such differentiation is a violation of the constitutional rights of your Petitioners as subjects of His Majesty." [68] The protests from the Cape Indians were, however, few and far between—perhaps because they felt the licensing law adequately protected the interests of those already established in the colony.

Gandhi criticized his compatriots for a want of courage. He was particularly incensed at the Cape Indians' failure to object strongly to the lack of appeal to the supreme court in cases involving the issue of new licenses. "On that question," he wrote, "it was necessary for the people of the Cape to take a lesson from the conditions in Natal and put up a strong fight. But it is to be regretted that this was not done. They remained altogether indifferent while the Bill was before Parliament. It needs to be dinned into the minds of the Indians in the South that having come to this country, they cannot afford to be asleep all the time." [69]

The British Government did not disallow the licensing bill because it could claim that nothing in the measure was specifi-

68. NAI, Dept. of Rev. and Ag. (Em.), January 1906, proc. 4, petition from the Indians of Griqualand West to sec. of state, Mar. 28, 1906.
69. *Works*, VI, 379–80.

cally detrimental to any racial group. But as it turned out, Gandhi's apprehensions were justified, for in practice the Cape Act operated in very much the same way as its Natal model. "At the monthly meeting of the Cape Divisional Council held at Capetown on the 5th inst.," the *Cape Times* reported,

. . . [a number of] applications were considered for permission to apply for licenses to trade as general dealers. Not much time was wasted in refusing the applications or referring them back for further information. . . . The procedure was something as follows: The Secretary read out the Sanitary Inspector's report on the state of the premises, usually to the effect that the ventilation needed looking into, the drains were bad, there was connection between the sleeping apartments and the shops and so on. Before Mr. Sorrie had read a half-dozen lines, Mr. Gibbs would shout out, "Not Granted," and the other Councillors followed suit.

"Indians," said Mr. Gibbs with scorn, "I want . . . none of their nationality. I am not in favour of these Indians coming here at all, and I would like to see as many of them as possible getting out of the country. They work the poor people out of the country, and I really think a good deal of the depression existing at this time is due to them. Why, they live on the smell of an oil-rag, and sleep on the butter (laughter). I'll do everything possible in my power, whatever Council I'm on, to drive them out." [70]

In August 1908 the house of assembly appointed a select committee to investigate Asian grievances under the immigration and licensing acts. Several Indians testified that, outside of Cape Town, Indians were denied licenses as general dealers or hawkers merely because of their color. The European merchants, on the other hand, demanded even stronger legislation and claimed, as usual, that they were being driven out of business by a people who represented a lower order of civilization. The committee found that there had indeed been some instances of discrimination against Indians, but it recommended only a few minor changes in the administration of the law. Lending credence to one of the more prevalent folk myths of

70. *Cape Times,* Nov. 6, 1907.

the time, the committee contended that Indians drove white men out of business, at least in part, because "Indians have as a rule, no domestic establishments to maintain." [71]

The situation in the Cape never achieved the level of complexity or the degree of threat to the Indian population that manifested itself in postwar Natal. There no sooner had the dust of battle cleared than the government determined to change the existing terms of Indian immigration and residence in Natal to its own benefit. All the stratagems, such as the £3 license, that had attempted to force Indians either to return to India or to re-indenture had failed, and the old dilemma of how to keep a steady supply of Indian laborers flowing to the plantations without at the same time increasing the permanent Indian population of the colony remained. A raising of the residence license fee to £10 was suggested, but rejected, as "there is no penalty attached to the non-payment of the license, no means to compel the payment of it, and no method by which Indians can be forced back to India." [72] Indians, one member of the legislative assembly remarked, thought the payment of the £3 license fee made them free men, when all the white colonists of Natal knew that this was not so.[73]

As a first step in its renewed campaign to make life increasingly less comfortable for the colony's free Indians, the postwar Natal legislature passed Act 2 of 1902, which remedied a weakness in the terminology of Act 17 of 1895—the failure to take proper cognizance of the status of Indian minors. The £3 tax was now clearly to be levied on boys of sixteen and girls after they had reached their thirteenth birthday.

Every point at which the Indian came into contact with the white man was minutely scrutinized. The shop-closing act of

71. Cape Colony, Report of the Select Comm. on Indian Grievances, Select Comm. Report no. 19, 1908.
72. NA, "Precis of evidence given before Select Committee of the Legislative Assembly appointed to consider the petition (no. 1 of 1902) of the Indian Immigration Trust Board."
73. *Ibid.*

1905 was passed largely because Europeans had, as one member of the legislative assembly put it, "to compete with the coloured races who have been introduced into this Colony." [74] More significantly, the bill "to amend and consolidate the laws relating to Municipal Corporation," originally passed in 1905, contained a number of articles designed to reduce significantly the rights of Indians in Natal. The trouble began as early as the definitions clause where Indians were referred to variously as "coloured persons," "coolies," and members of an "uncivilised race." The proposed law empowered town councils to regulate the use of pavements, footpaths and rickshaws by colored persons (section 182) and also authorized them "to make By-Laws establishing a system of registration of Natives or persons belonging to uncivilised races . . ." (section 200). Of greatest importance, however, was the attempt to remove the last vestige of Indian political influence in Natal by depriving of the municipal franchise all persons who were disqualified from the parliamentary franchise by Act 8 of 1896 or any like act, unless they were specifically exempted by the governor of the colony (subsection c of section 22).

The first reactions from the India Office were rather mild, and were confined to concern about the definitions clause of the bill.[75] The Colonial Office was similarly guarded.[76] But the Government of India was considerably more outraged. It objected to all the bill's differentiating clauses but particularly to the extension of the meaning of "uncivilised races" to include the *descendants* of indentured immigrants.[77] The strength of its protests compelled the India Office to take a more forceful stand,[78] drawing the Colonial Office with it.[79] But still the

74. Natal *Hansard,* July 27, 1905.
75. CO 179/239, IO to CO, Nov. 15, 1905.
76. CO 179/238, minute paper, Natal no. 40730, Nov. 16, 1905.
77. *Ibid.,* tel., Govt. of Ind. to IO, Dec. 27, 1905.
78. *Ibid.,* IO to CO, Jan. 31, 1906.
79. NA, Natal G. no. 1030/1905, no. 104, sec. of state to gov., Dec. 9, 1905.

attacks on the measure were limited to such questions as whether the term "coloured persons" should be construed as having a wider application to natives of India than the expression "uncivilised races."

What seems curious in retrospect is that the bill's most significant attack upon the rights of Natal's Indians was not even a point of issue at this stage.[80] The Indians of Natal had to send a memorial to the secretary of state for the colonies before it was officially realized that the municipal corporations bill, in its existing form, would disenfranchise Indians at the municipal level—their only remaining arena for any kind of political activity. They pointed out that while India had no national representative institutions, it certainly had municipal ones. Hence, under the rationale advanced at the time of their parliamentary disenfranchisement, no excuse existed to deprive Indians of the municipal vote. "Indians do not aspire to any political power in the Colony of Natal but they naturally resent interference with municipal liberty when they pay the same rates as other taxpayers." [81]

When the petition was forwarded to the India Office, Morley rose to its support.[82] The Colonial Office was dismayed and embarrassed by its oversight. One official minuted: "I scarcely think we can press the objection with regard to the Municipal franchise, if Natal holds out, in view of the late stage in the correspondence at which it has been raised by the I.O." [83] But Frederick Graham, now one of the assistant undersecretaries, disagreed. "We can afford to chop logic with Natal," he wrote,

80. NA, tel., gov. to sec. of state, Jan. 20, 1906, G. no. 396/1906, minuting by minister of justice, July 23, 1906; minute paper, sec. of state no. 23, Apr. 11, 1906, AG 1448/1906, MJ 2801/1906, PM 489/1906.
81. NA, G. no. 725/1906, minute paper, sec. of state no. 3, July 25, 1906, encl. Indian petition to the sec. of state, Apr. 13, 1906.
82. CO 179/238, IO to CO, Oct. 18, 1906.
83. *Ibid.,* minuting dated Dec. 12, 1906, Natal minute paper no. 45883, Dec. 13, 1906.

"as the Bill is not in operation. I should send a copy of I.O. letter and say that the objection though not taken before is of great force." [84]

It was to be many months before any sort of order emerged from the chaos. Meanwhile the issues raised by the municipal corporations bill became fused with the old problem of Indian trading licenses. After receiving reports from all parts of the colony, the South Africa British India Committee, the prime British defender of the South African Indians, addressed a letter to the Colonial Office giving figures as to the beleaguered state of the Indian merchants in Natal. "My Committee feel," L. W. Ritch, the body's secretary, wrote, "that the facts warrant the conclusion that the Natal Dealers' Licenses Act (Law 18 of 1897) is being deliberately used as an engine of oppression with the object of driving away British Indian trade competition, and [we] respectfully urge His Majesty's Government to take prompt steps to secure relief to those established British Indian traders whose licenses have been arbitrarily refused and to prevent any such future invasion of vested interests." [85] Several questions were posed in the Commons. Dr. V. H. Rutherford, for instance, on February 18, 1907, asked the undersecretary of state for the colonies whether he was aware of the injustices being perpetrated against Indian shopkeepers in Ladysmith, "and whether, seeing that the Licensing Officer is the appointee of the Town Council which is composed of merchants and storekeepers in competition with British Indian traders, he proposes to take any action in the matter." The secretary of state himself felt that "the incidents, if correctly reported, give rise to grave doubts whether the licensing boards can be trusted to deal with applications in a judicial spirit." [86]

84. *Ibid.*, minuting by Graham, Dec. 15, 1906.
85. NA, G. no. 285/1907, sec. of state to gov., Mar. 23, 1907, encl. So. Af. Brit. Ind. Comm. to CO, Mar. 13, 1907.
86. NA, Natal no. 30, sec. of state to gov., Mar. 23, 1907.

And as in the early years of the act, the evidence was embarrassingly clear. At Klip River eleven Indians lost their licenses, not because they did not keep proper books in English, but because they had hired a professional bookkeeper to do the accounting for them. In the Lower Umzimkulu Division, Mahomed Saduck Vahed was deprived of his license even though the licensing officer admitted that the books of the business were well kept and that the premises were sanitary. When the appeal was heard, a certain J. W. Godwin appeared against Vahed. He based his position on the presence of too many "Arab" stores in the district. The "Arabs," he contended, did not compete fairly. Why, "these fellows lived on practically nothing—on the smell of an oiled rag—and we Europeans have to live in a quite different way." J. F. Retham, representing the chamber of commerce, agreed that the "Arabs" were taking over. He contended that it was the duty of every man to protect European interests against them. "They had to take the initial steps for getting these people out of the country." [87] The board then retired and after some deliberation rendered its verdict. "The Board is unanimous," the chairman read, "in its decision that the action of the Licensing Officer should be upheld and the appeal is dismissed without costs." The governor, Sir Henry McCallum, despite being an opponent of the Indian intrusion into commerce, nevertheless urged access to the supreme court for Indians deprived of licenses. He felt that they should not be exposed to the vagaries of local municipal boards—although he had to admit that few in the colony agreed with him.[88]

Faced with such clear evidence of Natal's malfeasance, the Colonial Office did little more than temporize. "I should be glad," the secretary of state wrote, "if you would draw . . . [ministers'] attention to Mr. Chamberlain's confidential despatch of the 20th of November 1897, enclosing a letter from Mr. Escombe, in which he gave it as his opinion that the Act

87. See note 85.
88. NA, Natal conf. no. 1, gov. to sec. of state, May 18, 1907.

did not require books to be kept by the Indian trader personally."[89]

What caused the Government of Natal the greatest embarrassment, however, was the action of the colony's own supreme court. While the general dealers' licenses act did indeed not permit the direct appeal of a licensing board's decision to the supreme court, the court could rule on procedural matters concerned with hearings conducted by the boards. In mid-1907 some of the Indian traders of Ladysmith brought such a case. They claimed that despite numerous protests they had been deprived of their licenses without either the licensing officer or his notes being examined at the hearings. The chief justice, with the other two justices sitting on the case concurring, condemned the actions of the licensing board. He addressed himself only to the question of whether the board, sitting as a court of appeal, had the right to come to a decision without the complete record of the licensing officer's proceedings being introduced in evidence. Clearly the answer was no. "It was certainly extraordinary," the chief justice thought,

> that any Court sitting as a Court of Appeal should decide a question on appeal without having before it all the records that were available. . . . Quite apart from the principle, it seemed to him, having regard to the rules framed under the law, the rules themselves required that the Board should have the report of the Sanitary Officer, the remarks of the Licensing Officer, and also the record of the application, and all the minutes that the Licensing Officer had. . . . The proceedings seemed of the greatest irregularity. . . . The proceedings before the Licensing Board were set aside, the appeal to be recommended de novo.[90]

The court's decision gave eloquent witness to the need of an appeal to the supreme court in licensing cases and to the court's very limited powers under the law as it stood. Shortly afterwards, however, the Ladysmith licensing board reheard the

89. NA, G. no. 419/1907, conf., sec. of state to gov., May 25, 1907.
90. *Ibid.*, encl. *Times of Natal*.

cases and again turned down the appeals against the licensing officer's decision.[91]

Natal's free Indians as they looked about them saw little reason for joy. The white colonists only wanted to see the last of them. The India and Colonial Offices seemed to limit their efforts to preventing explicitly discriminatory terminology from being enacted into law, and the Government of India, on the few occasions that it attempted to intercede, was essentially impotent. As for the governor, emissary of the monarch and Whitehall and champion of the imperial philosophy of equality, he nearly always identified with the white colonists. Early in 1907 the same McCallum who opposed the operation of the licensing act scribbled an angry note referring to Gandhi. "The 'Bombay Wallah' has come here knowing the conditions," he wrote, "and he can leave if he does not like them. Because we wanted *indentured labour for agriculture* it is no reason why we should be swamped by black matter in the wrong place —namely storekeepers etc." [92]

But despite a marked reluctance to act, neither the Colonial Office nor the India Office could ignore the overt challenges of the franchise clause of the municipal corporations act and the egregious persecution of Indian storekeepers under the terms of the dealers' licenses act. In its agony, the Colonial Office discerned the seeds of a solution in a note from the India Office received in August 1907. "If the dealers' licenses act is not amended," Morley had written, "it [is] essential that Indian rate-payers should remain in possession of the municipal franchise, in order that their interests may be adequately represented on the Municipal Boards. I therefore trust that Lord

---

91. Gandhi, in *Indian Opinion*, Dec. 14, 1907, called attention to new licensing regulations which forced applicants to allow the taking of a thumbprint, to publish their intent in the newspaper, and to deposit £12-10-0 when making an appeal (the last point was not new). *Works*, VII, 427–28.

92. NA, minute paper, sec. of state, Dec. 29, 1906; note by McCallum, Jan. 21, 1907.

Elgin may be able to agree that, unless the Dealers' Licenses Act be amended, it is impossible to consent to the retention of section 22(c) of the Municipal Corporations Bill." [93]

Lord Crewe, who had assumed the colonial portfolio in Herbert Asquith's Liberal government, consequently decided that British honor would be sufficiently vindicated if Natal were given the choice of either disenfranchising Indians at the municipal level or maintaining the status quo on the licensing issue.[94] It was a rather cynical gamble. Crewe realized that from his viewpoint the vital issue was that of licenses, and he was convinced that Natal would permit appeals to the supreme court in preference to allowing Indians to retain the municipal franchise.

The secretary of state failed to recognize the high value the white colonists placed on the dealers' licenses act as it stood. At a meeting between the Government of Natal and the mayors and chairmen of local boards called in January 1908, the minister of justice (Carter) spoke bluntly. He thought it perfectly proper for municipalities to rid themselves of licensing officers who disregarded the wishes of the white community and issued licenses to Indians. The municipal officials when their turns came vied with each other in detailing how they had driven the Indians in their locales out of business. The minister of justice then returned to the rostrum to explain that "if there was one law which they should cherish it was the Licensing Law. If the Imperial Government had ever known in what direction the law was going to operate he was certain it would never have obtained the Royal Assent. Already the Imperial Government had asked them to alter the law so that there should be an appeal to the Supreme Court and that was one thing the Government would never agree to." The prime minister, F. R. Moor, "thought the time had come when they should most seriously consider the advisability of not issuing

93. CO 179/249, IO to CO, Aug. 24, 1907.
94. *Ibid.,* minuting on Natal minute paper, Sept. 2, 1908.

any more licenses [to Indians]." No doubt aware of the Natal Government's earlier duplicity, he cautioned his listeners not to "blazen the fact abroad, but it was their policy nevertheless." [95]

Thus, when Natal reacted to the secretary of state's proposed bargain, its decision ran contrary to Lord Crewe's expectations. The prime minister reported that by promising the municipal association that the government contemplated no amendment of the dealers' licenses act it had gained the association's unanimous consent to changes in the municipal corporations bill.[96] Virtually all the sections of the orginal bill to which the Colonial and India Offices had objected were removed from the version it was intended to introduce into the next session of the legislature. Indians retained the municipal franchise. They were no longer to be considered members of an uncivilized race, and the term "coloured persons" was defined as meaning "any Asiatic labourer or domestic servant (including Asiatic labourers but not including mechanics, artisans, clerks, and other persons of a status above labourer or domestic servant)." [97]

Having chosen one of the alternatives put forward by the Colonial Office, Natal confidently awaited a note of approbation from the secretary of state. But Crewe was, of course, on the horns of a dilemma. He had offered Natal a choice of paths to follow, confident that the colony would prefer to amend the dealers' licenses act, and he had been wrong. He now indulged in a series of delaying tactics in order to avoid acceptance of the bargain he had himself proposed. Minor faults were discerned in the revised municipal corporations bill and loud exception was taken to them.[98] The prime minister of Natal quite properly replied that "impediments should not be placed in the way of an otherwise unobjectionable measure because

95. NA, PM 74/1908, Conf., Jan. 23, 1908.
96. NA, Natal no. 74, gov. to sec. of state, May 7, 1908.
97. NA, tel., gov. to sec. of state, July 24, 1907.
98. NA, G. no. 400/1908, tel., sec. of state to gov., June 18, 1908.

White Colonist versus Colored Immigrant 231

the Association did not go further and repeal existing legislation which had never been questioned by the Imperial Government in the past nor even mentioned prior to the secretary of state's telegram under reply," and he went on to point out that the Natal legislative session was already far advanced and unless some indication was soon received from the Colonial Office, it would be too late for the revised bill to pass.[99]

As his bargain had not worked out to his expectations, Crewe determined to abrogate it. The municipal corporations bill might have been satisfactorily altered, but this was not after all enough. In July 1908, the secretary of state, while expressing his pleasure at the proposed amendment of the municipal corporation bill, could not help expressing his regret at Natal's failure to permit Indian storekeepers an appeal to the supreme court in licensing cases. He felt that "such an appeal [was] . . . necessary to secure due protection of vested interests [for] . . . traders who have carried on their businesses for many years without let or hindrance [and who] should not be suddenly deprived of their licenses on the plea of insufficient bookkeeping." [100]

Natal's answer to the renewed assault was the introduction of three of the most virulently anti-Indian measures into the legislative assembly. The first bill (Assembly Bill 5 of 1908) was designed to bring to an end the issue of new trading licenses to Asians. It defined as a new license: "(a) a license to any person who does not hold a license similar in every respect to the license applied for at the date when the application is made for the license; (b) a license in respect to premises for which a license similar in every respect is not held at a date when application is made for the license." The transfer of a license was, under the terms of the act, deemed to be the issuance of a new license. And the act stipulated that after December 31, 1908, no

99. See note 96.
100. NA, G. no. 54/1901, Natal conf. (2) sec. of state to gov., July 18, 1908.

new license would be issued to an Asian, although rights of inheritance were preserved. Only one member (Connolly) who claimed to represent the working class seemed in strong opposition to the proposed law. He contended that competition aided the consumer and that the presence of the Indian traders consequently allowed the white laborer to buy at the lowest possible price.[101]

The introduction of the measure allowed the members of the legislative assembly to give voice to a whole spectrum of prejudices. Although most of the colonists were really only worried about competition from the "Arabs," one member (Robinson) had a different point of view. "The Arab is undoubtedly an undesirable resident," he admitted, "but on the question of comparison of degree of danger, do members realise what I have pointed out before, that the sons of Indian immigrants are practising as barristers in this Colony today? . . . There are thousands of these men in the country. Their children are being admitted into all the professions. By a comparison of menace, the Arab is nil. The descendants of the coolie are a very serious menace." [102] Another member (Wylie) "would like to see the provisions of the Bill extended, as there were traders just as undesirable as Indians and Asiatics, such, for instance, as the Polish and other low-class Jews." A third speaker (O'Meara) was even more exotically anti-semitic. "[He] wanted the title to the Bill to be extended to include such people as Peruvian Jews, who were the most undesirable class of people he could conceive." [103]

It was at this juncture that Sir Matthew Nathan arrived as governor. The appointment did not turn out to be a particularly popular one. In the first place Nathan replaced Sir Henry McCallum, who had strongly supported the white colonists' views; secondly, he was a Jew, one of the first to achieve

101. Natal *Hansard*, July 15, 1908.
102. *Ibid.*, July 23, 1907; statement made in an earlier debate on a similar measure.
103. *Ibid.* It should be noted that Yiddish was considered a European language under the provisions of the immigration act of 1903.

prominence in the colonial service; and thirdly, he was much more sympathetic to the Indians than any of his predecessors—certainly at least in part because of his own struggle for success in a century when anti-semitism in public life was endemic. Nathan was critical of the bill "to bring to an end the issue of new trading licenses to Asiatics," [104] and there were those in the assembly who wished to modify the law. All attempted amendments were, however, rejected. The bill was read without a division for the third time on July 28, 1908, and sent to London for ratification by the secretary of state.

The passage of this first of the three pieces of anti-Indian legislation occurred while the assembly was debating the second bill, which would "put an end to further introduction of indentured Indian immigrants." The proposal was, of course, highly controversial, so much so that it was withdrawn to allow appointment of a commission, broadly representative of all shades of colonial opinion, which, under the chairmanship of Walter F. Clayton, was to investigate fully the various facets of the colony's labor situation.[105]

The third bill, the most destructive of the Indian position to date, was passed by the Natal legislature and sent to the governor on August 27, 1908. Its purpose was "to prohibit after a certain time the holding of trading licenses by Asiatics." The act stipulated that after December 31, 1918, "no license shall be issued or transferred to or be capable of being held by or on behalf of an Asiatic." Compensation was to be provided for those still holding licenses at the time the act went into operation, but the scale was singularly niggardly. In case of difficulty in determining the amount of compensation, article 5 of the law provided for adjudication under the terms of the arbitration act of 1898, or whatever similar act might be in force at the time.

104. NA, no. 289, gov. to sec. of state, Dec. 7, 1908.
105. Opposition to the bill was not limited to the coast planters. Up-country farmers had been making increasing use of Indian labor in the wattlebark industry and elsewhere, and the railways employed 1,500 indentured and 2,000 free Indians.

This final bill was so extreme that eleven of the thirty-three members of the assembly opposed it, mainly on the basis of the compensation clause, which the colonial secretary stated was more liberal than ordinarily would have been the case and was only included to disarm criticism in London. He also contended that Indians sent two and one-half million pounds out of the country annually, and that "it was their duty to hand down a clear land to their children, and he appealed to members to do their duty." [106] More even than those of the colonial secretary, the statements of a member of the Assembly (Taylor) characterized the attitude of the advocates of the bill. Taylor thought that the provision for a ten-year period during which Indians were permitted to continue in business was excessively generous when a license was issued for only one year at a time. If the licensing officers did not reduce the number of Indian licenses by half before the act went into effect, "he would endeavour to make it hot for them. It would behoove the young men of Natal to get up a Movement and let the rest of the world see that they were not going to allow the thing to go on. He was prepared to take a lead in the matter." [107]

On August 27, Marshall Campbell, the noted sugar planter and hence very familiar with Indians, rose in the council to oppose the bill in what he knew to be a losing effort. But his words represented the sentiments of the more liberal of Natal's white colonists: "He considered the Bill a most unjust one. The Arabs had been encouraged to come into the Colony to trade by the Government, the Corporations, and individuals. They had built up new houses and businesses, and to get notice that in ten years' time they had to leave everything that was dear to them was cruel. The Council had been especially constituted [in conjunction with the advent of responsible government in 1893] to protect the two races that were not directly represented. He would again oppose the Bill at the third reading."

Nathan was strongly critical of the measure. He felt that the

---

106. Natal *Hansard,* Aug. 19, 1908.   107. *Ibid.*

rationale so often used of passing anti-Indian laws to protect the natives was an obvious sham.[108] But as the governor of a colony possessing the rights of responsible government, he had to be circumspect in his official correspondence. "As in the case of the other Bill," he wrote to the secretary of state, "stress is laid on the present exodus of the Colony's white manhood, an exodus which it may be mentioned has taken place also from the Cape Colony where it has, as far as I am aware, never been attributed to the Asiatic trader." [109] In referring to the compensation arrangement, Nathan concluded that the stipulated terms were inadequate and designed to force Indians to sell out to Europeans at a loss during the grace period provided by the act. All in all, he was convinced that "the compensation clauses are illusory." [110] And so saying, he reserved the measure for the signification of His Majesty's pleasure.[111]

Yet Nathan was not totally hostile to the fears of the white population, and he searched his mind for a solution to the problem that the Indians presented. He had no doubt that the three bills, extreme as they were, would never achieve their aims, but the only alternative he could recommend was not really practicable. "Repatriation to India or removal to some Colony which Great Britain governs but does not colonise, for the bulk of the Indians outside of the Tropics in South Africa," he wrote, "is the only solution which would be completely satisfactory to the white races. . . . It might be worthwhile for the United Kingdom to contribute financially and otherwise to the gradual carrying out of the scheme with this view under such conditions of full compensation for injury to vested interests as would prevent it becoming unduly harsh on the persons removed." [112]

When news of the three bills reached the Colonial Office, Lord Crewe reacted with unaccustomed vigor. On July 22 he sent a long dispatch to Natal. He had little to say about the bill

108. See note 104.
109. NA, no. 290, gov. to sec. of state, Dec. 7, 1908.
110. NA, Natal conf., gov. to sec. of state, May 8, 1908.
111. See note 109.   112. See note 110.

to halt indentured immigration, but he condemned the other two acts in the strongest terms. Not only would they have a very unfortunate effect on India, but the disabilities imposed on the Indians of Natal were absolutely unconscionable. Consequently, the secretary of state informed the governor "that the inherent defects to which I have referred will make it impossible for me to advise His Majesty to assent to the Bills." [113]

Increasingly, the course of events in Natal angered the viceroy and his council in Calcutta. Not only did the Colonial Office, in September 1908, finally approved the Municipal Corporations Act, but Natal had, in order to gain uniformity in licensing decisions, appointed a single officer for the whole of the colony. The testimony he gave before the Clayton Commission must have been of interest to the Government of India. The new appointee, E. Wynne Cole, feared "the imminent risk of contamination which our children incur through daily contact with inferior, coloured races" and the commercial competition of the "Arab," whom he accused of having absorbed half of the trade of the Colony through fraudulent business practices and of having sent the proceeds to India. He concluded his testimony with a damaging confession. "Since my appointment as Licensing Officer for the Colony," he admitted,

> the Arab trader has generally come to understand that he will not get any more licenses issued to him in the future. . . . The reduction of the Arab and Indian licenses will mean prosperity to the Colony, and the settlement of Europeans in our midst in their places. I think this is already apparent from the fact that during the months of November and December, 1908 and in January, February and March 1909, I have refused 32 Arab licenses, many of whom have been trading for years, and during the same period I have issued about 32 new licenses to Europeans in different parts of the Colony.[114]

That the danger of Indians taking over much of the trade of Natal was exaggerated was evidenced by figures Nathan sent to

113. NA, G. no. 555/1908, no. 125, sec of state to gov., July 22, 1908.
114. NA, CSO 2783, Clayton Commission evidence.

Crewe. In 1895 Indians had held 393 licenses and Europeans 356. In 1908 there were 1,008 Indian and 2,034 European license-holders.[115] In addition, the Indian Government had assumed, at least since the Anglo-Boer War, that the indentured Indians in Natal, its chief responsibility, were well treated. It was surprised to discover that this was not always true. For instance, John P. Armatage, a plantation owner, cut off the ear lobe of one of his laborers, stating that as it was permissible so to mark sheep it should also be a legal method of identifying Indians.[116] A laborer named Ramsamy was whipped by the planter to whom he was indentured. He fled and was sent to jail for seven days while his employer was only fined ten shillings for assault.[117]

Not unaware of the growing tide of resentment in India, Natal did what it could to insure the continuation of indentured immigration. Act 22 of 1909, passed as the separate existence of Natal as a British colony was coming to an end, at last permitted shopkeepers deprived of licenses to appeal to the supreme court, which could either order the issuing of a license or remit the case for rehearing. Lord Crewe was delighted; he informed the Natal Indians that the amendment of the Dealers' Licenses Act of 1897 was the single most important reform that Natal could have implemented. In Natal itself the change was surprisingly widely applauded. The *Mercury*, on November 26, 1909, under the headline "Gross Injustice Removed," wondered how the law in its original form had ever been allowed to pass, "as it violated one of the most basic principles of the British Constitution, and was without precedent in any part of the Empire. To deprive any man of the right of appeal to the Courts of the Land was simply a monstrous piece of injustice."

If the Colonial Office and Natal at last basked in the warmth

115. NA, Natal Conf., gov. to sec. of state, July 9, 1908.
116. NA, no. 300, gov. to sec. of state, Dec. 28, 1908.
117. NA, no. 96, gov. to sec. of state, May 8, 1909.

of clear consciences, the Indians, though they welcomed the amendment, were less enthusiastic. They emphasized the limited nature of the change, for the granting of new licenses and the transfer of existing ones was still left, without appeal, to the discretion of the licensing officer and the licensing boards.[118] The Government of India was even more displeased. "Our position has always been," the viceroy telegraphed London, "that appeal to the Supreme Court should lie against all decisions of licensing boards, and we are not prepared to accept as sufficient a proposal to allow appeal against withdrawal of licenses only."[119] The Colonial Office did not dispute the validity of the points made by the Natal Indians and the Government of India, but Graham concluded that "it is useless to go to Natal again now and I have drafted the various letters required on that assumption."[120] Lambert perhaps most accurately reflected the Colonial Office's view when he minuted: "The Natal people of course are determined to reduce the number of Indian traders and no doubt feel that if licenses are to be freely transferred the number will never be reduced. This is no doubt from our point of view a blemish, but the amendment does clearly secure that a man trading is not himself thrown out of business by the jealousy of European rivals on the Town Council. The Indian can still transfer his business to a European if he wants to go."[121]

Frustrated on all sides and deprived of any rationalization for inaction, the Government of India determined to use the one weapon at its disposal—the termination of indentured emigration from India. London managed to delay the implementation of this decision, but it finally came to pass in July 1911.

118. CO 179/255, Anglia to CO, Dec. 7, 1909.
119. NAI, Govt. of India, Dept. of Comm. and Ind. (Em.), Mar. 1910, procs. 14–43, viceroy to sec. of state, Oct. 27, 1909.
120. CO 179/255, minuting on Natal minute paper no. 29775, Dec. 8, 1909.
121. *Ibid.*, Dec. 9, 1909.

The birth of the Union of South Africa in 1910, with Louis Botha and his newly-formed South African National Party at its head, concentrated the Indian question that had existed in four separate colonies into a single arena, at least as far as some issues were concerned. A most dramatic struggle ensued which pitted the Indians led by Gandhi, prophet of the revolutionary new technique of dissent, *satyagraha,* against General Smuts and the Afrikaner establishment. With the attention of at least the English-speaking world focussed on the struggle, the Indians forced the Union Government to moderate its position on a number of issues.

Under the terms of Act 22 of 1914—the Indian Relief Act—resident Indians were guaranteed the right to gain admission to the Union of one wife and her minor children. The legality of Indian marriages which had been called into question in the cases of *Sultina* v. *Rex* (1912) and *Esop* v. *the Minister of the Interior* (1913) was assured and Indian domiciliary rights were clarified. Of greatest importance to Indian morale was the repeal of Natal Act 17 of 1895, which had established the hated £3 residence tax in law.

But what seemed like a staggering victory against insuperable odds was significant only in terms of shadow rather than substance. The provinces of the new Union—the four former colonies—still maintained considerable jurisdiction over their own affairs. Law 3 of 1885, as amended in 1886, and the Transvaal Gold Law and Townships Act of 1908 remained on the statute books. Indians lacked the franchise (a provincial prerogative), license abuses were as common as ever, the municipal councils still held sway, and the situation was destined to grow worse. An imperial philosophy of equality before the law not withstanding, it was clear that British citizenship and the rights supposedly inherent to that status were not common to all subjects of the crown in South Africa any more than they were in the other Dominions.

"The principles by which we must be guided are clear," exclaimed the *Times* of September 12, 1910. "In the past we have conceived of British citizenship as conferring, in the same way as Roman citizenship of old, an equal *status* in all parts of the King-Emperor's Dominions." But this is not a principle which the colonies will accept. Consequently, "we must strive to make our Indian fellow-subjects realise that . . . inequality [is] inevitable . . . not due to inferior *status* but to facts of race. . . ."

Australia was as determined as South Africa to arrest the colored cancer that lack of vigilance had permitted to grow upon the continent. Immigration legislation and capitation taxes to which Chinese alone were subject were not deemed sufficient by the white colonists. Again, the franchise, naturalization and commercial competitiveness were all objects of colonial attention. New South Wales, for instance, had prohibited the naturalization of Chinese as early as 1861 (Act 3), an action which was rescinded in 1867 (Act 8) and reinstituted in 1888 (Act 4). Then in 1899 (Act 19), the colony disenfranchised all resident Chinese unless they were qualified freeholders. Queensland wanted only immigrants interested in settling permanently. The legislature had as a consequence in the same year as New South Wales's initial action passed a measure excluding Asian or African aliens from eligibility for naturalization unless they were married (with a wife in the colony) and had been in Queensland for three years.[122] Although it did not in the 1860s and 1870s pass anti-Chinese immigration legislation of the type that reached the statute books in Victoria, New South Wales and South Australia, Queensland did, unimpeded by the Colonial Office, pass Act 49 of 1885, article 6(1) of which stipulated that "no aboriginal native of Australia, India, China or of the South Sea Islands shall be entitled to be entered on any electoral roll prepared . . . for the purpose of election of a member of

122. Queensland Act 9, 1861. Repromulgated in Queensland Act 28 of 1867.

the Legislative Assembly, except in respect of a freehold qualification." [123]

Despite their declining number, the Chinese on the few remaining Australian goldfields were a continuing annoyance to the white colonists. Thus, Queensland in 1876 passed "A Bill to Amend 'The Gold Fields Amendment Act of 1874'," the stipulations of which were aimed directly at the Chinese. No doubt a major motivation for passage of the measure was the realization that there were 7,000 Chinese on the Palmer goldfield and that they greatly outnumbered the European miners.[124] Article 1 raised the fee an Asian or African alien had to pay for a miner's right from 10 shillings to £3 and for a business license from £3 to £10. Heavy penalties were prescribed for evasion, and the burden of proof in questions of race or nationality rested with the defendant. Summary justice was to be the order of the day.

The law initiated a major controversy. Governor Cairns wrote Lord Carnarvon, secretary of state, that his attorney general had recommended the allowance of the measure, but that he did not see his way clear to following this advice. It seemed to Cairns, who to his ministers epitomized Whitehall, that the bill was one of "an extraordinary nature and importance"; that it ran counter to established international conventions and that it violated Anglo-Chinese treaties in both the spirit and the letter. Besides, it offered no protection to Chinese British subjects, not to mention other British Asians and Africans. The governor concluded on a note which must have particularly

123. Western Australia emulated Queensland under the terms of Act 19 of 1899. Throughout the Australasian colonies, Europeans could normally become voters in several ways: (1) any 25-year-old male with six months' residence in the district was eligible; (2) so was the holder of a freehold without encumbrance valued at £100, or the occupier of a £10 leasehold estate, and (3) the holder of a six months' government license to pasture land. Finally, (4) a renter who paid £10 rent annually was entitled to vote.

124. CO 234/37, Q. 12192, speech by the postmaster-general, July 4, 1876.

enraged the white colonists of Queensland: "I question whether it can be shown, that man for man, the European miner . . . contributes at all more largely to the revenue and general prosperity of the Colony than does his Asiatic rival." [125]

Cairns, by espousing the imperial philosophy, had placed himself on a collision course not only with his own ministers and the majority in the colonial legislature but with public opinion as well. The cabinet pointed out that the governor was entitled to reserve a bill only when Her Majesty's prerogatives had been questioned, the rights or property of British subjects not residing in the colony endangered, or the trade and shipping of the United Kingdom and its dependencies threatened.

> It appears to Ministers to be of the utmost importance that the authority of the Colonial Legislature to pass laws on all subjects whatever which they may think necessary for the good Government of the Colony should be recognised and upheld and that no other limit to that power should be admitted than that which is imposed by the Royal Instructions to the Governor. They think that to go beyond those instructions, or to allow the unusual character of the proposed legislation not forbidden by them as a sufficient ground for not giving immediate effect to the wish of the Legislature would be a serious consequence to the independence and freedom of Parliament.[126]

Carnarvon rallied to the support of his governor. Emphasizing that both New South Wales and Victoria had repealed acts similar to the one under consideration, he strongly defended Cairns's right to reserve the measure under the royal instructions. The bill was imperial in nature, and it fell under the 11th clause of the instructions, which ordered the reservation of any bill of "an extraordinary nature whereby the rights of Her Majesty's subjects not residing in the Colony may be prejudiced. . . ." Besides, the proposed law contravened the friendly relations which prevailed between Great Britain and China.[127]

125. CO 234/36, Q. 14701, no. 80, Cairns to Carnarvon, Oct. 11, 1876.
126. *Ibid.*, encl. 4, George Thorn to Cairns, no date (first days of Oct.).
127. *Ibid.*, draft, Carnarvon to Cairns, Mar. 27, 1877.

Other officials of the Colonial Office also recorded their views. John Bramston asserted that it would be impossible for a British-born Chinese to prove his status, and he objected to the summary trial of suspected offenders at the point of apprehension. "If a Chinese cook sends up a bad breakfast to two J.P.'s in a gold field public house and is without a miner's right, he may be at once sent off for three months hard labour." Robert Herbert, then the ranking undersecretary, took a somewhat different tack. He thought the governor should carefully watch the operation of the act but that neither he nor Her Majesty's Government should actually impede its coming into operation. In general, the staff of the Colonial Office saw little reason to disallow the Queensland bill as it did not, in their view, run counter to treaty obligations.[128]

The Brisbane *Courier* accurately gauged the public pulse when it supported the bill. It referred to the violence the Chinese engendered and the amount their presence cost the colony.[129] "If the Chinese were treated more like Asiatics and less like Englishmen," the paper contended, "much, much trouble would be spared wardens and police, and revenue would be more effectually extracted from them. It is utterly absurd to try and administer government to these people strictly according to the spirit of English law which they cannot understand, and if they could, would not appreciate." [130]

Meanwhile, Premier John Douglas had asked other Australasian colonies for their support in the battle over the Chinese miners' bill. In a bitter letter, he invoked the danger of smallpox which the Chinese presence entailed and the threat to colonial self-government constituted by the action to reserve the measure. Next he addressed the Queensland agent-general in London, asking him to impress upon Carnarvon the strong feeling about the miners' bill manifested throughout Australia.

128. *Ibid.,* minuting of Jan. 1 and 9, 1877.
129. Bramston had asserted that this justification was pure rubbish.
130. Brisbane *Courier,* Aug. 4, 1876.

The agent-general was to point to the colonists' conviction that the Chinese, while industrious and frugal, did not make good settlers. They came without their women and sent their wealth back to China. The advent of the Chinese could well mean the replacement of European labor by an intelligent but servile and docile class which could well prove detrimental to the whole colony. Douglas hoped the agent-general would be able to persuade the secretary of state that Her Majesty's Government would be ill-advised to so interpret international agreements as to allow interference with the rights of colonial self-government.[131]

The Australasian colonies saw the disallowance of the Queensland bill as an attack on all of them. Sir Henry Parkes led his colleagues in the New South Wales cabinet in a minute addressed to the governor, Sir Hercules Robinson. The ministers expressed sympathy for Queensland's dilemma, and urged the governor to represent to Her Majesty's Government the expediency of modifying existing treaties with China so as to prevent "the present exceedingly undersirable flood of Chinese people coming into Australia . . . your Excellency's advisers would respectfully represent to Lord Carnarvon the expediency and sound policy of removing any impediments in the way of such measures of legislation as the Parliament of Queensland may consider necessary for the protection of the British population of the Colony." [132]

In writing to Douglas, Parks made it clear that the Chinese problem was one that concerned the entire continent. He felt that an excessive immigration of Chinese into northern Queensland could not but affect the other colonies and his desire to aid Queensland on the mining bill issue was based on "regard to the public safety of our own community not less than our

---

131. CO 15/76, paper 91 of 1877 on proc. 11, July 1877, John Douglas to all colonies and New Zealand, Apr. 20, 1877; Douglas to agent-general, same date.

132. CO 201/583, minute signed by Henry Parkes, July 6, 1877.

desire to aid in your efforts to protect society in Queensland." [133]

Graham Berry, in a long letter, assured Douglas of Victoria's support. He based his position both on a defense of the rights of self-government and on the need to fight the menace "of a race which carries with it serious social and physical dangers." Berry offered Queensland "the heart-felt sympathy and support of this Government" and urged joint Australasian action whenever one of the colonies was treated by the home government in the same manner as Queensland.[134]

Meanwhile in London, Queensland's agent-general had entered the lists against Lord Carnarvon. He denied that the miners' bill constituted a breach of existing treaties or that it infringed on the rights of British subjects not resident in the colony. Queensland, he asserted, was willing to receive Chinese who came to trade or settle, but ". . . at the same time it is said we cannot consent to vast hordes engaged by agents in China landing on our Northern Coasts and taking possession of our Northern goldfields." This, said the agent-general, was neither trading nor settlement and as the Chinese did not add to the welfare of the colony, it was only proper that they be asked to contribute to the support of the various government departments their presence in part necessitated. The new charges levied on Chinese by the miners' bill were thus totally justified.

On the question of British citizenship, the burden for proof of which rested, under the bill in question, on the Chinese on the goldfields, the agent-general's only defense was that "if the onus were removed from the Defendant and placed on the shoulders of the official prosecuting there would be an end of the Act. The Chinese are exceedingly astute regarding their own interests and every one of them would naturally set up

---

133. Queensland Archives, COL 13, Parkes to colonial secretary, Queensland, June 27, 1877.
134. *Ibid.*, no. 2759, Graham Berry, chief secretary, Victoria, to John Douglas, vice-president of the executive council, Queensland, no date.

the plea that he was a British subject. Of course there would be no evidence that he was not, and thus, the act would become a nullity." [135]

Carnarvon remained obdurate, and his attitude moved the Queensland legislature to new heights of fury and frustration. Griffith, at the time the attorney general, urged the secretary of state to reconsider and not finally to disallow the miners' bill.

> If he did [not do] so, he would incur a responsibility which he thought few ministers of the crown would care to assume, taking into consideration the result of that assumed by the Administration in reference to America in 1776. He thought that even if the colonies of Australia had had to resign whatever benefits they were likely to derive from their connection with Great Britain, it would be better for them to do so than to allow their country to become an appendage of the Chinese Empire.[136]

The minister for mines took umbrage at Carnarvon's assertion that the exclusion of the subjects of a state with whom Her Majesty was at peace from any part of Her Majesty's dominions was "highly objectionable in principle." "That was a matter of opinion. . . . His (the Attorney-General's) answer to this was that the colony of Queensland was the best judge, and not the Secretary of State in this matter." [137]

The Brisbane *Courier* reflected the views of the city's working men when it wrote: "The Government of this colony should not quietly submit to the defeat which they have sustained from the Colonial Office. . . . We hope that Parliament . . . will re-enact as often as may be necessary such measures as may be thought advisable to discourage too great an influx of Chinese immigrants." The Chinese problem was not limited to the goldfields, the *Courier* asserted. In the northern towns Chinese were beginning to gain control of trade. Soon they would monopolize whole industries to the detriment of the white man. Although both assertions were untrue, they were indicative of a fear not

135. *Ibid.*, G. W. Herbert to Carnarvon, July 12, 1877.
136. Queensland *Hansard*, June 26, 1877.   137. *Ibid.*, June 13, 1877.

only of Chinese labor but of commercial competition on a higher plane. "If the people of Queensland do not desire to see this state of thing," the paper concluded,

let them be up and doing—let them support their Government in a persistent attempt to recover the right of regulating the internal affairs of the colony of which they have been virtually deprived by the action which the Imperial Government has lately taken; and, above all, let them resolve not to give any support to any Government which does not plainly show that it is alive to the magnitude of the damage which threatens this colony, and is prepared to combat it by every legitimate means within its power.[138]

With a new spirit of defiance, the government, in mid-1877, introduced another goldfields act. Noting it was almost identical to the bill reserved by Cairns the year before, Sir Arthur Kennedy, the new governor, wondered what had motivated his ministers when they knew he had approved of Cairns's action.[139] The bill required the same special fees from Asian and African aliens for miners' rights and business licenses as the disallowed measure. And in its first draft it stipulated that no African or Asiatic alien would be permitted to mine upon any goldfield until two years after its proclamation, though this restriction was removed in the final version of the law. The attorney general advised the governor to allow the bill. He contended that major changes had been introduced. No longer would it be necessary for an African or Asian to prove that he was a British subject. He need only have a license, and the bill did not mention race in regard to the right to mine—only the need to hold a valid license.[140] Still, the law's purpose was clear, and it did maintain the main proviso of the original bill, the special levies on African and Asian (that is, Chinese) miners.

Kennedy, despite his basic opposition to the mining bill, was beginning to feel the heavy domestic pressure and asked the

138. Brisbane *Courier,* Apr. 11 and 16, 1877.
139. CO 234/37, Q. 10027, conf. Kennedy to Carnarvon, June 16, 1877.
140. CO 234/37, Q. 10919, no. 50, Kennedy to Carnarvon, c. July 1877, encl. att. gen. to gov., July 14, 1877.

Colonial Office for a speedy decision.[141] Not that the support for the act was unanimous. In the legislature, for instance, Henry Walsh of Warrego confessed to feeling humiliated. He thought the proposed law un-English and expressed his conviction that it would meet the same fate as its predecessor at the hands of the Colonial Office.[142] Walsh's faith was, however, not justified. Whitehall clearly had a bad case of cold feet. Herbert minuted: "I do not think we can at the present stage further resist the urgent demand of the Queensland legislature to be allowed to control, in the manner adopted by the Act, the influx of Chinese which is causing and threatening so much trouble. As the attorney general's Report shows—your [Carnarvon's] objections have been met to an extent which may be considered sufficient." Carnarvon had more important things on his mind and as a consequence telegraphed Kennedy that he might assent to the goldfields act but again without prejudice to the Queen's power of disallowance.[143] Once more a determined colonial government had shown just how far the Colonial Office was prepared to go (or not to go) to protect the imperial philosophy of equality of all subjects of the crown before the law. Lord Derby pragmatically remarked, "We are in the hands of the colonists and they must act in this matter as they please." [144]

With the dike successfully breached, Queensland the following year passed another act to amend the goldfields act of 1874 as it related to new goldfields.[145] It thus wrote into law restrictions which had been removed from the legislation of 1877 as a concession to imperial London. The measure defined a goldfield as being "new" for three years after its proclamation, and its heart was article 5 which stipulated: "No miner's right issued

141. *Ibid.* 142. Queensland *Hansard,* June 18, 1877.
143. CO 234/37, Q. 10919, no. 50, Kennedy to Carnarvon, minuting by Herbert, Sept. 21, 1877; tel., Carnarvon to Kennedy, Sept. 26, 1877.
144. *Hansard,* 3rd series CCCXXVI, 1518, quoted in *Cambridge History of the British Empire,* VII, pt. 1 (Cambridge, 1933), 42.
145. Queensland Act 2 of 1878.

to any Asiatic or African alien shall either when originally issued or by way of subsequent endorsement be made available for any new gold field," unless an Asiatic or African alien had discovered it. Article 6 stated: "No consolidated miner's right shall authorise the employment by virtue thereof of an Asiatic or African alien upon a new gold field."

What the law, of course, effected was the exclusion of nonwhites from all future gold discoveries until after most of the wealth had been removed. As has already been pointed out, the limiting of the law's restrictions to Asiatic and African *aliens* was in fact no protection at all. Yet Kennedy was somehow able to write Carnarvon that the new law was an attempt to mitigate the crude and unwise legislation of the previous year— an interpretation hard to understand except perhaps in purely economic terms; for Kennedy asserted that the law of 1877 had been a signal failure and had caused a serious loss of revenue. He thought the act of 1878 would be similarly unsuccessful, but he did not prevent it from reaching the statute books.[146]

Queensland's drive against Asian miners was emulated by South Australia, Act 368 of 1886. Among other things, it limited them to goldfields that were essentially worked out. The early efforts to exclude the Chinese from the goldfields of Victoria have already been recounted in Chapter 2, and by 1891 there were only 2,186 Chinese miners in the colony. The Western Australia Gold Fields Amendment Act (21 of 1892) excluded Asians from "new" goldfields even beyond the five-year period provided for in the original legislation of 1886. And mining or business licenses could no longer be issued to Asian or African aliens.[147]

Much more important than the possible presence of a few Chinese on a goldfield was the threat of commercial competition

---

146. CO 234/38, Q. 12124, conf., Kennedy to Carnarvon, July 24, 1878.
147. Act 3 of 1892. These limitations were confirmed in article 14 of Act 40 of 1895, the Goldfields Act of 1895, and article 4 of Act 16 of 1898, the Goldfields Act, 1895, Amendment Act, 1898.

by nonwhites in other spheres. South Australia, for instance, in its Northern Territory continued to strive for the best of both worlds—the benefits of nonwhite labor without the danger of permanent colored presence. On the one hand, the Constitution Further Amendment Act 278 of 1882 had limited the franchise in the Northern Territory to natural-born subjects of Her Majesty and naturalized subjects of "European nationality" or from the United States.[148] And the Government of South Australia, by administrative edict of May 1886, had empowered the resident to collect a £10 poll tax from every Chinese arriving in the territory—an act not sanctified by law and so illegal that the governor cautioned the premier that it would not stand up for a moment in the courts.[149] On the other hand, the contractors for the Pine Creek railway introduced 300 Chinese coolies to work on the line. The vast majority of the Chinese constituted a sort of floating population which worked on the railways, in the mines, and as servants. About 1,300, however, resided in the Darwin area, where they became proprietors of various kinds of stores, of laundries, restaurants and other commercial establishments—much to the discomfiture of the European population.[150]

Rising hysteria drove the South Australian Government with increasing frequency into actions that were blatantly illegal. When the resident in the Northern Territory reported an unusually large number of Chinese en route to Port Darwin, the government again, "subject to parliamentary sanction," authorized the collection of a £10 poll tax on all new arrivals and instructed the resident to keep all vessels arriving from Chinese ports in quarantine for twenty-one days. Chinese who were al-

148. A unique restriction which struck at one of the few principles of imperial equality the Colonial Office insisted on maintaining. It either passed unnoticed or for some reason was ignored.
149. Rendell, 102.
150. J. P. M. Long, "Asian Immigration into the Northern Territory to 1910" (Adelaide, 1964), 7; Rendell, 124.

ready in the territory but who ventured further than 200 miles from Port Darwin were also liable to the £10 exaction.[151]

Nevertheless, more and more Chinese made their way into the Northern Territory. In absolute terms their number was never great, but they made a large percentage of the total population. In 1889 there were 6,200 Chinese compared to some 1,000 Europeans.[152] "The interests of the Chinese extend into many fields of activity in the Territory," one observer noted. In Palmerston (Darwin), "the Europeans are almost entirely dependent upon them. There is a Chinese bootmaker, tailor, baker, and hairdresser; several dobies or washerwomen and gardeners unlimited. A Chinese company is being formed to bring cattle from Queensland to compete with European butchers." [153] The Chinese provided virtually all of the agricultural production of the Northern Territory and most of the labor on European plantations and in the mines. On the coast, sampans carried salt fish to China and brought copper ore from Daly when the mines there were in operation. They also fished extensively for shrimp.

The governor of South Australia, Lord Kintore, was a strong advocate of colored labor for the Northern Territory. In June 1891 he visited the area and wrote that Europeans were leaving the region due to the impediments being placed in the way of Chinese immigration. "Where the average White Labourer is incapable of sustained efforts," he wrote, "where European women and children do not thrive, it becomes necessary to rely on Asiatic assistance. Moreover, it is clear that no employer would be likely to continue to pay 10/- a day for European labor which as a rule is physically incapable of satisfactorily performing, seeing that Asiatics can work continuously and satisfactorily at a much lower wage." [154]

151. CO 236/10, tel., Playford to Griffith, Feb. 29, 1888.
152. Long, 22.   153. *Ibid.*, 12.
154. CO 13/147, S.A. 15080, no. 41, Kintore to Knutsford, June 23, 1891.

Kintore particularly favored the presence of the Chinese. "Only those who have lived in the territory," he wrote, "can realise what an important factor in its present social organisation the Chinese are. Remove them tomorrow, and residents of Palmerston would be left without fish, vegetables, or fruit, to a large extent without meat, without laundries for their washing, neither would there be any tailors, cooks or domestic servants." [155] A visitor to the territory wrote in 1894 that "the territory reminded one more of a little Asia or China than a European colony." [156] Colonial Office minuting correctly assessed the governor's position: "The sense and substance of these papers is that nothing can save the Northern Territory but the admission of Chinese." [157]

But Kintore was to be frustrated in his aspirations. The last Chinese was naturalized in April 1888. And Act 501 of 1890 stipulated that, "No Asiatic alien shall be entitled to acquire the fee simple of any land in the Northern Territory." For a moment it appeared that conversations with the Government of India might, at last, achieve fruition and provide indentured Indian labor for the Northern Territory. But it was all in vain. Despite lengthy negotiations the whole business fell to the ground much to the surprise of the authorities in Calcutta, who were not used to being treated so cavalierly by a mere colony just because the government had changed.

It is perhaps a commentary on the quality of life in China that Chinese continued to live in the Northern Territory at all —although their number did in fact drop to 2,760 by 1894.[158] In Palmerston, a harmless Chinese was savagely murdered by two Europeans. Despite the absolute certainty of their guilt, the jury would not convict them and Kintore was forced to write Ripon: "The occurrence seems to add weight to the asser-

155. Long, 12–13.   156. *Ibid.*
157. CO 13/147, S.A. 15080, no. 41, Kintore to Knutsford, June 23, 1891, minuting of 28/7.
158. Long, 22.

White Colonist versus Colored Immigrant 253

tion now commonly made that, owing to the antipathy of Australians to all Alien Races, few juries will convict in such cases as this one, however clear the evidence. No power to remove the trial of these cases from Palmerston exists." Robert Meade, the permanent undersecretary at the Colonial Office, minuted: "The truth is that juries in such cases cannot be relied upon to convict their fellow countrymen. Life is held cheaper than at home, and a Chinaman is not rated as of much value." [159] The *Northern Territory Times* told of an occurrence at Pine Creek when the resident justice had sworn at a Chinese from the bench and had shouted: "That's right, Sergeant, take the ——— out and lynch him." [160]

The Chinese encountered difficulties not only with the white man; their relations with the Aborigines of the area were also strained. Native attacks on Chinese and their property reached such a level that even the Europeans urged upon the government the duty of protecting them. On the other hand, the Chinese were not always totally innocent. At Pine Creek, Jimmy Ah Fat, after being repulsed by an Aborigine girl, threw a loaded charge of dynamite at her and wounded both the object of his affection and an innocent bystander.[161]

The future of the Northern Territory was sufficiently unclear for a royal commission to be appointed and to hold hearings during 1895. Its report came out in favor of the use of Asian labor for the agricultural development of the territory but urged the exclusion of the Chinese and other Asians from the goldfields. The first of the commissioners' recommendations was never successfully implemented in the sense intended, but the second resulted in the passage of a law (Act 608 of 1895) which banned "Asiatic aliens" from in future obtaining gold mining leases in the Northern Territory. In June 1901 the

---

159. CO 13/147, S.A. 19018, conf., Kintore to Ripon, Aug. 20, 1892; minuting by Meade, 28/9/92.
160. Rendell, 205, quoting the *Northern Territory Times*, Oct. 11, 1894.
161. Rendell, 205.

government instructed the resident in the Northern Territory not to issue or renew mineral leases or licenses even to Asians who were British subjects, pending Commonwealth action.[162] Finally, in 1911, the Commonwealth did assume jurisdiction over the Northern Territory.

In South Australia, Victoria, and later Queensland, Chinese furniture manufacturers were deemed a threat to white cabinetmakers. The number involved in South Australia must have been tiny, for the census of 1891 placed less than 500 Chinese in the colony proper, a fact which in no way diminished the fervor and hostility of the European artisans. A resident of Glenelg wrote in the *South Australia Register* of July 5, 1888, that the Chinese "turn out an excellent article . . . are civil, courteous, obliging, industrious, quiet, well-to-do, law abiding people." The writer found it strange that some shops would advertise, "We don't sell furniture made by Chinamen," but that "all these good people would not for a moment hesitate to sell to a Chinaman for cash." Four days later another reader responded in familiar terms. "Dealers," he asserted,

> are desirous that the furniture-making should be retained amongst men who have wives and families to support instead of falling into the hands of an Alien race who can afford to make furniture for less per week than will suffice to pay the European cabinetmaker's house rent. . . . Might I ask who was it that made America what it is today—was it the Chinaman or was it the Briton? I fancy I hear you say it was the Briton. . . . Let him plant his foot where he will, he seeks to elevate those around him, . . . whereas on the other hand, no matter where the Chinaman goes outside of his own country people begin to feel uncomfortable at once, and almost without exception seek to impose penalties to restrict his coming. . . . To sum up a Chinaman, he is a despoiler.

The Chinese furniture makers of Victoria not only produced an excellent article but undersold their European competitors. Consequently, they were accused of paying subsistence wages and of making a profit by virtue of the subhuman conditions

162. *Ibid.*, 182.

in which they lived. Above all, it was alleged that the Chinese contravened the various acts on the statute books which regulated factories and workrooms and limited shop hours. For some reason, Britain and her colonies always felt the need of enforcing the celebration of the Christian Sabbath by law and of rigidly controlling the hours during which shops might be open. Normally factory and shop legislation did not apply to family-run enterprises. Article 3 of Victoria Act 862 of 1885 defined a factory or workroom as "an office building or place in which six or more persons are engaged directly in working for hire or reward in any handicraft or in preparing or manufacturing articles for trade or sale . . . but shall not include any dwelling, office building or place in which the persons engaged in working are shown to the satisfaction of the chief inspector to all be members of the same family."

Two years later, the Government of Victoria determined to place all establishments which were Chinese-owned or which employed Chinese under the restrictions placed on factories. In Parliament, Alfred Deakin, the future prime minister of the Commonwealth of Australia and at that time premier of Victoria, boldly asserted that the Chinese were destroying the cabinetmaking industry in Victoria.[163] In other words, they were more successful than the European manufacturers. Act 961 of 1887 attempted to remedy the situation. Although a clause requiring that all furniture manufactured by Chinese be stamped "Chinese made" was dropped, article 3 of the measure stipulated: "Any office building or place in which Chinese are engaged directly or indirectly in working for hire or reward in any handicraft or in preparing or manufacturing articles for trade or sale shall be deemed a factory or workroom within the meaning of the Principal Act and any Act for the time being in force amending it." In future, a Chinese and his son manufacturing furniture by themselves were to be placed under the same regulatory control as a factory employing

163. Victoria *Hansard*, Dec. 8, 1887.

dozens of workmen. When the law reached the Colonial Office, this restriction on the rights of British subjects was either not noticed or ignored.

But the agitation of the Victorian furniture interests persisted. In conjunction with increased public fear of Chinese immigration, the United Furniture Trade Society of Victoria and its supporters in mid-1887 initiated an anti-Chinese campaign amongst the trade unions of the colony. To spread the scope of the attack, they solicited the support of the Australian Natives' Association, "a patriotic union of native born Australians" with great strength among the professional men of Melbourne and the small farmers of rural Victoria.[164] As the Melbourne *Age* of June 14 put it: "What is the use of the State restricting the legal hours of labour to eight for a European when a Mongolian can work for as long as he pleases? Or what is the use of the Trade Unions struggling to maintain the rate of wages when he can work for as little as he pleases?"

True to the stated needs of at least some of its constituents, the Victoria legislature did not relent. Article 57 of Act 1445 of 1887 stipulated that all furniture manufactured in the colony must be stamped "European labour only," or "Chinese labour," or "European and other labour." As Chinese frequently slept on or next to their premises, article 19 forbade the existence of sleeping places within a factory or adjacent to it. Article 23 addressed itself to the belief that Chinese profits were the result of their working excessively long hours. Thus it was prescribed that in any factory or workroom where any Chinese person was at any time employed or in any factory where furniture was made, no person could work before 7:30 in the morning or after 5 P.M. on weekdays, not after 2 P.M. on Saturdays, and not at all on Sundays. A £10 fine was established for the first offense, £25 for the second, while the registration of the factory could be cancelled for the third violation. Subsection 3 of this article is indicative of the intensity of colonial animosity:

164. Oddie, 57–59.

In any prosecution for an offence against this section evidence—
(a) that at any time during which work is prohibited by this section in any factory or workroom sounds have been heard such as would ordinarily be heard if made by persons engaged in such factory or workroom in the usual work therein carried on, and
(b) that during such time any member of the police force or inspector was refused or could not gain immediate admission to such factory or workroom—

shall be *prima facie* proof that the provisions of this section have been contravened by the defendant.

Once the principle of discriminatory commercial legislation had been established, it was only a matter of time until the other Australasian colonies fell into line. Queensland took nine years to emulate Victoria but then passed a measure defining a factory as "any building, premises, or place in which Chinese or other Asiatics are . . . engaged." [165] And New South Wales Act 37 of 1896 included an identical provision.

Chinese manufacturers were indeed the major irritant, but hawkers, many of whom were Indians, Afghans and Syrians, followed not far behind, resented because they provided competition for white merchants. In 1892 the County Traders' Association of Victoria asked the government to act against these hawkers. Consequently, after a cabinet meeting, the commissioner of police was ordered to issue no further hawkers' licenses to Asiatics (other than Chinese), while corporations and district councils were invited to follow his example.[166] Victoria provided the statutory machinery for suppression (Act 1097 of 1896) through the establishment of a licensing procedure complete with fees and fines. Although attempts to pass legislation more specifically to the disadvantage of Asian itinerant merchants were defeated by the legislative council, passions in both houses ran high. William McCulloch, the

165. Act 29 of 1896, A bill to make provision for the supervision and regulation of factories and shops and for the limitation in certain cases of the hours of working therein, and for other purposes. Article 2(2).
166. Rendell, 247.

minister of defense, in moving the first reading of the Hawkers and Peddlers Amendment Bill in the council claimed, "It was well known to Honourable members residing in the country that in some parts of the country the Hindoo and other foreign hawkers had become a nuisance. In many places the womenfolk were left to themselves the whole day, and the visits of these hawkers were often a terror to them." [167] In the assembly debate on the second reading, W. E. Hamilton of Sandhurst was forced to invoke the virtues of the Chinese in order to properly condemn the "Hindoos" and Afghans:

> I would say that by comparison with the Hindoo or Afghan the Chinese hawker is an angel: The Hindoo hawker is a large rough fierce-looking individual whereas the Chinese is a humble, "childlike and bland" individual. . . . I do not admire the Chinese in our country, but I must say that I always found the Chinese to be a civil man. The Hindoo hawker is the very reverse. They frequently try to force themselves into people's homes in the country district. . . . I have known lots of instances where women have been shamefully scared by these Hindoo hawkers. In some cases they have been ill-used.

Hamilton had to admit, "I have not known of such a case personally, but I have heard of instances which have been well authenticated." As a final argument for his position, the honorable member added that he knew it to be a fact that Asians never bathed.[168]

South Australia did not move against Asian hawkers and peddlers until 1898. Then Act 710 required an alien applying for a license to prove he had resided in South Australia for two years and had an adequate command of English to conduct his business. No license was to be required for those dealing in fish, dairy products, or vegetables they had themselves grown.

Western Australia's attitude was more reminiscent of that of Victoria. It felt itself greatly afflicted by Asian hawkers and peddlers, even though the census of 1891 counted only 183

167. Victoria *Hansard* (Council), Aug. 29, 1899.
168. *Ibid.* (Assembly), Aug. 17, 1899.

Indian males and 60 females in the population of the colony, and that of 1901, 4 Afghans. C. Harper of Beverley moved in the legislature: "That in the opinion of this House it is desirable that legislative action should be taken to prohibit the granting of hawkers' licenses to natives of India or other Asiatic countries." F. H. Piesse of Williams got to the heart of the matter in supporting his colleague: "These Indian peddlers were the scourge of the regular traders of the colony, and competed with them under conditions that were altogether in favour of the alien race. . . . They paid neither rates nor taxes and what money they made they took out of the country. . . . One could quite understand the power of intimidation exercised by these swarthy aliens, these dangerous-looking bravos, upon lonely women and children in the outlying parts of the colony." [169]

The motion was duly passed, but the problem was how to put it into effect as most of the hawkers were British subjects. The Honorable S. Burt, then the attorney general, suddenly hit upon the solution. He pointed out that until 1882 there had been no act to cover the issuing of licenses to hawk or peddle, and why one had been passed at that time he was unable to explain. He proposed the repeal of the legislation of 1882 and its replacement with a law which simply outlawed hawking altogether.[170] Act 35 of 1892 consequently defined the term "hawker" as meaning: "Any hawker, peddler, or other person who, with or without any horse or other beast bearing or drawing burden, travels and trades and goes from town to town or to other men's houses, carrying to sell or exposing for sale any goods, wares, or merchandise." Subsequent to December 31, 1892, no hawking was to be permitted under threat of heavy penalty. To make sure that only the true objects of the act were injured, it included language designed to exempt Europeans.

Obviously the general principle in all these actions was that

169. W.A. *Hansard*, Jan. 29, 1892.   170. *Ibid.*, Mar. 1, 1892.

colored enterprise and labor must never compete with white. Even the pettiest opportunities for persecution were not eschewed. In Queensland, for example, the Sale and Use of Poisons Act (31 of 1897) denied Asians the right to sell poisons. And when Victoria contemplated the establishment of a beet sugar industry, the legislature provided (Act 1440 of 1896) for government aid in the form of loans for colonists desiring to cultivate and render beet sugar, providing they used no colored labor. Of course, there were some who thought there was a place for the colored worker in Australia. A laborer from Sandhurst was heard to say: "We don't want the Chinese to go; we want them to stop here, and grow cabbages for us." [171] And the planters in Queensland and the financial interests of South Australia's Northern Territory thought there was room for the colored laborer as well. The former, at least temporarily, solved their problem with Kanaka recruits; for the latter the question was still unresolved.[172] Despite laws allowing the importation of indentured laborers, none, in fact, arrived, nor was any systematic arrangement for the importation of contract labor ever established.

As had become customary, action by the individual colonies was mirrored on the intercolonial level. Consequently, at the Hobart Postal Conference (1895), the delegates resolved: "That it be a condition in any future contracts that mail steamers should be manned by white labour." [173] This action had been based on the strong protest of organized labor against the hiring of colored seamen by the Pacific and Orient Line. "Cheap labour, in our judgement, is dear labour," the Trades

171. **Oddie, 161.**
172. Western Australia also wanted labor for its northern districts, but it would countenance no colored workers in Western Australia proper. Act 27 of 1897 therefore limited contract colored labor to the north of 27° of south latitude (originally the bill had specified 26° of south latitude, but this would have placed the pearl fisheries at Shark's Bay in the prohibited zone).
173. S.A. Archives, Parl. paps., 26, 1895, resolution of Feb. 2, 1895.

Hall Council in Melbourne had written the conference, "and though under ordinary circumstances coloured labour is endurable while everything is going right, they have neither the strength nor stamina nor the brain power to rise to the occasion if the necessity arose, and the consequences to a vessel so manned in a moment of calamity would be terrible to contemplate."

The remarks of the company's representative did little to soothe ruffled feelings. "The immediate reason for doing away with European crews in the lower grades," he wrote, "was that they caused an infinity of trouble through drunkenness and disobedience, etc." [174] But whatever the truth of the matter, the colonial representatives in Hobart knew the nature of their own prejudices and where the voting power at home lay.

The course of events in British Columbia showed once again that members of the "British race," wherever they might be, were singularly likeminded. As early as 1864, when the estimated number of Chinese in the province was less than 3,000, a motion to levy a special tax on the Chinese was tabled in the legislative assembly but did not receive the support of a majority.[175] Eight years later, John Robson, who represented Nanaimo, rose to move that a $50 head tax be placed on all Chinese in British Columbia. The motion lost by a count of 15–7, for the legislature was still not prepared to reflect the growing anti-Chinese sentiment of the public. When Robson claimed that Chinese were replacing white men in the coal mines of the province, his opponents derided him as a demagogue. But two days later Robson tried again. This time he moved that Chinese be barred from employment on public

---

174. *Ibid.,* J. G. Barrett, sec. Trades Hall Council, Melbourne, to chairman and members of postal conference, Jan. 29, 1895; G. D. Mitchie, agent for P and O Line, to the Hon. J. Cook, M.L.A., postmaster-general, Sydney, Jan. 28, 1895.

175. Andracki, 1.

works in British Columbia, whether they were provincially or federally funded. He planted his arguments in familiar ground. The Canadian Pacific Railway, he contended, had thirty million dollars to spend west of the Rockies. If Chinese were used to build the line, the money would go to Chinese merchants and eventually out of the country. Besides, the Chinese were merely birds of passage. They would not occupy the land or develop the province. Again the opposition of what today would be called the railway lobby was too strong, and the matter was allowed to fall into abeyance. In 1874, Robson urged the lieutenant governor to impose a per capita tax on Chinese, but the proposal was never implemented.[176]

Robson's persistence was, however, destined to be rewarded. The following year he introduced a bill declaring Chinese ineligible to vote in provincial elections even if they were Canadian-born. That measure did not threaten the labor supply for the railroad, and it was passed and put into operation as it infringed upon no right reserved to the Dominion,[177] and was really only a repromulgation of restrictions contained in legislation passed in 1872. Article 2 of the new law ordered every collector of an electoral district or polling division to remove all Chinese from the list of voters. If he failed to do so or allowed the introduction of a Chinese or Indian (native Canadian) to the list, he was liable to pay a $50 fine.

On the local level, the Victoria City Council decided in July 1875 to prohibit the employment of Chinese on city works. The

176. Cheng, 38–39.
177. Statutes of B.C., 1875, no. 2, an Act to make better Provisions for the Qualifications and Registration of Voters. The measure was essentially repromulgated by Act 35 of 1908. The Chinese were thus (except for the period 1885–1898) denied the Dominion franchise and precluded from sitting in Parliament by article 41 of the constitution act under which it was decreed that until Parliament provided otherwise, all laws in the provinces relative to the qualifications and disqualifications for persons to be elected as members of the legislative assembly should apply to the Dominion as well. Saskatchewan emulated British Columbia in 1908. Chapter 4, Revised Statutes of Saskatchewan, 1930.

Victoria *Daily Colonist* applauded the action and recommended it to other municipalities. But it cautioned its readers to bear in mind that the treaty between Great Britain and China prevented excessively overt action. It suggested that provincial and municipal governments include in their advertisements the statement that "the lowest tender would not necessarily be accepted," thus insuring that the bids of contractors employing Chinese laborers would not be successful.[178]

In 1878 the Walkem ministry, out of power for two years, returned to office in British Columbia determined to regulate and, if possible, eliminate Chinese labor. The government immediately introduced a bill barring Chinese from provincial public works and ordering all Chinese to take out a quarterly license at a cost of $10. Failure to obtain a license would result in a $100 fine, imprisonment or forced labor on the roads.[179] Although the measure duly became law, it was declared unconstitutional by Justice J. H. Gray of the British Columbia Supreme Court, who ruled it *ultra vires* because it was not designed primarily to raise revenue and impinged on powers granted exclusively to the Dominion.[180] Unabashed, the lieutenant governor, A. N. Richards, declared at the opening of the next session of the legislature: "Although your legislation upon the Chinese question has been considered unconstitutional, this circumstance should not deter you from adopting every legitimate measure for the attainment of the end your legislation had in view." [181]

The Chinese question was first mooted in Ottawa in March 1878, when two British Columbia representatives, Messrs. Bunster and Thompson, introduced a resolution into Parliament which provided heavy penalties on the Canadian Pacific Railway if it employed laborers whose hair was more than 5-½ inches long. The measure was, of course, aimed at the Chinese,

---

178. Wynne, 159.   179. Cheng, 40, Statutes of B.C., 1878, Chapter 35.
180. *Ibid.,* 41, "Report on Chinese Immigration, 1885," App. G.
181. *Ibid.,* 51, B.C. Journals, 1879, 2.

all of whom at that time wore queues, and it was not received with much sympathy by the House. During the debate on the motion, the prime minister, Alexander Mackenzie, denounced the proposal as "unprecedented in its character and altogether unprecedented in spirit and at variance with those tolerant laws which afforded employment to all who came into our country irrespective of color, hair, or anything else." He added that, "if its terms were strictly carried out, both these honorable gentlemen (the mover and the seconder) would be excluded from any employment on the Pacific Railway." The motion was defeated.[182]

Meanwhile, British Columbia continued to pass virulently anti-Chinese legislation. Chapter 2 of 1884, "An Act to Prevent Chinese from Acquiring Crown Lands," prohibited Chinese from acquiring title to crown lands in the province and voided any records or claims by Chinese, even though aliens were accorded the rights that the law denied by the Dominion naturalization act of 1870. The measure was consequently disallowed.[183] Frustration led the legislators of British Columbia into ever more extreme enactments. Chapter 4 of 1884 stipulated that every Chinese over fourteen years of age pay $10 upon passage of the law and an equal amount every June thereafter. The act also required Chinese to pay $15 for a free miner's license, as opposed to the $5 paid by Europeans, and placed a $100 fine on the nonmedical use of opium. The preamble of the law must surely have been unique—even in the mottled history of the British Empire—for legislation allowed to reach the statute books:

The coming of Chinese to British Columbia largely exceeds that of any other class of immigration, and the population so introduced are fast becoming superior in number to our own race; are not disposed to be governed by our laws; are dissimilar in habits and occupation from our people; evade the payments of taxes justly due to government; are governed by pestilential habits; are useless in in-

182. Canada *Hansard*, 1878, 1027 *et. seq.*   183. Huang, 27–28.

stances of emergency; habitually desecrate graveyards by the removal of bodies therefrom; and generally the law governing the whites is found to be inapplicable to Chinese, and such Chinese are inclined to habits subversive of the comfort and well-being of the community.

Lew Ta-jên was outraged. "The act which is to be cited as 'the Chinese Regulation Act of 1884'," he wrote Lord Rosebery at the Foreign Office," has for its preamble a series of charges such as was never perhaps before made in a public document against the people of a friendly nation. . . . Here we have a whole race accused of a series of the gravest and most revolting charges that could possibly be brought against the people of any country, and made against them in the name of H.M. the Queen. The Imperial Government cannot but think that the language of the Act has escaped the attention of H.M.'s Government." Lew reminded Rosebery that article 1 of the Treaty of Nanking conferred on all Chinese subjects "full security and protection for the persons and property" throughout the British Empire, and he appealed for adherence to this guarantee and for fair treatment to what were after all the subjects of a friendly nation.[184] In due time, the British Columbia Chinese Regulation Act of 1884 was declared *ultra vires* by the supreme court of the province, but Lew wondered why it had not immediately been disallowed by the Dominion Government.[185] He might also have asked why Her Majesty's Government had not intervened. Here the answer lay in the usual desire of the Colonial Office to remain uninvolved. Derby had written to Lord Lansdowne, the latest occupant of the governor's chair:

184. PAC, Governor General's Secretary's Office, General Correspondence Regarding Asiatics, file 226. Canada no. 181, Edward Stanhope to Lansdowne, Aug. 5, 1886, encl. Lew Ta-Jên to Rosebery, July 13, 1886.

185. *Ibid.*, draft, conf., Lansdowne to Derby, Mar. 31, 1885. The law had not been disallowed because Lansdowne felt it fell within the bounds of provincial competence under the terms of article 92 of the British North America Act, which granted provincial legislatures exclusive power to make laws regarding direct taxes for provincial purposes.

Her Majesty's Government have not held that the relations of this country with China require them to interfere with the Australian legislation on international grounds, and it has been treated as a matter of internal administration with which a responsible Colonial Government is competent to deal. When therefore the Dominion Ministers advise your Lordship with regard to these Acts, you may understand that the question is not held to involve Imperial interests and that you should deal with it as a Canadian question only.[186]

Even though the Chinese Regulation Act had been voided by British Columbia's own supreme court, the members of the provincial legislature could not contain their displeasure at being again, as they saw it, let down by the Dominion authorities. J. A. Mara, the speaker of the assembly, immediately fired off a long and angry telegram of protest to the governor general. He contended that British Columbia had acted only after thoughtful consideration of the issues at hand, and he emphasized that the province's objections to the Chinese were based on their failure to settle in the country. They were transients who came without their families and were interested only in making enough money to return to their native land, where they could spend the rest of their days in comfortable retirement. Besides, those Chinese who migrated to Canada were of the lowest class whose very presence "tends to the degradation of the white laboring class" and prevented the immigration of white laborers who would not work side by side with them. The Chinese, the speaker continued, were governed by secret societies which encouraged crime and hindered the administration of justice. Finally, "the use of opium has extended throughout the province to the demoralization of the native races, and the Chinese encourage the use of this drug amongst others of our own rising population and we urgently request that some restrictive legislation be passed to prevent our province from being completely overrun by the

186. *Ibid., Canadian Emigration,* Derby to Lansdowne, May 31, 1884.

Chinese." [187] To add insult to injury, the British Columbia Municipal Act of 1885 which placed a tax not to exceed $75 on laundries was declared *ultra vires* by the courts because its purpose was obviously not to raise revenue, the tax rate being fifteen times the normal.[188]

One source of provincial concern was the completion of the Canadian Pacific Railway, which resulted in many Chinese re-entering the labor market. Consequently, starting in 1886, a standard clause was inserted in all private acts—that is, measures passed by the legislature of British Columbia granting franchises to private companies to construct public works— prohibiting the employment of Chinese, either directly or indirectly, on any work authorized by such acts. The appearance of an increasing number of Chinese available for employment coincided with an economic slump in British Columbia and the result was a rise of hostility towards the Chinese population among white labor groups. In January 1887 the first act of physical violence against Chinese in Canada took place in Vancouver. Some Chinese were forced to flee the city, and all Chinese residents were commanded to leave with their belongings. The order, in the form of a public notice, was the work of the Anti-Chinese Committee of Vancouver in collaboration with the Knights of Labour. City authorities, the Victoria *Weekly Colonist* of January 21 reported, were "kindly cautioned not to risk their lives in trying to rescue the Mongolians." The provincial government did, however, intervene, and even the anti-Chinese *Colonist* on March 4, 1887, felt constrained to write, "The Chinese have as good a right to live in Vancouver as the whites and though an undesirable element, must be protected as long as they are there."

If the British Columbian legislators continued to push Ottawa, it was only a reflection of the pressure they themselves

187. *Ibid.*, J. A. Mara, speaker of the B.C. Legislative Assembly to Lansdowne, Mar. 3, 1885.
188. Huang, 231.

were under. At one point, the legislature received a petition signed by about 4,000 miners on Vancouver Island demanding that Japanese and Chinese be prevented from working underground in collieries for reasons of safety.[189] But although legislation to this effect was passed in 1890 (Chapter 28), it was struck down by the courts in *Union Colliery Co. v. Bryden* (1899).[190] Undeterred, the British Columbia legislature asked Ottawa to amend the Dominion naturalization act so that Chinese and Japanese would need ten years' residence to be eligible for Canadian citizenship and would, in addition, have to appear in person before a judge. As was so often the case, the privy council was uncooperative because of treaty commitments.[191] Nevertheless, British Columbia did what it could, and legislation of a purely provincial character was successfully carried into law. For instance, article 39 of the Municipal Act of 1892 (Chapter 33) stipulated: "No Chinese or Indian [native Canadian] shall be entitled to vote at any municipal election of a Mayor, Reeve, Alderman or Councilor."

There were less than 1,000 Japanese in British Columbia by 1896;[192] yet the provincial legislature felt impelled to place Japanese under the same restrictions regarding the provincial franchise as it had the Chinese.[193] When the trend continued, the Japanese consul general in Vancouver, S. Shimizu, addressed the governor general. He called Lord Minto's attention to the recent passage through the British Columbian legislature of several railway and other private bills which prohibited the employment of Japanese on the projects for which the legislation in question provided charters. A partisan only for his own countrymen, the consul general pointed out "that while the legislators of the Province of British Columbia apparently

189. CO 62/40, B.C. Sessional Papers, 1892.   190. Huang, 230.
191. CO 62/51, B.C. Sessional Papers, 1897, Privy Council Report, July 5, 1897.
192. CO 42/857, 13230, no. 135, Aberdeen to Chamberlain, encl. S. Shimizu, Japanese Consul General to Aberdeen, May 10, 1898.
193. B.C. Provincial Elections Act, 1897.

look upon the Japanese in the same light as Chinese, it is a well-known fact, that the education and character, customs and manners of the Japanese are entirely different from those of the Chinese." In conclusion, he felt compelled "in the name of His Imperial Majesty's Government, most respectfully [to] protest, as far as Japanese persons are concerned, against any such discrimination against the subjects of a friendly nation, whose Government I have the honour to represent here." [194] Ten days later Shimizu found the occasion once more to take up his pen—this time to protest the passage of the British Columbia "Alien Labour Act," [195] which forbade the employment of Chinese and Japanese under franchises granted by private acts. Shimizu also asked Dominion action against the British Columbia Public Works Loan Act Amendment Act [196] and the several railway and other private bills which carried similar provisos.[197]

The Colonial Office manifested some embarrassment. John Anderson, since the previous year one of the principal clerks, minuted: "The Governor General ought to have sent us copies of these offensive statutes. . . . We must at once ask the Governor General to send us copies of the obnoxious statutes and desire him to furnish us with his Ministers' observations on them as soon as possible, saying that we hope they will delay advising him as to their disallowance until we have had an opportunity of considering them." Hugh Cox, the assistant undersecretary for legal affairs, remarked: "It is important to stop these acts being sanctioned if possible." [198]

Still determined to persevere, British Columbia passed Chapter 39 of 1899, "An Act respecting Liquor Licenses," which in its 36th section stipulated: "No license under this Act shall be issued or transferred to any person of the Indian, Chinese or

---

194. See note 192.   195. Statutes of B.C., Chapter 1, 1897.
196. *Ibid.*, Chapter 30, 1898.
197. CO 42/857, 13240, no. 145, Aberdeen to Chamberlain, May 30, 1898, encl. Shimizu to Aberdeen, May 20, 1898.
198. *Ibid.*, minuting of June 14.

Japanese race." "Your Excellency will observe," Shimizu wrote Minto, "the discrimination in the Bill . . . is a decided advance upon the former measures aimed against Japanese labour, inasmuch as this Bill now imposes restriction on Japanese subjects in matters of Trade also. It may also be taken, I think, as an indication that these anti-Japanese measures will not stop here, in this Province, unless the Higher Authorities are pleased to exercise their powers." At the Colonial Office, Cox lapsed into a not unfamiliar mood of futility. "I see nothing else to be done," he minuted, "unless we can press the Dominion Govt. to disallow the obnoxious anti-Japanese laws, more strongly. The matter is really becoming serious." [199] The Canadian privy council and the Colonial Office tossed the issue back and forth. Each hoped the other would take action. Minto pointed out to Chamberlain that "the Provincial Government appears to be indisposed to take steps to alter the legislation in question in conformity with the wishes of the Japanese Government; and I point out that the power of disallowance reserved to the Governor General lapses on the 8th of June next." [200] In other words, Minto, on behalf of his privy council, wanted to be ordered to act or to have the job done for him by Her Majesty's Government in order to avoid Canadian responsibility.

Included with the papers Minto forwarded to London was a justification by British Columbia for the passage of the acts objected to by the Japanese consul general. "The economic conditions in British Columbia and Japan," wrote F. Carter-Cotton, the provincial minister of finance and agriculture,

and the standards of living of the masses of the people in the two countries, differ so widely that to grant freedom of employment to Japanese on such public works as are authorized to be carried out by Acts of the Legislature would almost certainly result in all such

199. CO 42/868, no. 46, Minto to Chamberlain, Mar. 9, 1899, encl. Shimizu to Minto, Feb. 28, 1899; minuting of Mar. 28, 1899.
200. CO 42/868, no. 54, Minto to Chamberlain, Mar. 16, 1899.

employment being monopolized by the Japanese to the exclusion of the people of this province. . . . That such restrictions are not only judicious but necessary has been shown by the manner in which cheap Asiatic labour has in many cases entirely supplanted white labour on works to which no such restrictions, as those referred to, were attached.

On the other hand, the minister pointed with pride to the fact that the legislature had "scrupulously abstained from any interference with the employment of Japanese by private individuals or companies," even though the provincial government was committed to seeing British Columbia peopled "by a large and thoroughly British population." In conclusion, Carter-Cotton reported that the Government of British Columbia could not see its way clear to repealing the statutes to which the Japanese Government took objection.[201]

Chamberlain, for his part, reminded Minto of the "principles of equality which have been the guiding principle of Br. rule throughout the Empire." He hoped that British Columbia could be induced to repeal the offensive legislation, but if the province proved intractable, he urged the governor general to press his ministers to invoke those powers vested in them by the British North America Act for the benefit of the Empire as a whole, and to disallow the British Columbia legislation to which Her Majesty's Government objected on the grounds of both principle and policy.[202]

Once the secretary of state had made London's attitude clear, the Dominion Government reluctantly determined to take action. David Mills, the minister of justice, thought "the advantages to be derived by the Province of British Columbia from these enactments are . . . very doubtful and not at all corresponding in importance to the advantages which may be expected both for the Province and the Dominion at large from

[201]. CO 42/868, lt. gov. of B.C. to sec. of state, Ottawa, Feb. 16, 1899, encl. report by F. Carter-Cotton, minister of finance and agriculture (British Columbia), Feb. 13, 1899.
[202]. CO 42/868, draft, Chamberlain to Minto, Apr. 19, 1899.

a friendly sentiment on the part of Japan in matters of commerce and otherwise." When the relations between Japan and the Empire as a whole were added to the balance, Mills could only advise the governor general in council to disallow the British Columbia legislation.[203]

In a final effort to avoid the loss of some political capital, Sir Wilfrid Laurier, the Dominion prime minister, wrote C. A. Semlin, the premier of British Columbia, pointing with some desperation to the fact that only four days remained to the Dominion Government in which to act on the legislation in question before it automatically became law. "Have you any suggestion," he asked hopefully, "as to this legislation as far as it relates to Japanese?" The following day, Semlin telegraphed that no change in the provincial position was possible, "in justice to the interests of labour in British Columbia." [204] Thus with no choice left, the prime minister on June 5, 1899, recommended the disallowance of Chapter 28 of 1898, "An Act relating to the employment of Chinese or Japanese persons on works carried on under franchises granted by Private Acts" and Chapter 44 of the same year, "An Act to amend the Tramway Incorporation Act." [205] The government did not, however, disallow the many private acts which contained restrictions on the employment of Chinese and Japanese because such an action would cause undue confusion and the disallowance of the principal act would ensure against future inclusion of the offending clause.[206] The liquor licensing measure was struck down by an order in council of April 24, 1900 (P.C. 1075).

The Government of Japan was for the moment satisfied. "I

203. PAC, Orders in Council, R.G. 2, series 1, V. 799, Laurier to Minto, June 5, 1899 (P.C. 1195), encl. report of David Mills, minister of justice, to the governor general in council, May 29, 1899.
204. PAC, Governor General's Secretary's Office, General Correspondence Regarding Asiatics, file 232, tel., Laurier to Semlin, June 2, 1899; tel., Semlin to Laurier, June 3, 1899.
205. PAC, Orders in Council, R.G. 2, series 1, V. 799 (P.C. 1195), Laurier to Minto, June 5, 1899.
206. *Ibid.*

am now directed by His Excellency the Minister for Foreign Affairs," K. Matsui, the Japanese ambassador in London, wrote to Lord Salisbury at the Foreign Office, "to express to your Lordship that the Imperial Japanese Government has been gratified with the just and enlightened policy which has been pursued by Her Majesty's Government on the matter, and to request that your lordship will kindly convey to Her Majesty's Secretary of State for the Colonies my Government's high appreciation of the good offices kindly taken by him and through his advice by the Governor General of Canada on the subject." [207]

By 1900 the Government of British Columbia determined to utilize the "Natal formula" in its efforts to curtail Oriental and Indian opportunities in the province, although in doing so the legislature removed what pretense still shrouded Chamberlain's favorite stratagem. Chapter 14, again an act dealing with employment carried on under franchises granted by private acts, in its fourth section demanded knowledge of a European language on the part of eligible employees. But then British Columbia was only following Chamberlain's advice. The secretary of state had claimed "the exclusion of Japanese subjects either from employment on public or quasi public works in the Province by the operation of an education test, such as is embodied in the Natal Immigration Law, is not a measure to which the Government of Japan can take exception." [208]

Shimizu did, however, object and once more took up the cudgels. "The provision embodied in the Section 4 of this Bill," he wrote the governor general, "will wholly deprive those Japanese residents in this Province who are unable to read in any language of Europe of the opportunity of employment on works specified in the section." When European languages other than English were countenanced, Shimizu

207. PAC, Governor General's Secretary's Office, General Correspondence Regarding Asiatics, file 232, K. Matsui to Salisbury, Apr. 28, 1899.
208. See note 202.

wondered why Japanese was not considered eligible, "in spite of the fact that Japanese may be educated to the highest degree in their own tongue." Furthermore, exemptions from the workings of the measure were available to some groups, but not to Japanese.[209]

As was usually the case, British Columbia passed anti-Oriental measures *en masse,* and Shimizu also objected to Chapter 18 of 1900, "An Act respecting Liquor Licenses," which declared "Mongolians" to be ineligible for classification as "householders" or "inhabitants," [210] and to Chapter 54 of the same year, which deprived Japanese residents in Vancouver along with Chinese and Canadian Indians of the municipal franchise. Finally, he pointed to the passage of another tramway incorporation bill, identical to the one disallowed the previous year, to the continued passage of private acts with discriminatory clauses, and to another coal mines act which again attempted to bar Japanese and Chinese from working underground unless they had a knowledge of English.[211]

Although the offending laws were by and large disallowed in Ottawa,[212] Chapter 18 of 1900 was not considered sufficiently discriminatory to merit disallowance,[213] and Chapter 54 was deemed wholly within the province's competence, although a subsequent legal decision enabled Japanese, if not otherwise ineligible, to enforce a claim to be placed on the voters' roll.

209. PAC, Governor General's Secretary's Office, General Correspondence Regarding Asiatics, file 232, Canada no. 186, CO to Canada, July 9, 1900, encl. Shimizu to Minto, Feb. 1, 1900.
210. *Ibid.,* encl. Shimizu to Minto, Feb. 15, 1900. This measure was essentially a repromulgation of an act disallowed in 1899, but the later version was allowed.
211. *Ibid.*
212. By two orders in council of 1902, British Columbia recommended that in all contracts, leases and concessions granted by the government, no Chinese or Japanese should be employed. These orders did not come to the notice of the courts until 1920.
213. PAC, Orders in Council, R.G. 2, series 1, V. 904, Mills to Minto, Jan. 5, 1901.

British Columbia nevertheless continued to find it possible to tighten the noose little by little. Chapter 17 of the provincial code (1903-4) successfully disenfranchised "Hindus" at the provincial level. To make sure there was no mistake about what the legislators had in mind, Chapter 16 of 1907 defined a "Hindu" as a native of India not born of Anglo-Saxon parents, whether he was a British subject or not. In addition, Japanese and Chinese had previously been made ineligible to cut timber.[214]

Year after year, the legislature of British Columbia persisted in passing inadmissible legislation with little change, knowing full well that the offending measures would be disallowed in Ottawa or declared *ultra vires* by the courts. For instance, Chapter 38 of 1902 was another attempt to pass the act dealing with public works carried out under franchises with all its restriction on the use of nonwhite labor. Whereas the Coal Mines Regulation Amendment Act of 1900 had stipulated that no person could work underground who was unable to read to the satisfaction of an inspector the special rules for the mine which were printed in English, Chapter 48 of 1902 tried to achieve its purpose through a slightly altered mode of expression. "No Chinaman, Japanese or person unable to speak English," article 2 explained, "shall be appointed to or shall occupy any position of trust or responsibility in or about a mine subject to this Act, whereby through ignorance, carelessness or negligence he might endanger the life or limb of any person employed in or about a mine." But the changed wording had little effect in Ottawa, where the law failed to be sanctioned. A further attempt— Chapter 39 of 1904—was declared *ultra vires* by the supreme court of British Columbia.

When Japan, victor over China, challenger of Russia, and ally of Great Britain, remonstrated, His Majesty's Government reacted with alacrity. In September 1902 the Japanese Government protested the wave of anti-Japanese legislation passed by

---

214. Section 50, Chapter 113, Revised Statues of British Columbia, 1897.

British Columbia and the Foreign Office, in some alarm, wrote the Colonial Office: "Lord Lansdowne [now the foreign secretary] fully realises the strength of Colonial feeling on the subject and the difficulty of running counter to it, but His Lordship would point out that that attitude of the Colonies is deeply resented by the Japanese Government and that, in his opinion, no pains should be spared in order to prove to them that His Majesty's Government are not in sympathy with the extreme measures which have been resorted to in some of the British Colonies." [215]

But despite their more favored status, the Japanese continued to be the victims of discrimination. British Columbia was able to promulgate regulations further limiting their involvement in the fishing and timber industries,[216] actions which the premier explained away in terms singularly temperate by the standards of British Columbia but familiar to the rest of the British Empire. He observed that he had

> on frequent occasions publicly endeavoured to make clear that such apparent discrimination is not intended to reflect upon Japanese and Chinese as being inferior to the white races. . . . That the Oriental standards of living—of civilization—belong to a distant ethnographical zone and are unsuitable for transplantation to this continent where a different standard prevails. That the two must, and do come into conflict, and so far as the white race is concerned the question resolves itself ultimately into an alternative of maintaining a standard essential to social peace and uniform prosperity, or that of accepting a reduced scale of wages, and as a consequence, a different plane of living.[217]

Or as put more lyrically in "White Canada Forever":

> This is the voice of the West and it speaks to the world
> The rights that our fathers have given

215. CO 42/890, 38823, FO to CO, Sept. 16, 1902.
216. PAC, Orders in Council, R.G. 2, series 1, V. 1281, Dec. 20, 1913 (P.C. 3088).
217. *Ibid.*, encl. copy of a report of a committee of the Honourable Executive Committee of B.C., July 14, 1913.

> We'll hold by right and maintain by might,
> Till the foe is backward driven.
> We welcome as brothers all white men still,
> But the shifty yellow race,
> Whose word is vain, who oppress the weak
> Must find another place.

[Chorus]

> Then let us stand united all,
> And show our fathers' might,
> That won the home we call our own
> For white man's land we fight.
> To Oriental grasp and greed
> We'll surrender, no, never.
> Our watchword be "God save the King."
> White Canada for ever.[218]

218. Khushwant Singh and Satindra Singh, *Ghadar 1915: India's First Armed Revolution* (New Delhi, 1966), 2. It should be noted that Canada continued to refine its body of discriminatory legislation well into the twentieth century. The Manitoba Factories Act of 1913 defined a "factory" as any building or premises in which three or more persons were employed, and any laundry operated by Chinese. Chapter 220 of the Revised Statutes of Saskatchewan (1930) treated Chinese laundries and tailor shops in the same manner as Manitoba. Alberta defined laundries as not being included under the meaning of the term "commercial business" as defined in the Early Closing Act, and hence they were forced to operate under a disadvantage (Huang, 234). British Columbia defined "every laundry run for profit" as a factory (Chapter 27, 1919), and another enactment prohibited the use of a factory as a dwelling house (Huang, 234–38). Quebec placed a heavy license fee on every laundry not run by women, charitable societies, or incorporated companies, leaving only the Chinese (Cheng, 88, Statutes of Quebec, Chapter 22, 1915). The British Columbia Produce Marketing Act of 1928 forbade Chinese from selling their products at less than the price established by a local committee (Huang, 234–38). Chinese in British Columbia were also excluded from the practice of law or pharmacology (*ibid.*) and from obtaining licenses for hand logging (Forest Act, 1923, article 22). By virtue of their exclusion from the voters' roll, Asian British subjects were also denied the right to stand for the provincial legislature (Revised Statutes of British Columbia, 1924, Chapter 45, article 27), and for municipal office (Revised Statutes of British Columbia 1924, Chapter 75, article 42), to be nominated as a school trustee (Revised Statutes of British Columbia, 1924, Chapter 226, article 37), or to serve on a jury (Revised Statutes of

It is true that historians must be very careful about making moral judgments. The world has looked quite different in other ages. But taking things at their best, it is difficult to justify, especially in the context of British liberalism and the imperial philosophy of racial equality, the treatment of the nonwhite residents of the British colonies of settlement, many of whom were, after all, British subjects. Even Gandhi tended to differentiate between immigration restriction and a policy of mistreatment of Indians, and by inference other colored persons, who were legitimately domiciled in the colonies. The former was unfortunate, unfair and ungenerous; the latter was nothing less than immoral. And both violated the officially proclaimed precepts of an Empire which in Chamberlain's words: "makes no distinction in favour of, or against any race or color."

British Columbia, 1924, Chapter 123, article 4). British Columbia prevented white women and girls from being employed by Chinese (Revised Statutes of British Columbia, 1924, Chapter 273). Saskatchewan barred white females from employment in restaurants, laundries and other places of business or amusement owned by Japanese, Chinese or other Orientals (Statutes of Saskatchewan, 1912, Chapter 17). Owing to Japanese protests and British advice (PAC, Governor General's Secretary's Office, file 7683, Canada, secret, Harcourt to Duke of Connaught, Aug. 7, 1912) the wording of the enactment was changed so that no white girl could be employed in a restaurant, laundry or other place of business or amusement (with no reference being made to the race of the owner or operator) unless it were specifically licensed (Revised Statutes of Saskatchewan, 1920, Chapter 188, Cheng, 88). Japanese, Chinese and Indians would as a matter of course not obtain licenses. The march of events in Manitoba was almost identical (PAC, Governor General's Secretary's Office, file 7683, undersec. external affairs to sec. to the gov. gen., Nov. 3, 1913). Saskatchewan disenfranchised Chinese in 1908 (Revised Statutes of Saskatchewan, 1930, Chapter 4).

5 The Classic Example— "White Australia"

In a sense, what occurred in Australia before the creation of the Commonwealth was prelude. And although post-1901 developments in South Africa and Canada have already been discussed, it seems appropriate to devote a separate chapter to Australasia in this period, as regards both immigration policy and the treatment of colored, nonindigenous inhabitants. Of all the constituent parts of the British Empire, Australia and to a lesser extent New Zealand seemed the most determined to make themselves bastions of Anglo-Saxon civilization preserved forever against the colored races of the earth.[1] The resulting combination of legislation and public attitudes, which history has remembered as the "White Australia" policy, constituted the greatest triumph for the "Natal formula" and the philosophy it represented.

The Commonwealth's first Parliament started in pursuit of the national goal immediately. Act 12 of 1901 stipulated that Australia would be party to no mail contract which did not contain the provision that only white labor would be employed on vessels carrying the Australian mails. It was the first pillar of the legal arch to support "White Australia." The second was Act 16 of the same year, which was designed to end the presence

---

1. Article 51 of the Constitution Act awarded the Commonwealth Government jurisdiction over external affairs, naturalization and aliens, and people of any race for whom it was deemed necessary to make special laws.

of South Sea Island labor in Australia forever. Whereas the Queensland planters had been able to fight a better than even battle with the white labor interests in their own colony, they were no match for the opposition of a united Australia. The law stipulated that no islanders were to enter the Commonwealth after March 31, 1904, and between the promulgation of the act and that date importations would steadily decrease. The repatriation of islanders would commence on December 31, 1906.

The keystone of the whole "White Australia" edifice was Act 17 of 1901, "To place certain restrictions on Immigration and to provide for the removal from the Commonwealth of prohibited Immigrants." The act was based on the "Natal formula" and was very similar to the laws passed by the separate colonies after the 1897 conference in London. The heart of the measure was article 3(a), which defined as a prohibited immigrant: "Any person who when asked to do so by an officer fails to write out at dictation and sign in the presence of the officer a passage of fifty words in length in an European language dictated by the officer." Article 3 also described several classes of exemptions—members of the King's regular land and sea forces, diplomats, wives and children under eighteen of nonprohibited immigrants and most significantly, "any person possessed of a certificate of exemption . . . signed by the Minister." This last provision allowed the temporary residence of useful kinds of laborers, such as divers for the pearling industry, who might otherwise have been excluded. If a worker on temporary status tried to change his employment, his certificate of exemption would be cancelled, and he would be submitted to the dictation test. He would fail and then be deported. It is worthy of note that there was again no special protection for British subjects.

The whole of Act 17 was considered a concession by many Australians. The Labour Party, for instance, had wished to exclude colored persons from Australia explicitly, and in regard to article 3, there had originally been a general inclination to require that the dictation test be taken in English. Although in time he conceded the point, one of those who favored the exclusive use of English was Prime Minister Edmund Barton, who exclaimed in the newly constituted Parliament on August 7, 1901:

> I do not propose to say that we do not want a man who can only speak Austrian, Italian or another language that is not the English language. But, I do say this also, that we shall not work an act of this kind without national complication, unless we are able to lay something down which in the outset distinguishes nothing between race and colour; but as to language there is not the same complication at all. The English language is our language, and the man who wants us to impose a test of another language should show some reason for his preference. Ours is the right language to use.

Once the principle of the dictation test had been established, other sections of the act made its purpose crystal clear. Article 5(2) stipulated that an immigrant could be given the dictation test at any time up to a year after his arrival in Australia.[2] Article 8 provided that any person not a natural-born or naturalized subject of the United Kingdom or Australia might, after a term of imprisonment, be forced to take the dictation test. Most illuminating of all was article 9, which prescribed a maximum penalty of £100 on a master or ship owner for each prohibited immigrant entering the Commonwealth from his vessel: "Provided that in the case of an immigrant of European race or descent no penalty shall be imposed under this section on any master, owner or charterer who proves to the satisfaction of the Court that he had no knowledge of the immigrant being landed contrary to this Act, and that he took all reasonable precautions to prevent it."

The change from "English" to "an European language" was ostensibly designed to mollify the Japanese, who demanded equality of treatment with all other peoples. But the real object

---

2. Raised to two years by an amending act in 1910 (10) and to three years in 1920.

of the amendment was to mollify the Colonial Office. The Japanese were, of course, not fooled. H. Eitaki, the Japanese consul general in Sydney, wondered why Japanese were not the equals of Russians, Greeks, Turks or Poles, and why if these people could be examined in their own languages the privilege was denied his countrymen. He thus asked, on behalf of his government, that Japanese be made an eligible language for the dictation test.[3] The proposal was, naturally, destined to fall on deaf ears.

The whole debate over the "Natal formula" and its relevance to Australia made embarrassingly clear the shallowness of the imperial philosophy and the whole liberal rationale for Empire. The Colonial Office was delighted at the new Commonwealth's attitude. Chamberlain wrote Sir John Forrest, the former premier of Western Australia and the minister for defense in the Commonwealth government:

> I think the Australians are right in taking steps to prevent the country from being over-run by the coloured races but I also feel, as you do, that the matter is full of difficulty, and that we, as Imperialists, must take care not to make invidious distinctions between the different races who live under the British flag, and that we must also avoid unnecessary offence to powerful nations like Japan whose friendship in the future may be of the greatest importance to the States of the Pacific.

The secretary of state concluded with his customary praise for the "Natal formula," which could exclude undesirables without recourse to such invidious distinctions. He was convinced that "No nations would have the right to object to legislation which is of universal application . . ." and was "sure that the future will justify your wise moderation in regard to this matter."[4]

But surely Chamberlain could not have been so naive as to anticipate a favorable reaction from the proud and sensitive Japanese, who had only to study the Commonwealth Parlia-

3. CO 418/10, Eitaki to Barton, Sept. 20, 1901.
4. Chamberlain Paps., JC/14/1/1/17, private, Chamberlain to Sir John Forrest, Nov. 13, 1901.

mentary debates to resolve any lingering doubts as to the true purpose of the immigration act. As Barton on October 1 replied to a colleague's question:

> If a Swede were asked to write a passage at dictation, I should not dream of instructing the officer to subject the immigrant to a test in Italian. That would be unfair, and is not what this House has in mind in pressing this legislation. . . . Honourable members may rely upon it that this Act will not be worked unfairly or oppressively in regard to those whom it is not our common desire to exclude, but that every care will be taken to prevent its being defeated by those whom we desire to keep out.

The Japanese were infuriated by the tone of the debate on the immigration bill. Not that they were great egalitarians; it was rather the other way around. "The Japanese," wrote Eitaki, exhibiting his own form of racism, "belong to an Empire whose standard of civilisation is so much higher than that of Kanakas, Negroes, Pacific Islanders, Indians or other Eastern peoples, that to refer to them in the same terms cannot but be regarded in the light of reproach, which is hardly warranted by the fact of the shade of the national complexion." Eitaki also protested the post and telegraph bill with similar lack of success, and when both it and the immigration act had been irrevocably passed into law, he wrote one further time protesting that both measures "make a racial discrimination," and expressing "high dissatisfaction" on behalf of his government.[5]

It is doubtful that the Japanese were cheered by the words of Alfred Deakin, the attorney general and future prime minister, even though they were a more tactful expression of the sentiments of most of his colleagues. "I contend," Deakin said, "that the Japanese require to be excluded because of their high abilities. I quite agree . . . that the Japanese are the most dangerous because they most nearly approach us, and would, therefore, be our most formidable competitors. It is not the bad qualities, but the good qualities of these alien races that make them

---

5. CO 418/10, Aus. 41695, Eitaki to Barton, Sept. 11, 1901; Eitaki to Hopetoun, Oct. 5, 1901.

dangerous to us." [6] Fundamentally, Deakin felt that the Empire and hence Australia were strong because they were British. "It is not British in the colour of all its subjects, but in the number of its white citizens, who control it, who give it authority, force and weight; whose character and courage sustain it in the day of battle as well as in industrial tasks from hour to hour. The Empire is great because it is British, and the stronger and more numerous our Britons the stronger our Empire must become." [7]

The Japanese were not the only Asians affronted by the immigration and postal laws. But the Chinese could speak only in muted tones and the Government of India was, when all is said and done, British. The Calcutta Bengali weekly, *Sanjivani*, however, wrote:

> Every part of the British Empire will send troops to Australia to celebrate the federation of the Australian Republics on the 1st January next. India too will send Gurkha, Pathan and Sikh soldiers to take part in the ceremony. Cannot Lord Curzon take this opportunity to have that obnoxious Australian law repealed which prohibits the Indians, who do not know English, from entering that colony and imposes a heavy tax on all Indians who are allowed entrance? Australian colonists are allowed to come freely to this country. Why then should not the Australians give the same privilege to Indians? [8]

Unfortunately for them, the nonwhite residents of Australasia were often their own worst enemies. As was the case in other parts of the British Empire, each colored group refused to look at the problem as a whole and tended to be interested only in its own welfare. The Japanese had already been heard from. In Queensland, some Singhalese protested:

> We are not cheap labourers, the cheap labourers are: Hindoos, Chinese, Pacific Islanders, Japanese, the British Cingalese are not cheap labourers. . . . Are the Government of His Majesty indiffer-

6. Quoted in John La Nauze, *Alfred Deakin* (Melbourne, 1965) I, 279.
7. *Ibid.*, II, 482.
8. IOL, Reports of the Native Press, Bengal, *Sanjivani,* Nov. 15, 1900.

ent to do Justice for the British Cingalese? The Labour Party are decidedly wrong in classing the British Cingalese as: Chows, Japs, Hindoos, Kanakas etc. etc. we do no like to trated [sic] as Chows. . . . The British Cingalese are honest, educated and civilised same any white nations.[9]

The post and telegraph and immigration acts may have been attacked from outside Australia, but they received universal support within the new nation. Not so the Pacific Islands laborers act, which aroused great antipathy in the sugar districts of Queensland. The storm in Parliament had been relatively mild when the prime minister had announced that his government was pledged to rid Australia of the Kanakas, but then not even the Queensland delegation was unanimous in support of the Polynesian work force, as labor in the north and south tended to oppose the sugar interests of central, coastal Queensland. When the measure actually passed and the news reached Brisbane, the planters rose in indignation. Sir Samuel Griffith, the former premier and now the lieutenant governor, took the high line of moral rectitude and indignation in telegraphing the governor general on behalf of his government. The bill, he contended, ran counter to the principle recently articulated by the secretary of state that any attempt to impose disqualifications based on place of origin, race or color was contrary to the conception of equality which was the guiding principle of British rule throughout the Empire. Furthermore, the law demanded the forcible expulsion from Queensland of a people whose original immigration had been legal and who had, for many years, enjoyed the protection of British laws. Finally, the measure would inflict a grievous wrong on Queensland as opposed to the rest of the Commonwealth. So saying, Griffith asked Lord Hopetoun to reserve the act. But this the governor general would not do.[10]

9. CO 418/12, Q. no. 141, Griffith to Chamberlain, Dec. 25, 1901.
10. CO 418/10, Aus. 3604, no. 134, Hopetoun to Chamberlain, Dec. 19, 1901, encl. tel., Griffith to Hopetoun, Dec. 12, 1901; Hopetoun to Griffith, Dec. 17, 1901.

Griffith was not to be easily mollified; in a letter directly to the secretary of state, he enclosed a paper by Queensland's premier, Robert Philp, contending that the Pacific Island laborers act would emasculate the Queensland sugar industry, and that, furthermore, the Government of Queensland, in 1892, had promised that no steps would be taken to inhibit the flow of island labor into the colony, on the basis of which undertaking many farmers had gone into the cultivation of sugar. It was now the responsibility of the Commonwealth Government to respect this pledge. Besides, Philp felt it was too early in the history of the new Dominion to start playing politics.[11]

Public meetings were frequent in the sugar districts, and the Kanakas went into battle on their own behalf by addressing a petition, with 3,000 apparently bona fide signatures, to Edward VII. The petitioners referred to their vested interests and to guarantees of continued residence provided by Queensland legislation. They reminded their sovereign that they were Christians as opposed to their heathen brethren on the islands.[12] A collection of papers entitled *The Sugar Question in Queensland* placed the planters' case before the Australian public. Most of the arguments were familiar. E. Sayne, of the Pioneer River Farmers Association, asserted that the white man could not physically survive plantation work in northern Queensland: "The utter unreliability of white labourers in the tropics, which is often adduced as the cause why industry cannot be successfully prosecuted, if dependent entirely upon them, is wrongly termed—it is simply the effect of a cause, the primary reason being the natural repugnance of white men to work under conditions to which they are not constitutionally adapted." [13]

11. CO 418/12, Q. 699 01/02, Q. no. 129, Griffith to Chamberlain, Nov. 29, 1901, encl. Robert Philp to President and members of the Senate of the Commonwealth of Australia, Nov. 15, 1901.
12. Queensland Archives, PRE-87, Q. no. 57, Griffith to Chamberlain, June 23, 1901, encl. the Kanaka petition.
13. *The Sugar Question in Queensland* (Brisbane, 1901), 17.

One of the papers was by a Dr. Walter Maxwell, who had been commissioned by Barton to investigate the problems of the sugar industry in Queensland, and whose views were, consequently, bound to be influential. His thesis was that the Commonwealth could afford to be more sympathetic to Queensland. He pointed to the increase in the white population of the north, the growth of sugar production and the decline in the number of islanders. In fact, "under the current condition of given natural laws, and particularly in certain latitudes, the Pacific Islander is a relatively declining factor in sugar production in Australia." [14] But time was needed and Maxwell was convinced that, at that particular moment in history, the provisions of the Pacific Island laborers act "will paralyze the industry." [15] That Barton was not going to be easy to convince was manifested by the tone of a letter he addressed to Premier Philp:

The savage employed by the white man is, in our judgement, more or less a slave, even under an agreement, because of the intellectual inequality between them. This inequality, while it accentuates the duty of humanity, forbids forever that the two races can contract upon an equal basis, for nothing can be done by enactment to undo the external difference. The islander may be grateful for kind treatment as the negro was: the negro cannot be deported now, because of his numbers, and because his race has become rooted in American soil. We do not propose that either of these conditions should ever arise in Australia, but we do propose to prevent them by such conditions, legislative and fiscal, as may least impair the islander or the white.[16]

Both the proponents and opponents of island labor emphasized the depth of their concern for the physical and moral welfare of

14. *Ibid.*, 32–67.
15. Alan Birch, "The Implementation of the White Australia Policy in the Queensland Sugar Industry, 1901–1912," *Australian Journal of Politics and History*, Aug. 1965, 201.
16. CO 562/3, H. of R., copy of letter from Barton to Philp, Nov. 12, 1901.

the islander. The former would save him by allowing him to remain in Australia; the latter by sending him home.

The passage of the Pacific Island laborers act seemed to many to have settled the Kanaka question once and for all, and in a sense it had. Even the planters seemed to acquiesce in the prohibition of further islander immigration. But the enforced repatriation of *all* the islanders already in Queensland was another matter, and an acrimonious correspondence between Queensland and the Commonwealth Government was destined to continue for many years, a conflict reflected in the newspapers of the Commonwealth. "The advocates of a 'white Australia' would like to see . . . a preventative measure of legislation set up like a stone wall against the danger of race pollution," boomed the *Sydney Morning Herald* on September 11, 1901. "On this point all thinking men and women are agreed, and no one with even the slightest personal knowledge of life in the Asiatic East will harbour a moment's doubt on the subject." The *Colonist* of sugar-growing Maryborough in Queensland wrote on October 12 that Barton had admitted that it was only a matter of time until the planters so improved conditions that white labor would replace colored, "and yet it [Queensland] is to be bludgeoned with this brutal piece of legislation. . . . The premier of Queensland has entered his protest none too soon. With ignorance at the helm, there is a grave need for prompt action on the part of those who perceive the dangers that lie ahead." To discourage a dependence on colored workers, Parliament made provision (Act 11 of 1902) for excise rebates on sugar grown through the use of white labor only. The measure was, however, found to be faulty and was replaced by two acts (4 of 1903 and 23 of 1905) that offered bounties for sugar grown entirely by white labor.[17] These achieved the desired effect, and an increasing percentage of Australian sugar came to be produced exclusively through white effort. In 1902,

17. Article 10 of the second measure permitted the employment of Australian aborigines.

12,254 tons of sugar was grown by white labor and 65,581 by colored. In 1907 the figures were 162,480 and 22,583 tons, respectively.[18]

As the deadline for the repatriation of all islanders in Australia approached, the Queensland planting interest, humanitarians, and the Kanakas themselves agitated with increasing urgency for a revision of the existing law. They argued that it was grossly unfair to uproot islanders who had been in Queensland for years and had vested interests. Besides, many of them were Christian, some had European wives, and they were being asked to return to islands which were no longer home and where they would be at best unwelcome and at worst the objects of murderous assault.[19]

For the first time the Commonwealth authorities indicated some flexibility. Although "the reversion of the policy embodied in existing law is not possible, . . . in effecting the work of returning Islanders to their homes no effort will be spared to prevent any hardship or injustice arising." To this end, the government was prepared to grant exemptions to islanders who had been in Australia for over twenty years, to those married to Australians or to women from islands other than their own, and to islanders too infirm to earn a living.[20]

The emerging new attitude, prompted by the success of the sugar bounty legislation, was encouraged by the report of the 1906 Queensland Royal Commission on the Repatriation of Kanakas which urged exemption from repatriation in certain cases.[21] As a consequence the Commonwealth Parliament passed a measure amending the act of 1901, which came into operation

---

18. J. W. Gregory, "White Labour in Tropic Agriculture," *The Nineteenth Century*, LXVII, no. 346, Feb. 1910.

19. C[ommonwealth] A[rchives] O[ffice], A–1 06/6324, Pacific Islanders Assoc. to Dept. of External Affairs, Sept. 4, 1906.

20. *Ibid.*, Atlee Hunt, sec. to Dept. of External Affairs, to Pacific Islanders Assoc., Oct. 2, 1906.

21. CO 418/47, Q./W. Pac. 33204, Commonwealth Parliamentary Paps., CA no. 75.

just before the first Kanakas were due to be deported.[22] On the whole, the concessions made in the new law were minor. They covered only a very few islanders, and immediately after December 31, 1906, the repatriation of the Kanakas commenced, leaving behind only a handful to sully the purity of "White Australia."

With the advent of Commonwealth, the jurisdiction of the former colonies, now states of the new union, of course became more limited, and their efforts were thus directed increasingly towards the position of nonwhites resident within their jurisdictions. The determination of eligibility for the state and consequently also the federal franchise remained a state prerogative.[23] The Queensland Elections Amendment Act of 1905 provided that no aboriginal native of Australia, Asia, Africa or the islands of the Pacific be placed on the electoral roll, and

22. Under the terms of Act 22 of 1906, the minister was empowered to exempt islanders from the workings of the principal act. General certificates of exemption were to be made available to any islander who convinced the minister that he had been introduced into Australia before Sept. 1879 (as in the principal act); that he was so aged or in such ill health as to preclude his earning a living on his native island; that he had been married before Oct. 9, 1906, to a native of another island and could not return to his home without grave physical danger; or that he had been married before that date to a female who was not a native of a Pacific island. Finally, islanders who were before Oct. 9, 1906, registered as the beneficial owners of freeholds in Queensland which they still held were exempted, as were those who had been continuously in residence in Australia for a period of not less than twenty years prior to the thirty-first day of December, 1906. Special certificates (not to remain in effect after June 30, 1907) were to be issued to islanders whom the minister judged it would be inconvenient to return to their native islands immediately after Dec. 31, 1906.

23. Article 41 of the Australian constitution specified that any person who had acquired a right to vote at elections for the more numerous House of Parliament of a State would not, while the right continued, be prevented by any law of the Commonwealth from voting at elections for either House of Parliament of the Federation. The electoral law, 1918–1929, repealed the Franchise Act of 1902 and disenfranchised aboriginal natives of Australia, Asia, Africa and the islands of the Pacific unless they were entitled to vote under the constitution.

Western Australia, two years later, in its election act, disenfranchised aboriginal natives of Asia and persons "of the half-blood." The other states apparently felt that restrictions effected previously or at the Commonwealth level provided sufficient protection.

The main object of concern, however, continued to be those Asians who offered or might conceivably offer commercial competition to Europeans—hawkers, manufacturers, especially of furniture, and to a lesser extent plantation workers. Again the rhetoric was familiar. In the Western Australian legislature, Arthur Diamond averred, "If we were going to make Australia a nation it must be a nation of white men," and rhetorically asked, "What were the rights of these coloured people? They had no rights." Frederick Illingsworth of Murchison urged his fellow legislators to "restrict the Asiatics to such channels of labour as leave them hewers of wood and drawers of water." [24] In Victoria one member of the assembly (David Gaunson) urged his colleagues to recollect that without further restrictive legislation "the possible danger is incurred of licensing a number of those dirty greasy Syrians and Indians, and God knows what." [25] Vincent Lesina, who represented Clermont in the Queensland legislature, exclaimed, "If we were going to be frightened of a 'White Australia,' and allowed wretched Annamese and Japanese to keep open until 12 o'clock at night, while Christians closed at the proper time, we would never be able to deal with it." [26] In New South Wales, the Chinese were accused of infiltrating the ladies' underwear market, for which garments could be made silently at night. To make matters worse, they slept in rooms where garments were manufactured and subsequently sold as clean! [27]

24. W.A. *Hansard,* Oct. 27, 1903; Aug. 23, 1903.
25. Victoria *Hansard,* Aug. 28, 1903.
26. Queensland *Hansard,* Aug. 23, 1906.
27. N.S.W. *Hansard,* Aug. 11, 1909. But Act 23 of 1909 said little that was new or of note. Article 42 specifically stated that in no factory where any Chinese were employed could work be commenced before 7:30 A.M. or

Inspired by such evidence, colonies without mining, pearl shell, factory, shop, and licensing laws proceeded to place them on the books, while those already protected made their legislation even more stringent.[28] The most imaginative measure was read a second time in the Victoria Assembly. On the totally unproved assumption that Chinese worked after hours in violation of the law, the bill stipulated that Chinese employees of a factory must be required to work on the ground floor and all be visible through a window no less than three feet from the ground.[29] Fortunately, the council did not see fit to pass the proposed act.

On another front, Queensland Act 13 of 1904, "A Bill to Amend 'The Agricultural Bank Act of 1901'" stipulated in article 3(3): "No advance under the Principal Act or this Act shall be made to any aboriginal native of Asia, Africa or the Pacific Islands." When the Japanese vehemently complained to the Colonial Office, which in turn passed on the protest to the Commonwealth and Queensland, the state was still able to achieve its purpose by generalizing the prohibition so that the amending act (15 of 1905) stated: "No advance under the Principal Act or this Act shall be made to an alien."

Queensland was less successful in a tangential area. In 1901 the legislature attempted to amend the sugar works guarantee acts, 1893–1895, in such a way as to prohibit the employment of

---

continued after 6:00 P.M. On Saturdays closing time was at 1 P.M., and all factories had to be shut on Sundays. Huang, 243, points out that in the area of state factory legislation, Queensland and Tasmania designated as a factory any buildings or premises where either Chinese or other Asiatics were employed, while Victoria, New South Wales and South Australia singled out Chinese alone.

28. Examples are: Western Australia Acts 1, 30, and 37 of 1904; Victoria Acts 1975 and 2008 of 1905; South Australia Act 763 of 1901, the Northern Territory Pearl Shell Act of 1901, the Northern Territory Mining Act of 1903, Acts 839 of 1903, 856 of 1904, 890 of 1905, 915 and 946 of 1907; Queensland Acts 5 of 1905 and 4 of 1908; New South Wales Act 28 of 1909.

29. Victoria *Hansard,* Nov. 17, 1904.

aboriginal natives of Asia, Africa or the Pacific Islands by companies that had received or might in the future be made advances under the provisions of the principal act. The Colonial Office, in opposing the law, deprecated any disqualification based on place of origin which, it contended, was little different from removal of certain rights due to race or color. The secretary of state hoped the Commonwealth Government would join that of His Majesty in opposing "legislation of the character of that provision in the Bill to which His Majesty's Government have felt bound to take exception." [30] With no terminological escape in view and, as the only Australasian colony to have adhered to the Anglo-Japanese treaty, Queensland was unable to prevail on the sugar works guarantee issue. And when the earlier acts were finally amended by means of Act 10 of 1908, the controversial clause was excluded.[31]

30. Commonwealth Parl. Paps. Sess. 1901–1902, p. 845.
"Any attempt to impose disqualifications on the base of such distinctions, besides being offensive to a friendly power, is contrary to the general conceptions of equality which have been the guiding principle of British rule throughout the Empire. Disqualification by educational tests such as are embodied in the immigration laws of the various colonies, is not a measure to which the Government of Japan, or any other Government, can take exception in behalf of its subjects; and if the particular tests in these laws are not regarded as sufficiently stringent, there is no reason why more stringent ones of a similar character should not be adopted. But disqualifications for certain employments on the sole ground of place of origin is a measure to which any Government concerned may reasonably object; and in the present Bill the aboriginal natives of two continents and of the Pacific Islands are disqualified solely on that ground."
31. Huang, 239–68, identifies several other areas of state interference with the rights of nonwhite residents. Among those listed are Queensland Act 16 of 1901, which reiterated the prohibitions of Act 11 of 1892 in regard to the employment of Asians in the construction of railways, etc., and the Queensland Local Authority Act, 1902–1920, which stipulated that unless a person not of European descent held a certificate indicating that he had passed a dictation test in the English language, he might not be employed in connection with tramways or omnibuses. This same certification requirement applied also to sugar (Acts 3 and 4 of 1913),

New Zealand never contemplated becoming part of the Commonwealth of Australia, but its racial policy rarely strayed far from that adopted by the new state and its constituent parts. In fact, the virulence of New Zealand rhetoric almost outdid anything to be heard on the neighboring continent. As in the Australian colonies, immigration restriction, the consequent barrier to the reuniting of families, and the dearth of commercial opportunities all combined to diminish the Chinese population of New Zealand. But these facts seemed in no way to lessen the European settlers' zeal. The census of 1901 showed 2,857 Chinese out of a total population of 815,862. Of this number, 1,313 were gold miners; 591, market gardeners; 172, fruiterers or greengrocers; 82, laundrymen; 117, laborers; 47, farm laborers; 43, storemen; 41, hotel cooks and servants; 26, boardinghouse keepers; 24, fish hawkers; 25, rabbiters; 13, carpenters and cabinetmakers; 9, fishermen; 7, restaurant keepers; 5, clerks and accountants; 2, butchers; 2, hawkers; and 5, of independent means. The census also listed 23 Chinese lunatics. Under the circumstances, it is surprising there were not more.

That much of the anti-Asian agitation verged on the irrational was manifested by the case of Lionel Terry, "The Yellow

---

bananas (Banana Industry Reservation Act, 1913), dairy products (Dairy Produce Act, 1904–1920), and margarine (Margarine Act, 1910–1930). A similar certificate was required under the terms of the Queensland Land Act, 1910–1931, for an alien to hold land. No alien might hold land if he were not naturalized within five years, and Asians were, of course, denied this privilege. The Queensland Mining Act, 1899–1930, precluded an alien who by lineage belonged to any of the Asiatic, African, or Polynesian races from being either a purchaser, a lessee, or a mortgagee of a miner's homestead. And under the terms of the Queensland Petroleum Act, 1918–1927, only a person in possession of a certificate attesting to his having passed the dictation test (where relevant) could qualify for or hold a petroleum permit or lease. The New South Wales Crown Lands Act, 1913–1927, prohibited the holding of land by an alien unless he had resided in the state for one year and had lodged a declaration of intent to become naturalized within five years. The South Australia Irrigation and Reclaimed Lands Act of 1914 disqualified persons of Asiatic race who were not British subjects from holding leases of land in irrigation areas.

The Classic Example—"White Australia"   295

Terror Fanatic," as he became known. Terry, a well-educated, upper-class Englishman, murdered an elderly Chinese to dramatize his opposition to the Asian presence in New Zealand. "As a protest against immigration," he wrote the governor, "I had deemed it advisable to put to death a Chinaman that evening." [32] When Terry came to trial in 1908, there was a good deal of public sympathy for him. *The Truth* of December 3, 1908, described the presence of the defendant in the court:

> Terry presented a striking appearance in the dock. His, by far away, was the most distinguished personality in court. As he stood at the bar to plead he was neither aggressive nor assertive and spoke with quiet and dignified composure.
> Every inch of his 6 ft. 4 in. of stalwart well-built manhood betokened his military training in a crack cavalry regiment, and his clean-cut, fine, classical features portrayed him as the least discomposed person in the whole crowded throng.

Terry was adjudged insane and he lived (it is said very comfortably) for many years at the Seacliff Asylum in Dunedin.[33] There is little doubt that the verdict of the court was appropriate. While in prison, Terry had written a poem which in its last verse had predicted the fate that would befall New Zealand as a result of having admitted Chinese immigrants.

> As bursts the thunderbolt from blackened
> Heaven,
> So shall the awful truth burst o'er thy land,
> As falls the mighty rock by lightning
> riven,
> So shalt thou fall.[34]

---

32. Fong, 27.   33. *Ibid.*
34. *The Dominion*, of Sept. 24, 1908, published all of Terry's poem. It is worthy of repetition in its complete form as an example of the anti-Asian sickness in its most extreme state, although it was probably the product of a deranged mind:

> i
> Athwart the northern sky dark clouds
> assembling

Yet, if Terry represented the abnormal mind in action, only a thin line separated him from his thoroughly normal confrères. In the reply to the address from the throne on July 2, 1907, the Chinese question came in for some discussion. T. K. Davey of Christchurch confessed to being "astonished that the people of

---

Cast o'er the earth a shroud of dreadful gloom
An evil nation. . . panic stricken . . .
awaits the crash of doom.

ii
For o'er the silent sea the blood light gleaming
Proclaims the rising of the pagan foe.
Steel fortresses in grim procession steaming
Herald the hour of woe.

iii
Thou hast no hope O blind and foolish nation!
Thou woulds't not heed the prophet's warning cry
The ancient law decrees its consummation
All things corrupt shall die.

iv
When the pagan cry "Banzai!" "Banzai!" shall ring in the bloody street,
And the fortress shall totter and fall to the guns of the pagan fleet,
Thou shalt once more move the ancient Law from the throne of God above
Which thou woulds't not heed in thy cowardly greed when t'was taught in pity and love.

v
When thy women stand in the market place mid the taunts of a hideous throng
To be bought and sold for the pagan gold and to suffer the deadly wrong,
Thou shalt feel the flame of thy burning shame and bitterly shalt thou rue
The day thou dids't brand the prophet as mad and follow the lure of the Jew.

The Classic Example—"White Australia" 297

Wellington have for so many years found it necessary to deal with Chinamen, and will not patronise the white fruiterer and greengrocer. It is an everlasting disgrace to the people of New Zealand that they support Chinamen after reading—as most of us have done—of the way in which Asiatics and Chinamen in particular live." It appeared that the colonial housewife, like her counterparts in other parts of the Empire and regardless of her racial feelings, bought where the prices were best. Davey went on to say: "I think it is our duty as legislators to pass a law, and at once, saying that no Chinamen shall be allowed to land in New Zealand. I suppose it would be extremely difficult to get rid of those already in the country. Once being here, I presume they must stay. It would cost a great deal of money to get rid of them, but I think we should bolt the door and say, 'No more of you shall land in the colony.'" H. J. H. Oney, the member from Taranaki, noted with glee that the white settlers of Taihape had the right idea: "In Taihape five Chinese tried to make a living but the settlers determined that they should not

---

vi
So now amid despair and desolation,
the wrath of God revealed throughout thy land;
Flood, fire, and strife shall end devastation
the ancient law shall stand!

vii
Where are thy fighting men? Where are
thy fortresses?
Slaves cannot keep the furious foe at bay!
The thousand miles of mortgaged wilderness,
thy impotence betray.

viii
A country bare of human habitation;
Slave-crowded cities open to the foe;
A people steeped in vice and degradation;
O thou hast fallen low!

The last of the nine verses appears above. The excerpts from *The Truth* and *The Dominion* are from the files of the Mitchell Library in Sydney.

stay in the district, and so they starved them out." [35] F. M. B. Fisher of Wellington Central reminded the prime minister, Sir Joseph Ward, that upon leaving Fremantle, in Western Australia, on a recent visit, he had exclaimed: "Make it white; keep it white." And Ward agreed that, "My desire is to have the purity of race maintained in our country." [36]

The Maori representative, Hone Heke, famous son of a still more famous father, rivaled his white colleagues in the virulence of his anti-Chinese sentiments.[37] Perhaps he had been influenced by Seddon's address to the Maoris of South Island, in which he had warned them that the Chinese presence meant the "deterioration of your race. They bring evils amongst you worse than the bubonic plague. It may be strong language to use, but I would rather see a case of the plague here than see a hundred Chinese land." [38] But then the Maoris were afflicted with their own sense of ethnocentrism.

It remained, however, for A. W. Rutherford, the member from Hurunue, to bring the debate to its lowest level:

I have never liked the idea of Chinese being admitted. I take exception to them not only because they come into competition with our workers, but on higher racial grounds. It was only the other day that I was walking down Lambton Quay and saw four little slant-eyed whitey-brown steps-and-stairs enter a Chinese fruiterer's shop, showing that the cradle had been in frequent use. The Premier gave the Australians the advice to keep Australia white. My idea would have been to give the Chinese three years to wind up their business and clear out, and return them their poll-tax.[39]

Parliamentary and public sentiments were, of course, translated into legislative action. Act 26 of 1901, "An Act to Prohibit the Importation or Smoking of Opium," in article 3(3) singled out Chinese as being ineligible for permits to import opium. Article 8 required a warrant for the search of places

35. N.Z. Hansard, July 2, 1907.   36. Ibid., Nov. 13, 1907.
37. Ibid.
38. R. M. Burdon, *King Dick* (London, 1953), 72.
39. N.Z. Hansard, Nov. 17, 1907.

The Classic Example—"White Australia" 299

where it was suspected opium was being smoked, "Provided that a search warrant shall not be required in the case of any entry on premises occupied by Chinese." Six years later, the New Zealand Parliament determined that the immigration restriction act of 1899 was not sufficient protection against the threatening yellow hordes and passed Act 79, "An Act to Amend the Chinese Immigration Act, 1881." The measure's third section violated the "Natal formula" by prescribing that a *Chinese immigrant* in order to be admitted to New Zealand had to be able to read a printed passage of not less than 100 words in English selected at the discretion of the immigration officer. The law was duly reserved for imperial action by the governor, Lord Plunket, while 750 Chinese residents of the colony sent him a long petition requesting redress. Among other things they pointed out that the new law required the dictation test to be given in English, though the principal act permitted the choice of any European language.[40] Sir Joseph Ward disdainfully replied to the governor:

The difference is immaterial. . . . The long and consistent course of legislation on the subject shows conclusively the fixed determination of the people of New Zealand that the presence of Chinese is undesirable. It is not necessary to offer reasons for this, though reasons in abundance could be given. It is sufficient to state that fact; and Your Excellency's advisers are profoundly convinced that any action by the Home authorities tending to fetter the policy of the New Zealand Parliament on this matter would be regarded by the people with feelings of the liveliest dissatisfaction. . . . In conclusion it is submitted that, the right to legislate on the subject being conceded, the details are matters entirely for the New Zealand Parliament in the exercise of the power conferred by the Constitution Act to make laws for the peace, order and good government of New Zealand.

The pressure was apparently sufficiently great for the Colonial Office once more to concede defeat. The draft of a letter from Elgin informed the governor that His Majesty's Government

---

40. CO 418/62, N.Z. 14053, no. 12, Plunket to Elgin, Mar. 17, 1908.

was assenting to the bill, "as the question of the immigration of aliens into the Dominion is one which must be determined according to the will of the Parliament and people of New Zealand. You should add that His Majesty's Government have every confidence that the Government and Parliament of New Zealand will afford all just relief to Chinese residents who are domiciled in New Zealand and who may have occasion to pay temporary visits abroad." Minuting by A. B. Keith was more to the point. He urged that New Zealand not be pressed to amend the Chinese immigration act of 1907, as Ward had been very cooperative in regard to the passage of a £100,000 subsidy for the carrying of the mails! [41]

To add insult to injury, the minister of internal affairs, in 1908, determined that no more Chinese should be naturalized— a decision upheld by the cabinet and destined to remain unaltered for forty-four years.[42] When the newly appointed Chinese consul was asked about the edict, he remarked: "Why the Chinese wish to become British subjects passes my understanding . . . for I cannot see where they are to benefit while they are held in contempt by the people who grant them the privilege." [43] What motivated the continued and increasing stringency of New Zealand legislation dealing with Chinese and Asians in general can only be ascribed to a "Yellow peril" mentality. The New Zealand census for 1911 showed 2,611 persons born in China and 1,315 in India and Ceylon.

Still, whatever transpired in the local affairs of the Australian states and even in New Zealand was of secondary importance to the course of events in that robust young giant, the Commonwealth of Australia. Although its Parliament found time to pass Act 11 of 1903, excluding Asians, Africans and Pacific

41. *Ibid.*, Ward to Plunket, Mar. 14, 1908; draft, Elgin to Plunket, May 15, 1908; minuting by A. B. K., of Apr. 23.
42. Fong, 37.
43. *Ibid.*, quoting the *Wellington Evening Post,* Apr. 7, 1909.

Islanders from the privilege of naturalization and empowering the governor general to revoke without reason certificates already issued,[44] as well as to revise the Kanaka legislation, most of the government's attention on the "White Australia" front was directed towards the international sphere. And here the chief protagonists were the acutely sensitive Japanese. Their unwillingness to forget the affronts afforded by the immigration act of 1901 and the growing importance of Japan in the defense plans of the British Empire forced a reassessment of the terminology and administration of the law.

Baron Hayashi, the Imperial Japanese Government's emissary to London, continued to demand British intervention. He was incensed at both the spirit and the letter of the law. He referred to Australian parliamentary debates which stated explicitly that one of the purposes of the measure was the exclusion of the Japanese and to the hypocrisy of Commonwealth ministers who "explain that the measure imposes an educational qualification without distinction of race or colour." Hayashi found the combination of the two "monstrous!" The Colonial Office, knowing that the disallowance of the bill would

---

44. Section 117 of the Constitution Act establishing the Commonwealth of Australia guaranteed: "A subject of the Queen resident in any State, shall not be subject in any other State to any disability or discrimination which would not be equally applicable to him if he were a subject of the Queen in such other State." Yet attempts were made to deprive non-white Australians of the protection of this clause. Alfred Deakin, the Commonwealth's first attorney general, found himself able to write: "The refusal to recognise as a British subject in one State a person upon whom the privilege of naturalization has been conferred in another State does not in my opinion constitute a disability or discrimination within the meaning of section 117" (CAO, Victoria Branch, Dept. of Trade and Customs, C. and E. 02/2793, opinion of Alfred Deakin, attorney general, Feb. 14, 1902). Huang, 194–95, points out that the Commonwealth Invalid and Old Age Pensions Act, 1908–1931, which insured naturalized subjects of at least three years' standing against sickness, incapacity, and old age, did not cover Asian British subjects unless they were born in Australia. The Commonwealth Maternity Act of 1912 excluded Asian women from its benefits.

only result in an explicitly insulting one, urged the Foreign Office to explain to Hayashi that words uttered in the heat of debate were of little moment.[45] Hayashi was not mollified. He objected to the requirement that the dictation test had to be given in a European language, but more significantly he withdrew his government's acceptance of the "Natal formula" because of the very obvious anti-Japanese bias manifested in the administration of the act. "This is of course a total change of position," the Colonial Office minuted in some dismay. "Formerly the Jap. Govt. said they did not mind the exclusion of Japanese from Australia, so long as it was done in a quiet way without naming Japanese or classing them as Asiatics: now they object to exclusion in itself, irrespective of method." [46]

The whole debate with the Japanese was complicated by the fact that Queensland, as a consequence of being a party to the Anglo-Japanese treaty of 1894, guaranteed Japanese certain rights. From the first, the Commonwealth wanted to sever the connection. Alfred Deakin, the attorney general, contended that with the creation of the Commonwealth, Queensland's adherence to the treaty lapsed because Queensland had never signed in its own right but rather as a dependency of Great Britain. The Queensland Parliament at that time also held exclusive jurisdiction over the colony's immigration policy. Now Queensland was part of a new international entity which did not wish to adhere to the Anglo-Japanese treaty, and immigration into all of Australia was governed by the Commonwealth Parliament, which had already expressed itself through the federal immigration restriction act.[47]

The Japanese Government was willing to abrogate the agree-

45. CO 418/16, Aus. 45375, Hayashi to Lansdowne, Dec. 16, 1901; draft, CO to FO, Jan. 2, 1902.

46. CO 418/23, Aus. 25097, FO to CO, June 11, 1902; minuting by Dale of 23/6.

47. Queensland Archives, PRE-105, Barton to Philp, Feb. 8, 1902, encl. minute by Deakin, Jan. 16, 1902.

ment⁴⁸ but Queensland was not eager to do so, for the treaty conveyed some real commercial advantages to the state. For the time being the law officers of the crown came to Queensland's rescue. They ruled that the creation of the Commonwealth did not affect Queensland's adherence to the Anglo-Japanese treaty. The treaty was not concluded between Japan and Queensland but between Japan and Great Britain. Since Queensland and the Commonwealth of Australia were both parts of His Majesty's dominions, the Queensland protocol was still binding.⁴⁹

Australian animosity towards the Japanese was indeed intense. Poetically, the *Morning Bulletin* of Rockhampton in Queensland wrote:

> Followers of Siva and Hanuman
> With Mahomedans may stand,
> Side by Side and Sweep the Land
> Bare of British as your hand—
> Thank Japan! ⁵⁰

Nevertheless, the Commonwealth Government was sufficiently enamored of the potential rewards of increased trade with Japan that it seriously proposed the adhesion of Australia to the Anglo-Japanese treaty.⁵¹ The Japanese not surprisingly suggested a *quid pro quo* in the form of a revised Australian immigration policy,⁵² and the whole matter, in due course, came to nought.⁵³ Two years later, the Commonwealth was able to bring enough influence to bear on Queensland that both the

---

48. *Ibid.*, PRE-106, R. Tayui, Japanese Consul General to Philp, Jan. 30, 1902.
49. CO 418/24, Aus./Q. 10190, Law Officers, Law Officers Dept., Royal Courts of Justice, to Chamberlain, Mar. 11, 1902.
50. D. C. S. Sissons, "Attitudes to Japan and Defence, 1890–1923," (M.A. thesis, University of Melbourne, 1956), 43.
51. CO 418/49, Aus. 37478, FO to CO, Oct. 10, 1906, encl. Sir Claude MacDonald to Sir Edward Grey, Oct. 6, 1906.
52. *Ibid.*, Aus./Gen. 44676, conf., FO to CO, Dec. 3, 1906.
53. CO 418/66, Aus./Q. 3151, FO to CO, Aug. 28, 1908.

state and the Commonwealth requested the abrogation of the protocol by the legal means established. On October 14, 1908, the Foreign Office informed the Colonial Office that the Japanese Government had been informed that under article 11 of the protocol, Queensland's adherence to the Anglo-Japanese treaty would terminate in twelve months.[54]

During the first full year of the operation of the immigration restriction act, 653 persons were refused admission to the Commonwealth. Four hundred fifty-nine were Chinese; 22, South Sea Islanders; 17, Japanese; and 11, "Hindus." Thirty-three persons to whom the dictation test was administered passed it, and, most significantly, 45,468 immigrants, nearly all of whom must have been white, were admitted without being required to take the test.[55] At the end of 1901, the Commonwealth was 54,856 persons short of being a totally "White Australia." Of this number, 31,836 were Chinese (compared to 38,533 in 1881), and 9,841 were South Sea Islanders.[56]

Nor were the Japanese the only non-Europeans to demand redress; Quong Tart, a prominent Chinese merchant of Sydney, was worried about the right of domiciled Chinese to return to Australia after a visit abroad. He also wondered if the time had not come to repeal the New South Wales Chinese immigration restriction act which was still in effect. The prime minister replied that certificates permitting re-entry would be issued to resident Chinese. On the latter issue the solicitor general thought the act was probably illegal as it imposed £100 poll tax on Chinese even if they entered New South Wales by land, that is, from another part of the Commonwealth.[57] Nevertheless,

54. Ibid., Aus./Q. 37516, FO to CO, Oct. 14, 1908.
55. CO 562/6, 1903, Imm. Rest. Act 1901, returns for 1902.
56. Ibid., paper 43, 1903. On Mar. 31, 1901, 47,104 or 1.246 percent of the total Australian population was Asian-born. By Apr. 3, 1911 the number had been reduced to 36,442 or 0.82 percent. Campbell, 77.
57. CAO, A–1 03/2900, Quong Tart to Barton, Jan. 8, 1903; Barton to Quong Tart, Mar. 9, 1903, encl. opinion by Hugh Pollack.

New South Wales was not willing to repeal the measure of its own volition.[58]

The most disturbing aspect of the Commonwealth immigration act from an imperial point of view was that it discriminated against certain types of British subjects more than it did against aliens. The Coloured Progressive Association of Sydney wrote the secretary of state for the colonies: "We are free to roam about, free to stand, free to hunger, free to starve, also free to die, for what?—Starvation under the Union Jack! . . . We are not making unfair demands, we only wish to be classed as our fellow subjects of the Empire." The Colonial Office replied with a straight face that it did not appear to the secretary of state that the act discriminated against His Majesty's colored subjects.[59]

There were 4,383 Indians in the Commonwealth at the end of 1901,[60] and they were ostensibly represented by an entire government and a British cabinet department. The Indians of Victoria addressed a letter to the Colonial Office in which they asked what the difference was between an Indian and other British subjects. Why should they be classed with Chinese and Japanese in being judged by the color of their skin when there was no mention in the immigration act of Germans, Russians, Frenchmen, Italians, and so on? When they loyally fought Great Britain's wars, how was it possible that they were treated so unfairly in Australia? [61] Indian residents from all over the Commonwealth filed similar complaints.[62]

The Government of India was unwilling to devote much time

---

58. *Ibid.*, premier of New South Wales to Barton, May 19, 1903.

59. CO 418/25, Aus. 41733, Misc., Coloured Progressive Association of Sydney to Chamberlain, Aug. 30, 1902 (60 signatures); CO to Commonwealth, Oct. 15, 1902.

60. CO 562/6, 1903, paper 43.

61. CO 418/17, Aus./Vict. 42811, Victoria Indians to Chamberlain, Oct. 25, 1901.

62. CO 418/30, Aus./W.A. 29384, IO to CO, Sept. 4, 1903, encl. Western Australia Indians to Curzon, Jan. 19, 1903.

to the matter because of the small number of Indians on the continent. While his government would regret restrictions acting to the detriment of British Indians, Lord Curzon was not prepared to intervene actively and preferred to leave matters in the hands of the India Office.[63] The Colonial Office answered the Victoria Indians much as it had the Coloured Progressive Association: "HMG appreciate the anxiety shown by them [the Indians] on behalf of their fellow-countrymen in India, but so far as the Govt. can judge . . . it [Commonwealth immigration legislation] does not appear to cast a reflection on any class of HM's subjects." Minuting by Dale added, "Their point of view is mainly sentimental," but admitted, "their protest against the 'White Australia' cry as *prima facie* anti-Imperial goes to the root of the whole matter." [64]

Should there have been any lingering doubts about how the immigration act was to operate, Atlee Hunt, the secretary of the Department of External Affairs and the officer charged with the implementation of the measure, made his government's policy unequivocally clear. "It is not desirable that [coloured] persons should be allowed to pass the test," he wrote the collector of customs at Fremantle, "and before putting it to anyone the Officer should be satisfied that he will fail. If he is considered likely to pass the test if put in English, it should be applied in some other language of which he is ignorant." [65] In a letter to a certain J. A. Nuno da Cunha, Hunt wrote: "With regard to the Dictation Test under the Immigration Restriction Act, it may be mentioned that its purpose is to prevent the in-

63. IOL, Govt. of India, Dept. of Rev. and Ag., May 1903, proc. 54, no. 22 of 1903, Dept. of Rev. and Ag. (Em.), Curzon in Council to Hamilton, May 21, 1903.

64. CO 418/17, Aus./Vict. 42811, draft, CO to Commonwealth, Dec. 24, 1901; minuting of Dec. 12, 1901.

65. CAO, CP. 235, Atlee Hunt to Collector of Customs, Fremantle, 1903. Quoted in C. F. Yong, "The Chinese in New South Wales and Victoria, 1901–1921, with Special Reference to Sydney and Melbourne," (Ph.D. dissertation, Australian National University, 1966), 20.

flux into Australia of coloured persons. It has never yet been applied to a white person." [66]

Hunt never relaxed his efforts to impress the purposes of the immigration restriction act on his subordinates. In the second year of the operation of the law, he wrote the collector of customs at Brisbane:

> In any case where enquiries indicate that a coloured person seeking admission to the Commonwealth intends to remain, the test, if administered in English, should be put in such a form and with such stringency as to place its sufficiency beyond doubt. Officers are, of course, free to select a passage from any other European language, and the services of your Interpreter, if necessary, may be employed for dictation of the passage in the tongue selected.[67]

That the dictation test was a most flexible tool was manifested by the case of a certain Hans Max Stelling, the son of a German doctor and an Egyptian mother. He was the second mate of the S.S. *Lita* and a German citizen. The vessel arrived in Australia in May 1903, and Stelling immediately absconded along with several thousand of the captain's cigars. He was duly arrested, tried and convicted. After serving six months in the Maitland jail, he was examined by a doctor who certified "him to be a half-caste with a large proportion of black blood in his veins." As a consequence, Stelling was submitted to the dictation test in Greek, which he failed, and was deported.[68]

When Harry Young Yan, a Chinese resident of Newcastle, requested that his fiancée be allowed to enter the Commonwealth, the Department of External Affairs would permit only a nonrenewable six-month visa requiring a £100 bond.[69] The

66. CAO, A–61, Imm. Rest. Act, Dept. of Ext. Affs., 09/6012, Atlee Hunt, sec. Dept. of Ext. Affs., to J. A. Nuno da Cunha, June 16, 1909.
67. CAO, AC and E. 03/0513, Atlee Hunt to Collector of Customs, Brisbane, June 24, 1903.
68. A. T. Yarwood, "The Dictation Test: An Historical Survey," *Australian Quarterly*, XXX, no. 2, 1958, 25–26.
69. CAO, A–1, 09/7192, sec. to Dept. of Ext. Affs. to Harry Young Yan, July 2, 1909.

many uses of the dictation test and the certainty of the outcome were manifested in a letter the Department of External Affairs wrote to the Japanese consul general concerning a Japanese couple who were engaged in prostitution. Now that the nature of their profession had been discovered, they would immediately be given the dictation test, "and on their failing to pass it they shall be charged as prohibited immigrants and deported from the Commonwealth." [70]

The stringency with which the immigration restriction act was administered only increased the foreign and imperial pressure for amendment. In mid-1904 the Commonwealth Government determined to permit merchants, students, and tourists from friendly powers, who were in possession of passports, to enter Australia temporarily without being subject to the act.[71] By 1905 it decided that it would be to its advantage to amend the immigration legislation of 1901. The amending measure (Act 17 of 1905) was in its own way a stroke of genius. The administration of the principal act was made more stringent at the same time that the Japanese and many other foreign opponents of the measure were largely disarmed.[72]

70. CAO, A-1, 09/5309, sec. to Dept. of Ext. Affs. to consul general of Japan, July 5, 1909.
71. CO 562/15, Dept. of Ext. Affs., minute paper, July 27, 1904, signed by Atlee Hunt.
72. Article 4(c) deleted section 3(m) (originally suspended in March 1903), and section 3(n) of the principal measure, thus removing the right of a wife and children under eighteen of an immigrant to enter the Commonwealth and of persons who could satisfy an officer that they had formerly been domiciled in the Commonwealth or in any colony which had become a state. Article 8 empowered the government to exempt citizens of certain countries from the dictation test and was designed to encourage other nations to control emigration to Australia themselves. This same section also provided for temporary exemption certificates to be issued to Australian residents of not less than five years' standing who wished, for a time, to absent themselves from the Commonwealth. However, "The officer may in his discretion give the certificate on payment of the prescribed fee, or, without assigning any reason, withhold it." Article 14 was designed to discourage shippers from bringing potentially prohibited immigrants to the shores of Australia. It required the master or

The essence of the new law lay in article 4(a). Whereas article 3(a) of the principal act had prescribed a dictation test in "an European language," article 4(a) of the new bill substituted "in any prescribed language." The Government of Japan, whose main objection to the original measure had been that it unfairly discriminated against its nationals by prescribing a European language for the test, found itself neatly boxed. The terminology of the laws was now above reproach when in fact the new bill, by broadening the selection of languages available to an examining officer, made it easier than ever to exclude Japanese, and for that matter anyone else, from the Commonwealth.[73]

The Colonial Office was delighted:

The important point of this Bill is that it substitutes for the test in a European language the test in a "prescribed" language: i.e., in appearance at least it definitely removes any trace of discrimination between Asiatics (Japanese) and Europeans.

There is no reason why we should object: on the contrary, there is every reason why we should applaud this amendment. The practical effect as far as actual immigration is concerned, is nil—since everything depends on the way in which the Act is administered: but the act itself will now contain nothing which can offend the Japanese except niceties.[74]

Alfred Deakin, Barton's successor as the Commonwealth's prime minister, was, for his part, full of bonhomie. He saw the new measure as a means of making the Japanese and his Hindu fellow subjects happy. Besides, the Japanese were "allies of the

---

owner of any vessel bringing a prohibited immigrant to the Commonwealth to return him whence he came at no cost to the state and to recompense the Government of Australia for any expenses incurred in the interim.

73. Article 4(a) did, however, stipulate: "No regulation prescribing any language or languages shall have any force until it has been laid before both Houses of the Parliament for thirty days and, before or after the expiration of such thirty days, both Houses of the Parliament by a resolution of which notice has been given, have agreed to such regulation."

74. CO 418/37, Aus. 44643, minuting, no date.

Empire to which we belong . . . [and] we can convey to them [now] our appreciation of their qualities, and, while excluding permanent settlers from among them, inflict no sense of offense." When a member of the House misunderstood the purpose of the amending bill, Deakin was quick to reassure him "that the object of applying the language test is not to allow persons to enter the Commonwealth, but to keep them out." [75]

But if most branches of the imperial tree seemed pleased with the act of 1905, the same could not be said of the Government of India, although its protest was mild and without visible effect. "We have carefully examined the new Act," Calcutta wrote, "and notice with regret that the effect of the proposed changes in the law will render still more stringent the provisions of an enactment already sufficiently severe." The Government of India had not objected to the principal act because it had not received a copy until long after the measure had been approved, but now that the law was being amended the viceroy and his advisers, "as guardians of the interests of the British Indian subjects of His Majesty" felt impelled to remark that "the history of the Anti-Asiatic movement in Australia justifies the apprehension that the Act may be worked in a spirit of hostility to British Indians in the Commonwealth." [76]

When it came right down to it, the India Office was just as much interested in appearances, as opposed to substance, as the Colonial Office. Hence, if Australia would not freely accept all Indians, perhaps some form of reciprocity would be possible. It was accordingly proposed that only a limited number of Aus-

75. Commonwealth *Hansard*, Nov. 10, 1905.
76. IOL, Govt. of India, Procs. of Dept. Comm. and Ind. (Em.), JP/7399, Apr. 1906, proc. 7, Dept. of Comm. and Ind. (Em.), no. 20 of 1906, Denzil Ibbetson, E. M. Baker, C. L. Tupper to Morley, Apr. 12, 1906. The Government of India also objected to the Australian custom's tariff (British preference) of 1906, because it restricted preferential treatment to such British goods as were imported into Australia on British ships manned exclusively by British crews and because the measure did not provide for preference for Indian goods. CO 418/56, Aus. 10209, IO to CO, Mar. 20, 1907.

tralians be permitted to enter India, with the same figure governing Indian admission to Australia. Further immigration would be barred by legislation on both sides. It was all rather laughable, a charade which pretended that large numbers of Australians wished to emigrate to India.[77] Lord Morley, at the India Office, wrote the viceroy in all seriousness, asking "Your Excellency's Government to give this suggestion your most careful consideration." The secretary of state realized the acceptance of the proposal would require the Government of India to abandon the principle of complete freedom of movement within the Empire, but as "there is little chance of persuading either the Australian or any other Colonial Government to accept it," perhaps India could gain some advantage it did not currently enjoy by condoning a form of reciprocity that was clearly "rather nominal than real."[78]

The Colonial Office tried to cajole the Commonwealth into acceptance of its part of the proposal,[79] but Lord Minto, who had become viceroy in 1905, wrote *finis* to the whole unlikely scheme when he identified it as a transparent piece of chicanery. "We cannot . . . hope," he wrote, "that the one-sidedness of the arrangement proposed would escape detection, and we are convinced that our acceptance of it would be regarded, and justly so, as a betrayal of the cause of the Indian people." The viceroy finished his dispatch in a less lofty but thoroughly pragmatic vein. "On the whole," he wrote with almost audible relief, "the Indian question in Australia is not one that has received much public attention. . . . So why not let sleeping dogs lie?"[80]

The level of Australian concern with the immigration ques-

77. IOL, Govt. of India, Procs. of Dept. of Comm. and Inc. (Em.), July 1909, proc. 1. At the time of World War I, Australia agreed to ease the terms for the temporary admission of Indians to Australia and to admit the families of Indians resident on the continent.
78. *Ibid.*, Morley to Minto, Mar. 5, 1909.
79. *Ibid.*, annex 1, conf. Crewe to Dudley, Sept. 1908.
80. *Ibid.*, proc. 2, Minto in Council to Morley, June 24, 1909.

tion was manifested by a curious exchange between the acting collector of customs at Adelaide and the Department of External Affairs. The former asked: "Is it necessary [under the terms of article 9 of the Immigration Restriction Act of 1901] that persons should be absolutely of European descent, as in the case of inhabitants of the United States, or can, say, South American races being a mixed breed of Spanish and Indian descent be included?" Not without charity, the attorney general ruled: "My view is that, the words 'European descent' having reference to race and not nationality, the test should be the prepondering blood, and that in cases of half-blood the person charged is entitled to the benefit." [81] Four years later, the secretary of the Department of External Affairs wrote Percy Hunter, who ran an immigration and tourist bureau in Sydney: "I may state that it is not the practice of the Department to admit half-castes, but we do not lay down any general rule that they are inadmissible. Special cases may often occur requiring special consideration. I would, however, certainly advise that no encouragement or inducement be held out to such persons to migrate here." [82]

Why Australia continued to fear invasion by hordes of Asians, protected as it was by a legal curtain of awesome effectiveness, is hard to explain, and the answer must lie more in the realm of the romantic and emotional than the rational. For some unknown reason a wave of illegal Chinese immigrants was anticipated in 1909, and H. Robinson, the inspector of police at Perth, urged that twenty officers instead of just one should be placed on steamers sailing for Western Australia from Singapore; that no Asiatic be allowed to leave a vessel until identified by a ship's officer; and that all ships from Singapore be fumigated at Broome as a deterrent to stowaways.

81. CAO A-1, 05/6378, act. collector of customs, Adelaide, to Atlee Hunt, Mar. 24, 1905; sec. to Dept. of Ext. Affs. to attorney general, Aug. 29, 1905, minute paper by attorney general's dept., Sept. 30, 1905.

82. CAO, A-1, 09/5309, unofficial, sec. to Dept. of Ext. Affs., to Percy Hunter, July 9, 1909.

Masters of vessels should possess photographs of all Asian members of their crews so that deserters might be traced.[83] And as if these precautions were not enough, the assistant comptroller general urged the establishment of a travelling corps of officers, a coastal patrol, and the assignment of detectives to all vessels while in Australian waters. When it came to applicants for exemption from the dictation test who based their case on former residence, a cumbersome system of interviews and the comparison of photographs taken at various times was recommended.[84] Despite the miniscule number of Chinese scholars who came to Australia to study under the revised regulations of 1904, the Department of External Affairs determined "that this practice is not wise, and [we] do not propose to continue it. Applicants may be informed in future that the Minister does not see his way to grant the desired exemption." [85]

The leaders of the two major political parties continued the crusade against colored immigration when it must have been clear, at least to them, that whatever danger there might once have been had long since been allayed by the corpus of stringent legislative measures. The Labour Party based its support of "White Australia" on its historic role as protector of the white working man against the threat of cheap colored labor. It was a stance that had always had an appeal at the polls, and there was no need to abandon it just because the issue was not real or alive, especially as the voter did not seem aware of that. The Liberal Party did not have the same philosophical attachment to "White Australia" as its rival, but its senior members recalled that Samuel Griffith had cost the party heavily when he had supported the planters in Queensland on the Kanaka issue. Realistic Liberal leaders like Parkes and Sir Isaac Isaacs, the

83. CAO, A–1, 09/14282, recommendation by H. Robinson, inspector of police, Perth, no date (circa Nov. 1908).
84. CAO, A–1, 10/770, asst. comptroller general to sec. Dept. Ext. Affs., Nov. 6, 1908.
85. CAO, A–1, 11/17896, ministerial decision re. the admission of Chinese for ed. purposes, Dept. of Ext. Affs., Oct. 20, 1911.

future governor general, saw an emphasis on the common appeal of "White Australia" as a way to avert the political disaster of a Labour victory. They therefore adopted one of their rivals' most potent weapons—one which cut across conventional loyalties and affiliations. As Carlotta Kellaway summed it up in her article in the *Australian Quarterly:* "It seems as if the Liberals realised the value of 'White Australia' as a catchcry for drawing the radicals into support of Federation. And it seems as if the Labour groups saw it as a good rallying-point for drawing their rather disunited supporters into some sort of uniform Labour movement." [86]

The passage of Act 17 of 1905 notwithstanding, the Japanese continued to protest the immigration restriction acts. But all three major protagonists—the Australian, British and Japanese Governments—knew that the battle, in any substantive sense, was over. "I am tempted," a Japanese visitor to Australia wrote in frustration, "to point out that already your cry of 'racial purity' is farcical. Practically every country in the world has contributed to your population. You fall back on the objection of 'colour'—and forget that many Chinese and Japanese are whiter skinned than the average Australian. You are glad to avail yourself of the discoveries of our scientists, and yet you object to having such scientists—far greater than you have produced—in your midst." [87]

In consonance with the policies of both major parties and despite the international victory represented by Act 17 of 1905 and the now essentially completed legal outworks for "White Australia," public attitudes remained constant. Fear of the "Mongolian" hordes poised to descend on the continent continued to preoccupy white Australians. In 1909 both a play by F. R. C. Hopkins, *Reaping the Whirlwind,* and a novel by

86. Carlotta Kellaway, "White Australia: How the Political Reality Became a National Myth," *Australian Quarterly,* XXV, no. 2, 1953, 7–17.
87. Y. Nagano, "The Other Side: A Japanese in White Australia," *Australian Magazine,* VIII (new series), no. 4, 1908, 473–74.

C. H. Kirness, *The Australian Crisis,* dealt with this theme. The concluding lines of the latter work eloquently captured the Australian point of view: "In this struggle the still larger issue is bound up with whether the White or Yellow Race shall gain final supremacy. Christian civilisation cannot afford the loss of this continent. *For Australia is the precious front buckle in the White girdle of power and progress encircling the globe.*" [88]

It might be worthwhile to point out that in the development of its racial policy, Australia felt that it had gained both knowledge and inspiration from the American example. The unfortunate result of so many Negroes being permanent residents of the United States of America received frequent mention (although the blame was placed more on Britain than the United States). California was deemed exemplary in its attitudes and actions toward Chinese, Japanese and Indians. A short-lived journal named *White Australia* displayed on the cover of its maiden issue of August 8, 1908, a large colored cartoon depicting an Indian and a Chinese with their heads thrust through a gate labeled Northern Territory. The cartoon was titled "Teddy's Warning," and in a field on the other side of the gate Teddy was addressing a robust, bearded figure called "White Australia." President Roosevelt: "Mind that back gate, my boy, you might have trouble!" White Australia: "All right Teddy! I haven't forgotten your warning." The next issue showed Uncle Sam and Lady Australia together bemoaning the lack of sufficient whites and the consequent black threat to the Northern Territory. The front of each issue was emblazoned with American, British and Australian flags.

A survey of the period from the mid-nineteenth century to 1910 shows the slow evolution of a policy that started out as nothing more than a set of colonial laws basically designed to keep Chinese off the Australasian goldfields into a racial philosophy that enjoyed many of the trappings of a state religion.

88. Quoted in Sissons, 68–69. Italics in original.

Australia and New Zealand had to be kept pure and white and this meant the exclusion of not only Chinese, but Japanese and Indians—in fact, all men of color. It also seemed to mean the harrying of nonwhite residents, although this was more difficult to justify in terms of the messianic role Australasia had chosen for itself.

Conclusion

The "Natal formula," the "White Australia" policy, and the whole array of discriminatory legislation which grew up in Australia, New Zealand, Canada, and South Africa represented a triumph not so much for the white working man, concerned as he was about "cheap" labor, as of the prevailing ethos that saw the colored man worth intrinsically less than the white. Although this book has dealt with the question of nonwhite immigrants in the British Empire of Settlement, the white racial attitudes exhibited applied just as surely to black men in Africa (and America) and Indians in their own native land.

To a singularly law-abiding people used to what A. P. Thornton has called "the habit of authority," [1] the one force that might have inhibited legal sanctions against colored persons was Her Majesty's Government. But, despite its roles of enunciator of the imperial philosophy of equality and fair play within the Empire and the whole British community's spokesman to the outside world, Whitehall remained largely ineffective. On the basis of many of its pronouncements, one might have assumed that the rights of British subjects, regardless of race, would have been rigorously preserved and affronts to friendly powers such as China and Japan avoided. From the first, however, the fight against white colonial sentiments was a losing battle. The Colonial Office knew that London could not really stand up against the determination of colonial governments if the Empire was to survive. And, given the essential homogeneity of the

1. A. P. Thornton, *The Habit of Authority* (Toronto, 1966).

Anglo-Saxon world view, most of the officials in the corridors of power agreed with the racial attitudes of the colonists.

Furthermore, London was a very long way from the overseas settlements. And if Great Britain's ability to interfere in colonial affairs was limited before the advent of responsible government, it was almost nonexistent afterwards. The right to disallow colonial legislation remained, but it could be invoked only on questions having imperial or international implications. Her Majesty's Government, therefore, found itself in the position of constantly developing or supporting schemes which preserved the letter but violated the spirit of Britain's international agreements and the imperial philosophy. Thus, Newcastle, in 1853, suggested a formula for Chinese exclusion based on a ratio of Chinese passengers to ship tonnage. This idea, which allowed the Australasian colonies to achieve their goal under the guise of ensuring adequate shipboard comfort for Chinese passengers en route to the Antipodes, was the kind of solution the Colonial Office avidly sought.

The effect of this attitude was that so long as colonial legislatures made sure the letter of any act was nonracial and placed the teeth of implementation in the regulations under which the law was administered, the British Government kept its hands off. Even when colonies violated that rather general precept (e.g., the New Zealand Chinese Immigration Act of 1907), they could usually achieve success in the end, if they were sufficiently obstinate.

One might assume that were it not for the constitutional rights of the self-governing colonies, the British Government would have defended the imperial philosophy more boldly. After the Boer War, however, the British authorities were clearly free to administer the conquered territories of the Transvaal and the Orange Free State in any way they saw fit. They nonetheless adhered more rigorously than even their republican predecessors to the racial precepts held by the Afrikaners, at least to the degree that they applied to those other

British subjects, the resident Indians. Given the wealth of the region and the makeup of the white population, however, such a policy, if not laudatory, was at least understandable. A less excusable case was that of Zululand, a province under the Colonial Office's immediate supervision, and hence not subject to the jurisdiction of a colony enjoying the rights of responsible government. By the early 1890s, Indian traders had filtered into Zululand from neighboring Natal to be greeted with familiar hostility by the few white colonists. For once the Colonial Office could have taken the high road and forthrightly applied the imperial philosophy without risk. But it did not do so, and Indians in Zululand became subject to just the same kind of restrictions they had encountered in Natal.

Politicians in the colonies of settlement were not unobservant, and once they understood the rules of the game as established in London, they played it with great skill, always bearing in mind that in matters of great urgency they did not really have to play at all. On the immigration front, the "Natal formula" became accepted as the key to success. And as we have seen, it was a most effective technique. The law merely implied that the various colonies wanted settlers who were at least moderately educated and that to achieve this end immigrants would be examined as to literacy. On the surface it even appeared that the frequent stipulation permitting the use of any European language (and after 1905 in Australia of any language) made it possible for a non-English-speaking immigrant to take the examination in his native tongue, when the real intent was quite to the contrary. Canada, of course, added its own innovations to the "Natal formula" by conceiving the direct passage doctrine and in the Immigration Act of 1910 sealed any loophole that might have remained by disingenuously empowering the governor general to prohibit the entry into Canada of "immigrants belonging to any race deemed unsuited to the climate or requirements of Canada, or of immigrants of any specified calling, occupation, or character."

The next step was to make sure that any colored person who had entered a colony before the gates were barred did not obtain the rights of citizenship. The Indian immigrants to Natal were virtually all British subjects, so that naturalization was not an issue. The franchise of course was. Here the colonial officials, having failed to disqualify Indians from the voters' rolls by direct assault, resorted to the kind of subterfuge which, in dealing with the Colonial Office, almost always succeeded. The Franchise Act of 1896 achieved its purpose by denying the vote to those "who (not being of European origin) are Natives or descendants in the male line of Natives of countries which have not hitherto possessed elective institutions." Nowhere in the legislation were Indians specifically mentioned, but the white colonists achieved their goal nonetheless and with the blessings of Westminster into the bargain.

If an economic motivation for anti-color enactments existed anywhere, it was surely lacking in the case of the Natal franchise. Under existing legislation, all eligible voters had to possess £50 in property or pay £20 in annual rent. Consequently, only very few Indians would ever have reached the voters' rolls. In fact, in 1894 there were only 251 Indians so enrolled compared to 9,650 Europeans—a ratio of 1/38—at a time when the two elements of the population were close to equal in numbers.[2]

In Australia, where the vast majority of nonwhite immigrants were not British subjects, they were kept off the voters' rolls either through direct prohibition or by denial of naturalization. Both courses of action affronted friendly foreign governments, but in British eyes they did not pose the same moral and philosophical dilemma as interference with the rights of British subjects. As early as 1861 Queensland passed a measure excluding Asian and African aliens from eligibility for naturalization unless they were married with a wife in the colony and had been in Queensland for three years.[3] Victoria Act 723 of 1881

2. Huttenback, *Gandhi*, 74.
3. Act 9 of 1861, repromulgated in Act 28 of 1897.

in its eleventh article excluded Chinese from the voters' rolls for parliamentary and municipal elections even if they were ratepayers. Although British subjects were theoretically exempted, local officials were empowered each to "decide upon his own belief or view or knowledge or judgment whether any ratepayer is or is not such an alien immigrant." [4] South Australia Act 278 of 1882 stipulated in regard to the colony's Northern Territory that the vote be denied to naturalized British subjects who were not of "European nationality" or from the United States of America. Article 6(I) of Queensland Act 49 of 1885 declared that "no aboriginal native of Australia, India, China or of the South Sea Islands shall be entitled to be entered on any electoral roll prepared . . . for the purpose of any election of a member of Legislative Assembly, except in respect of the freehold qualification." Western Australia later emulated Queensland,[5] but neither the Colonial Office nor the Foreign Office manifested much concern. New South Wales under the terms of Act 3 of 1861 prohibited the issuance of any further certificates of naturalization to Chinese. Act 8 of 1867 repealed this provision, but Act 4 of 1888 reinstated it. Victoria suspended the naturalization of Chinese by edict in 1887. Finally, the Queensland Elections Amendment Act of 1905 provided that no aboriginal native of Australia, Asia, Africa or the islands of the Pacific be placed on the electoral roll, and Western Australia, two years later, in its election act, disenfranchised aboriginal natives of Asia and persons "of the half-blood."

The establishment of the Commonwealth of Australia in 1901 in no way altered the prevailing situation. The determination of voter eligibility remained a state prerogative, and section 41 of the Australian constitution limited itself to guaranteeing that any person who had or acquired a right to vote at elections for the more numerous House of Parliament of a state would not, while the right continued, be prevented by any law of the Commonwealth from voting at elections for either House

4. Article 13.   5. Act 19 of 1899.

of Parliament of the federation. The Electoral Law, 1918–1929, however, disenfranchised aboriginal natives of Australia, Asia, Africa and the islands of the Pacific, unless they were entitled to vote under the constitution. The Commonwealth Act 11 of 1903 excluded Asians, Africans and Pacific Islanders from eligibility for the privilege of naturalization and also empowered the governor general to revoke certificates already issued, without having to show cause. But then the possession of British nationality did not protect nonwhites from discriminatory treatment under the law.

The situation in Canada was very similar to that in Australia, though two significant differences existed: virtually all the Orientals and Indians gravitated to one province, British Columbia, and the immigration occurred after confederation. Thus British Columbia had no opportunity to carry a corpus of discriminatory legislation into a new union, and all laws directed against Chinese, Japanese, and Indians had to pass through the filter of a Dominion government situated far from the source of the problem and more interested in trade with the Orient than in the dilemma of a province which sent to Parliament less than one-tenth the number of representatives elected in Quebec or Ontario. The result was that a great deal of British Columbian legislation was disallowed in Ottawa, although many matters of significance such as the franchise remained under provincial jurisdiction.

As early as 1872, when "an Act to Amend the Qualification and Registration of Voters Act, 1871" was passed, Chinese in British Columbia were denied the franchise. Act 2 of 1875 ordered the removal of any Chinese who might still be on the voters' roll. And the Provincial Elections Act of 1897 reinforced the previous enactments by stipulating that no Chinese, Japanese or Indian (Canadian native Indian), whether naturalized or not, could have his name placed on the voters' roll for any election. The Chinese were denied the municipal franchise in 1892 and the Japanese were similarly treated eight years later.[6]

6. B.C. Chapter 33 of 1892; Chapter 54 of 1900.

When Indians (East Indians) began arriving in British Columbia, they too were made ineligible for the franchise by Chapters 17 of 1903-4 and 16 of 1907. The Dominion Government never barred Chinese and other nonwhites from naturalization, but being a British subject in itself provided so little protection against discriminatory actions by the provinces that the privilege was largely meaningless.

The bounds of prejudice were clear-cut and direct in such essentially legal questions as the right to vote and naturalization. A more complex dilemma was faced when the white settlers in Australasia, South Africa, and Canada attempted to express their animosity toward their nonwhite fellow subjects in such areas as business opportunities, employment, taxation, and residence—in fact, the very right to exist at a level other than that of "a hewer of wood and a drawer of water."

Again, it would be easy to assume that the sole motivation for such action was the fear of a kind of economic competition which would debase the quality of life for all settlers. The evidence presented in the foregoing pages does not bear out this contention. Race hatred was the vital driving force behind legislation that withheld education from nonwhites, submitted them to special forms of taxation, and denied them the use of liquor, employment on public works, access to goldfields, and even the right to run a business. In South Africa, Indians were required to carry passes, forbidden to use the sidewalks, and relegated to special locations. Everywhere nonwhites were deprived of equal treatment before the law, were harried and exposed to every manner of indignity. The white settlers were convinced, as we have seen, that men of color were "a great curse. . . . Incapable of improvement . . . [and] nothing better than filthy harbingers of disease." [7]

Some of the pronouncements in the preceding chapters also give evidence of the same psychosexual terrors and frustrations

7. PAC, Orders in Council, R.G. 2, series 1, V. 566, George Gagan, sec. Vancouver Trades and Labour Council to George Dower, sec.-treas., Dominion Trades and Labour Congress, Sept. 1, 1892.

discussed in recent histories of race relations in the United States. The white man, it is asserted, has always attributed greater sexual potency to the black and has imputed to him an insatiable lust for white women.[8] Sexual hostility towards colored persons was an important element in the "White Australia" mentality. When a Japanese naval squadron visited Australia in 1906, the local press alleged the sailors were distributing pornographic postcards and that the ships were filled with naked prostitutes. William Lane wrote that he would rather see his daughter dead than kissing a black man or "nursing a little coffee-coloured brat she was mother to." [9] The Australian writer, Henry Lawson, created his own nightmare in which:

> I saw the stricken city fall . . .
>   The pure girl to the leper's kiss
> God, give us faith for Christ's own sake,
>   To kill our womenkind ere this.[10]

It was a vision very similar to that expressed in the apocalyptic poetry of Lionel Terry:

> When thy women stand in the market place
> mid the taunts of a hideous throng
> To be bought and sold for the pagan gold and
> to suffer the hideous wrong,
> Thou shalt feel the flame of thy burning shame
> and bitterly shalt thou rue
> The day thou dids't brand the prophet as mad
> and follow the lure of the Jew.[11]

Had Asians wished to assimilate with the white settlers, their attempts would have spawned even more violence than actually occurred. On the other hand, the unwillingness of Asians to mingle more closely with whites, and the Chinese, Japanese and

8. Calvin C. Hernton, *Sex and Racism in America* (New York, 1966).
9. S. Encel, "The Nature of Race Prejudice in Australia," in Stevens, I, 33.
10. H. O. McQueen, "Racism in Australian Literature," in Stevens, I, 110.
11. *The Dominion* (Wellington, N.Z.), Sept. 24, 1908.

Indian sense of their own cultural identity and racial purity, served only to infuriate their detractors rather than to assuage white fears.

In time the varying efforts of the Dominions to turn themselves into white men's countries imbued what was really just another tawdry form of racism with the aura of an evangelical movement. As late as 1921 one prominent Australian, Sir James Connolly, saw the "White Australia" policy as "a national ideal, to the Australian mind as unalterable as the laws of the Medes and the Persians. . . . Australia's white ideal," he concluded, "has the whole-hearted sympathy and practically the whole-hearted support of the British race," [12] and so, he might have added, had the "white ideal" of New Zealand, Canada, and South Africa.

As Sir West Ridgeway, a former Indian provincial governor and erstwhile chairman of an investigatory committee sent to the Transvaal, wrote to the *Times*, it was a delusion to

dream of a Utopian Empire where all citizens enjoy equal rights. This dream can never be realised; at least for generations to come. If the Government were to make any attempt to enforce this policy, or even to support it by argument, the break-up of our Empire would follow. Our self-governing colonies—at least at this stage of their development—will not tolerate the entry of coloured races into their midst in any number. It is a question of life and death with them. Theirs must be a white man's country.[13]

For the nonwhite resident of the Dominions, life must have been a sort of nightmare. Cut off from his native land, with his relatives and dependents unable to join him, he suffered continuing attacks on his economic, political, and social position as well as direct physical assaults, alone. "Will not the British Government do anything to save the poor Indians of Australia?" asked the Bengali weekly, *Bangavasi*. "They are British subjects

12. Frazer Hunt, "White Australia and Pink Queensland," *Nineteenth Century*, CXCIII, Dec. 1921.
13. The *Times*, Dec. 6, 1913.

and Australia is a British territory. Where will they go if they do not get protection from oppression in the dominion of their Sovereign?"[14] To this and many similar questions no reply was ever forthcoming, and therein lies one of the tragedies of Empire.

It is admittedly much too easy to judge the past through the eyes of the present. The nineteenth century was not the most tolerant of ages. Discrimination of all sorts, racial, national, economic, and class, was almost universally practiced. What Philip Mason terms "patterns of dominance"[15] had been established by all European nations wherever they ruled overseas. Germans, Belgians, French, Portuguese, Italians, Spaniards, and Dutch slaughtered indigenous populations whenever it suited their convenience. Those nations without colonies managed to indulge the same dark art in a different context, by practicing it on elements of their own domestic populations.

The British Empire of Settlement was not alone in denying the brotherhood of all men, and its history is in many ways more typical than exceptional, if not of the European mentality, then certainly of the Anglo-Saxon. Generations of British and American schoolchildren have grown up with the conviction that Britain, if not the birthplace of all liberal ideas, was, with the states she spawned, at least where they flowered the most perfectly. And the generalization may indeed be a valid one. But the study of the "White Australia" policy and its counterparts in the context of the liberal rhetoric of Empire brings to light perhaps the major skeleton in the British imperial cupboard.

14. IOL, Reports of the Native Press, Bengal, *Bangavasi*, June 28, 1905.
15. Philip Mason, *Patterns of Dominance* (New York, 1970).

Bibliography

GENERAL SOURCES

BOOKS

Allport, Gordon W. *The Nature of Prejudice.* Boston: Beacon Press, 1954.
Barzun, Jacques. *Race: A Study in Superstition.* New York: Harper and Row, 1965.
Blainey, Geoffrey. *The Tyranny of Distance.* London: Macmillan, 1968.
Blanton, Michael. *Race Relations.* New York: Basic Books, 1967.
Bolt, Christine. *Victorian Attitudes to Race.* London: Routledge and Kegan Paul, 1971.
Buchan, John. *Prester John.* New York: Popular Library, 1938.
Cambridge History of the British Empire. Cambridge: Cambridge University Press, I–III, VII, VIII, 1929–1963.
Campbell, P. C. *Chinese Coolie Emigration to Countries Within the British Empire.* London: P. S. King, 1923.
Carrington, C. E. *The British Overseas.* Cambridge: Cambridge University Press, 1950.
Cox, Oliver C. *Caste, Class, and Race.* New York: Doubleday, 1948.
Curtin, Philip D. *The Image of Africa.* Madison: University of Wisconsin Press, 1964.
Curtis, L. P., Jr. *Anglo-Saxons on Celts: A Study of Anti-Irish Prejudice in Victorian England.* Bridgeport: Conference on British Studies, 1968.
Dilke, Sir Charles. *Greater Britain.* London: Macmillan, 1869.
Fredrickson, George M. *The Black Image in the White Mind.* New York: Harper and Row, 1971.
Garvin, J. L. *The Life of Joseph Chamberlain.* London: Macmillan, I–III, 1933–35; Julian Amery, IV, 1951.
Hernton, Calvin C. *Sex and Racism in America.* New York: Grove Press, 1966.

Houghton, Walter E. *The Victorian Frame of Mind, 1830–1870*. New Haven: Yale University Press, 1957.
Huang Tsen-ming. *The Legal Status of Chinese Abroad*. Taipei: China Cultural Service, 1954.
Huttenback, R. A. *The British Imperial Experience*. New York: Harper and Row, 1966.
Johnston, Sir Harry. *The Backward Peoples and our Relations with Them*. London: Oxford University Press, 1920.
Jordan, Winthrop D. *White Over Black*. Chapel Hill: University of North Carolina Press, 1968.
Kiernan, V. G. *The Lords of Human Kind*. London: Weidenfeld and Nicolson, 1969.
London, Herbert I. *Non-White Immigration and the "White Australia" Policy*. New York: New York University Press, 1970.
Mason, Philip. *Prospero's Magic*. London: Oxford University Press, 1962.
———. *Patterns of Dominance*. London: Oxford University Press, 1970.
Montagu, M. F. Ashley. *Man's Most Dangerous Myth: The Fallacy of Race*. New York: Harpers, 1942.
Price, A. Grenfell. *White Settlers and Native Peoples*. Cambridge: Cambridge University Press, 1950.
Russell, A. G. *Colour, Race and Empire*. London: Victor Gollancz, 1944.
Seeley, J. R. *The Expansion of England*. London: Macmillan, 1911.
Swinfen, D. B. *Imperial Control of Colonial Legislation, 1813–1865: A Study of British Policy Towards Colonial Legislative Powers*. Oxford: Clarendon Press, 1970.
Thornton, A. P. *The Habit of Authority*. Toronto: University of Toronto Press, 1966.
Tinker, Hugh. *A New System of Slavery: The Export of Indian Labor Overseas 1830–1920*. London: Oxford University Press, 1974.

ARTICLES

Farley, M. Foster. "The Chinese Coolie Trade, 1845–1875," *Journal of Asian and African Studies*, III, nos. 3 and 4, 1968.

NEWSPAPERS

Indian Press Reports (India Office Library).
The Times (London).

Bibliography   329

OFFICIAL SOURCES

Great Britain. *Hansard*, 1860–1914.
C. 8596, 1897. *Proceedings of a Conference Between the Secretary of State for the Colonies and the Premiers of the Self-Governing Colonies.*

PRIVATE PAPERS

Birmingham University
Chamberlain Mss.

AUSTRALIA AND NEW ZEALAND

BOOKS

Barnard, Marjorie. *A History of Australia.* New York: Praeger, 1966.
Battye, J. S. *Western Australia: A History, From its Discovery to the Inauguration of the Commonwealth.* Oxford: Clarendon Press, 1924.
Borrie, W. D. *Immigration: Australia's Problems and Prospects.* Sydney: Angus and Robertson, 1949.
Borrie, W. D. et al. *A White Australia: Australia's Population Problem.* Sydney: Australian Institute of Political Science, 1947.
Buchanan, W. F. *Australia to the Rescue: A Hundred Years' Progress in New South Wales.* London: Gilbert and Rivington, 1890.
Burdon, R. M. *King Dick.* London: Whitcombe and Tombs, 1955.
Chidell, Fleetwood. *Australia: White or Yellow?* London: William Heinemann, 1926.
Cilento, Sir Raphael, and Jack, Clem. *Triumph in the Tropics: An Historical Sketch of Queensland.* Brisbane: Smith and Paterson, 1959.
Cowan, James. *Suwarrow Gold and Other Stories.* London: Jonathan Cape, 1936.
Deakin, Alfred. *The Federal Story.* Melbourne: Melbourne University Press, 1944.
Docker, Edward W. *The Blackbirders.* Sydney: Angus and Robertson, 1970.
Fong, Ng Bickleen. *The Chinese in New Zealand: A Study in Assimilation.* Hong Kong: Oxford University Press, 1959.
Hogan, James F. *The Australian in London and America.* London: Ward and Downey, 1889.

Bibliography

Huck, Arthur. *The Chinese in Australia*. Melbourne: Longmans, 1967.
Jupp, James. *Australian Party Politics*. Melbourne: Melbourne University Press, 1968.
La Nauze, John. *Alfred Deakin*. 2 vols. Melbourne: Melbourne University Press, 1965.
Lubbock, Basil. *Coolie Ships and Oil Sailors*. Glasgow: Brown, Son and Ferguson, reprinted in 1953.
Madgwick, R. B. *Immigration Into Eastern Australia, 1788–1857*. London: Longmans, Green, 1937.
McIntyre, W. David. *The Imperial Frontier in the Tropics, 1865–75*. London: Macmillan, 1967.
Markham, Albert Hastings. *The Cruise of the "Rosario" Amongst the New Hebrides and Santa Cruz Islands, Exposing Recent Atrocities Connected With the Kidnapping of Natives of the South Seas*. London: Sampson, Low, Marston, Low and Searle, 1873.
Nairn, N. B., Sente, A. G., and Ward, R. B. *Australian Dictionary of Biography*. 4 vols. to date. Melbourne: Melbourne University Press, 1969.
Overaker, Louise. *The Australian Party System*. New Haven: Yale University Press, 1952.
Palfreeman, A. C. *The Administration of the White Australia Policy*. Melbourne: Melbourne University Press, 1967.
Parkes, Sir Henry. *Fifty Years in the Making of Australian History*. London: Longmans, Green, 1892.
Patterson, J. A. *The Goldfields of Victoria in 1862*. Melbourne: Wilson and Mackinnon, 1862.
Ross, I. Clunes (ed.). *Australia and the Far East: Diplomatic and Trade Relations*. Sydney: Australian Institute of International Affairs, 1936.
Rivett, Kenneth (ed.). *Immigration: Control or Colour Bar*. The Immigration Reform Group. Melbourne: Melbourne University Press, 1962.
Serle, Geoffrey. *The Golden Age: A History of the Colony of Victoria, 1851–1861*. Melbourne: Melbourne University Press, 1963.
——. *The Rush to be Rich: A History of the Colony of Victoria, 1883–1889*. Melbourne: Melbourne University Press, 1971.
Sinclair, Keith. *A History of New Zealand*. London: Oxford University Press, 1961.

Stevens, F. S. (ed.). *Racism: The Australian Experience.* 3 vols. New York: Taplinger, 1972.
Turner, Henry G. *A History of the Colony of Victoria.* 2 vols. London: Longmans, Green, 1904.
Wawn, William T. *The South Sea Islanders and the Queensland Labour Trade.* London: Swan Sonnenschein, 1893.
Wilkinson, H. L. *The World's Population Problems.* London: P. S. King, 1930.
Willard, Myra. *History of the White Australia Policy.* Melbourne: Melbourne University Press, 1923.
Wise, B. G. *The Making of the Australian Commonwealth, 1889–1900.* London: Longmans, Green, 1913.
Yarwood, A. T. *Asian Immigration to Australia: The Peopling of Australia.* Edited by P. D. Phillips and G. L. Woods. Melbourne: Melbourne University Press, 1930.
——. *Asian Migration to Australia: The Background to Exclusion, 1896–1923.* Melbourne: Melbourne University Press, 1964.

ARTICLES

Birch, Alan. "The Implementation of the White Australia Policy in the Queensland Sugar Industry, 1901–1912," *Australian Journal of Politics and History*, August 1965.
Carrington, D. L. "Riots at Lambing Flat, 1860–61," *Journal of the Royal Australian Historical Society*, XLVI, Pt. 4, October 1960.
Forbes, Archibald. "The Kanaka in Queensland," *New Review*, VI, no. 37, 1892.
Hunt, Frazer. "White Australia and Pink Queensland," *Nineteenth Century*, CXCIII, December 1921.
Kellaway, Carlotta. "White Australia: How the Political Reality Became a National Myth," *Australian Quarterly*, XXV, no. 2, 1953.
Kelly, Pat. "The Working Man in Queensland," *Journal of the Historical Society of Queensland*, IV, 1951.
Kneipp, Pauline. "The Seaman's Strike, 1878–1879: Its Relation to the White Australia Policy," *Australian National University Historical Journal*, I, 1965/66.
Lyng, J. "Non-Britishers in Australia," *University of Melbourne Pubs.*, no. 10, 1927.
Moles, I. M. "The Indian Coolie Labour Issue in Queensland," *Journal of the Historical Society of Queensland*, V, no. 1, 1953.

Nagano, Y. "The Other Side: A Japanese in White Australia," *Australian Magazine*, VIII, no. 4, 1908.
Nairn, N. B. "A Survey of the History of the White Australia Policy in the Nineteenth Century," *Australian Quarterly*, XXIII, no. 1, 1957.
Nationalist Chinese Kuo Min Tang Association Journal. "The Development of the Party in Australia." (Translation) Sydney? 1935?
"The North Queensland Sugar Conference," reprinted from the *North Queensland Herald*, October 29, 1904. Sydney: The Mitchell Library.
Pike, L. H. "White Australia and Tropical Queensland," *Journal of the Royal Society of Arts*, June 10, 1938.
Phillips, O. E. "The Administration of Asian Immigration Into Australia: A Comparative Study," *Australian Quarterly*, XXVIII, no. 4, 1956.
Stoodley, June. "The Queensland Gold Miner and the Chinese Question (1873–1890)," *Journal of the Historical Society of Queensland*, IV, no. 2, 1951.
Yarwood, A. T. "The Dictation Test: An Historical Survey," *Australian Quarterly*, XXX, no. 2, 1958.
———. "The 'White Australia' Policy. A Re-Interpretation of Its Development in the Late Colonial Period," *Historical Studies: Australia and New Zealand*, X, no. 39, 1962.
Yong, C. F. "The Chinese Revolution of 1911: Reactions of Chinese in New South Wales and Victoria," *Historical Studies: Australia and New Zealand*, XII, no. 46, 1966.

NEWSPAPERS AND PERIODICALS

Aborigines Friend and the Colonial Intelligencer, 1859–1866.
The Antipodean. An Illustrated Annual. Sydney: George Robertson and Company, 1893. In the Mitchell Library.
Chambers' Journal of Popular Literature, Science and Art. Sydney: 1888. In the Mitchell Library.
The Colonist (Maryborough).
The Courier (Brisbane).
The Daily Telegraph (Sydney).
The Dominion (Wellington).
The Morning Herald (Perth).
The Morning Herald (Sydney).
The New Zealand Mail (Wellington).
The New Zealand Times (Wellington).

The South Australian Register (Adelaide).
The Truth (Wellington).

UNPUBLISHED THESES AND PAPERS

Choi, C. Y. "Chinese Migration and Settlement in Australia with Special Reference to the Chinese in Melbourne." Ph.D. dissertation. Melbourne: Australian National University, 1971.
DeGaris, Brian. "The History of Asian Immigration Into Western Australia." Perth: The Battye Library, no date.
Hack, W. "Japanese Immigration, 1876–77," Research Paper 358. Adelaide: South Australia Archives, 1959.
Hicks, Bonnie. "A Study of a Minority Group: The Chinese in Albany." Perth: The Battye Library, 1967.
Long, J. P. M. "Asian Immigration into the Northern Territory to 1910," paper read to the Historical Society of the Northern Territory. Adelaide: South Australia Archives, June 22, 1964.
Macafie, M. "Are the Laws of Nature Transgressed or Obeyed by the Continuous Labour of White Men in the Australian Tropics?" Paper read before the Royal Geographic Society of Australasia (Victoria). Melbourne, 1910.
Morris, Constance. "The Chinese in Geraldton and the Case of Irene Fong, 1895." Perch: The Battye Library, 1955.
Oddie, Geoffrey A. "The Chinese in Victoria, 1870–1890." M.A. thesis, University of Melbourne, 1959.
Rendell, Margaret P. "The Chinese in South Australia and the Northern Territory in the Nineteenth Century." M.A. thesis, University of Adelaide, 1952.
Sissons, D. C. S. "Attitudes to Japan and Defence, 1890–1923." M.A. thesis, University of Melbourne, 1956.
Yong, C. F. "The Chinese in New South Wales and Victoria, 1901–1921, With Special Reference to Sydney and Melbourne." Ph.D. dissertation, Australian National University, 1966.

PAMPHLETS

Calwell, Arthur A. *Immigration Policy and Progress*. Canberra: Commonwealth of Australia, 1949.
Dixon, R. *Immigration and the "White Australia Policy."* Sydney: Australian Communist Party, no date.
Hurst, J. (ed.). *The Chinese Question in Australia, 1880–81*. Sydney: The Australian Printing Works, 1880. In the Mitchell Library.
Meng, L. Kong; Cheong, Cheok Hong; and Ah Mouy, Louis. *The*

Chinese in Australia, 1878–79. Melbourne: F. F. Bailliere, 1879. In the Mitchell Library.

DIARIES

W. D. Ponder in Archives of South Australia (Adelaide).

OFFICIAL SOURCES—GREAT BRITAIN

Public Record Office
  Australia (Commonwealth)
    CO 558, Acts.
    CO 559, Government Gazettes.
    CO 560, Miscellanea.
    CO 562, Parliamentary Papers.
  New South Wales
    CO 201, Correspondence, original, Secretary of State.
    CO 202, Colonial Office to Governor, Entry Books.
    CO 203, Acts.
    CO 204, Sessional Papers.
    CO 205, Government Gazettes.
    CO 206, Miscellanea.
  Queensland
    CO 234, Correspondence, original, Secretary of State.
    CO 235, Acts.
    CO 236, Sessional Papers.
    CO 237, Government Gazettes.
    CO 238, Miscellanea.
    CO 423, Colonial Office to Governor, Entry Books.
  South Australia
    CO 13, Correspondence, original, Secretary of State.
    CO 14, Acts.
    CO 15, Sessional Papers.
    CO 16, Government Gazettes.
    CO 17, Miscellanea.
    CO 396, Colonial Office to Governor, Entry Books.
  Tasmania
    CO 280, Correspondence, original, Secretary of State.
    CO 281, Acts.
    CO 282, Sessional Papers.
    CO 283, Government Gazettes.
    CO 284, Miscellanea.
    CO 408, Colonial Office to Governor, Entry Books.

Victoria
CO 309, Correspondence, original, Secretary of State.
CO 310, Acts.
CO 311, Sessional Papers.
CO 312, Government Gazettes.
CO 313, Miscellanea.
CO 411, Colonial Office to Governor, Entry Books.
Western Australia
CO 18, Correspondence, original, Secretary of State.
CO 19, Acts.
CO 20, Sessional Papers.
CO 21, Government Gazettes.
CO 22, Miscellanea.
CO 397, Colonial Office to Governor, Entry Books.
Australia (General)
CO 12, Acts, Federal Council, 1886–1897.
CO 381, Colonies (General), Colonial Office to Governors, Entry Books.
CO 418, Correspondence, original, Secretary of State, 1894–1922.
CO 433, Sessional Papers, Federal Council.
CO 537, Supplementary original correspondence, 1841–1897.
New Zealand
CO 209, Correspondence, original, Secretary of State.
CO 210, Acts.
CO 211, Sessional Papers.
CO 212, Government Gazettes.
CO 213, Miscellanea.
CO 406, Colonial Office to Governor, Entry Books.
Colonial Office Confidential Prints
CO 881/2, Print 15, October, 1869, Queensland. Correspondence Relating to the Importation of South Sea Islanders into Queensland.
CO 881/3, Print 23, 1871, Queensland. Murder of Bishop Patteson, Correspondence.
Co 881–3, Print 24, January 29, 1872, Queensland. Abuses of Polynesian Immigration; Memorandum by Mr. Dealtry.
CO 881/3, Print 25, September 19, 1871, Queensland. Labour Traffic; Proceedings on board the *Anna;* Letter from Consul March.
CO 881/3, Print 36A, February 10, 1873, South Sea Islands. Return to an address of the House of Lords for Copies of Extracts

of any Communications of Importance respecting Outrages Committed upon Natives of the South Sea Islands which may have been received from the Governors of any of the Australasian Colonies from the Senior Naval Officers Commanding in Australia and China, or from Her Majesty's Consul in the Pacific since the last issue of papers upon this subject.

CO 881/6, Print 84, 1882, Western Pacific. Labour Trade in Western Pacific; Memorandum by Commodore Wilson, R.N.

CO 881/8, Print 129, 1888, Australia and Canada. Chinese Immigration into Australasia and Canada.

CO 881/9, Print 130, 1890, Australia. Further Correspondence relating to Chinese Immigration into the Australasian Colonies.

CO 881/9, Print 144, January 15, 1889–May 26, 1892, Australia. Chinese Immigration. Further correspondence.

CO 881/10, Print 160, 1894, Queensland. Further Correspondence relating to Polynesian Labour in the Colony of Queensland.

CO 881/11, Print 181, 1906, Western Pacific. Memorandum on Bill to amend the Pacific Islanders Protection Act, 1872.

Foreign Office Papers

FO 405, December 1890. Memorandum on the Question of Chinese Immigration into the Australasian Colonies.

Colonial Office Library

Hansards and census reports of the Australian colonies, the Commonwealth of Australia and New Zealand.

Parliamentary Papers

Papers 391 and 496, H of C, 1868. South Sea Islanders, Queensland. Return to an Address of the House of Commons, Copies or Extracts of all Correspondence Relating to the Importation of South Sea Islanders into Queensland.

C. 4222, H of L, 1869. Correspondence respecting the Deportation of South Sea Islanders.

Paper 408, H of C, 1869. South Sea Islanders, Queensland. Further Correspondence.

Paper 79, H of C, 1871. Copies or Extracts of Correspondence between the Board of Admiralty and the Commanders of the Australasian and South Pacific Stations in regard to the Exportation of South Sea Islanders subsequent to August 10, 1869.

Paper 468, H of C, 1871. South Sea Islanders, Queensland. Further Correspondence.

C. 479, 1872. Correspondence between the Governor of New

South Wales and the Earl of Kimberley respecting certain statements by Captain Palmer, R.N., in his book entitled *Kidnapping in the South Seas.*
C. 496, 1872. Further Correspondence respecting the Deportation of South Sea Islanders.
C. 793, 1873. Correspondence relative to the Introduction of Polynesian Labourers into Queensland.
Paper 232, H of C, 1874. Copies of Correspondence respecting Outrages committed on the Natives of the South Sea Islands.
Paper 29, H of C, 1876. Return of South Sea Islanders introduced into Queensland.
C. 3641, 1883. Correspondence respecting the Natives of the Western Pacific and the Labour Traffic.
C. 3814, 1883. Correspondence respecting New Guinea and other Islands and the Convention at Sydney of Representatives of the Australasian Colonies.
C. 3839, 1884. Further Correspondence (continuation of C. 3641).
C. 5448, 1888. Correspondence relating to Chinese Immigration into the Australasian Colonies with a Return of Acts passed by the Legislatures of those Colonies and British Columbia on the subject.
C. 6686, 1892. Correspondence relating to Polynesian Labourers in the Colony of Queensland.
C. 6808, 1892. Further Correspondence (continuation of C. 6686).
C. 7000, 1893. Further Correspondence (continuation of C. 6808).
C. 7912, 1895. Further Correspondence (continuation of C. 7000).

OFFICIAL SOURCES—AUSTRALIA AND NEW ZEALAND

Australia (Commonwealth)
Records of the Department of External Affairs—Immigration.
New South Wales
Colonial Secretary's Records.
Governor's Records.
Naturalization Records.
Queensland
Colonial Secretary's Records.
Governor's Office Records.

Bibliography

Immigration Department Records.
Premier's Department Records.
South Australia
   Chief Secretary's Records.
   Governor's Records.
Tasmania
   Chief Secretary's Department Records.
   Premier's Department Records.
Victoria
   Chief Secretary's Records.
   File on Buckland Riots of 1857.
   Governor's Records.
   Premier's Records.
   Premier's Secret Records.
Western Australia
   Chief Secretary's Records.
New Zealand
   Government House Records.
   Internal Affairs Department Records.
   Justice Department Records.

CANADA

BOOKS

Barth, Gunther. *Bitter Strength: A History of the Chinese in the United States.* Cambridge: Harvard University Press, 1964.
Borden, Henry. *Robert Laird Borden, His Memoires.* Toronto: Macmillan, 1938.
Brown, George W. *Canada.* Berkeley: University of California Press, 1954.
Cheng, Tien-fang. *Oriental Immigration in Canada.* Shanghai: The Commercial Press, 1931.
Corbett, David C. *Canada's Immigration Policy.* Toronto: University of Toronto Press, 1957.
Creighton, Donald. *John A. Macdonald.* 2 vols. Toronto: Macmillan, 1952–55.
Garis, Roy L. *Immigration Restriction.* New York: Macmillan, 1928.
Howay, F. W. *British Columbia: The Making of a Province.* Toronto: Ryerson Press, 1928.

La Violette, F. E. *The Canadian Japanese and World War II*. Toronto: University of Toronto Press, 1948.
Lower, A. R. M. *Canada and the Far East*. New York: Institute of Pacific Relations, 1940.
McKenzie, R. D. *Oriental Exclusion*. Chicago: University of Chicago Press, 1928.
Miller, Stuart C. *The Unwelcome Immigrant: The American Image of the Chinese, 1785–1885*. Berkeley: University of California Press, 1969.
Ormsby, Margaret A. *British Columbia: A History*. Toronto: Macmillan, 1971.
Saxton, Alexander. *The Indispensable Enemy: Labor and the Anti-Chinese Movement in California*. Berkeley: University of California Press, 1971.
Schull, Joseph. *Laurier: The First Canadian*. Toronto: Macmillan, 1965.
Seward, George R. *Chinese Immigration*. New York: Charles Scribner's, 1881.
Singh, Khushwant, and Singh, Satindra. *Ghadar 1915: India's First Armed Revolution*. New Delhi: R and K Publishing House, 1966.
Skelton, Oscar D. *Life and Letters of Sir Wilfrid Laurier*. 2 vols. Toronto: Carleton Library, 1965.
Sung, Betty Lee. *Mountain of Gold*. New York: Macmillan, 1967.
Woodsworth, Charles J. *Canada and the Orient*. Toronto: Macmillan, 1941.
Young, Charles H., and Reid, Helen. *The Japanese Canadians*. Toronto: University of Toronto Press, 1938.

ARTICLES

Boggs, T. H. "Oriental Immigration," *Annals of the American Academy of Political and Social Science*, CVII, 1923.
Brown, Giles T. "The Hindu Conspiracy, 1914–1917," *Pacific Historical Review*, XVI, 1948.
Dignan, Don K. "The Hindu Conspiracy in Anglo-American Relations During World War I," *Pacific Historical Review*, XL, 1971.
Kawakami, K. K. "White Canada: A Japanese View of Canada's Oriental Problem," *Canadian Magazine*, III, 1913.
Mitchell, George W. "Canada: Savior of the Nordic Race," *Canadian Magazine*, LXI, 1923.
Singh, Sunder. "The Hindu in Canada," *Journal of Race Development*, VII, 1917.

The Spectator. "Japan and Canada," C, 1908.
Timlin, Mabel F. "Canada's Immigration Policy, 1896–1910," *Canadian Journal of Economics and Political Science,* XXVI, no. 4, 1960.

NEWSPAPERS AND PERIODICALS

The Colonist (Victoria).
Daily Province (Vancouver).
The World (Vancouver).

UNPUBLISHED THESES

Andracki, Stanislaw. "The Immigration of Orientals into Canada With Special Reference to the Chinese," Ph.D. dissertation, McGill University, 1958.
Lowes, George R. "The Sikhs of British Columbia," Graduation Essay, History 449, University of British Columbia, 1952.
Morse, Eric W. "Immigration and Status of British East Indians in Canada: A Problem in Imperial Relations," M.A. thesis, Queens University, Kingston, Canada, 1936.
Wynne, Robert E. "Reactions to the Chinese in the Pacific Northwest and British Columbia, 1850–1910," Ph.D. dissertation, University of Washington, 1970.

OFFICIAL SOURCES—GREAT BRITAIN

Public Record Office
 CO 42, Correspondence, original, Secretary of State.
 CO 43, Colonial Office to Governor, Entry Books.
 CO 44, Acts.
 CO 45, Sessional Papers.
 CO 46, Government Gazettes.
 CO 47, Miscellanea.
 CO 62, British Columbia Sessional Papers.
 CO 881/8, Print 129, 1888. Australia and Canada. Chinese Immigration into Australasia and Canada.
Colonial Office Library
 Hansard—Canada
 India Office Library
  Proceedings of the Department of Commerce and Industry (Emigration).

Bibliography   341

OFFICIAL SOURCES—CANADA

Public Archives of Canada
Canadian Census Reports.
Canadian Statute Law.
Cd. 4118, 1908, "Report of Mr. W. L. Mackenzie King of His Mission to England in Connection with Immigration of Asiatics into Canada."
Governor General's numbered files, 1887–1914 (R.G. 7, G. 21).
Governor General's Secretary's Office, General Correspondence Regarding Asiatics, files 226 and 232.
Orders in Council, Canada (R.G. 2).
Records of the Immigration Branch, Department of the Interior.
Provincial Archives, British Columbia
Files of the Office of the Lieutenant Governor.
Journals of the Legislature of British Columbia.
Prime Ministers' Papers.
Records of the Provincial Secretary's Office.

PRIVATE PAPERS—PUBLIC ARCHIVES OF CANADA

Borden Mss.
Laurier Mss.
Lemieux Mss.
Macdonald Mss.
Mackenzie King Mss.
Sifton Mss.

SOUTH AFRICA

BOOKS

Ashe, Geoffrey. *Gandhi*. New York: Stein and Day, 1968.
Burrows, H. R. *Indian Life and Labour in Natal*. Durban: South African Institute of Race Relations, 1953.
Calpin, G. H. *Indians in South Africa*. Pietermaritzburg: Shuter and Shooter, 1949.
Desai, D. M. *The Indian Community in Southern Rhodesia*. Salisbury: Herold, 1949.
Dotson, Floyd, and Dotson, Lillian O. *The Indian Minority of Zambia, Rhodesia and Malawi*. New Haven: Yale University Press, 1968.

Ferguson-Davie, C. J. *The Early History of Indians in Natal.* Johannesburg: South African Institute of Race Relations, 1952.
Fisher, L. *The Life of Mahatma Gandhi.* New York: Collier, 1966.
Gandhi, M. K. *The Collected Works of Mahatma Gandhi.* Delhi: Government of India, 1958–.
———. *Satyagraha in South Africa.* Ahmedabad: Navajivan, 1928.
———. *The Story of My Experiments with Truth.* Boston: Beacon, 1957.
Hancock, W. K. *Smuts: The Sanguine Years, 1870–1919.* Cambridge: Cambridge University Press, 1967.
———. *Survey of British Commonwealth Affairs.* Vol I, *Problems of Nationality, 1918–1936.* Oxford: Oxford University Press, 1957.
Hancock, W. K., and Van Der Poel, J. *Selections from the Smuts Papers.* 4 vols. Cambridge: Cambridge University Press, 1960.
Headlam, C. (ed.). *The Milner Papers, 1897–1904.* 2 vols. London: Cassell, 1931–1933.
Hellman, Ellen (ed.). *Handbook of Race Relations in South Africa.* Cape Town: Oxford University Press, 1949.
Huttenback, R. A. *Gandhi in South Africa: British Imperialism and the Indian Question, 1860–1914.* Ithaca, N.Y.: Cornell University Press, 1971.
Joshi, P. S. *The Tyranny of Colour: A Study of the Indian Problem in South Africa.* Durban: Commercial Printing Co., 1942.
Kondapi, C. *Indians Overseas, 1838–1949.* Bombay: Oxford University Press, 1951.
Kuper, H. *Indian People in Natal.* Pietermaritzburg: Natal University Press, 1960.
Kuper, L., Watts, H., and Davies, R. *Durban: A Racial Ecology.* London: Jonathan Cape, 1958.
Nanda, B. R. *Mahatma Gandhi.* London: George Allen and Unwin, 1958.
Narain, Iqbal. *The Politics of Racialism.* Ahmedabad: Navajivan, 1957.
Palmer, Mabel. *The History of the Indians in Natal* (Natal Regional Survey No. 10). Cape Town: Oxford University Press, 1957.
Pyarelal. *Mahatma Gandhi: The Early Phase.* Ahmedabad: Navajivan, 1965.
Pyrah, G. B. *Imperial Policy and South Africa, 1902–1910.* Oxford: Oxford University Press, 1955.
Sacks, Benjamin. *South Africa: An Imperial Dilemma.* Albuquerque: University of New Mexico Press, 1967.

Bibliography   343

Smith, William R. *Nationalism and Reform in India.* New Haven: Yale University Press, 1938.
Thompson, L. M. *Indian Immigration into Natal (1860–1872).* Cape Town: Archives Year Book of South African History, 1952.
——. *The Unification of South Africa, 1902–1910.* Oxford: Oxford University Press, 1960.
Woods, C. A. *The Indian Community of Natal: Their Economic Problem* (Natal Regional Survey No. 9). Cape Town: Oxford University Press, 1954.

NEWSPAPERS AND PERIODICALS

Cape
   Cape Times, 1885–1916.
Natal
   Indian Opinion, 1903–1916.
   Natal Mercury, 1859–1916.
   Natal Witness, 1859–1916.
Transvaal
   Rand Daily Mail (Johannesburg), 1899–1916.
   Standard and Diggers News, 1892–1900.
   The Star (Johannesburg), 1899–1916.
   De Volkstem, 1882–1888.

OFFICIAL SOURCES—INDIA

National Archives of India
   A and B Proceedings from the following departments:
      Home, Public, 1859–1870.
      Revenue, Agriculture and Commerce—Emigration, 1873–1879.
      Home, Revenue and Agriculture—Emigration, 1879–1881.
      Revenue and Agriculture—Emigration, 1881–1906.
      Commerce and Industry—Emigration, 1906–1914.
      Legislative Proceedings, 1863–1914.
      Papers with Acts, 1864–1910.

OFFICIAL SOURCES—GREAT BRITAIN

Public Record Office
   CO 3, British South Africa Company Ordinances.
   CO 48, Cape Colony, 1880–1910.
   CO 179, Natal, 1859–1910.
   CO 224, Orange River Colony, 1901–1910.
   CO 291, Transvaal, 1877–1881, 1901–1919.

CO 292/6, 7, Transvaal Acts.
CO 417, High Commissioner, South Africa, 1880–1914.
CO 427, Zululand, 1891–1896.
CO 525, Nyasaland, 1904–1914.
CO 549, Transvaal and Orange River Colony, 1903–1908.
CO 551, Union of South Africa, 1910–1914.
CO 632/1, Union Acts.
Colonial Office
Statute Law of the Transvaal.
Parliamentary Papers
C. 7911, 1895. Papers relating to the grievances of Her Majesty's Indian subjects in the South African Republic.
C. 7946, 1896. Continuation of C. 7911, further papers.
Cd. 1640, 1903. Minutes of the proceedings of the South African Customs Union Conference, Bloemfontein.
C. 1683, 1903. Correspondence relating to a proposal to employ Indian coolies under indenture on railways in the Transvaal and Orange River Colony.
Cd. 1684, 1903. Despatch from the Governor of the Transvaal respecting the position of British Indians in that colony.
Cd. 2239, 1904. Correspondence relating to the position of British Indians in that colony [Transvaal].
Cd. 3251, 1906. Transvaal Asiatic Law Amendment Ordinance of 1906.
Cd. 3308, 1907. Correspondence relating to legislation affecting Asiatics in the Transvaal.
Cd. 3404, 1907. Published proceedings and precis of the Colonial Conference, 15–30 April, 1907.
Cd. 3406, 1907. Published proceedings and precis of the Colonial Conference, 30 April–14 May, 1907 (continuation of Cd. 3404, 1907).
Cd. 3887, 1908. Further correspondence relating to legislation affecting Asiatics in the Transvaal.
Cd. 3994, 1908. Correspondence relating to the Transvaal Indentured Labour Laws Temporary Continuance Act, 1907.
Cd. 4327, 1908. Further correspondence relating to legislation affecting Asiatics in the Transvaal.
Cd. 4584, 1909. Further correspondence relating to legislation affecting Asiatics in the Transvaal.
Cd. 5194, 1910. Report of a committee on emigration from India to the crown colonies and protectorates.

Cd. 5363, 1910. Further correspondence relating to legislation affecting Asiatics in the Transvaal.
Cd. 5579, 1911. Correspondence respecting a bill to regulate further immigration into the Union of South Africa, with special reference to Asiatics; together with the draft bill, and the acts, regulations and statistics relating to immigration into the Commonwealth of Australia.
Cd. 6087, 1912. Correspondence relating to the position of British Indians under the Gold Law and Township Amendment Acts, 1905, of the Transvaal.
Cd. 6283, 1912. Continuation of Cd. 5579. Further correspondence respecting a bill to regulate further immigration into the Union of South Africa, with special reference to Asiatics.
Cd. 6940, 1913. Continuation of Cd. 6283. Further correspondence respecting a bill to regulate further immigration into the Union of South Africa, with special reference to Asiatics.
Cd. 7111, 1913. Correspondence relating to the Immigrants Regulation Act and other matters affecting Asiatics in South Africa.
Cd. 7265, 1914. Report of the Indian Enquiry Commission.
65 (Lords). Transvaal Registration Bill. Further papers as regard the Transvaal Registration Bill (The Lord Ampthill).

OFFICIAL SOURCES—REPUBLIC OF SOUTH AFRICA

Cape Archives (Cape Town)
Acts of the Cape Parliament, 1870–1910.
Cape Government Gazettes, 1870–1910.
Cape Parliamentary Debates, 1870–1910.
Letter Books, Administrative and Convict Service, 1899–1904.
Votes and Proceedings of the House of Assembly, 1870–1910.
Natal Archives (Pietermaritzburg)
Government House Series, 1859–1910.
  Confidential Despatches.
  Correspondence with the High Commissioner.
  General and South African Correspondence.
  General Despatches.
  Minutes to Ministers.
  Secret Despatches.
  Telegrams and Despatches to and from the Secretary of State for the Colonies.
Prime Minister's Office
  Letters Dispatched and Received, 1900–1910.

Minute Papers and Confidential Minutes, 1900–1910.
Minutes of Meetings, 1903–1909.
Prime Minister's Meetings, 1904–1910.
Prime Minister's Private Papers, 1899–1910.
Archives of the Executive Council
   Minutes of Meetings, 1871–1910.
   Original Certified Bills, 1898–1910.
   Register of Papers Laid before the Executive Committee, 1879–1889.
Colonial Secretary's Office, 1880–1910.
Documents Presented
   Clerk of the Legislative Council—Letter Books.
   Legislative Council (Responsible Government).
      Bill Passed.
      Documents Presented.
      Government Notices.
      Sessional Papers.
   Minutes of the Provincial Council, 1910–1914.
   Natal Blue Books, 1859–1914 (containing annual reports of the Protector of Indian Immigrants, the Indian Immigration Trust Board and the report on Indian schools).
   Natal Government Gazettes, 1859–1910.
   Natal Government Notices and Proceedings, 1859–1910.
   Natal Parliamentary Debates, 1857–1910.
   Natal Provincial Gazettes, 1910–1914.
   Ordinances of the Provincial Council, 1910–1914.
   Select Committees.
      Bills.
      Messages.
      Miscellaneous (Legislative Assembly and Council).
      Petitions.
      Rough Minutes.
   Statutes of Natal, 1845–1910.
Natal Parliamentary Papers, 1857–1910.
Votes and Proceedings.
South African Republic (in South African National Archives, Pretoria)
   Correspondence of the British Agent in the Transvaal, 1890–1899.
   Correspondence of the British Resident in the Transvaal, 1881–1884.
   Executive Council Resolutions, 1886–1899.

Gazettes and Minutes of the Volksraad, 1856–1899.
Notule Volksraad, 1856–1899.
Volksraad Debates, 1856–1899.
Wetboek, 1854–1899.
ZAR Green Books.
Correspondentie van de Zuid-Afrikaashe Republik met betrekking tod de Kwest van Asiatische Gekleurde Personnen.
ZAR–No. 1 van 1894.
ZAR–No. 2 van 1894.
ZAR–No. 1 van 1899.
Officiele Bescheiden Gewisseld met de Engelse. Refeering in zake de Conventie van London. Geslotten den 27 sten Februarie, 1884, ZAR–9 Juni 1884.

Transvaal, 1902–1910 (in South African National Archives, Pretoria)
Executive Council Minutes, 1902–1910.
Gazettes, 1900–1910.
Governor's Papers, 1902–1910.
Legislative Assembly Debates, 1907–1910.
Legislative Council Debates, 1903–1910.
Minutes and Correspondence of the Executive Council, 1903–1906.
Minutes, Votes and Proceedings of the Legislative Assembly, 1907–1910.
Minutes, Votes and Proceedings of the Legislative Council, 1902–1910.
Ordinances and Laws, 1900–1910.
Records of the Colonial Secretary's Office, 1901–1907.
Records of the Lieutenant Governor of the Transvaal, 1903–1906.
Records of the Prime Minister of the Transvaal, 1907–1910.

Union of South Africa, 1910–1914 (in South African National Archives, Pretoria)
Archives of the Secretary to the Department of the Prime Minister.
Government Gazettes.
Minutes, Votes and Proceedings of the Union Parliament.
Select Committee Reports.
Union Debates.
Minutes by the Governor General.
Union Government Blue Books.
U.G. 55, 1913. Witwatersrand Disturbances.

U.G. 56, 1913. Witwatersrand Disturbances.
U.G. 6, 1914. Industrial Disturbances.
U.G. 14, 1914. Report of the Indian Enquiry Commission.

PRIVATE PAPERS

Bodleian Library (Oxford)
   Nathan Mss.
British Museum
   Gladstone Mss.
   Kimberley Mss.
   Ripon Mss.
Cambridge University Library
   Hardinge Mss.
India Office Library
   Argyll Mss.
   Cross Mss.
   Curzon Mss.
   Elgin (9th Earl) Mss.
   Hamilton Mss.
   Kilbracken (Godley) Mss.
   Lansdowne Mss.
   Lytton Mss.
   Northbrook Mss.
Public Record Office
   Carnarvon Mss.
Rhodes House (Oxford)
   Nathan Mss.

Index

Afghan incident, 105–107, 108–110, 115
Afrikaners, 24, 145, 213, 239
Ah Mouy, Louis, 78
Anderson, John, Colonial Office official, 100, 163, 269
Anglo-Boer War, 145, 210
Anglo-Saxonism, 15–21 *passim*, 26, 157, 317–318, 326
Aoki, Viscount, 156
Australasia
  and Anglo-Japanese treaty of 1894, 157
  and Australian union, 155, 166
  and Chinese question, diplomatic solution to, 100–101, 103–104, 109, 111, 115, 116, 117, 118–119
  Conference of Premiers (London, 1897), 162–164, 280
  discriminatory legislation, joint: commercial restriction, 260–261, 323; effect of gold discovery on, 59; exclusion bills, 117–118, 121, 154, 164; and Natal formula, 162–164, 166–167, 279, 280; and "White Australia" policy, 155, 162
  Hobart Postal Conference (1895), 260–261
  intercolonial conferences (1881), 79–80, 83, 84; (1888), 97–98, 99, 101, 115–116, 117–118; (1896), 160–161, 162; (1898), 166–167
  intercolonial Trade Union Congress, 78–79
  nonwhite immigrants in, 21, 27, 41, 59, 155, 156, 158, 160–161, 240; and joint action toward, 75, 79–80, 95, 97, 101, 154, 160–161, 260–261, 320, 323; labor attitudes toward, 75–77, 78–79, 104, 110–111; and rights of as British subjects, 117, 163, 278, 320
  as outpost of the British race, 21–22, 26
  and responsible government, 23
  see also names of specific Australasian colonies
Australia, Comonwealth of
  and Anglo-Japanese treaty of 1894, 303
  census figures (1901), 304, 305
  discriminatory legislation: commercial restriction, 288, 291, 316, 317; disenfranchisement, 321–322; exclusion bills, 280–281, 285, 288, 316; immigration restriction, 279–281, 283, 285, 301, 302, 304–311, 312, 313, 314; and Natal formula, 279, 280, 282; and "White Australia" policy, 279, 281, 283, 285, 301, 313–315, 316, 317, 324, 325, 326
  nonwhite immigrants in: from China, 284, 304, 312, 314, 315, 316; from India, 305–306, 310–311, 316, 325–326; from Japan, 281–283, 301–304, 308–310, 314, 316, 324; labor attitude toward, 280–281, 313, 314; from Polynesia, 279–280, 285–291; repatriation of Polynesians, 285, 288, 289–290, 301; rights of as British subjects, 281, 284–285, 301n, 305, 310, 322, 325–326; white attitudes toward, 279, 281, 283–284, 313–315
  and white emigration to India, 310–311
  see also Australasia

Australian Natives' Association, 256
Australian Steam Navigation Company, 77

Barton, Edmund, Prime Minister, Commonwealth of Australia (1901–1904), 281, 283, 287, 288
Begbie, Sir Matthew, Chief Justice of British Columbia, 131
Berry, Graham, Premier of Victoria, 80, 84, 245
Borden, Robert L., leader of Canadian Conservative Party, 182, 191–192
Botha, Louis, Prime Minister, Transvaal (1907–1910), Union of South Africa (1910–1919), 218, 239
Bowen, Sir George, Governor of Queensland, 35–40
Bowser, William J., Attorney General of British Columbia, 192
Bramston, John, Colonial Office official, 123, 243
British Columbia
census figures (1880–84), 128; Chinese (1881, 1891), 126, 135; (1880–84), 128; (1901), 171; (1911), 194n; (1864), 261; Indian (1900), 170; (1906), 178; (1911), 194n; Japanese (1901), 171; (1911), 194n; (1896), 268
discriminatory legislation: commercial restriction, 261–276 passim, 277n–278n; disenfranchisement, 262, 268, 274–275, 277n, 322–323; effect of gold discovery on, 126; immigration restriction, 130–131, 133, 170, 179–180, 181; and Natal formula, 170, 172, 179, 192, 273
and Dominion Government, 130, 131, 133, 138, 170, 180, 184–185, 191, 192, 264–275 passim, 322; and Chapleau Commission Report (1885), 132; petitions to Canadian Parliament, 128, 129–130, 135, 137–138
nonwhite immigrants in: and anti-Asian associations and activities, 128, 183–185, 267; and Canadian Pacific Railway, 128, 129, 136, 178, 262, 267; from China, 126–133 passim, 168, 169, 170, 171–172, 181, 183, 184, 191, 261, 269, 274, 275, 276; from India, 27, 168–169, 174–178, 180–181, 182, 184, 186, 274, 275; from Japan, 135, 168, 169, 170, 171–172, 173, 174, 182, 183–184, 185, 191, 268–276 passim; labor attitude toward, 51, 137–138, 175–176, 262, 267; need for, 126–127, 129–130, 177; and rights of as British subjects, 168, 175, 177, 182, 275; white attitudes toward, 126–129, 131–133, 168, 175–178, 183, 191–192, 266, 267–268, 270–271, 276–277
see also Canada, Dominion of
British Empire, 13–14; attitudes toward nonwhite subjects, 18–19, 20–22, 26, 96; and colonies of settlement, 21–23, 26–27, 54; imperial philosophy, 13–14, 21, 22, 23, 89, 91, 114, 138, 142, 213, 228, 239, 241–242, 271, 278, 282, 285, 318, 319
British Honduras, and Indian immigrants from British Columbia, 181
British Indian Association, 214
Buchan, John, 18, 19
Bulwer, Henry, Governor of Natal, 55n
Burt, S., 95, 259

Cairns, Sir William, Governor of Queensland, 41, 241–242
Canada, Dominion of
census figures: Chinese (1886–89), 135 and n; (1903), 173; (1904–8), 181 and n; (1906–7), 182; Indian (1905–7), 174–175; (1906–7), 182; (1907–13), 188; Japanese (1906–7), 182
discriminatory legislation: commercial restriction, 323; disenfranchisement, 262n; effect of gold discovery on, 59, 125–126; immigration restriction, 51, 126, 130, 133–137, 168, 169, 171, 172–173, 179, 187–188, 192–194, 319; and Lemieux formula, 185–186, 190, 192, 193n; and Natal formula, 169, 179, 194, 319

Index 351

Dominion Trades and Labour Congress, 137–138
French population of, 24
government of: and British Columbia anti-Asian activities, 184–185; and British Columbia anti-Asian legislation, 130, 131, 133, 138, 170, 180, 191, 182, 264–275 *passim*, 322; and British North America Act, 130, 131n; and Chinese question, 263–264; and provincial discriminatory legislation, 277n–278n; relations with China, 190–191, 193, 263, 265; relations with Japan, 169, 170, 174, 182, 184, 185–186, 193, 268–272; relations with the United States, 188–189, 194; and responsible government, 23; royal commissions on Asian immigration, 131–132, 171–172
nonwhite immigrants in, 21, 51; and Canadian Pacific Railway, 128, 129, 130n, 136, 173n, 263; from China, 27, 184, 185, 190–191, 193n, 278n; from India, 175, 180–181, 186–188, 193n, 194, 278n; from Japan, 27, 169, 174, 182, 183, 184, 185, 191, 193n, 278n; labor attitude toward, 137–138, 182–183; need for, 130n, 133, 173n; and rights of as British subjects, 171, 187, 188, 190, 194, 278, 323
as outpost of the British race, 21–22, 26
Parliament of: and Chinese immigration, 126–128, 129–130; Select Committee on Chinese Labor and Immigration, 127–128
see also British Columbia
Canadian Pacific Railway, 128, 129–130, 135–138, 173n, 263
Cape Colony
census figures (1904), 148; (1903–11), 147n; (1904, 1912), 206n
discriminatory legislation: disenfranchisement, 206; immigration restriction, 148–149, 150–152; and Natal formula, 148; nonwhite resident restriction, 206–207, 219–221
nonwhite immigration in: ex-indentured from India, 150, 206; free from India, 206; indentured from India, 149; political activities of, 206, 220; and rights of as British subjects, 149, 220

Carnarvon, Henry Howard Herbert, 4th earl of, Secretary of State for the Colonies (1867–1868, 1874–1878), 241, 242, 243, 244, 245, 246, 248, 249
Carrington, Sir Charles Robert Wynn-Carrington, 1st earl, Governor of New South Wales (1885–1890), 104, 111, 113, 117
Carter-Cotton, Francis, Minister of Finance and Agriculture, British Columbia, 270–271
Chamberlain, Joseph, Secretary of State for the Colonies (1895–1903), 15–16, 21–22, 278; and Indian rights in South Africa, 145–146, 202, 204–205, 213, 217, 226; and Japanese rights in Canada, 169, 271; and Natal formula, 141, 162–164, 273, 282
Chapleau, J.-A., Secretary of State of Canada, 131–132
Cheok Kong Cheong, 78
China, Government of: and Chinese rights in Australasia, 102–103, 115–116, 317; and Chinese rights in Canada, 190–191, 265, 317; and diplomatic solution to the Chinese question, 111–112, 119–120; and emigration, 29; and Treaty of Nanking, 74–75
Clayton, Walter F., 233
Clayton Commission, 233, 236
Clute, R. C., 171
Cole, E. Wynne, 236
Connolly, Sir James, 325
Cox, Hugh, Colonial Office official, 269, 270
Crewe, Robert Offley Ashburton, 1st marquis of, Secretary of State for the Colonies (1908–1910), Secretary of State for India (1910–1911), 188, 220–231, 235–236, 237
Curtis, Lionel, 145
Curzon of Kedleston, George Nathaniel Curzon, 1st baron, Viceroy of India (1899–1905), 284, 306

Customs Union Conference, 149, 212n

Deakin, Alfred, Premier of Victoria, Attorney General and Prime Minister of Australia, 255, 283–284, 301n, 302, 309–310
Derby, F. A. Stanley, 16th earl of, Secretary of State for the Colonies (1885–1886), 248, 265–266
de Villiers, Melius, Chief Justice, Orange Free State, 210, 214
Dibbs, Sir George, Premier of New South Wales, 113
Dickson, James, Premier of Queensland, 160
Douglas, Captain Bloomfield, 32
Douglas, John, Premier of Queensland; later Resident on Thursday Island, 158–159, 243, 244, 245
Duncan, Patrick, Governor-General of Union of South Africa, 212
Dunsmuir, James, Lt. Governor of British Columbia, 180, 183

Eitaki, H., Japanese Consul General in Sydney, 282, 283
Elgin, Victor Alexander, 9th earl of, Secretary of State for the Colonies (1906–1908), 299–300

Faure, Sir P., Colonial Secretary of Cape Colony, 148–149
Fitzroy, Sir Charles, Governor of New South Wales, 29, 31
Fraser, Sir M., Colonial Secretary of Western Australia, 124
Fuller, Frederic W., Colonial Office official, 113–114, 125
Fysh, P. O., Premier of Tasmania, 118

Gandhi, Mohandas K., 14, 25; and Anglo-Boer War, 210; and Bambata Rebellion, 210–211; and Indian rights in South Africa, 214–216, 220–221, 228 and n, 239, 278
Gillies, Duncan, Premier of Victoria, 99, 101
Gipps, Sir George, Governor of New South Wales, 28
Glenelg, Charles Grant, 1st baron, Secretary of State for War and the Colonies (1835–1839), 28

Gorst, Sir John, 121
Gouger, Robert, Colonial Secretary of South Australia, 27
Government of India: and emigration of indentured Indians, 23; and ex-indentured Indians in Natal, 140, 143; and free Indians in Natal, 58, 143; and indentured Indians in Natal, 52–53, 54–56, 196, 199; and Indian emigration to Australasia, 32, 36–37, 38, 252; and Indian emigration to Canada, 176–177, 178, 186; and the Natal formula, 143; and rights of Indians in Australasia, 168n, 284, 305–306, 310, 311; and rights of Indians in Canada, 190; and rights of Indians in Natal, 202–203, 204, 223, 224, 228, 236, 238; and rights of Indians in the Transvaal, 219
Graham, Frederick, Colonial Office official, 224–225, 238
Gray, John Hamilton, Judge of British Columbia Supreme Court, 131–132, 263
Great Britain, and racial superiority, 15–21 passim, 26, 82, 325, 326; see also Anglo-Saxonism
Great Britain, Government of
and China diplomacy, 74–75, 100–101, 103–105, 111, 115–116, 118–119
Colonial Office: and Australasia, rights of nonwhites in, 28–30, 33, 124–125, 162, 167–168, 282; and Commonwealth of Australia, rights of Asians in, 301–302, 305, 306, 309, 310–311; and Canada, rights of Asians in, 61, 172, 176, 256, 265–266, 269–272; and Cape Colony, rights of Indians in, 148–149, 150, 151–152, 206, 207; colonial secretary defined, 27n; and diplomatic solution to Chinese question, 105, 111–112, 118–119, 121; and imperial philosophy, 22–23; and intercolonial conference (1888), 115–118; and Natal, rights of Indians in, 54, 58, 140–142, 196, 199, 200, 201–202, 204–205, 223–238 passim, 320; and Natal formula, 162–164,

Index   353

Great Britain (cont.)
  167; and New South Wales Eurasian immigrants, 30; and New South Wales immigration restriction legislation, 90–91, 92–93, 100–101, 113–114, 115; and New Zealand, rights of Asians in, 299–300; and Orange Free State, rights of Indians in, 207–208; and Queensland discriminatory legislation, 122–124, 242–243, 244, 245–246, 248–249, 252, 292, 293; and Queensland, indentured labor in, 35–38, 40–41, 42, 45–46, 48–51; and Queensland Japanese immigration, 156; and rights of nonwhite British subjects, 119, 125, 144, 167–168, 317, 321; and the Transvaal, rights of Indians in, 146, 208–209, 210, 213; and Western Australia, rights of Asians in, 83–85; and Zululand, rights of Indians in, 319
  and Dutch republics in South Africa, 145–146
Foreign Office: and anti-Asian activities in Canada, 184, 276; and Asian rights in Australia, 302, 321; and diplomatic solution to the Chinese question, 119, 120n–121n; and Japanese immigration to Queensland, 156; see also Treaties
India Office: and Indian emigration to Canada, 176, 186–187; and Indian rights in Australia, 306, 310–311; and Indian rights in the Cape Colony, 152; and Indian rights in Natal, 223, 224–225, 228, 230; and Natal formula, 152–153 and Japan diplomacy, 163–164, 173–174
House of Lords, and *Afghan* affair, 110
and London Convention (1884), 208–209
and the Natal formula, 24, 143, 144
Parliament: and the Chinese question, 121; and Indian rights in South Africa, 144; and Polynesians in Queensland, 42
and rights of its subjects, 13–14,

145–146, 147, 156–157, 167, 217–218, 220–221, 317–318, 325–326
Grey, Albert Henry George Grey, 4th earl, Governor-General of Canada (1904–1911), 183–184
Grey, Sir George, Governor and Prime Minister of New Zealand, 81–82
Grey, Sir Henry George Grey, 3rd earl, Secretary of State for War and the Colonies (1846–1852), 30
Griffith, Sir Samuel, Premier and Lt. Governor of Queensland, 43, 47–48, 101, 157, 246, 285–286, 313

Hamilton, Lord George Francis, Secretary of State for India (1895–1903), 217
Hawaii, and Japanese immigrants, 182, 187
Hayashi, Baron, Japanese emissary to London, 301–302
Hely-Hutchinson, Sir Walter Francis, Governor of Natal (1893–1901), Governor of Cape Colony (1901–1910), 141, 148, 149, 150, 151, 202n
Henty, G. A., 19
Herbert, Sir Robert, Colonial Office official, 114, 116, 119, 122, 125, 196–197, 243, 248
Hotham, Sir Charles, Governor of Victoria, 60–62
Hunt, Atlee, Secretary of Dept. of External Affairs, Australia, 306–307

Iijima, K., Japanese consul at Townsville, 159–160
Imperial philosophy, see British Empire: imperial philosophy
India, Government of, see Government of India
India, people of: British racial attitudes toward, 18, 20, 21; and treatment of Indians in Australia, 284; and treatment of Indians in Canada, 168–169, 194; see also Government of India
Irish, British racial attitudes toward, 17, 18, 20, 21, 82
Isaacs, Sir Isaac, 313

Jameson, Dr. L. S., Prime Minister of Cape Colony, 151
Japan, Government of: and Anglo-Japanese treaty, 302–303, 304; and Japanese emigration to Canada, 169–170, 174, 182, 184, 185–186; and Japanese emigration to Queensland, 156–157, 159–160; and Japanese rights in Australasia, 163–164, 281–283; and Japanese rights in Canada, 268–274, 275–276; and Japanese rights in Commonwealth of Australia, 301–303, 308–309, 314; and Japanese rights in Queensland, 292–293; and Natal formula, 302; see also Treaties
Jervois, Sir William, Governor of South Australia and of New Zealand, 94, 124–125

Kanaka, defined, 47n; see also Queensland, entries for Polynesians
Keith, A. B., Colonial Office official, 300
Kennedy, Sir Arthur, Governor of Queensland, 247–249
Kimberley, John Wodehouse, 1st earl of, Secretary of State for the Colonies (1880–1882), 84–85
King, W. L. Mackenzie, 184, 185, 188–191, 192
Kintore, Sir Algernon Keith-Falconer, 10th earl of, Governor of South Australia, 251–252
Knutsford, Henry Thurstan Holland, 1st baron, Secretary of State for the Colonies (1887–1892), 115, 116–117, 122–123

Lagden, Sir Godfrey, Commissioner of Native Affairs, the Transvaal, 211 and n
Lambert, H. C. M., Colonial Office official, 151, 238
Lane, William, 158, 324
Lansdowne, Henry Charles Keith Petty-Fitzmaurice, 5th marquis of, Governor-General of Canada, British Foreign Secretary, 133, 179–180, 276

Laurier, Sir Wilfrid, Prime Minister of Canada (1896–1911), 174, 182, 183–184, 192, 194, 272
Lawley, Sir Arthur, Lt. Governor of the Transvaal (1902–1905), 216–217
Lawson, Henry, 324
Lemieux, Rodolphe, Postmaster General of Canada, 184, 185
Lew Ta-Jên, Chinese minister to London, 103, 115, 119–120, 265
Liang Ten-yen, Acting President of Chinese Foreign Office, 190–191
Loch, Sir Henry, Governor of Victoria, 107–108
Loftus, Lord Augustus William Frederick Spencer, Governor of New South Wales (1879–1885), 90–91
London Convention (1884), 208
Lorne, John George Edward Henry Douglas Sutherland, styled marquis of (later 9th duke of Argyll), Governor-General of Canada (1878–1883), 129

McBride, Richard, Premier of British Columbia, 170, 192
McCallum, Sir Henry, Governor of Natal, 211, 226, 228, 232
McCulloch, William, Minister of Defense, Victoria, 257–258
Macdonald, Sir John A., Prime Minister of Canada, 126–127, 131, 134n
Macdonald, William, Canadian senator, 127, 129–130
McIlwraith, Sir Thomas, Premier of Queensland, 116
McInnes, T. R. E., 184
Mackenzie, Alexander, Prime Minister of Canada, 264
Maoris, 8, 298; British racial attitude toward, 18–19
Matsui, K., Japanese emissary to London, 273
Maxwell, Dr. Walter, 287
Meade, Robert, Colonial Office official, 253
Mercer, W. H., Colonial Office official, 49

Index 355

Mills, David, Minister of Justice of Canada, 271-272
Milner, Sir Alfred Milner, 1st viscount, High Commissioner for South Africa (1897-1905), 212-214, 215
Minto, Gilbert John Murray Knynmond Elliot, 4th earl of, Governor-General of Canada (1898-1904), 169, 268, 270, 271, 311
Moor, F. R., Prime Minister of Natal, 141, 142, 229-230
Morehead, Boyd, Premier of Queensland, 122
Morgan, William, 84
Morley of Blackburn, John Morley, 1st viscount, Secretary of State for India (1905-1910, 1911), 194, 224, 228, 311
Murdoch, Sir Clinton, 40
Musgrave, A. W., 109
Musgrave, Sir Anthony, Governor of Queensland, 44-46

Naoroji, Dadabhai, 144
Natal
  census figures (1891), 55; (1880-91), 140
  commissions: Clayton, 233, 235; "Coolie," 54; Wragg, 55-56
  discriminatory legislation: contract labor laws, 52-53, 54, 55n, 140, 233, 237; disenfranchisement, 196-197, 198, 200-202, 223, 224, 228-229, 230, 320; free Indian exclusion, 140-141, 152, 153; licensing acts, 203-205, 225-230, 231-232, 233-234, 236, 237, 238; and Natal formula, 141, 152-153, 163; nonwhite resident restriction, 195-196, 197, 198, 199-200, 203-204, 222-224, 228-236, 237, 320; quarantine act, 144-145
  nonwhite immigrants in: and Anglo-Boer War, 210; and anti-Indian activities, 205-206; and Bambata Rebellion, 210-211; ex-indentured Indians, 54-55, 56, 57, 130, 140, 198, 199; free Indians ("Arabs"), 58, 139, 142, 153-154, 197, 198, 205, 222, 226, 228, 232, 234, 236; indentured Indians, 24, 52-58, 139, 196, 197, 223, 228, 233, 237, 238; mistreatment of indentured Indians, 53-54, 55, 237; need for, 26, 52, 56-57, 228, 233n; political activities of, 153-154, 197-198, 201, 203, 224, 238; Protector of Indian Immigrants, 54, 55; and right of as British subjects, 141, 142-143, 153-154, 202, 225, 320; white attitudes toward, 56-57, 58, 196, 197-198, 204, 205-206, 226, 228, 232, 234-235, 237
  and self-government, 198
Natal formula, 24, 194, 195, 317, 319; see also under specific colonies
Nathan, Sir Matthew, Governor of Natal, 232-233, 234, 236
Nelson, Sir Hugh, Prime Minister of Queensland, 167
Newcastle formula, 61-62, 318
Newcastle, Henry Pelham Clinton, 5th duke of, Secretary of State for the Colonies (1852-1854; 1859-1864), 36, 37-38, 39, 61-62, 91
New South Wales
  and Afghan incident, 108-109, 115
  census figures, 29, 88, 90; (1861, 1871), 68, 97; (1881), 79, 87, 97
  Chinese question: diplomatic solution to, 244; intercolonial conference on, 80; Parliamentary debate on, 89-90, 112-114
  Coloured Progressive Association of Sydney, 305, 306
  discriminatory legislation: commercial restriction, 257, 291n-292n, 294n; disenfranchisement, 240; effect of gold discovery on, 62; immigration restriction, 68-69, 86, 88, 89-93, 99-100, 112, 114-115, 118, 161, 165-166, 240, 304-305; and Natal formula, 166; and Newcastle formula, 61-62; nonwhite resident restriction, 321; and Queensland's Chinese miners' legislation, 244
  nonwhite immigrants in, 29, 30; Eurasians, 30-31; from China, 27, 28, 29, 31, 304; from India, 155, 160-161; indentured from India, 27-30; labor attitude toward, 29,

New South Wales (cont.)
  77–78, 79, 90; need for, 27–28; rights of as British subjects, 91–92, 114–115, 161; and smallpox scare, 85–87, 88; white attitudes toward, 69, 78–79, 88–89, 95–96, 98–99, 161–162, 291; white violence toward, 70–71, 78
  Trades and Labour Council, 77
  see also Australasia
New Zealand
  census figures (1867–74), 72; (1876), 83n; (1881), 93; (1887), 94; (1896), 165; (1901), 294; (1911), 300
  Chinese question, and intercolonial conferences on, 80, 118, 124, 125
  discriminatory legislation, 317; commercial restriction, 298–300; effect of gold discovery on, 59, 72–73; immigration restriction, 81–83, 93, 124, 162, 165, 166, 294, 299, 318; and Natal formula, 166, 297, 299; nonwhite resident restriction, 300
  and Maoris, 82, 298
  nonwhite immigrants in, 21; attacks on, 72–73; from China, 27, 72–74, 81–83, 294–299; and Chinese Immigration Committee, 73–74; exclusion of, 108, 164–165, 297–298; from India, 27; labor attitude toward, 72–73; need for, 51; and rights of as British subjects, 166; white attitudes toward, 73–74, 93–94, 294–298
  as outpost of the British race, 21–22, 26
  and responsible government, 23
  see also Australasia
Norman, Sir Henry, Governor of Queensland, 47–49, 123
Normanby, George Augustus Constantine Phipps, 2nd marquis, Governor of Queensland, 40, 41
Northern Territory (South Australia)
  census figures, Chinese, 69n, 251, 252
  discriminatory legislation: disenfranchisement, 250, 321; effect of gold discovery on, 32
  nonwhite immigrants in: from China, 32, 69n, 105, 250–251; indentured from India, 252, 260; from Japan, 161; mistreatment of, 252–253; need for, 32, 250, 251–252, 253, 260; white attitudes toward, 105, 251–252, 253
  see also Australasia and South Australia

Oliver, Frank, Minister of the Interior, Canada, 184
Orange Free State
  as British possession, 145; discriminatory legislation, 208–209; nonwhite immigrants in: ex-indentured Indians, 206; free Indians, 206; and rights of as British subjects, 318–319
Orange River Colony, see Orange Free State

Palmer, Sir A. H., Colonial Secretary and Administrator of Queensland, 79–80, 122
Parkes, Sir Henry, Premier of New South Wales: and Afghan incident, 109; Australasian support for, 110–111, 113; and British Government, 111, 121; and Chinese question, 104–105, 112–113, 117; and discriminatory legislation, 88, 89–90, 92, 98, 99–100, 112–114, 244, 313; and intercolonial conferences, 79–80, 84–85, 97–98, 99, 117; and smallpox scare, 85–87
Patterson, J. A., 69
Philip, Robert, Premier of Queensland, 287
Playford, Thomas, Premier of South Australia, 102
Plunket, William Lee Plunket, 5th baron, Governor of New Zealand, (1904–1910), 299
Polynesians, see under Queensland
Ponder, W. D., 70–71
Pope, J. H., 128–129
Pretoria Convention (1881), 208

Queensland
  bêche-de-mer and pearl fisheries, 43, 156, 158

Index 357

Queensland (cont.)
census figures: Chinese, 241; Japanese, 155, 160; Polynesian, 41, 42, 45
Chinese question, intercolonial conference on, 80
cotton and sugar cane cultivation, 35–36, 37, 40
discriminatory legislation: Chinese miners' restriction, 241–244, 245–249; commercial restriction, 257, 260, 292n, 292–293 and n; and Commonwealth Polynesian exclusion bills, 285–290; and conference exclusion bill, 121–124; contract labor laws, 38; disenfranchisement, 240–241, 290, 321; immigration restriction, 69, 90, 240, 241–244, 245–249; nonwhite resident restriction, 240–241, 320; Polynesian recruiting restriction, 43–49
foreign white immigrants, 97, 158
nonwhite immigrants in: from China, 35, 37, 39, 40, 41, 97; ex-indentured Polynesians, 42–43, 44, 51; indentured, 35–51 *passim*; from India, 35, 36, 37–38, 39, 40, 41; from Japan, 155–158; labor attitude toward, 38–39, 41, 42–43, 44, 45, 47, 51, 158, 244, 246–247; need for, 35–36, 39, 40, 45, 47–48, 52, 158, 260, 285–286, 288; from Polynesia, 41–51 *passim*, 97, 155, 158, 260, 280, 285–290; Polynesian litigation, 46–47, 49–50, 51; repatriation of Polynesians, 288, 289–290, 313; rights of as British subjects, 241–242, 243, 245–246, 247; Royal Commission on the Repatriation of Kanakas, 289; white attitudes toward, 50–51, 156, 158, 159, 243, 286–287, 288, 291
see also Australasia

Rhodes, Cecil, 16
Richards, A. N., Lt. Governor of British Columbia, 263
Ridgeway, Sir West, 325
Ripon, George Frederick Samuel Robinson, 1st marquis of, Secretary of State for the Colonies (1892–1895), 206
Ritch, L. W., 225
Robinson, Sir Hercules, Governor of New South Wales, 244
Robinson, William, Governor of Western Australia, 83, 84, 85
Robson, John, 261–262
Roosevelt, Theodore, and Asian immigration, 188–189
Rose-Innes, Sir James, 217–218

Salisbury, Robert Arthur Talbort Gascoyne-Cecil, 3rd marquis of, Secretary of State for Foreign Affairs (1878–1880, 1885–1886, 1887–1892, 1895–1900), 111, 115, 122
satyagraha, 147, 239
Saunders, J. R., 56
Scott, W. D., 176
Scurrah, Vernon, 81
Seddon, Richard, Prime Minister of New Zealand, 80–82, 93, 164–165
Semlin, C. A., Premier of British Columbia, 272
Shakespeare, Noah, 128–129, 130
Shimizu, S., Japanese Consul General at Vancouver, 268–269, 270, 273–274
Singapore, and emigrants to New South Wales, 30
Smuts, General Jan C., 25, 239
South Africa (general): Afrikaner population of, 24, 145; and discriminatory legislation, 323; effect of gold discovery on, 59; and nonwhite immigrants, 21, 24, 27; as outpost of the British race, 21–22, 26; and responsible government, 23; *see also names of specific South African colonies*
South Africa British India Committee, 225
South African Customs Union Conference, 153, 212n
South African National Party, 239
South African Republic, *see* Transvaal
South Australia
census figures, Chinese, 69 and n, 250, 254
discriminatory legislation: Chinese

358 Index

South Australia (cont.)
miners' bills, 249, 253–254; commercial restriction, 258, 292n, 294n; and conference exclusion bill, 124; immigration restriction, 67, 69, 93, 102, 108, 162, 250–251, 252; and Newcastle formula, 69
nonwhite immigrants in: from China, 28, 32, 69–71, 250; from India, 28, 32; need for, 31–32, 250; rights of as British subjects, 102, 125, 321; white attitudes toward, 70–71, 108, 164, 254
see also Australasia and Northern Territory
Sprigg, J. Gordon, Prime Minister of Cape Colony, 149, 150
Stanley, Edward George Geoffrey Smith, Lord (later 14 earl of Derby), Secretary of State for War and the Colonies (1841–1844), 28–29
Stout, Sir Robert, Prime Minister of New Zealand, 165
Streatford, H. L., 178

Tasmania
census figures (1881), 80; (1891), 94
Chinese question, and intercolonial conferences on, 80, 98, 118, 125
discriminatory legislation: commercial restriction, 272n; immigration restriction, 94, 121, 166; and Natal formula, 166
nonwhite immigrants: and rights of as British subjects, 118, 162; white attitudes toward, 94
see also Australasia
Terry, Lionel, 294–296, 324
Towns, Captain Robert, 41
Transvaal, the
and Afrikaners, 145, 213
as British possession, 145
census figures, Indian (1899), 209n
discriminatory legislation: immigration restriction, 146; and Natal formula, 146–147; nonwhite resident restriction, 208–219 *passim*
and London Convention, 208–209
nonwhite immigrants in: ex-indentured Indians, 206; free Indians, 206, 209, 210; indentured Chinese, 47, 149, 150; indentured Indians, 149; litigation involving, 217; political activities of, 214–215; rights of as British subjects, 208–209, 211, 217, 219, 318–319; white attitudes toward, 211–213, 215, 216–217
and Pretoria Convention, 208
and responsible government, 146
Treaties: Anglo-Chinese (1860), 68, 75; Anglo-Chinese draft treaty (1888), 117, 120n–121n; Anglo-Japanese Alliance (1902), 173–174; Anglo-Japanese Convention of 1905, 174; Anglo-Japanese of 1894, 157, 169, 174, 182, 293, 302–303, 304; of Nanking (1842), 75, 265; Sino-American (1880), 104, 116

Union of South Africa
and Afrikaners, 239
discriminatory legislation, 193n, 239, 323; and Natal formula, 154
nonwhite immigrants in: litigation involving, 239; political activity of, 239; and rights of as British subjects, 239
United States: and Anglo-Saxonism, 16, 17; anti-Oriental organizations, 183, 184; attitudes toward nonwhites, 20–21, 315; and Chinese immigrants, 87, 108, 131–132, 183; Chinese population figures (1880s), 90, 125–126; Indian entry figures (1907), 182, 183; Japanese entry figures (1907), 182

Victoria
and *Afghan* incident, 105–107, 115
census figures (1851–52), 59; (1857), 63 and n; (1861), 67; (1870s), 77, 79; (1891), 249
Chinese question: and intercolonial conference, 80; and Victoria legislature, 79
County Traders' Association, 257
discriminatory legislation: Asian opposition to, 66–67, 103; Chinese miners' bill, 245; commercial restriction, 255–258, 260, 291, 292 and n; conference exclusion bill,

Index   359

Victoria (cont.)
124; disenfranchisement, 320–321; effect of gold discovery on, 59–61, 62; immigration restriction, 62–63, 65–66, 67, 68, 93, 99, 101–102, 110; and Newcastle formula, 61–62; nonwhite resident restriction, 321; quarantine acts, 107–108
goldfields: Bendigo Miners' Union, 75; described, 60–61, 69–70; miners' strike at, 75–76
nonwhite immigrants in: anti-Asian organizations and activities, 60, 61, 63–65, 66, 76, 106, 256, 257; from China, 59–70 *passim;* and exclusion litigation, 109–110; and the goldfields, 59–61, 63–64, 69–70; from India, 305; labor attitude toward, 75–76, 77, 256, 260; rights of as British subjects, 99, 106–107, 256, 305, 321; white attitudes toward, 60, 65, 66, 68, 69–70, 254–255, 256, 258, 291
Trades and Labour Council, 175–176
see also Australasia

Wakefield, Edward Gibbon, 26
Walkem, George Anthony, Prime Minister of British Columbia, 263
Walsham, Sir John, British Ambassador to China, 120
Ward, Sir Joseph, Prime Minister of New Zealand, 298, 300
Western Australia

census figures (1868), 33; (1891), 83n; (1891, 1901), 258–259
Chinese question, intercolonial conference on, 83–85
discriminatory legislation: Chinese miners' bill, 249; commercial restriction, 258–259; conference exclusion bill, 124; contract labor laws, 33, 260n; disenfranchisement, 241n, 291, 321; effect of gold discovery on, 95; immigration restriction, 94–95, 121, 166; and Natal formula, 166
nonwhite immigrants in: from China, 33–34, 83–84; labor attitude toward, 34, 259–260; and rights of as British subjects, 95, 167–168; white attitudes toward, 291; white violence toward, 34
see also Australasia
Westland, J., 143
Wingfield, Edward, Colonial Office official, 92–93, 163, 201–202
Wolseley, Sir Garnet, Administrator of Natal, 57
Wong Young Ho, General, 102
Woodburn, J., 143
Wragg, Walter, Justice of Natal, 55–56
Wragg Commission, 55–56
Wybergh, W., 211–212

Younghusband, Sir Francis, 14–15

Zululand, and rights of Indians in, 319

Library of Congress Cataloging in Publication Data
(For library cataloging purposes only)

Huttenback, Robert A
    Racism and Empire.

    Bibliography: p.
    Includes index.
    1. Great Britain—Colonies—Emigration and immigration—History. 2. Contract labor—Great Britain—Colonies—History. I. Title.
JV1041.H88 1976   325'.341   75-30257
ISBN 0-8014-0974-8